DANCING THE AFROFUTURE

UNIVERSITY PRESS OF FLORIDA

Florida A&M University, Tallahassee
Florida Atlantic University, Boca Raton
Florida Gulf Coast University, Ft. Myers
Florida International University, Miami
Florida State University, Tallahassee
New College of Florida, Sarasota
University of Central Florida, Orlando
University of Florida, Gainesville
University of North Florida, Jacksonville
University of South Florida, Tampa
University of West Florida, Pensacola

Dancing the

Afrofuture

Hula, Hip-Hop, and
the Dunham Legacy

Halifu Osumare

UNIVERSITY PRESS OF FLORIDA

Gainesville/Tallahassee/Tampa/Boca Raton
Pensacola/Orlando/Miami/Jacksonville/Ft. Myers/Sarasota

Publication of this work is made possible by a Sustaining the Humanities through the American Rescue Plan grant from the National Endowment for the Humanities and a University of California, Davis, Edward A. Dickson Emeriti Professorship Award.

29 28 27 26 25 24   6 5 4 3 2 1

Library of Congress Cataloging-in-Publication Data
Names: Osumare, Halifu, author.
Title: Dancing the Afrofuture : hula, hip-hop, and the Dunham legacy / Halifu Osumare.
Description: 1. | Gainesville : University Press of Florida, 2024. | Includes bibliographical references and index.
Identifiers: LCCN 2023017148 (print) | LCCN 2023017149 (ebook) | ISBN 9780813069876 (hardback) | ISBN 9780813080345 (paperback) | ISBN 9780813070643 (pdf) | ISBN 9780813073026 (ebook)
Subjects: LCSH: Osumare, Halifu. | Dunham, Katherine—Influence. | Dance, Black—History—Biography. | Hula (Dance)—History—Biography. | Hip-hop dance—History—Biography. | Afrofuturism. | BISAC: BIOGRAPHY & AUTOBIOGRAPHY / Personal Memoirs | PERFORMING ARTS / Dance / General
Classification: LCC GV1603 .O78 2024 (print) | LCC GV1603 (ebook) | DDC 784.18/86—dc23/eng/20230513
LC record available at https://lccn.loc.gov/2023017148
LC ebook record available at https://lccn.loc.gov/2023017149

The University Press of Florida is the scholarly publishing agency for the State University System of Florida, comprising Florida A&M University, Florida Atlantic University, Florida Gulf Coast University, Florida International University, Florida State University, New College of Florida, University of Central Florida, University of Florida, University of North Florida, University of South Florida, and University of West Florida.

University Press of Florida
2046 NE Waldo Road
Suite 2100
Gainesville, FL 32609
http://upress.ufl.edu

To my mother, Tenola, who gave me life and love

My father, Leroy, who gave me my rebellion
My stepfather, Herman, who insisted on education
and
Katherine Dunham, who allowed me to understand I have always been free

Contents

Figures

Acknowledgments

After writing *Dancing in Blackness: A Memoir,* I realized I had only told the first half of my story. I knew I had to continue reflecting on the next chapters, often saying to myself, "I have lived some life since the early nineties." Continuing the saga of my life's journey, more people emerged to whom I owe gratitude. My husband, Gene Howell, has to be high on the list, as he not only supported me in every way for the ensuing book tour of *Dancing in Blackness,* but encouraged me to continue writing this sequel and revisit my personal journals that served to jog my memory. My "adopted" daughter, Ayo Walker, has to be second, always lending a sympathetic ear to my ideas and concepts. Her encouragement, "You can do it, Mama," became a mantra that nudged me along. Of course Stephanye Hunter, the editor-in-chief at University Press of Florida, deserves a shout-out because of her belief, encouragement, and patience in guiding me to this finished tome. And I would also like to thank my sensitive and detailed copy editor, Lyric Dodson, for her excellent work.

As *Dancing the Afrofuture* chronicles my transition from artist to scholar, several institutions and administrators also deserve my gratitude. In remembering my transition into academia, I must thank the late Dean Victor Kobayashi of the Summer Session Office of University of Hawai'i at Manoa for believing in me and my vision for Black dance in Hawai'i when I first moved to the islands. I also thank Dr. Kathryn Waddell Takara for her friendship and promotion of my work at that institution during my PhD graduate years. My late friend and scholarly mentor, Dr. VèVè A. Clark, is also high on my list because, without her academic guidance I would not have become the "thinking outside the box" scholar that she encouraged me to be. During those graduate years on Oahu, while living on the Big Island, I could not have done it without the kindness and accommodations of Sidney Wesley, Dhira DiBiase, Amy Kogut, and my dear spiritual advisor, the late great artist Gladys Crampton.

Once arriving at my final academic institution before retirement, the University of California, Davis, I was encouraged and assisted by several people. John Ortiz-Hutson, as the African American and African Studies student advisor for many years, was particularly helpful and encouraging, as well as our secretary-office manager Aklil Bekele. They helped me tremendously as both faculty and director of the then program. I would also like to thank the Edward A. Dickson Professorship Award for emeriti faculty at UC Davis for giving me a small grant to aid in the publication of this book. I also recognize that while climbing the academic ladder and doing my hip-hop research, I was inspired by the late great musicologist Dr. Kwabena Nketia of Ghana, and was aided greatly by Dr. Terry Ofosu as my research assistant. *The Hiplife in Ghana: West African Indigenization of Hip-Hop* would not have been possible without him.

Finally, my deep gratitude goes to my spiritual mother, Madame Katherine Dunham. The late great dance doyen of the twentieth century was not only my dance teacher but became my spiritual mentor. The model she established as the artist-scholar, dancer-academic, and community activist-world humanitarian created the template that I attempt to emulate today. I do my part to carry on her legacy along with many others—Albirda Rose, Penny Godboldo, Patricia Wilson, Jan Blunt, Keith Williams, Saroya Corbett, Amansu Eason, Leslie Arbogast, Molly Christie González, and so many others. Miss Dunham demonstrated the deep *caring* at the foundation of a real artist, and I hope I model a small part of the legacy she established. *Dancing the Afrofuture: Hula, Hip-Hop, and the Dunham Legacy* reveals how I carry that legacy.

Introduction

From Dancing on the Stage to "Dancing" on the Page

As I sat on the plane next to my first husband in the middle of the Pacific Ocean on our way to live in Hawai'i, I began to second-guess myself about the decision to reinvent myself yet again. I was leaving behind all to whom I was close and all that I had accomplished—my twenty-five-year dance career, twenty years of cultural activism and community-building, my friends and colleagues in the Oakland Bay Area, and most importantly my family, mother, father, sisters, nieces—for the unknown, chasing my destiny again. As I peered out at the billowy white clouds taking on imaginary shapes thirty thousand feet up above the earth, I wondered what this new pursuit of my dreams would really bring. Sure, I had applied to the doctoral program of anthropology at the University of Hawai'i, but I had not received an acceptance letter yet. Yes, we had purchased a small house on an acre of land on the Big Island of Hawai'i, but I didn't know how I was going to fare in everyday island living. Was I going to get what they call "rock fever" and crave the mainland again? Was I really going to be able to continue my driving "mission" in the Hawaiian Islands? Was taking a needed break from urban America to live in a developed area of the Hawaiian rainforest really going to give me what I was looking for? I had made the decision with Kimathi Asante, my first husband, to make this life-changing move, but now I was going to have to literally live with it.

We had done all the right things to confidently leave our established Bay Area life. We had a proper going-away community bash, and I had earned my master's degree in dance ethnology and Kimathi his public school teaching certificate. But were we ready to tackle a whole new life adventure? I had said goodbye to "my baby," CitiCentre Dance Theatre, which I had spent the last seventeen years building. I left it in good administrative and artistic hands with my friend Linda Goodrich as artistic director and Lynn Rogers as general manager. I had ensured that my national dance initiative, Black Choreographers Moving Toward the 21st Century (BCM), would continue with strong committed organizational presenters in San Francisco, Los Angeles, and San Diego. In hindsight, I realize I was already conceiving of a kind of "Afrofuture" toward the end of the twentieth century with that dance initiative. With BCM I was deconstructing the old Black dance stereotypes to construct a future with the freedom of self-definition in the present, leading to an empowering future.

Looking out at the vast sky, I couldn't help but wonder what this life-changing decision would bring. But, as I had already done many times before, leaving for long sojourns in Europe, Africa, New York, and Boston, I was willing to put all my energy into embracing this new geographic location in the Hawaiian Islands. I was anxious to continue sharing the transformative power of dance, Black dance, Black culture, Black people, now in Hawai'i halfway between California and Asia. But were the Hawaiian Islands ready to *hear* and really *see* me?

The Rapprochement of Dance and Race

As I said in my first memoir, *Dancing in Blackness* (*DinB*), I understand *dancing* and *blackness* as a confluence between the art of expressive movement and the socio-cultural construct that has become "a fluid constant." The concept of blackness—that which binds people of African descent—is ever shifting, changing, and ephemeral, just like dance, with one telling difference: the global racial hierarchy is an edifice historically etched in stone. Since 1968 I have explored the rapprochement of dance and race throughout my career as a dancer-choreographer, and then in the early nineties as a budding researcher-writer. My career propensities, developing out of my innate rebellious character, was evidenced in a brash boldness in my twenties and thirties. It revealed itself again—albeit more maturely—as I approached my forty-eighth year on my way to live in the Hawaiian Islands. Tempered by middle age, I began to deploy my predisposition for personal rebellion, alternative narratives, and adventurous leaps into new geographical and conceptual territory toward *analyzing* dance and the culture(s) generating it.

As a dancer, I saw my penchant for improvisation as my most salient methodology of exploring the fluid constant of blackness. For example, at age twenty-five when I danced in New York with the famous saxophonist Ornette Coleman at his Artist House in Greenwich Village, I was investigating who I was becoming through dance improvisation in relation to the musical explorations of his ensemble of musical geniuses. Back in 1972, we artists were interrogating in creative conversation what it meant to be human from a Black perspective, on the heels of the legal successes of the Civil Rights Movement, the challenge and awakening of the Black Power Movement, and the continuing pursuit of "the need to develop a black aesthetic,"[1] as Larry Neal mandated in his Black Arts Movement treatise in the 1960s.

I discovered a different focus on dancing in blackness four years later in the coastal Fante village of Arkrah in Ghana when I was conducting my own self-motivated African dance research. As I was coaxed to dance *Adzewa* by the village women, they made me relinquish the researcher role to become a part of their dancing community. Those Ghanaian women insisted on my embodied participation, which in the dancing process became an exploration of the relativity of the fluid constant of blackness as it manifests across the Black Atlantic. As our bare feet displaced the sandy Atlantic coastal earth, as we danced in blackness, bending low in the Adzewa stance—I in my African American manner and they in their Fante style—we improvised an embodied diasporan conversation. As Thomas DeFrantz has observed, "This black is action; action engaged to enlarge capacity, confirm presence, to dare."[2] My dancing "dare" with the Fante women was about enlarging our capacity as Africans to see each other across time and space. But it was also about being sentient beings sharing our humanity through the rhythmic body. My move to Hawai'i was also about further exploring the soul dialogue possible in the Black dancing body.

"Dancing" on the Page and the Dunham Legacy

Dancing the Afrofuture: Hula, Hip-Hop, and the Dunham Legacy continues the review of my life and career in relation to the shifting political, cultural, and aesthetic contexts of my artistic, academic, and personal choices. In this sequel memoir I focus more on how I use Katherine Dunham's dance and philosophy to navigate this multilayered terrain. I followed the Dunham model of artist-scholar as I became a burgeoning writer and academic as a second career. But my love of dance in relation to an activism illuminating Black culture, which I argue is central to the US and the world, remains at the core of my story. *Dancing in Blackness* revealed hints of my future as a scholar, but *Dancing the Afrofuture* foregrounds the gradual shift from active performer to observer-commentator. In the process I find the relationship between the two—dancing on the stage to dancing on the page. I transform what I learned in the first part of my life as dancer-choreographer-activist into a career as academic in the second part. Hawai'i became the entry way for that transformation.

My shift in career dictated that I decipher how to use the artistic principles I had mastered as a dancer-choreographer to become a dance and Black popular culture scholar. As I said in *DinB,* I read about a dance artist who had followed a similar path: New Zealand dancer and education scholar Karen Nicole Barbour, who found that she could "dance across the page." Barbour, understanding dance as embodied knowledge, was able to translate that understanding into her actual writing.[3] Like Barbour, my process of writing dancing becomes a way to represent what I learned from my multiple experiential roles. She found, like me, one must be willing to be self-reflexive in one's representations of subject matter, not hiding behind some kind of impossible *objective* observer while trying to obscure one's own biases in imitation of the positivist etic method.

As I reflected on this self-reflexive approach in my new craft of scholarly writing, I realized that I had a mentor that had already modeled the road from dancer to scholar. During my master's degree program at San Francisco State University, I had discovered the so-called new methodology of postmodern anthropology, where one was allowed to put oneself into the writing of one's research. But I had already experienced this method in the writings of Katherine Dunham, particularly in her layered representation of her lifelong dance research in Haiti woven into a deeply personalized story in *Island Possessed,* first published in 1969. Dunham, by example, gave me permission to include, in varying degrees, my own personal experiences within the context of the representation of my research. And she continues to mentor me as an Ancestor, guiding me from the other realm, as I continue to comprehend the complexity of the artist-scholar.

Born during the turn of the century in the small town of Glen Ellyn, Illinois, Katherine Dunham (1909–2006) became one of the first dance anthropologists. She started the first internationally touring predominantly Black dance company with its own codified dance technique, and simultaneously became one of Hollywood's first African American choreographers, all while authoring many scholarly books and news articles on dance in the Caribbean.

Her personal life is a fascinating tale. She was born to a French Canadian mother, Fanny June Taylor, and Albert Millard Dunham, who could trace his ancestry to Madagascar and West Africa. After her mother's early death, her father raised her and her older brother Albert in Joliet, Illinois. She later followed her brother, a brilliant philosophy student, to the University of Chicago, where she was exposed to some of the key figures of Black culture and theater who were shaping the 1920s Jazz Age. In that metropolis she had her first exposure to the vaudeville theater, the only genre open to African Americans at that time. However, she studied ballet and the developing early modern dance from Ruth Page at the Chicago Opera while also studying anthropology at the University of Chicago with some of the founders of the discipline. Dunham also studied with the famous Africanist Melville Herskovits at nearby Northwestern University. Her professors encouraged her to integrate dance with anthropology, which she did during her fieldwork for her master's thesis in Jamaica, Trinidad, Martinique, and what was to become her second home, Haiti.

Established after her sixteen-month fieldwork in the Caribbean, the Katherine Dunham Dance Company became Dunham's vehicle for her major contribution to the concert stage. She translated her vision of dance in the Africa diaspora, including the United States, into vivid works of choreography that revealed diasporic cultures and their overarching social structure, such as her famous *Rite de Passage* (1941) and *Shango* (1948). After performing between Chicago and New York, the company began to tour the world between 1943 and 1965, becoming one of the major internationally recognized American dance companies. During this period, she created a repertoire of over one hundred ballets for the concert stage, Broadway, nightclubs, and opera.[4] The success of her dance company was also due to her artistic collaboration with her brilliant husband, Canadian John Pratt, who became the costume and set designer for the Katherine Dunham Dance Company.

However, during this period in her own country she encountered many instances of racial discrimination, both in the lack of accommodations for her company members and being forced to perform in segregated theaters, where Blacks were either relegated to the back row balcony or not allowed in at all. Dunham always fought against racial discrimination in the US and abroad, filing several lawsuits and using her celebrity to bring attention to systemic racism and the African American plight.

During the dance company's touring years, she instituted The Katherine Dunham School of Arts and Research in New York City in the 1940s and 1950s, where the famous Katherine Dunham Technique, combining Caribbean folk movement with ballet and modern, was born. The school demonstrated her equal love of dance and the humanities, with professional dance classes in several genres besides Dunham Technique, as well as music, drama, languages, and anthropological fieldwork techniques. Her New York school became the institutional base where the Dunham Technique was developed and codified, with many theater and film celebrities studying at the Dunham school, which was an accredited institution offering certificates of completion through its affiliation with nearby Columbia University.

Part of the Dunham acclaim and mystique was due to her unique combining of dance and scholarship. In anthropology, she continued to lecture after her years at the University of Chicago, including at Yale University and the Royal Anthropological Society in Brussels and London. While she directed her company, she published several ethnographies and autobiographies, including *Dances of Haiti* (1947, 1956, 1983), *Journey to Accompong* (1946, 1971), *Island Possessed* (1959, 1994), and the biography of her early life, *A Touch of Innocence* (1969, 1994). Miss Dunham received numerous honors and awards, such as the 1957 Chevalier of Haitian Legion of Honor and Merit, Haiti's highest honor, and the Kennedy Center Honors for Lifetime Achievement in the Arts in 1983.

Yet it is the Dunham Philosophy—dance as a "way of life"—that underpinned the next stage of her life after disbanding the Katherine Dunham Dance Company in 1965. She began to apply her dance technique and philosophy to community development in the economically depressed Black community of East St. Louis, Illinois. The foundation behind Dunham Technique was the integration of mind, body, and sprit, which became her tool to test if the arts could make a difference in such a social setting, and in 1967 her Performing Arts Training Center (PATC) was born. During this period, she lived both in Port-au-Prince, Haiti, and East St. Louis, and as a world humanitarian she was ever vigilant to social injustices, whether in Haiti or the United States, bringing attention to them through her celebrity.

I directly inherited this great legacy from Katherine Dunham, studying with her from the late 1980s, as well as working closely with her while producing several major Dunham projects. She empowered me to forge my own way of combining the arts and humanities—dance and scholarship—in the service of community activism for social justice. There will only be one Katherine Dunham, but she mentored many in my generation, and my unique synthesis of the Dunham legacy and how I accomplished it is a central theme of this book.

Shifting Blackness and the Politics of Race

As I began writing *Dancing the Afrofuture,* the overarching political conditions and narrative of race and racial hierarchy in the United States continued to rage around me, and my inheritance of the Dunham legacy underpins my representation of these conditions. Now at the other end of my career shift, having negotiated academia for sixteen years, rising to the rank of full professor and publishing many book chapters, journal articles, and three books, including my first memoir, it is imperative that I reflect on the shifting political dynamics. The current generation is initiating what I consider the new civil rights movement, the Black Lives Matter (BLM) Movement. Beginning with the 2012 killing of unarmed seventeen-year old Trayvon Martin by an acquitted neighborhood vigilante; growing with the killing of eighteen-year old unarmed Michael Brown by a white policeman in Ferguson, Missouri, in August 2014 and the death of Freddie Gray while in police custody in April 2015 in Baltimore, Maryland; and reaching a crescendo with the 2020 killing of George Floyd, when the world watched the life drain from his body for nine minutes and twenty-nine seconds as he called out for his deceased mother. A new generation of Black activists have emerged in the hashtag digital age as #BlackLivesMatter Movement, posing the existential question: will the world finally acknowledge the humanity of people of African descent?

The Black Lives Matter Movement website states that they are "a chapter-based national organization working for the validity of black life." The organization naturally makes a connection with previous Black activist movements: "Our network centers those who have been marginalized within Black liberation movements," and the founders clearly understand BLM is a part of a continuum, "The call for Black lives to matter is a rallying cry for ALL Black lives striving for liberation."[5] It is notable that unlike the 1950s civil rights organization, the co-founders of this contemporary activist movement are Black women: Alicia Garza of Oakland, *Ayǫ* (Opal) Tometi of Nigerian descent from Phoenix, and Patrisse Cullors from Los Angeles. Given these millennials' engagement with social media, the network of BLM chapters has become truly national and international, engaging in the 2016 US presidential campaign to ensure the continuing plight of Black people in America is on the national agenda.

I have echoed these exact sentiments in the many incarnations of my lecture-demonstration "The Evolution of Black Dance," performed throughout the 1970s and 1980s and continued in a new iteration in the Hawaiian Islands. The Hawaiian production was accomplished while I simultaneously worked on my doctorate and studied hula. Learning and performing the Indigenous dance form of my new home was out of respect and using my "[dancing] body as a transactional space,"[6] just as Katherine Dunham did in her Caribbean fieldwork. It is heartening to see the next generation receiving the baton of activism within the shifting "fluid constant" of blackness.

BLM's strong Black positioning within the culturally diverse landscape of the United States, like the Dunham legacy, is a smart way to proceed in fighting for what is now called "restorative justice."[7] Everyone, whether white, Latino, Asian, gay, straight, or transgender, joined in public protests and demonstrations with Black people demanding the acknowledgment of their humanity at every level of society, often with engaging thematically driven dance theater, such as the "die-in" demonstrations that became popular in the wake of the George Floyd protests. The Black Lives Matter organization has forged a path to intentionally build and nurture a community that is bonded together through a struggle that is restorative, not depleting. This approach reflects a Black feminist perspective that infuses political activism with a nurturing dimension into this new Black empowerment movement.

As I was moving to Hawai'i, I focused on fostering a blackness that engenders love and human connections between people, bolstering the factual cultural diversity of the US and indeed the world. This is why my community activism in Oakland, manifesting as Everybody's Creative Arts Center/CitiCentre Dance Theatre, was so successful; I often said, "I set a Black table where everyone is welcome to eat." This intercultural approach was also my motivation to study Hawaiian hula. Dunham always taught us to share in the local dance as a way of understanding one's social and cultural context. Turning fifty in Hawai'i, I continued to promote Black culture through dance while becoming a professional hula dancer. Dance has always been my way of continuing the beautiful "struggle that is restorative, not depleting."

The Soul Power of Dance in the Racial Hierarchy

When I first started penning this sequel to *Dancing in Blackness: A Memoir*, the dance phenomenon of Misty Copeland hit the news cycle with much fanfare. As the first African American *prima* ballerina in American Ballet Theatre, one of the most respected ballet companies in the world, she represents only the third African American ballerina in that company's now over eighty year history. In the lily-white world of ballet, Copeland was being touted as a major breakthrough. As the back cover of her *New York Times* best-selling autobiography, *Life in Motion: An Unlikely Ballerina*, states, "Picture a ballerina in a tutu and toe shoes. What does she look like?" Even though Copeland is a light-skinned Black woman with long straight hair, her blackness became a rupture in the notorious hierarchical white-wall of ballet.

The racial insinuation in ballet has always been apparent, front and center. After all, one of the famous edicts of George Balanchine, founder of New York City Ballet, was, "A ballerina has skin the color of a peeled apple." Even though Arthur Mitchell became the first Black male dancer with New York City Ballet in 1962, the ballerina—viewed as the epitome of the white woman—has always been mounted on a pedestal and visually touted as the pinnacle of the aspirational ethereal realm, particularly when she is lifted high above the marley dance floor by her male partner. Misty Copeland shattered that idolatry of the iconic white prima ballerina.

Copeland's elevation to the role of American Ballet Theatre's prima ballerina shattered that *racial* hierarchy in ballet in more ways than mere surface image. She did it also by debunking the long-held myth that Black dancers could not master the technical prowess of the form. In her autobiography, she suggests, "The difference between being an amazing technician and being a soloist or principal is mastering those interpretive flourishes to tell the best story. Otherwise, you aren't a ballerina—you're just another dancer."[8] At every level, she demonstrated her ability to own her status in the ballet world. I argue that her groundbreaking success goes beyond her technical skill and is actually her emphasis on "mastering interpretive flourishes" in the act of dancing.

Brenda Dixon Gottschild has offered an important premise about the essence of dance itself that speaks to Copeland's assessment of true dancing:

> First, spirit and soul are embodied, meaning that their location and means of expression for all human beings are in the flesh; secondly, through soul power, the body manifests spirit. Soul represents the attribute of the body/mind that mediates between flesh and spirit. It is manifested in the feel of a performance.[9]

Good [Black] dancers like Misty Copeland, in any dance style, including the often-stilted ballet form, move beyond the obvious physical manifestation of dance to "soul power" that is the quintessence of dance. This is the spirit I have always sought through dance, with my propensity for dance improvisation guiding me to the authority of the soul force that only dance can conjure. During movement improvisation one literally embodies the moment-by-moment mind and heart enactments emanating from the manifestation of spirit itself.

Throughout my dance career, I became known for dance improvisations, often inserting room for improvised movements and phrases into my set choreography and giving the dancers an opportunity to co-create in the moment. Soul power became the motivating force behind my dance, the fusing of mind, body, and spirit, as Dunham always preached. The following is a passage from my late friend and dance student poet-playwright Ntozake Shange's posthumously published *Dance We Do* (2020), describing the first time she saw me improvise a dance in 1972 at the Village Vanguard in New York City:

> On a muggy summer night, the Village Vanguard was warm and crowded. The line to see the legendary Pharoah Sanders, saxophonist, snaked around the block. Seventh Avenue was abuzz with black people in dashikis and geles. I was sweating and tired from dance class. But

I was determined to get down the steps and around the winding hall to the very dark space that looked like a French café but was the Village Vanguard, a spot where so many jazz musicians had honed their skills.

When I finally got in, after showing my ID there was only standing room, so I stood as close to the bandstand as was possible without offending someone. Pharoah picked up his horn and a booming tenor saxophone captivated the audience. Leon Thomas, the vocalist, began *The Creator Has a Master Plan,* and people's faces just lit up. The drummer Norman Connors had everybody's feet moving. Then suddenly on the far-right elevated portion of the club, a young woman with short-cropped hair, thin of body and long of legs, began to dance. The loose clothing she had on floated through the air as her arms swept across the sitting patrons. She was so vibrant and innovative demonstrating west African, Cuban, and what seemed like Haitian movement and fabulous improvisation. Everyone's gaze bounced between Pharoah and this dancer who was attracting so much attention, yet her movements did not distract from the music; they amplified it. They made the human body part of the band. She was golden and glistening as the night went on, and she danced until the music ended. She got as much applause as the band. And she hugged Pharoah when he put his horn down. They had made a fabulous ensemble.[10]

Although Ntozake and I did not meet that night—I didn't even know she was in the audience—when she moved to San Francisco, she became my dance student, and we began a lifelong friendship. During our developing relationship she only briefly mentioned she had seen my dancing spirit that night at the Village Vanguard with the late saxophone master Pharoah Sanders. But it was her witnessing the power of my soul through dance that initiated our relationship.

But "soul" is a tricky term. It has been associated with Black people—"soul music," "soul man," "you've got soul," "it don't mean a thing, if it ain't got that swing." Using it can reinforce stereotypes, but my meaning of "soul" here is the essence of dancing at the deepest human level. And yes, African diasporan cultures allow access to that depth of being through the ontology of dance and music. That human depth can manifest in Ghanaian Ewe drummers, Haitian vodou yanvalu ceremonial dancers, the Nicholas Brothers in their famous *Stormy Weather* tap dance, and the Rock Steady Crew getting down literally in a Bronx break battle cipher. But soul surpasses those cultural genres; if the performers are transcendent in their skillful execution, soul power emerges and the *human* spirit is made manifest.

The problem arises when hierarchical perceptions are interjected, and "race" is superimposed to articulate the power of Black movement and music. Historic racial stereotyping, what I have called "the marginality of culture" in my global hip-hop scholarship, is deleteriously invoked, thereby limiting the opportunities available for those purveyors of the soul force through discrimination and overt racism, while many appropriate that very culture. Luckily, the ancestral legacy of Black resilience has prevailed and stubborn, dogged cultural agency has resulted. Humanity has greatly benefited from determined Black resilience (witness a good performance of Ailey's *Revelations* and you'll experience it), producing one of the world's great narratives of resistance. My dance story is but one among many that have negotiated this personal soulfulness in a duplicitous American cultural and artistic landscape.

The Horizon of Afrofuturism and Dance

In these pages I consider Afrofuturism as the current manifestation of Africanist culture, where past, present, and future collide. With popular slogans like "Black Lives Matter," "Get Woke," and "The Next" becoming central in the public discourse at organized street protests, in social media posts, published treatises, and science fiction novels and films, Black folks are not only concerned with how the past begot the present, but with seizing control of the future narrative. Viewing time and space holistically, we are no longer focused on the then and the now, but the next and how we can imaginatively shape it to manifest an awesome salutary future reality.

We clearly understand that we stand on the shoulders of our ancestors— on their superhuman resilience—as well as the grace of our Elders. My own website's home page proudly announces, "I write and dance for my Ancestors, for I have empowered myself to be their Wildest Dream!"[11] I acknowledge that the past figures decisively in our continuing present struggles, but the current moment is pregnant with Black future possibilities. The most obvious examples are the blockbuster Marvel Studio films *Black Panther* (2018) and *Wakanda Forever* (2022) with their record-breaking global box office numbers. Their futuristic vision of Black possibilities is occurring in the most oppressive and ambiguous of times. But our survival has always depended upon our ability to imagine a future that holds the potential of real freedom. Was not the historical focus on the North Star during Underground Railroad escapes from slavery a futuristic beckoning to the promised land of the North? Though still fraught with enormous white-supremacist challenges in the Afro-Present, after Barack Obama's two-term presidency and Kamala Harris's gender and racial groundbreaking rise to vice president of the United States, Black Twitter often conjectures a limitless future that motivates us again today.

Katherine Dunham's oeuvre offers an Afrofuturistic model through dance. While negotiating the vagaries of institutional racism and stereotyping, she researched the past for a self-empowered vision of blackness, and in the process performed on some of the world's largest stages. Her brilliant groundbreaking dance sequence in the 1943 all-Black Hollywood film *Stormy Weather* was a tour de force of a futuristic modern vision of blackness in the midst of lingering WWII blackface minstrelsy, stereotypic vaudevillian tap, exhibitionist acrobatic routines, and popular Lindy Hop dances. The WWII all-Black musical film featured tap master Bill "Bojangles" Robinson and a young Lena Horne as featured singer, along with a dizzying array of Black dancers, comedians, and musicians. To be sure, the film showcased some excellent social and tap dance sequences, including the Nicholas Brothers' jaw-dropping "flash dance" tap dance to the Cab Calloway band. But the choreography of the Katherine Dunham Dance Company was worlds apart in vision and representation of blackness in the *Stormy Weather* film.

The late Black culture scholar VèVè A. Clark has opined about the meaning of what she calls the Dunham "Stormy Weather Break" in the film:

> The section in which the Dunham company appears occurs during the break as Lena Horne performs Harold Arlen's urban white version of the blues, *Stormy Weather.* Her blues is uptown, sophisticated, and smooth, stylistically well removed from the Ma Rainey and Bessie Smith . . . Dunham's choreography literally replaces the section in a blues song during which musicians improvise on the theme; in this instance, black dance is improvising, and it is here that Dunham's visions of modernism in black dance are expressed forthrightly.[12]

What makes Dunham's *Stormy Weather* choreographic dance break such a modernist contrast is her reversal of the director Andrew L. Stone's image of Black street people (read: pimps and prostitutes) engaged in social partnering dancing under overhead train tracks to escape the deluge of the storm. At a key moment in the outdoor scene Dunham, as the "Madam" of the streets, peers up at the ominous cinematic storm clouds just as lightning streaks across the sky, and the entire scene changes. Her choreography develops into a dream sequence with the same dancers, now appearing in flowing modernist costumes by her husband John Pratt, transformed into a new vision of Black humanity.

Dunham's *Stormy Weather* choreography becomes the first vision we have through dance of the possibilities of Black self-envisioning beyond the white stereotypic gaze. As Dunham herself descends a ramp, seemingly manifesting out of the storm clouds, she meets the former street dancers now metamorphosed into a dignified community dancing in a futuristic self-empowered vision. They perform modernist leg extensions, elegant sultry walks, Caribbeanist shoulder rolls, low hinges into the floor, and balletic jumps. For the first time in American film, we witness Black dancers signifying a modernist aesthetic that is steeped in their cultural roots. Tommy Gomez and Lucille Ellis, long-term Dunham company dancers, along with Talley Beatty, who would go on to become a recognized choreographer himself, were now dancing an agency of self-definition, surrounded in a future vision of freedom to be their unencumbered selves. The *Stormy Weather* dream sequence represented choreography that was far beyond what 1940s audiences had witnessed performed by Black dancers. Even now when one views the film, one realizes this is a 1940s vision of Afrofuturism in dance.[13]

It is crucial to note that Dunham knew exactly what she was doing politically because she had to negotiate the shift into the dream sequence with Stone, the director. She told me she had to convince him that her modernist futuristic idea would work as a dream because his only vision was for her to create a street jazz number reminiscent of the other dances in the film. Stone wanted Dunham to replicate the stereotypic Black dance of the 1940s coming out of earlier ragtime and then current swing era dances, but Dunham saw her filmic chance for another representation. She convinced him to trust her futuristic vision, and in her astute process gave contemporary Black choreographers our first vision of Afrofuturism in dance.

Decades later, in 2020, I was awarded the Distinction in Dance Award by the Dance Studies Association for "Artistry, Scholarship, and Service to the Field." In my online broadcast acceptance speech, I voiced the following, "We are now imagining ourselves in a future not tied to a narrative of oppression, a future where we are free to fully express ourselves and be heard." This is the aspiration of Afrofuturism stated straightforwardly simple. At the heart of Afrofuturism is the mandate not just to imagine, as Dunham did in *Stormy Weather,* but to actually be any manifestation of ourselves our minds and spirits can conjure. What a novel idea for a people on whose backs the template for oppression has been built. This would be a state of being totally unimaginable by our ancestors, a state of being separate from the almighty white gaze.

Afrofuturism and Technology Writ Large

Afrofuturism is becoming mainstream in popular culture, literature, and art. Black expressive speculative fiction and imagery is flooding the global populace with counternarratives about how we interpret the past and speculate the future. An empowering Afrofuture was depicted in the 2018 blockbuster film *Black Panther* with the technologically advanced African country of Wakanda (discussed further in chapter 8), while the 2020 haunting horror TV series *Lovecraft Country*, lodged in the 1950s pre–Civil Rights era, presented the racist past from a mind-controlling otherworldly perspective. And the 2019 galactic travel film *Star Wars: The Force Awakens*, with its controversial Black leading man Stormtrooper character, played by John Boyega, depicted Blacks in a non-racialized future. New filmic visions of Black people are indeed training us to think beyond the historic stereotypic images constructed by the edifice of white supremacy. American film and television have been tools of erecting Black stereotypes, and now are attempting to create important building blocks to constructing a future beyond racial hierarchy. New Afrofuturistic cinema is imagining a self-empowered future, as well as reexamining the past from a humanistic perspective that exposes the horror of American history.

At the beginning of the third decade of the twenty-first century in the US, Afrofuturism acts as a palimpsest that imagines new aspects of Black possibilities while deconstructing the edifice of our oppressive past. As artist and comic book author Turtel Onli has said, "The times didn't change, but we the people changed. We refused to be contained."[14] We clearly saw this refusal in a radiating young twenty-two-year old Amanda Gorman when she delivered her penetrating poem *The Hill We Climb* on January 20, 2021, for the inauguration of President Joe Biden and Vice President Kamala Harris. She described an America "Where a skinny Black girl, descended from slaves and raised by a single mother, can dream of becoming president only to find herself reciting for one."[15]

Now that the Biden-Harris administration has hired Columbia University sociology professor and Afrofuturism theorist Dr. Alondra Nelson to the position of Deputy Director for Science and Society, there is the potential for the nation's policies concerning science and technology to be informed by an African diasporic perspective. Nelson has publicly articulated a strong Black feminist perspective. For her, science should be "valuing nurturance and cooperation over aggression and competition."[16] Afrofuturism is no longer viewed as imaginative speculative fiction, but an inevitable needed reality that is revealing itself in our contemporary times.

Throughout *Dancing the Afrofuture* I interweave my reflective musings about our collective past with current manifestations of Afrofuturism in US culture and its potential for moving the entire nation closer to its founding ideals of equality and inalienable human rights.

But I also argue that this imaginary materialized almost from the beginning of the African American experience. Myths abound of enslaved flying Africans who lifted upward out of their dire circumstances and were teleported back home to safety and cultural nurturance. From the beginning of the diasporic experience, conjuring a different fantastical reality became a necessity for survival that already had its roots in magical realism of African spirituality.[17] The invoking of that cultural imaginary has now grown into a cultural brand in the twenty-first century. Witness Camille A. Brown's contemporary statement about the meaning of flight in her dance piece *Ink* (2017), which appears in concert programs: "I lift up our real-life superheroes of the past who paved the way for us to fly and 'be fly.' In flight, we see the superpower of Black people in America." Indeed!

My generation and subsequent ones have been nurtured on Afrofuturism without naming it such. Haven't we baby boomers grown up on a *Star Trek* franchise that included a dignified and elegant Uhuru, portrayed by the late Nichelle Nichols as translator and communications officer specializing in linguistics and cryptography on the Starship Enterprise? Didn't I improvise to the celestial rhythmic sounds of jazz composer and orchestra leader Sun Ra and his Solar Arkestra that lived by his philosophy of "space is the place"? Weren't we all *One Nation Under a Groove* with George Clinton & Parliament Funkadelics' Mothership descending to the stage from an imagined outer space realm? And don't today's millennials dance to Janelle Monáe's music on her *Archandroid* album inspired by her messianic android alter ego, singing of love, identity, and self-realization?

We have explored, and continue to investigate, the potential of our lives from an Afrofuturist viewpoint. Futuristic perspectives have permitted Black folk to create vital worlds that project our consciousness beyond the continuing terror of being Black in America, elevating us to new heights via science fiction and fantasy, offering a futuristic respite. Afrofuturism has allowed Black people to see ourselves as an integral part of a future that defies a horrific past and resists a precarious present. The seed of this futurism lies in the Ghanaian symbol of the Sankofa bird, with its head turned back to the past as a foundational seed to understand who we are in the present. What I call in this text the "sankofa process" reinvents the past to move forward into a hopeful future and becomes the basis of Afrofuturism as I define it.

Besides film, television, art, literature, and music, as we saw in Dunham's early vision, dance has also played its part in creating this Afrofuture. Brooklyn's Renegade Performance Group, formed in 2007, created "The Afrofuturism Series" that joins their dancers in dialogue with writers and musicians to bridge the past, present, and possible future. Their website tells the story of "choreography, sound-design, and technology expounding on African American folklore built from stargazing into the night sky to find the North Star during the escape from enslavement on the Underground Railroad."[18]

New York Trinidadian choreographer Makeda Thomas mediates dance and technology through what she calls "radical interdisciplinarity," intersecting diaspora theory, dance studies, ethnography, and Black feminism. Thomas's 2015 performance work, *Speech Sounds*, is based on Black science fiction author Octavia Butler's collection of stories, *Bloodchild*. And Butler's literary work is at the forefront of Pittsburgh's STACYEE PEARL Dance Project with her major choreographic series *Octavia: Bringing a Literary Inspiration to Life*. Along with her sound designer husband, Herman "Soy Sos" Pearl, she developed and performed *Octavia* internationally. These are just a few dance artists who are plummeting twenty-first century dance through the lens of Afrofuturism. The theme of an empowering Black future has become increasingly intriguing to me during my own scholarship years after I stopped dancing, and I explore my own work in Afrofuturism throughout these pages.

Through the themes of hula, hip-hop, the Dunham legacy, and Afrofuturism I continue my life's story in *Dancing the Afrofuture: Hula, Hip-Hop, and the Dunham Legacy*. In this sequel to *Dancing in Blackness*, Black culture and my art form take on new, as well as familiar, turns as technology and the internet have come to dominate our lives, directing us from face-to-face interactions to a virtual reality not even imagined during the height of my performing career in the 1980s.

The virtuality of race, Black Twitter, and Black cyberculture in general have ushered in a brave new world that both facilitates and renders far more complex a positive Afrofuture. But as this new Wild West phenomenon of the internet provides mindboggling new possibilities and quagmires for our lives, the old haunting stereotypes and preconceived racist notions of blackness also take on new and unexpected turns.

Breaking It Down

I recount my perception of all these issues in this memoir, beginning with leaving my Bay Area home to live in Hawai'i in chapter 1. I examine the beginning of the transition from artist to scholar and the development of my approach to scholarship, based in my experiential focus in dance and cultural activism as I follow the Dunham legacy in my own unique way.

Chapter 2, "Dancing in Hawai'i: Scholarship and Black Dance," explores a new cultural site of my work, the Hawaiian islands, and how I negotiate the complex culture of the islands by learning and performing hula while simultaneously continuing to dance in blackness artistically and culturally. I produce a major dance project early in my island sojourn by bringing Katherine Dunham to Hawai'i for a two-island residency that galvanizes the dance, academic, and Black communities. I enroll in the doctoral program in American Studies at the University of Hawai'i at Manoa and begin to learn its theories, which I apply to my increasing interest in the internationalization of hip-hop culture. In the process I begin to carve out a second career as an academic. I also continue to choreograph, dance, teach, and create a new iteration of my career theme of the history of Black people through dance while contributing to the modern dance scene on both the Big Island and in Honolulu.

In chapter 3, "Dancing in Hawai'i: Performing Hula and A Hip-Hop Doctorate," I chronicle my emersion into the world of hula as Hawaii's indigenous dance, all while finishing my doctoral program. Joining Kumu Hula Ehulani Stephany's hula halau (school), I progress in my knowledge and performance of hula, including the accompanying chants and crafts, and eventually go through hula uniki (graduation). Simultaneously I write my dissertation on how hip-hop globalizes while retaining its foundational Africanist aesthetic, and graduate with my PhD in American Studies. I begin applying to myriad of tenure-track academic positions, and after obtaining an appointment on the mainland, I close this chapter saying farewell to Hawai'i.

My transition from artist to scholar is solidified in chapter 4, "Dancing in Ohio and Nigeria," after I complete my doctorate and receive my first tenure-track Assistant Professorship at Bowling Green State University (BGSU) in Ohio, establishing my new home in Toledo. As I settle into my dance faculty position, I explore my growing hip-hop scholarship, publishing my first book chapters and journal articles on the youth culture's globalization. I also officially become a Certified Instructor in Dunham Technique at Miss Dunham's behest and conduct a hula workshop in East St. Louis for her Dunham Children's Workshop. I remember the first years of the new millennium as ones that brought me great personal transformation: finding a unique mother-daughter relationship, divorcing my husband, becoming a Yoruba priestess, and traveling to Nigeria to visit spiritual shrines. I end the Ohio part of my career after being accepted for an Assistant Professorship in African American and African Studies at University of California, Davis, solidifying my transition from the arts to the humanities.

Chapter 5, "'Dancing' in Sacramento and Davis" captures a major transition period in my life when I returned to live again in Northern California while beginning to exclusively teach *academic* lecture courses at University of California, Davis (UCD). I explore how being a dancer-performer and my focus on Black popular culture analyses aided my maturation as a lecturer. I achieve tenure and associate professorship at UCD within one year and publish my first book, *The Africanist Aesthetic in Global Hip-Hop: Power Moves.* As I rejoin my Bay Area Dunham dance roots with Ruth Beckford, Katherine Dunham herself makes her transition to the ancestral realm, and I find myself in the right place at the right time to pay ultimate homage to her monumental legacy. Personally, I continue healing from my divorce and find another mate, Gene Howell. We begin to travel together, including journeying to Ghana, my first trip back to my West African home in thirty-two years, when I receive a Fulbright fellowship to study hip-hop in Accra.

I devote an entire chapter to remembering my five-month Fulbright fellowship in chapter 6, "Hip-Hoping Back to Ghana." With Gene accompanying me for the first month, I start by showing him the important Ghanaian sites, including the infamous African slave castles. I explore what I call the continuing Black Atlantic dialogue between Africans and African Americans, making it the center of my hiplife pop music research in Ghana, a synthesis of Indigenous highlife music and American hip-hop. I also investigate my teaching assignment in the Department of Dance Studies at the University of Ghana, Legon, as well as a short stint teaching Dunham Technique to the Ghana National Dance Theatre. I also travel to neighboring Burkina Faso to a Francophone hip-hop festival, allowing me to put Ghanaian hiplife into a larger African pop music context. I finish the Fulbright fellowship ready to start writing *The Hiplife in Ghana.*

In chapter 7, "Becoming a Public Intellectual and Celebrating Blackness," I explore my eleven-year tenure at UC Davis and my growth as a scholar and professor. Teaching lecture courses full-time, I trace how my performing career informs my classroom teaching methodology. I also survey how my past arts administration experience figures into producing several campus projects with artists of note, including Ntozake Shange and Blitz the Ambassador. My reputation grows as a Hip-Hop Studies scholar as the *Power Moves* book becomes a part of the canon studied by students internationally and as I give keynote addresses at a growing number of hip-hop conferences. I become a local public intellectual, sharing my research in local civic talks and news articles.

In chapter 8, "The Sankofa Process: Afrofuturism at Home and Abroad," I continue tracing my path as a public intellectual while simultaneously climbing the academic ladder at UCD. I teach one of my few graduate courses introducing the Black classics and, in the process, meet a graduate student who grows into my "adopted daughter." I also explore my first trip to Brazil to present my hip-hop research and discover the famous city of Salvador, Bahia, that invokes ancestral memory. I finish *The Hiplife in Ghana: West African Indigenization of Hip-Hop,* and its publication allows me to become full professor in 2012. The book's publication kicks off an international book tour beginning in Ghana and continuing in the United Kingdom. I also investigate my concept of the Sankofa process, which I argue the hiplife music culture in Ghana represents, as well as the concept of the Afrofuture.

I finish the memoir with chapter 9, "We Got Next! From the Afro-Present to the Afrofuture," as a deep dive into the convolutions between digital technology that shapes and directs our contemporary lives and the construct of Afrofuturism. The chapter starts with a juxtaposition of the 1960s' Age of Aquarius Pollyanna notion of post-racial celestial harmony with the four years of Trumpian overt racism and demagoguery. I personally chronicle the last years before my retirement from academia, including the directorship of UC Davis's African American and African Studies Program and helping several dance protégés achieve their terminal degrees. I also explore how Black dancers survived the coronavirus pandemic and the visions of a few select choreographers who focus on Afrofuturism in their work. I also delve into the socio-cultural issues of Big Tech that drives our current "shape-shifting" lifestyle changes, along with "digital Blackness" and what the concept of the Afrofuture really means. Finally, I end with the publishing of the prequel to this book, *Dancing in Blackness: A Memoir,* and my embarcation on another national and international book tour.

Dancing the Afrofuture: Hula, Hip-Hop, and the Dunham Legacy chronicles my transition from a dance artist to an academic scholar. Along the way I continued to find ways to dance, whether on the stage or on the page, putting the principles of life that I learned from my spiritual mother, Katherine Dunham, into full practice. My journey exposes the resilience of the past, the precarity of the present, and a beckoning proactive future as I continue to dance in blackness.

1

Dancing Out of the Bay Area

Leaving your home area, knowing you might never really live there again, is like the original letting go—cutting the umbilical cord. I had left the San Francisco-Oakland Bay Area many times, as I am a fearless traveler who had a three-year sojourn in Europe, two years living on the East Coast, and a one-year pilgrimage to West Africa. I am no stranger to leaving home to follow my dreams. But the move to Hawai'i in early 1994 felt different. I sensed a different kind of leaving home; it felt permanent. Thankfully, the big transition happened over a number of years, where in the beginning I barely noticed I was about to sever the geographical umbilical cord.

As I explored in my first memoir, my personal story creates a synergy between the micro level of my career and the macro level of race, culture, and dance. My life's mission has been fearlessly dedicated to what Melissa Harris-Perry calls the "politics of recognition."[1] She explores the lack of recognition for many Black women's efforts, and my career in dance advocated for recognition of being a "triple minority": Black, a woman, and a dancer. Even before I was truly conscious of my purpose—what I call my mission—I struggled to have dance be an integral part of the Blacks Arts Movement-West in the sixties at San Francisco (SF) State University. As a Black woman, an innate fearlessness allowed me to leave the US at a young age to develop my dance career, thereby making my mark on the world while increasing my artistic and cultural knowledge base.

As I became aware of the inequalities in the dance field, my Bay Area arts and cultural activism galvanized the East Bay Black community, advancing Oakland's African and diasporic dance and music community. After founding Everybody's Creative Arts Center/CitiCentre Dance Theatre, this nonprofit organization became the site and core of my dance activism driving my mission. That mission, through the collective of supporters I gathered, allowed Oakland to become one of the major centers of Africanist dance forms in the country, now known as the Malonga Casquelourd Center for the Arts, which I also chronicled in a book chapter.[2] From the late sixties through the eighties, I had danced in Europe, Africa, Mexico, Jamaica, and Trinidad and Tobago, which I explored in my first memoir. In this sequel I continue my story as I became a hip-hop scholar.

My mission has been partially determined by the place where, and the time when, I came of age. Graduating from high school in 1965, the same year Malcolm X was assassinated and President Lyndon Baines Johnson signed the Voting Rights Act, the US was only beginning to reckon with the historic inequities against Black people. By 1968, the country experienced one of the biggest eras of Black rebellion in most of the major cities. Oakland became the home of the Black Panther Party for Self-Defense (BPP), and simultaneously, the hippie counterculture, with its free love and pot-smoking culture, raged all around me in the Bay Area. These cultural and political forces motivated me as a rebellious, independent young Black woman, inspiring me to insert my voice through dance and choreography and encouraged my larger cultural activism. That same rebellion was channeled into my research agenda as a scholar.

My major transition from the Bay Area to Hawai'i in 1994 actually started in 1989, which became a fateful time in my life as well as my dance career. It was the year I produced the historic Katherine Dunham Stanford University Residency and inaugurated the first two-city Black Choreographers Moving Toward the 21st Century dance initiative. Personally, it was also the year when my first husband Kimathi and I found a house in Hawai'i that we would buy the following year. That summer after the Stanford Dunham Residency, he accompanied me to teach at the annual Multicultural Dance Festival on the Big Island of Hawai'i, produced by the retreat center, Kalani Honua. As jammed-packed with artistic projects as 1989 was, it also became my preparation to leave my San Francisco-Oakland Bay Area home.

Preparing for Hawai'i and Transition to Scholar

Before we could make such a drastic life-change we had to prepare for new jobs and career possibilities in the islands. We learned enough about Hawai'i over the years to understand the local adage: "There's a price for paradise." With the Hawaiian economy so intricately tied to tourism and most consumer goods being imported from the mainland, Hawai'i is expensive, and job opportunities are not on the scale of the other forty-nine states. We analyzed correctly that education and teaching was the only sure profession for us in Hawai'i, as the state's public school system recruited many teachers from the US mainland.

Therefore, from 1990 through 1993 we both focused on preparing ourselves for our move from California to Hawai'i by going back to school. I focused on earning a master's degree so I could eventually apply to a doctorate program at the University of Hawai'i, while Kimathi entered a teacher-credentialing program in preparing to become a public school teacher. The dance ethnology master's program I entered in the spring semester of 1991 was an interdisciplinary Special Major, combining anthropology, ethnic studies, and dance. With 75 percent of my course work in anthropology, I focused on applying to the anthropology PhD program at University of Hawai'i at Manoa even before we moved to the fiftieth state. Kimathi entered Holy Names University to enroll in its Education Department's Teaching Credential Program that could be completed in two years. As I was slated to finish my master's program in the same two-year period, both our educational programs could be completed by the end of 1993, allowing us to then move to Hawai'i the following year.

My SF State master's degree was my transitional plan from artist to scholar. As I furiously read, researched, and wrote essays in anthropology and dance, I saw myself as a 1990s Katherine Dunham, the first Black dancer to bridge anthropology and dance at the University of Chicago in the 1930s. The following is a journal entry written on my forty-fifth birthday in 1991, revealing my personal psychology as I re-entered academia. I consciously negotiated a complete career change by analyzing how I saw the relationship between dancing and researching dance as a discipline:

As I sit here in the Reserve Book Room of the S.F. State University library, I realize this is poetic justice in action. I always take off on my birthday, but can't this year because of the rigors of my master's program. As I make this transition from performer to writer/researcher, I wonder about the different processes involved in and between these two completely different tasks related to dance. Did Katherine Dunham sit in some library in the early 30s going through this same process? Scholarly writing can bring insights to dance performance: how it relates to society, culture, philosophy, and personal identity; but it can never capture the act itself. I dance to communicate that which I cannot speak or write. I dance to tell stories that only the silence of the body knows. I dance to dig deep into my soul, to know that which is within myself that is almost unknowable. Speaking and writing can never express the fullness of a gesture, or the complexity of an embodied ritual. Description falls short of the thing.

This level of inner probing was necessary for my psychological and emotional shift into my new life of the mind and scholarship.

Along with Julinda Lewis-Ferguson, I had just finished editing and publishing *Black Choreographers Moving: A National Dialogue* that chronicled the first year of my Black Choreographers Moving Toward the 21st Century project. I was also preparing for the second year's festival with Theater Artaud in San Francisco and First Impressions Performances in Los Angeles. I was focused, as usual, in many simultaneous projects, but now also focused on my graduate education because I knew that was the key to my future.

My last months on the US mainland in the Bay Area from September 1993 through January 1994 were intense, as I brought my multiple Bay Area roles to a close. I finished my master's degree with honors in Spring 1993, writing my thesis on the *Beni* dance of East Africa that I had researched during my 1990 dance consultancy for the US Information Service in Malawi, Central Africa. While finishing my last quarter teaching at Stanford, my various functions as artist, administrator, teacher, and now budding scholar were all called into full relief as I brought the various projects of "my mission" to an end.

As a choreographer, I was also in intense rehearsals for the American Conservatory Theater's (ACT) production of Steve Carter's *Pecong,* a complex play about Caribbean carnival and Greek myth told through a mélange of West Indian themes. With only a four-and-a-half-week rehearsal period, I created several culturally defining dances for the play with thirteen dancers who came from both sides of the Bay. I collaborated with the musical director, trombonist-composer Wayne Wallace, and the play's director, my friend Benny Ambush of the old Oakland Ensemble Theater days. There were also several community experts hired to provide traditional cultural context for this demanding and complex theater production, including Yoruba priestess Luisah Teish (who would eventually become my "spiritual mother" in the tradition), Cuban musician Guillermo Cespedes, Caribbean scholar Judith Bettelheim, one of my master's thesis committee members, Trinidadian dancer Wilfred Marks, Cuban traditional drummers David Frazier and Carolyn Brandy, and the late Haitian drummer Zeke Nealy. These were heavy-hitting artistic and cultural leaders of the Bay Area, who provided "authenticity" to the multiple African diasporic nuances in *Pecong*.

It was a wonder I made it through the rehearsal process of the play with any kind of sanity. But somehow I did, and even received the Bay Area's Critic Circle Award for Choreography in Drama to boot. But the intense collaborative process with so many consulting voices for *Pecong* as my last SF choreographic commission let me know that I needed a break from the communal collaboration that dance theater takes, and I was indeed ready for the solitary process afforded a researcher-scholar.

I had a chance to test out that relatively new role of researcher-scholar with an October 1993 lecture at Stanford. I had participated in Allegra Fuller Snyder's dance ethnology conference at UCLA in 1992, which led to my first scholarly essay published in the now defunct *UCLA Journal of Dance Ethnol-*

ogy the following year. My essay "'An Aesthetic of the Cool' Revisited: The Ancestral Dance Link in the African Diaspora" was an application of African art historian Robert Farris Thompson's well-known theory of the "aesthetic of the cool" applied to African American fraternity and sorority stepping. Thompson, as a white Africanist scholar who had immersed himself in West and Central African dance, music, and visual art, had found a common thread across thirty-seven different African language groups in his 1960s research, from which he coined the term "aesthetic of the cool." He defined the concept as "an all-embracing, positive attribute that combines notions of composure, silence, vitality, healing and social purification."[3]

Most importantly, he made the connection to the African diaspora: "The re-occurrence of this vital notion in tropical Africa and in the Black Americas, I have come to term the attitude 'an aesthetic of the cool' in the sense of a deeply and complex motivated consciously artistic interweaving of elements serious and pleasurable, of responsibility and of play."[4] In applying his cool concept to African American popular culture, and fraternity and sorority stepping in particular, I argued that the cool aesthetic, at the foundation of African secular festivals and sacred rituals that helped maintain social equilibrium, had become a survival tool to maintain personal composure in the face of slavery and Jim Crow segregation in the US. Today, I recognize the "aesthetic of the cool" represents more than mere Black American reaction to sociopolitical marginalization; but at the time, my adaptive concept served me well, as I was beginning to prove my competency as a scholar.

Another major opportunity that teaching at Stanford as a lecturer provided was moderating a post-performance talk with Garth Fagan on his evening-length 1992 *Griot New York,* along with the great jazz trumpeter Wynton Marsalis as the music composer of the work. Moderating a forum with both of these artistic geniuses gave me the chance to explore the Fagan choreographic work from both the dance and music perspectives. I wrote about the experience in my journal: *I knew I was in the presence of two masters who would go down in history as important culture-makers. I realized each had one foot in the 20th century and the other in the 21st century.* Toward the end of the twentieth century, Black artists of note usually had an Afrofuturist perspective just a few years before the millennium shift. And as I predicted, Fagan would continue to compound his dance accolades, while Marsalis would go on to become the Pulitzer Prize–winning leader of Jazz at Lincoln Center. Even though the twenty-first century was still unimaginable, I was getting glimpses of a shift into an Afrofuture that had me in awe.

Personal Preparations for the Big Move

On the personal level, Kimathi and I continued to ready our lives for the big transition. I spent more time with my family, and I packed away all my files from CitiCentre Dance Theatre, Stanford, Black Choreographers Moving, and my many choreographic projects.

In February 1994, before we left, I met my mother Tenola at the Berkeley Transcendental Meditation Center, where she had planned to become initiated as a transcendental meditation (TM) practitioner. My stepfather Herman unfortunately had passed away a few years earlier, and for the first time in her life she was now free from any authority figures, able to follow her own dreams. Tenola Hall could now actualize her own inner desires, like learning to meditate. Like so many women of her generation, she had lived for her children and spouse, and was now beginning to think about her own self-care. Even more interesting, NaNa, my former lover and producing partner, and now a certified Teacher of Transcendental Meditation, traveled up to the Bay Area to serve as Tenola's TM Initiator. Facilitating this familial liaison brought life full circle; I was helping my mother and NaNa (new name: Sananda) form a relationship that would foster my mother's growth, while I was transitioning into a new career and life shift.

As a part of saying goodbye to my family, I took a trip to Texas to visit Mama Ethel Wallace, my eighty-seven-year-old paternal grandmother in the small rural Texas town of Bay City. Until I was eight years old, I used to leave my birth town of Galveston in the summer months to stay with her in the Bay City. During my visit, a major national news event occurred. I remember sitting peacefully with Mama Ethel in her living room watching television when a breaking news story said after thirty-one years Byron De La Beckwith, the assassinator of Mississippi Civil Rights leader Medgar Evers, was finally convicted of that horrendous murder. I said to my grandmother, "It might take a long time for those who have committed crimes against us to eventually receive their payback, but it will happen." Mama Ethel, who had worked as a cotton-picking sharecropper most of her life for the major landholder in Bay City, just quietly looked at me and nodded her head. She told me she had already found her peace in Jesus Christ, which had to be the only solace for so many of her generation.

My father Leroy, whom I called Bubber, was also there in Texas during my visit. Usually quiet and taciturn, I was happy to hear his willingness to talk more intimately about his childhood memories. Mama Ethel had raised him and his three siblings, Nelson, Lily, and Melvin, as a single mother after her husband Leroy Miller, Sr., who, according to family stories, was a "Jack-Leg" preacher, had left them. Bubber described how he himself had left Bay City as a young teenager, driven to find his own life's path that did not include picking cotton like his mother. My father Bubber had walked away from Bay City at age fourteen, hitching a ride on a freight train to the "big city" of Galveston, where he lived with relatives and would eventually meet and marry my mother at age eighteen.

That Texas trip, before leaving for Hawai'i, allowed me insight into family sources of my own life choices, such as my father's bold move to leave home as a young boy. I realized that my decision to leave my family and move to Europe at age twenty-one was a drastic extension of his choice to leave the familiarity of his hometown in his early life. I was discovering the familial roots of my independence—my cultural and political iconoclasm—embedded in my family history. My father had chosen to leave his dead-end sociopolitical environment to find his own way into a larger world; I too had chosen to follow my inner-directed destiny during the infamous 1968 revolutionary period, making the entire world my life's canvas. My visit to Texas before moving to Hawai'i gave me a new understanding into my sense of personal autonomy.

Before we left for Hawai'i, I also made a major spiritual commitment. I had been attending workshops and ceremonies in the Yoruba spiritual tradition, in which I had become interested in the late eighties. I found Ile Orunmila Oshun, a Cuban Lucumi/Yoruba religious house in Oakland, headed by celebrated author Luisah Teish (Iya Osunmiya), and her then husband Baba Falokun Fatunmbi. I was attracted to the deep metaphysical tenets of the Yoruba belief system based in the forces of nature, the most organized of the African belief systems surviving the ravages of the Middle Passage and slavery in the Americas. I read about the *orisas* (or saints) at the basis of the tradition, as well as the concept of ancestor reverence. Priestess Luisah Teish became my spiritual mentor, and before we left for Hawai'i I went through a ceremony to receive the sacred *elekes,* beaded rosary-like necklaces representing the different orisas, as spiritual fortification for the new phase of my life.

We were both leaving behind years and decades of Bay Area life experiences. Kimathi was departing after twenty years of living in the East Bay, while I was exiting a lifetime of San Francisco's and Oakland's defining mark on my life. Three days before we left for Hawai'i we had our culminating community "Aloha Benefit Farewell Party" on February 19, 1994, at Oakland's Asmara Ethiopian Restaurant on Telegraph Avenue. Kimathi had made a deal with Asmara to have the party in the bar room adjacent to the restaurant, with us providing free hors d'oeuvres for our guests and the restaurant selling drinks. As entertainment, he had created one of his signature R&B mixtapes that kept our friends dancing on Asmara's dance floor, while our musician and dancer friends were arriving to perform as a going-away gift.

Many of our CitiCentre Dance Theatre artist colleagues came out in full force to dance and drum for our leave-taking: Malonga Casquelourd, Mabiba Baegne, drummer Fred Simpson and dancer Shadidi Harding, Mosheh Milon's Bantaba West African Dance Company, featuring Linda Johnson and Raheema Yenbere; Haitian drummer Zeke Nealy; Matome Somo of Uzulu Dance Theatre; and of course, my friend Linda Goodrich. Black Polynesian dance master Mahealani Uchiyama brought her ensemble, giving us a cultural sense of what was awaiting us in our new island home. Bantaba's performance, with the heat of their *DunDunba* and *KuKu* dances brought me out on the dance floor for my own "thank you" performance. Even though it was a rainy and stormy night, our "Aloha Benefit Farewell Party" lasted until 1:00 a.m., becoming our last Bay Area community festival. The whole affair allowed Kimathi and me to experience the artistic and cultural force we had become and the cultural legacy we were leaving behind.

2

Dancing in Hawai'i

Scholarship and Black Dance

The relatively few accounts of experiences of black individuals residing in Hawai'i by their absence or erasure reveal and document a unique perspective of an unexplored dimension of race, immigration and class history in Hawai'i.

Kathryn Waddell Takara

I first fell in love with Hawai'i during a refuge trip from my busy life in the mid-1980s when I was in the demanding throes of running Everybody's Creative Arts Center (ECAC) in Oakland. After producing one of the organization's last Multicultural Festivals of Dance Music, I was so physically, emotionally, and psychically drained that I booked a one-week condo and rental car package on the Ka'anapali coast of the island of Maui. I felt I had to be alone and in silence for one week to recover from overextending myself in multiple roles: organizing, choreographing, and negotiating with recalcitrant individuals, not to mention physically dancing myself in the annual year-end concert in a major Oakland union-run theater. I discussed my need with Kimathi, telling him I simply had to go to my island retreat alone to find my spiritual center again, and he supported me in my one-week Hawaiian sojourn. That first trip to the islands caused me to fall in love with the beauty of Hawaii's *aina* (land) and its relationship with the omnipresent *kai* (ocean), as well as the people's magnanimous *aloha* spirit.

After that initial solo Hawai'i trip Kimathi and I visited the islands together several times, enjoying the beauty and love at the foundation of Native Hawaiian culture, even shining through the pervasive tourism gloss in the fiftieth state. In 1987, right after Talley Beatty's choreographic stint with CitiCentre Dance Theatre, our resident dance company, and my first trip to the Katherine Dunham Seminar, he and I went for the first time as a couple to Hawai'i. We first visited Oahu, the Gathering Place, and had the typical tourist experience in Honolulu. We had a top floor penthouse condo with a view of the beautiful Ko'olau mountain range. We did go together to a hotel luau, where we witnessed for the first time the typical dance fare of Waikiki: a Polynesian dance show that included Hawaiian hula as well as Tahitian and New Zealand Māori dance.

We soon left Oahu's Waikiki Beach for the beautiful Garden Island of Kaua'i. Staying at a hotel only a few yards from the ocean, I was in heaven with "our piece of paradise," as I called it in my journal. On Kaua'i I also became more aware of the effect of the illegal annexation of Hawai'i by the US government on the Native Hawaiian population preceding its eventual statehood. I wrote in my journal about the political awareness I was developing from my second visit:

> *Looking out at the ocean waves lapping up on the Kapa'a coast of Kaua'i, I realize that the outrigger canoes I view today once rode these waves for transportation and survival, rather than simply for sport. Back then, during pre-European contact, it was a time when brown-skinned broad-featured Hawaiians owned their own land and knew their gods. Today the islands boast of a multicultural society, a mixture of colors and cultures that meet in the same ocean, the same changing tides, but the original people are dispossessed.*

I had learned about the Indigenous Native Hawaiian perspective on their islands a few years earlier when we met the venerable pure-Hawaiian Auntie Agnes Cope, artistic director of the Wai'anae Coast Cultural Center in the poor Wai'anae coastal area of Oahu, where many Native Hawaiians live. The National Endowment of the Arts' Expansion Arts Program had sent me as a site evaluator, and Kimathi had come with me. She taught us much about Native Hawaiian culture and made us her *hanai* (adopted) children, calling us *kama'aina* (children of the land). She gave us a cultural foundation that I carry with me today, allowing me to respect the true *kanaka* (Native Hawaiian) culture, and to be acutely aware of what the *haole* (white foreigner) invasion has done to the islands.

But it was the Big Island of Hawai'i that became our destiny in the islands. During the years before we moved to the islands, I had begun teaching Haitian and Dunham Technique in the Multicultural Dance Festival at Kalani Honua Retreat Center on the rugged black lava Kalapana Coast of Hawai'i Island, better known as the Big Island. It is indeed big because all the other five major islands—Oahu, Maui, Kaua'i, Lana'i, and Moloka'i—could geographically fit into it. Kalani Honua Retreat Center was founded by white American Richard Koob and the late African American Earnest Morgan, a gay couple who had traveled the world together as dancer-artists. They wanted to create a center "to celebrate art, nature, health and spirit" and settled on Hawai'i, as it was the place where Earnest had grown up.

They established the center on the southeast coast of the district of Puna, where Kimathi and I would eventually live, to create a retreat center for arts, healing, and spirituality. Kalani Honua (Where Heaven and Earth Meet) was the result, and today the retreat center is called Kalanimua (Heaven Forward). In those early days, the Multicultural Festival of Dance was an annual summer festival that became a part of its ongoing programming. Somehow, Richard Koob heard about my dance work in the Bay Area and sent me an invitation to teach at their Multicultural Dance Festival one summer in the late eighties.

In moving to Hawai'i, Kimathi and I took a Hawaiian Airlines flight to Oahu on February 21, 1994. As usual I had my usual journal in hand, writing reflections on our final farewell from the Bay Area. Thousands of miles in the air I wrote a prayer for our future endeavors in our new island home: *As we begin to descend onto the main islands of the South Pacific, the 50th U.S. State, I pray for the same charismatic authority that comes through me to bring people together for community sharing and belonging that we have just experienced in Oakland in the true Dunham legacy.*

Adjusting to the Hawaiian Islands

We moved to the Hilo side of the Big Island of Hawai'i in the Puna district. Our home that we bought in 1990 was situated in a developed area of the rainforest in the subdivision of Leilani Estates, just outside of the town of Pahoa. Our rental tenant, the real estate agent who sold us the house, had built his dream home just across the street and had our home cleaned and waiting for us when we arrived. At last we could enjoy our tropical paradise, with its 127 inches of yearly rain. In fact, our subdivision did not have county piped-in water. Because of so much rainfall our subdivision had "water-catchment," with large galvanize tanks in the backyards that catch the abundant rainwater from the roof's gutters that then flow into large PVC pipes directly into the backyard tank. When we turned on the water faucets, rainwater was drawn from the catchment tank through a tank filter and then is filtered again under our sinks for the best drinking water one could want. The rainfall pattern was often short downpours, with most people not bothering to use umbrellas; one simply got wet and naturally dried off in the normally eighty-four-degree tropical heat. Unlike neighboring subdivisions, Leilani Estates had smooth paved roads and electricity, making it one of the more desirable areas of Puna, particularly for expatriate mainlanders like us.

East Hawai'i, the windward side of the Big Island where we lived, is considered the "local" side, as opposed to the leeward side or West Hawai'i that is drier and more tourist-oriented. The leeward side has large sprawling five-star hotel grounds, with Kailua-Kona as its main town, while East Hawai'i has Volcano National Park with the active Kilauea volcano where the Hawaiian goddess Pele lives. The unpredictable active volcano kept big developers from building large resort hotels on our side of the island. Local people put this geo-social dynamic of East Hawai'i into a Native Hawaiian context: "Madame Pele blessed us by saving us from the tourists and keeping our property values reasonable."

Pele's active volcano in East Hawai'i continually spews its molten lava from the *Halemaumau* crater of the Kilauea volcano atop Mauna Loa. Although keeping real estate developers away from building in the town of Hilo and the East Hawai'i coastline, the volcano draws worldwide tourists to Volcano National Park to witness one of earth's natural phenomena: a continually lava-spewing volcano flowing into the Pacific Ocean and solidifying into new land daily.[1] Therefore, the property values are kept lower than any other place on the four major Hawaiian Islands. This was why we, as artists, could afford to buy property in Leilani Estates. This reality was perfect for the back-to-the-land types that had migrated to Puna particularly from Berkeley and the Bay Area.

For Kimathi and me, Leilani Estates was perfect because it gave us the best of both worlds: amenities like electricity and paved roads, but also a chance to live closer to nature and to extricate ourselves from US urban life, the kind of new lifestyle I desperately needed. Our front yard was already landscaped with the sacred Hawaiian *ti* leaf plants, fragrant plumeria and gardenia bushes, and three tall Norfolk pines that lined our driveway. Once we learned we could grow our own pineapples by simply cutting off the tops and planting them in our porous lava rock land, Kimathi grew some of the sweetest white and yellow pineapples I have ever tasted. These simple nature-oriented activities, which had initially attracted me to Hawai'i, became part of our new lifestyle, bringing us closer together as a couple.

We found other African Americans in the Puna area who also wanted to live and raise families outside of urban America, growing their own food and living closer to nature. In fact, the African American population on the Big Island was second only to the military towns on Oahu like Pearl City. That was where War World II-generated military bases were entrenched, housing thousands of Black military families, some of whom had come back to live after their military service. When I entered my doctoral program at the University of Hawai'i at Manoa on Oahu and had to commute by plane to my classes in Honolulu, I got to know both African American populations of the Hawaiian Islands: many middle-class professional Blacks on Oahu and the back-to-the-landers on the Big Island where we lived.

After two months, Kimathi and I were becoming well entrenched in the islands, both personally and professionally. Because I was already known on the Big Island artistically through my summer teaching at Kalani Honua, Richard Koob asked me to join some artists he was assembling into a lecture-demonstration called "Appreciating the World's Cultures through Hawaii's Heritage." The show consisted of five artists: Richard himself, a Hawaiian *kumu hula* named Ehulani Stephany, two other dancers, Lily Chan-Harris, Delton, and me. The lecture-demonstration was a scripted performance booked into the public schools on the Big Island. The theme of "Appreciating the World's Cultures" was about different cultures—Chinese, European, and African—centered within Native Hawaiian culture in the islands, with a theme of celebrating Hawaii's cultural diversity and acceptance of difference. With so many Asian and Polynesian ethnicities in the Islands, our lecture-demonstration was important in the larger socio-cultural scheme of Hawai'i. Performing in this show immediately allowed me to get to know the local culture in which I now lived, sharing my African American and African cultures (I introduced the *kpanlogo* dance and children's song that I had learned in Ghana), with school children and faculty. It also allowed me to immediately make some initial income in my new island home.

The "Appreciating the World's Cultures through Hawaii's Heritage" lecture-demonstration traveled around the Big Island and occasionally to other islands. Touring with this performance also allowed me to realize how much the fiftieth state is often less aware of certain social and political dynamics that are taken for granted on the mainland. But as I wrote in my journal, *the trade-off is the aina and the aloha spirit as I sit here on the deck of our home looking out into the jungle of the rainforest that is our backyard. I know why I am here.*

Kimathi and I quickly situated ourselves within the employment and cultural dynamics on the Big Island. He easily got a teaching position at the nearby high school, and immediately became entrenched in the educational infrastructure of Puna. Within two months of our arrival, our friends Mabiba and Fred arrived on the Big Island to teach Congolese and West African dance for the "Big Island Ethnic Cultural Project," run by Lasensua, a white woman who taught African dance on the Big Island. I thought of her as like Susanne Wenger (1915–2009), a German artist who became integral to Yoruba religion and culture in Nigeria, of the Big Island. Mabiba and Fred galvanized the Black and white African dance community that had developed in East

Hawai'i, arriving to teach their well-attended dance and drum workshops while providing us with the opportunity to have one of our first of many "Afro-Hawaiian Luaus" at our home.

This Afro-Hawaiian luau also became a housewarming party, bringing together the African American community with mainland expatriate whites who were into African culture, along with native locals we were getting to know. I was becoming friends with several African American sisters in Puna, like Mandisa, an African dancer from Oakland, Katheryn Craytonshay, Harriet Kaufman, Chioke, Kavelle, and Ina. I had already joined Ehulani Stephany's hula halau—*Halau Hula Kama'Kani Hali Ala O Puna*—and she and other halau members, like Lily Chan-Harris and her family, came to our luau for Mabiba and Fred. Like in the Bay Area, Kimathi and I immediately began serving as a cultural bridge within our new community in Hawai'i.

Several Big Island African Americans were what I call "expatriate freedom fighters" who had been on the front lines of the Black political struggle and had made Hawai'i a refuge and retreat from the heat of the struggle. On May 29, 1994, a banquet was held at the Seven Seas Luau House in Hilo for El Hajj Malik El Shabazz's (Malcolm X) birthday, produced by former Bay Area political activists Halima Shabazz and her partner Skeets. It was a free event with only donations accepted, and was produced to keep the Black freedom struggle in our minds and to honor Malcolm X.

Halima made sure that Native cultural traditions were honored, opening the event with a Hawaiian welcoming chant, followed by Black singers leading the audience in the Black National Anthem. There were Black children's performances of poems and dances, Rastafarian drumming, and I performed a dramatic presentation of Sojourner Truth's famous 1851 Akron, Ohio, speech "And Ain't I A Woman." Halima gave a heartfelt speech about the primacy of the land, the *aina,* and our interdependence as humans, as well as a talk on Malcolm X's legacy of courage, truth, and defiance. She also spoke directly to the Native Hawaiians in the audience, drawing parallels between the Black freedom struggle and the contemporary Native Hawaiian struggle for sovereignty: "*We* may be new here in Hawai'i, but your *struggle* is not new to us." Kimathi and I were quickly becoming entrenched in the Big Island's political, as well as cultural, battles.

My Black women friends and I formed a private Big Island cultural organization we called a "Sister Circle" as a Black women's support group. Once a month we met in one of our homes in East Hawai'i to share our personal triumphs and struggles. The Black brothers were in awe of our ability to come together. Each month we back-to-the-land sisters—Harriet, Aina, Kathy, Halima, and at least ten others—rotated our meetings at each other's homes. We started the Sister Circle with a meditation or prayer, held hands, and shared our month's work and personal issues since the last meeting. If a woman was experiencing some particular challenge or trauma, we allowed her to be vulnerable and share it, sometimes offering advice, sometimes simply listening and empathizing.

As a group we also organized various community events, such as the end of the year Kwanzaa celebration; in this way, we maintained a sense of mutual support and community cultural unity. We were a small enclave of Black people culturally isolated on the Big Island, and we needed this kind of community-oriented support group. The women of Puna had decided that mutual support and affirming each other were crucial to our survival in Hawai'i, and we made it happen.

University of Hawai'i and Ethnicity and "Race" in the Islands

I was also involved in the urban scene of Honolulu, as I had immediately applied to the University of Hawai'i at Manoa for a doctorate. Applying to the anthropology department even before we moved to Hawai'i, I was declined after we arrived. The department wanted me to get a master's degree in their discipline, not accepting my interdisciplinary degree in dance ethnology. Plus, noted dance anthropologist Adrienne Kaeppler was no longer teaching in the department and there was no other faculty member in the dance subdiscipline with whom I could be paired. The anthropology graduate advisor suggested I apply to the Department of American Studies, and I quickly investigated the department's website and was introduced to its interdisciplinary theoretical approach combining history, literature, anthropology, and some popular culture. American Studies seemed to match my research interests, and I immediately set up an appointment to talk to their then Chair, David Bertelson.

As an older student, I had no time to waste, and my strategy was placing the onus on the department to prove to me that it had what I needed. I was clear with Bertelson that my research interest was "the contributions of African American performance to American culture." If American Studies was open to that research emphasis, then I would be willing to apply to their department. American Studies at UH-Manoa had only one African Americanist on faculty, Professor Mark Helbling, a Jewish scholar who focused on literature and the Harlem Renaissance. Helbling agreed to take me on as a graduate student, with the caveat that he didn't really know much about the performing arts. My April 1994 acceptance letter from Bertelson into the department was a positive sign, and in fall 1994 I enrolled as an unclassified student in AMST 600, Method Approach to American Studies, the first in the *required* graduate courses while I applied to the university. My formal admission to the university and the Department of American Studies came in May 1995 when I was forty-eight years old. I was officially entering my second career. Although it was not in anthropology like Katherine Dunham, it was in a field that was allowing me to further investigate Black culture, including dance.

In July 1994, during our first summer in Hawai'i, the UH Summer Session Office produced its first major program on African American culture called "African American Visions: A Celebration," with two weeks of events occurring throughout Honolulu. Some of the visiting Black scholars and artists from the mainland and abroad included in African American Visions were my past mentors: Black feminism scholar Barbara Christian and Guyanese Caribbeanist scholar Percy C. Hintzen, both from UC Berkeley's African American Studies Department; historian Manning Marable of Columbia University; Bay Area novelist and essayist Ismael Reed; South African poet and activist-scholar Dennis Brutus; and the late New Orleans–based actor and playwright John O'Neal, whom I had produced at Everybody's Creative Arts Center in the 1980s. I too became a part of this rank of luminaries, listed as a dancer-choreographer-educator who emphasized dance of the African diaspora. I was very proud to be a part of Hawaii's first major acknowledgment of African American culture, and to be upholding the discipline of dance as a part of such a prestigious celebration.

The historic presence of African Americans in Hawai'i became an important aspect of "African American Visions." Dr. Kathryn Takara, the only African American professor at UH-Manoa in the humanities and social sciences, who eventually became my friend and a member of my dissertation committee, presented a talk on her lifelong research about the history of African Americans in Hawai'i. The epigraph that begins this chapter is from one of her major journal articles, "The African Diaspora in 19th Century Hawai'i: Colonialism and Erasure," published in *Western Journal of Black Studies* in 2003.[2] "African American Visions: A Celebration" made me feel like I had come to live in Hawai'i at just the right moment, when my people were getting their long overdue recognition in my newfound home.

To comprehend the monumental importance of the African American Visions program, one must understand the nature of ethnicity and race in the Hawaiian Islands. African diaspora scholar Elisa Joy White in her "Representations of Blackness and the *Popolo* Problematic" examines the complexity of the perceptions of blackness in Hawai'i in the context of its multiethnic society. When it was published, she was a professor in the Department of Ethnic Studies at UH-Manoa, and later became my colleague in the African American and African Studies Department at UC Davis. In her article, she explains several important terms: *haole* refers to white foreigners, but in post-plantation era Hawai'i a new pidgin English term, *popolo,* emerged to delineate Black Americans, literally meaning the juice of the blackberry. As White analyzes the situation of Blacks in the islands, she explains that:

> The slang *popolo* is significant because even as ethnicity in Hawai'i can be a mitigating factor in how one negotiates social hierarchies in the Islands, African-Americans not only contend with the perception of cultural difference but are clearly identified in explicitly racial terms: the color of one's skin. In a multiethnic space where the majority of people are "of color," color is still of highest relevance in determining the acceptance of African Americans . . . Blackness is reserved for individuals of African descent and, as a result, trumps all other aspects of the individual and automatically qualifies one for outsider status.[3]

This double-edged sword of difference based on ethnicity *and* "race" is the plight of African Americans in Hawai'i, and this was the reason why "African American Visions: A Celebration" in the mid-nineties was so important in raising the visibility and the potential status of Black culture and Black people in the islands.

My Participation in "African American Visions: A Celebration"

My reputation in Black dance and my Hawai'i artistic connections had all but guaranteed me a place in the African American Visions program. Besides presenting a scholarly presentation on dance's centrality to African American culture, I also participated in the kickoff to the entire two-week project: a major concert with the internationally renowned acapella singing group Sweet Honey in the Rock. Their opening concert was at Dillingham Auditorium in Punahou School, the prestigious college preparatory high school that former President Barack Obama had attended, and performing with them became my introduction to the larger Honolulu community.

During their first performance, my long-term association with the Black female singers group allowed me the opportunity to dance to one of their songs. I improvised to "Breaths" about the place of the ancestors in our lives. One of the Sweet Honey singers, Aisha Kahlil, is my close friend; but I had also become friendly with the other members—Founder Bernice Johnson Reagon, Isaye Barnwell, Natanju Bolade Casel, Carol Maillard, and the late ASL signer Shirley Childress. Previously, I had created an opening act with dance, theater, and music for one of their late eighties performances at the Great American Music Hall in San Francisco. Hence, Sweet Honey in the Rock invited me to perform on their opening of the African American Visions two-week program. I started the concert by introducing the group to the sold-out crowd at Punahou, and later appeared for my improvisational "Breaths" solo dance.

As their engagement was for two nights, the singers begged me to perform my solo dance again during their second night. According to Isaye, "You brought 'Breaths' to life in a way that was transformative." My second-night's performance to "Breaths" became a spiritual experience that I recorded in my journal:

I gave that night's performance up to the orisas (the gods) and egun (the ancestors). I asked that they simply come through me and make their power manifest. As I stood in the wings on stage right waiting for Isaye's first note, I said, "Not me, spirit, but thy will expressed through me." The ancestral spirit took over, as the lyrics invoked a phenomenon of forces all around us that should be listened to more than to the chattering of people. Those that we bury are not under the ground, but are all around us, ready to help us if we only take a deep breath.

The dance ended with the spirit sending me flying like a bird across the stage and landing me in a reverent crouching position in front of the seated singers with my back to the audience. As I had been dancing on stage right, slightly separated from the singers, the spirit moving through me seemed to want direct physical contact between us. After my reverent bow in front of the singers, they finished the song with angelic flurries of breath sounds as I trailed offstage into the wings with a spiraling turning movement. This performance allowed me to make my introduction to Honolulu through my dancing spirit, facilitated by Sweet Honey in the Rock. What a first experience after moving to the islands, dancing in blackness in Hawai'i.

The African American Visions project continued for the next two weeks, and for the first time, through specific artists, Hawai'i was recognizing African American and African cultures situated in the islands. UH-Manoa's Summer Session Office produced all of these events, and I had several conversations with the director Dr. Victor Kobayashi about the importance of Hawai'i recognizing African American culture and its influence in the islands. He agreed and acknowledged the struggle he had getting "African American Visions" approved and funded while recognizing the input of Kathryn Takara as a Black faculty member in conceiving the scope of the project.

With the islands having its own history of inequality and oppression involving the Native Hawaiian, Polynesian, and Asian populations in the islands, I began to realize how much work there was to be done in Hawai'i regarding

Black culture. I began to recognize that dealing with African American issues of inequality in the islands had not been a priority because it was only
marginally a part of Hawaii's own history of racial and ethnic inequalities.
Like Katherine Dunham did with Haiti, I would eventually use my Hawaiian
sojourn to explore this issue in my dissertation.

African Americans in Hawai'i and Obama

One can only imagine the issues with which former President Barack Obama
had to grapple while growing up in Hawai'i. In his autobiography, *Dreams
From My Father* (1995), Obama explores the ethnic complexity of the state
when his mother and maternal grandparents first came to the islands in 1959,
the same year as Hawaiian statehood. He captures the conundrum of Hawaii's
so-called racial tolerance against a multidimensional socio-historical backdrop: Native Hawaiian death through disease brought on by nineteenth-century Calvinist missionaries from the mainland; imported Asian immigrants
to work the sugarcane and pineapple plantations that rapidly built the islands'
economy; "the ugly conquest" of the Hawaiian monarchy by American busi-
nessmen; and Japanese American internment during WWII that greatly affected the islands. Blacks were nowhere represented in that early historical
picture.

Obama's white family, destined to have an African son-in-law and grandson, would have to deal with where he fit into a contemporary Hawai'i with
its multilayered ethnic history. Early in the memoir he reflects on "historical
amnesia" and the myth of Hawaiian racial accord:

> And yet, by the time my family arrived, [the sordid Hawaiian history]
> had somehow vanished from collective memory, like morning mist that
> the sun burned away. There were too many races, with power among
> them to diffuse, to impose the mainland's rigid caste system; and so few
> Blacks that the most ardent segregationist could enjoy a vacation se-
> cure in the knowledge that race mixing in Hawai'i had little to do with
> the established order back home. Thus, the legend was made of Hawai'i
> as the one true melting pot, an experiment in racial harmony.[4]

This was an observant summary of his eventual realization of the Hawaiian reality he was born into. Having an absentee Kenyan father also played
into his reality as a Black youth growing up in the islands: "I would not have
known at the time, for I was too young to realize that I was supposed to have
a live-in father, just as I was too young to know that I needed a race."[5] He, like
most *popolos,* or Blacks, in Hawai'i, found out that Hawai'i was nowhere near

racial harmony, and he had to negotiate the islands' own unique social and cultural hierarchy like any other place in America.

Because of the sidelined context of African Americans in Hawai'i, each time I gave a scholarly talk at the university on Black dance or taught an actual dance class, I felt I was chipping away at the edifice of our peripheral and stereotypic status in Hawai'i. I visited UH-Manoa's Department of Theatre and Dance, presenting them with my credentials even before I was formally enrolled as a PhD student. In April 1994, I gave a series of three lectures for the department, using my African dance knowledge as well as that of African American concert dance. My first talks, "Asante and Ewe Dance" and "Bakongo Dance," were in dance ethnologist Judy Van Zile's class, allowing me to validate the variety of African dance styles on the continent. The department then presented me at their Kennedy Theatre on campus for a talk on "African-American Dance Traditions." Unfortunately, these early lectures on Black dance traditions became the only formal affiliation that I would have with the department, leaving me to think that these Black dance lectures were merely a perfunctory "tip of the hat" to my reputation in the dance field, and my knowledge would not be used on an ongoing basis. I began to experience the marginalization of African Americans in the islands almost immediately.

But as usual, I created my own avenues to reach students through dance. My community-based evening African and Caribbean dance classes were usually packed with African dance enthusiasts, many of whom became my trusted friends on Oahu.

Back on the Big Island, just as he had done in Oakland, Kimathi was also continuing his music career in his spare time as a public school teacher. He found musicians in Puna and taught them his original musical compositions, forming another incarnation of his band, this time appropriately called Black Lava. Saxophonist Khensu-Ra, percussionist Ras Am, and trap drummer Joel Shanka joined him on his electric bass, rehearsing his music at our house. Kimathi got the support of promoters and local musicians and scheduled gigs performing his familiar songs: "Yelewa," "Roscoe Brown," and "Sno Joke," as well as "Two Birds," his James Brown funk piece. At some of his music gigs I performed my signature dance improvisations, particularly at Kalani Honua's twenty-fifth anniversary of Woodstock, an all-day concert in late July 1994. Kimathi's band brought an African jazz flavor to what became a day of Country Joe and the Fish and Jefferson Airplane cover bands. The local musicians were purely imitative of the bygone era of Bay Area hippiedom that I knew all too well. After only five months, both Kimathi and I had become thoroughly entrenched in contemporary alternative Big Island culture.

Katherine Dunham in Hawai'i

Living in Hawai'i, I had more opportunities to simply wake up and smell the roses, or in this case the plumeria, but I continued to take on large arts projects that required all the administrative, artistic, and spiritual skills I developed in the Bay Area. The "Katherine Dunham in Hawai'i" two-island project was one such undertaking. Like me, infectiously vivacious choreographer and artistic director Cleo Parker Robinson of Denver had also been teaching at Kalani Honua's annual Multicultural Festival of Dance, and in the summer of 1994 Kimathi and I hosted her at our home. Cleo envisioned the idea of giving Miss Dunham a "vacation" in the islands by setting up some appearances for her in Honolulu and the Big Island to reintroduce contemporary Hawai'i to her, as the Katherine Dunham Dance Company had performed in Honolulu many times during her world touring years. At this point Miss Dunham was eighty-five years old, living in East St. Louis, and exiled from her second home in Haiti due to yet another coup that had ousted her friend and duly elected president Jean Bertrand Aristide. We both knew that she missed going to her villa Habitation LeClerc on her adopted island, and that being in Hawai'i, with its beautiful Pacific Ocean, although not the Caribbean Sea, would replenish her spirit.

Sitting on our lanai overlooking the humid rainforest, Cleo and I hatched the plan to create "Katherine Dunham in Hawai'i" to present her to a new generation of dancers and the general public in Hawai'i, and gift her a working island vacation. Our strategy was for Cleo to raise the funds back home in Denver, and I would create and produce the two-island program, using my newly acquired Hawai'i contacts of movers and shakers.

Creating the Dunham in Hawai'i project on Oahu and the Big Island—Honolulu and East Hawai'i—brought the polar opposite Black communities, with which I was involved, into vivid relief. In Honolulu I was dealing with the Black middle class "who's who" of Oahu—lawyers, judges, administrators, and national organization leaders like the long-standing Links organization. On the Big Island I was organizing Black "hippie" back-to-the-landowners who started meetings with meditation and a lit candle, conducting them in the manner of what Hawaiians call "talk story." But I was prepared for both Black constituencies in the islands, and I fit right into each group to get the job done.

As I had just worked with Victor Kobayashi and the UH-Manoa's Summer Session Office, he was easy to bring on board for the university's sponsorship of a scholarly panel discussion on Dunham. After our initial meeting about the Dunham project, Victor suggested we host a Honolulu hotel dinner banquet, where the Black and Hawai'i-local middle class could hob-nob to honor Miss Dunham. On the Big Island, I naturally used the Sister Circle and their significant others as my Dunham committee, and Kimathi took responsibility for organizing a video team to document the entire Big Island project.

I constructed the two-island Dunham Hawai'i Residency to be a tight seven-day period, allowing her a short, but meaningful, stay in the Hawaiian Islands. I planned the details of the events while I was in Honolulu working with the African American Visions project, designing a series of two-island events in one month.

Miss Dunham arrived, along with her administrative assistant Jeanelle Stovall and her goddaughter Kati Stovall, at the Hilo airport to an arranged performance of African dance and drumming. It was led by Mandisa, performing the *lamban* dance of Guinea in the open-air Hilo airport lobby. Miss Dunham was pleasantly surprised and seemed particularly strong after what had to be a grueling twelve-hour trip from St. Louis.

In hindsight, I must have been half-dazed to have scheduled the first public event that very first evening of Miss Dunham's arrival at the University of Hawai'i-Hilo. But I had prepared her dressing room at the University of Hawai'i-Hilo with an abundance of *Hawaiiana*—a flower display of heliconia, ginger, and anthuriums, papaya and mango fruits, and chocolate-covered macadamia nuts. In case she needed it, I also had an oxygen tank for her. She went on the university stage within two hours of her arrival and of course "wowed" the audience, as I knew she would. She spoke of Haiti, her controversial ballet *Southland* about southern lynchings that had premiered in Santiago, Chile, in 1950, which had brought the wrath of the US State Department.[6] She also philosophized on the state of human collective consciousness: the need for humans to think less in linear time and more in cosmic eons of time. Yes, Miss Dunham was in true form, focusing on issues from the political to the metaphysical and speaking in her inimitable conversational and familial style that drew everyone in, no matter the subject. I was continuing to be mentored by the dance master simply by example.

After her opening greeting at the University of Hawai'i-Hilo theater, I presented a dance demonstration for Miss Dunham, featuring choreography I had arranged with my recent Kalani Honua dance class students. They performed a simple Dunham Technique class progressions across the stage followed by a Trinidadian calypso dance I performed with my students as a background chorus. Miss Dunham's response after my performance is something I will never forget. When I came offstage from my solo, seated in her wheelchair in the wings, she said, "You really love what you're doing, don't you?" I responded with, "I guess I do," and fell into her open arms as we embraced. The look

Figure 2.1. Author embraces Katherine Dunham, Miami, Florida, 2004. Photo courtesy of author.

on Miss Dunham's face when I came offstage was worth more than any *New York Times* dance review I could have ever gotten. After such a grueling day of travel and her major introductory public stage event, Miss Dunham, Jeanelle, and Kati collapsed at the Naniloa Surf Hotel that night in Hilo.

Her second public appearance on the Big Island was the next day at Kalani Honua. It was the perfect setting, with the rocky lava Kalapana Coast, to have the Native Hawaiian and Black communities meet and greet Katherine Dunham. The two communities performed for the "queen," and Richard Koob charged a nominal fee for the event to cover his costs and donated a percentage of the proceeds to Miss Dunham. It was a breathtaking multi-generational community event, and Miss Dunham, sitting in a regal high-backed chair, received all the children in her typical queenly elegance. Cleo and Kimathi took charge of this part of the continuing Big Island Dunham residency because I had to fly to Honolulu to prepare for the second leg of her trip. My greatest regret was that I was not able to attend the Kalani Honua community ceremony and Miss Dunham's address. I was rehearsing in Honolulu with a Honolulu African dance group, Dara Dara, to prepare for her airport arrival on Oahu.

When Miss Dunham arrived in Honolulu for the second leg of the residency, her reception was no less honorific, though culturally different. Dean Victor Kobayashi had organized an impressive Dunham residency infrastructure, partnering with my own Black Choreographers Moving, Inc. The official co-sponsors of the Honolulu Dunham Residency were my organization and his UH-Manoa Summer Session Office. Dean Kobayashi outdid himself by obtaining a donation of Miss Dunham's hotel suite on the twenty-ninth floor of the then newest five-star Honolulu hotel—The Waikiki Beach Marriott Resort. I remember watching Miss Dunham sitting in her wheelchair in the living room of her suite, starring at the panoramic view of the Pacific Ocean for a long time. Cleo and I stood behind her with our arms around each other, savoring that magic moment and knowing we had accomplished our personal goal of bringing Miss Dunham to Hawai'i.

One of the highlights of Dunham's 1994 Honolulu residency was the dinner in her honor. Held in the hotel ballroom where she was staying, all she had to do was descend from her hotel suite to the banquet. This event brought together many of Honolulu's prestigious personalities, from key University of Hawai'i administrators like the vice-chancellor and the dean of the College of Arts and Humanities, Department of Dance Chair Greg Lizenberry and dance ethnologist Judy Van Zile, as well as Honolulu Black middle-class luminaries, including Honolulu Appeals Circuit Judge Faye Kennedy (1941–2005) who served on the Hawai'i Women's Political Caucus and Hawai'i Civil Rights Commission. Also vibrantly present were well-known older modern dancers and Honolulu residents Jean Erdman and former José Limón dancer Betty Jones. Miss Dunham was very happy to meet the university, dance, and Black communities, and in her speech to the banquet audience she reminisced about her company's past performances in Honolulu, particularly about her warm relationship with Hilo Hattie (ne. Clarissa "Clara" Haili, 1901–1979), the Hawaiian dancer-comedienne who became a famous international personality.

I had choreographed "Caribbean Suite" for myself and four student dancers accompanied by three drummers for the classy banquet event, performing the dance on a raised platform constructed by the hotel. During one of my solos, I was supposed to execute a typical body roll up from the floor to a standing position; when the crucial moment came, I struggled as I had trouble using my quadricep thigh muscles to execute the roll up. I played it off with an improvised, comedic, awkward stand, holding my back as if it was hurting. My improvised gesture to cover up my lack of correct movement execution evoked the expected laughter from the audience. But for me it was no joke, becoming one of my first indications that my usual body strength was beginning to fail me at forty-eight years old. I realized I was no longer a young strong acrobatic dancer, forcing me to think of my pending PhD degree as even more important as a gateway to an impending necessary second career. However, Miss Dunham truly appreciated the dance and gave me much praise to the prestigious audience. Because of that Dunham island residency, within six months of my taking up residence in Hawai'i, I had established my reputation as a dancer-scholar.

The last Dunham event in Honolulu was the University of Hawai'i campus academic panel titled "Conversation with Katherine Dunham," a tried-and-true theme at the Dunham Seminars in East St. Louis as well as during my 1989 Dunham Stanford Dunham Residency (chapter 6, *DinB*). Dean Kobayashi had gotten several university departments to financially contribute to this scholarly event, comprising six university panels, including me, seated at a conference table on stage with Miss Dunham in her wheelchair at the center. She also insisted that Jeanelle and Kati join her on stage: "I do not do things alone" was one of her mantras. "Conversation with Katherine Dunham" opened with Miss Dunham's address to the gathered university crowd, which covered several contemporary political issues about which she was concerned, particularly the political situation in Haiti and the Haitian refugees in Guantanamo Bay, for which she had conducted her famous 1992 forty-seven-day hunger strike. Miss Dunham always positioned contemporary political issues as humanitarian ones, taking strong public stances whenever the opportunity presented itself, again a role model for my own community activism.

After her formal remarks, each panelist asked her a question concerning her art, company, or social justice issues. Given my signature rabble-rousing rebellion, I had a hidden agenda for this academic event: to expose her non-recognition by the discipline of anthropology for her contributions to the subfield of *dance* anthropology. I started by asking her about her relatively recent 1983 publication of *Dances of Haiti* by UCLA's Center for Afro-American Studies. The original version of the text was her University of Chicago master's thesis and the first ethological treatises clearly positioning dance as a social system reflecting Indigenous cultural values and overarching social structure in Haiti. By extension, *Dances of Haiti* created an anthropological template for any dance culture. Before the recent UCLA publication in English, it had only been published in Spanish in Mexico in 1947 and in French in France in 1957[7]; US scholarship had never recognized her important contribution to anthropology. I considered academia's oversight of Dunham's *Dances of Haiti*, which was prescient of the establishment of dance anthropology, as a travesty.

It took the development of African American Studies during my generation to finally publish her great work in English in the United States. This indisputable fact obviously smacked of American racism in academia.

But to my surprise, she brushed my righteous indignation off with typical Dunham grace. She quietly stated that she was unconcerned about people who had academically spurned her, for she had continued her work regardless. In that moment, Katherine Dunham demonstrated her wise eldership, teaching us all about how to live with self-examination, discrimination, and most of all detachment, her three-pronged philosophy that we teach in the certification of official Dunham instructors: do the work, and do not be attached to the result! What is meant for you will eventually happen. Katherine Dunham, as one of the great humanitarians of the twentieth century, continued to be just that during her 1994 Hawai'i residency.

After the one-week Dunham in Hawai'i Residency, Cleo and I reflected on our prodigious accomplishment. She had raised the money for the Dunham entourage's transportation and expenses, and I had produced the events that constituted the highly successful residency. We were pleased that even within the whirlwind tour of two islands, Miss Dunham did feel personally renewed from being in Hawai'i. It wasn't Haiti, but she felt the Pacific Ocean and the island lifestyle that she so loved. Once back in Denver, Cleo wrote me the following:

> *Mahalo* (Thank You) for taking a leap of faith with me and then doing everything possible to make it a wonderful spiritual/spirited experience. It is our love for Miss Dunham and our trusting each other that made the entire project feel so good.[8]

Cleo Parker Robinson, the diva of Denver dance, and I became sisters in the process of making the Dunham in Hawai'i Residency a reality.

Making a Life of Scholarship in Hawai'i

Between 1995 and 1999 I worked hard on my PhD in American Studies, continued my dance and choreographic career, and studied hula by performing with Ehulani Stephany's Puna halau. Being accepted into the American Studies doctoral program meant the road to my doctorate was now solidified. At forty-nine years old I knew I had to matriculate through in record time, often joking to my doctoral dissertation committee that it was a priority to finish in four years because I had to enter the academic job market before it was time for me to retire.

Living in Pahoa on the Big Island and going to school in Honolulu on the island of Oahu meant I had to commute by plane each week, leaving Hilo on Tuesday morning and returning late Thursday evening on the last flight. My one-pointed tenacity grew from the discipline acquired by juggling the artistic and administrative roles I had grown accustomed to. Kimathi would drive me to the Hilo Airport on Tuesday mornings, and then I would take a bus from the Honolulu airport to campus, using the commute to finish my reading for that week's classes. Once I finished a day of graduate classes—usually three per semester, each of which required reading one book a week—I would stay at the home of one of my dance students or friends in Honolulu. My UH-Manoa community dance classes produced caring student-friends, who often vied with each other for whose home I would stay at each week. I made sure to rotate between them, spreading my energy among my friendly supporters so as not to wear out my welcome with any one student. On Thursdays, at the end of each week's three-day Honolulu school trip, I would either take a bus or taxi back to the airport for that last flight to the Big Island. In this way, each week I negotiated a two-island lifestyle between Hawai'i and Oahu to achieve my academic goals.

The course of study for my first two years in the Department of American Studies was rigorous. I took both required core courses as well as classes in my emphasis on Black Studies, even if that meant taking undergraduate upper-division courses in other departments. American Studies courses like Patterns of American Culture, Women and Culture, Film in America, Twentieth-Century National Literature, and American Minds represented some of my graduate courses taught by my main advisor Mark Helbling, the late James McCutcheon, or the late Floyd Matson. I also took classes with David Stannard, known as the political radical on the faculty, married to the late Haunani-Kay Trask, founder of the Hawaiian Studies Department at the university and a staunch advocate of Hawaiian sovereignty. Besides several of my graduate courses, Stannard taught an undergraduate course called Race and Racism that utilized many of the classic Black texts on the subject, important to my concentration.

I also went over to the Music Department to take a course that had considerable Black music content, The History of Rock & Roll taught by Jay Junker. I wondered if this was Katherine Dunham's strategy when she took an important seminar at Northwestern University from the Caribbeanist Melville Herskovits while she was a student in anthropology at the University of Chicago. In this way, I pieced together a curriculum that taught me the discipline of American Studies while focusing on Black Studies and culture, turning every required term paper into an opportunity to explore African American history and culture.

I used my term papers to reinvestigate Black icons in American history, such as Frederick Douglass and W.E.B. DuBois, and their relationship to an Africanist knowledge base. For example, W.E.B. DuBois's belief in his "talented tenth" that would save and uplift the Black masses was steeped in his Harvard Enlightenment education. He often rejected jazz music and dance that were a part of Alain Locke's 1920 and 1930s "New Negro" aesthetics.[9] I wrote in one essay, "They unwittingly perpetuated an elitist European philosophical rationalism, while at the same time seeking to eradicate America's white-supremacist practices through the doctrine of advancing their (colored) race."[10] In this way I used my American Studies doctoral program to interrogate African American history in relation to my focus on Africanist beliefs and performance practices.

Teaching Dance to Support Graduate Education

During my intense graduate studies, my community dance classes on both islands were partially the way I financially supported myself, supplementing what Kimathi earned. In Honolulu, I taught at the university through student-sponsored groups. In the fall of 1994, the UH-Manoa student newspaper, *Ka Leo o Hawai'i (The Voice of Hawai'i)*, published a feature story on my classes entitled "Dance Instructor Crosses Cultural Bounds," announcing to the campus that I was teaching African dance styles. I appreciated the way the writer started the article, positioning my dance classes within the influential vitality of Africa itself:

> If there is an entire civilization founded upon dancing, it is probably that of sub-Saharan Africa. In few places does dance play such an integral role in daily life, integrating a complex of storytelling, ritual, healing (both spiritual and physical) and the transmission of history and knowledge. And so, according to former Stanford University dance instructor Halifu Osumare, dance is a window into the African heritage, one of the most vital world cultures.[11]

This article set the tone for my dance classes in Honolulu. The writer understood my focus on culture and history perpetuated through the dance in the true Dunham legacy, as opposed to the usual stereotype of African dance as exotic hot frenzy. The article also emphasized that I was studying hula on the Big Island, linking my approach to embodied knowledge by "again finding dance [as] a window into a new world." By summer 1995, I was teaching a three-pronged class series in African and Caribbean dance and the Katherine Dunham Dance Technique. I was starting my dance teaching in Hawai'i on a substantive level, aided by the UH-Manoa student-led Dara Dara Dance Company that sponsored my classes using free campus gymnasium space. And the media coverage helped spread my reputation that attracted a large dance following for my classes on Oahu.

Several of my Oahu dance students allowed me to "crash" at their homes on Tuesday and Wednesday evenings. Prime among these special supporters was Sidney Wesley, an expatriate white woman from my home state of Texas. Sidney's first husband was in the US diplomatic core, and they lived for long periods with their three daughters in Ethiopia and Kenya. After moving to Hawai'i after her divorce, she became a communications specialist for the East-West Center on the UH-Manoa campus, and my African dance classes allowed her a simulated return to an African cultural milieu that she missed. Sidney was now married to Mike Savage, a retired Nigerian science expert who worked for the Ford Foundation, traveling throughout Africa implementing the foundation's various science projects. They became close friends with whom I always felt welcomed to stay in their apartment on busy Kapi'olani Boulevard in Honolulu.

Several other student-friends rounded out my crash-pad options. Amy Kogut, a Jewish family practitioner medical doctor originally from Kentucky, and Dhira DiBiase, also known as Dhira Nalo, an Italian American expatriate mainlander who loved African dance and drumming and was a member of the Dara Dara Company, were among my supporters with whom I stayed while on Oahu.

But it was the late Gladys Crampton (1932–2013), an older Black female artist from Philadelphia, who became my spiritual mentor in Honolulu. I had met Gladys on one of my first trips to Honolulu before we moved to Hawai'i, having been introduced to her by another friend Allison Jacobs. Gladys lived in a small apartment on Ke'eaumouku Street and had moved to Hawai'i decades ago for health reasons. She was a painter par excellence, with an apartment filled with her compelling colorful artwork of celestial cosmic themes from a Black perspective. She was an Afrofuturist before it was a buzz term, seeing Black people from a cosmic perspective in the past, present, and future. Gladys was also a psychic healer, with many of her paintings reflecting her supernatural visions. She allowed me to stay in her spare bedroom stacked with her paintings and books, and when I arrived in the evening, we would often stay up late into the night talking about spirituality, Katherine Dunham

(Gladys had spent time in Haiti), and the Black middle class in Honolulu, many of whom she thought had forgotten their cultural roots.

Besides her art, I was fascinated by Gladys's healing ability, and I had one opportunity to experience it firsthand. One evening I limped into Gladys's apartment, having sprained my ankle after simply stepping off a street curb while walking to her home. She said, "Sit down and put your foot up, baby," and proceeded to massage my swollen ankle with her eyes closed. She told me to close my eyes and focus on my ankle. After she had finished her mojo, my ankle did feel a little better and I was able to fall asleep. The next morning, I got up and put my full weight on the foot without a hint of the previous evening's pain or swelling; such was the healing powers of Gladys Crampton.

Another important Gladys story has to do with one of her paintings that I purchased. One day when I arrived at her Keʻeaumouku apartment, I smelled a strong odor of oil paint and looked at her current easel to discover a work of art that overwhelmed me: "Eternal Dancer" is a nude Black woman straddling the earth floating in a black universe, with her arms raised high above her head holding two red spirals. The painting mesmerized me, and I could not take my eyes off it. I asked Gladys about the red spirals that the power woman held, and she said they represented the rotating axes that keep the celestial bodies in motion, one rotating clockwise and the other counterclockwise. That made me contemplate the logic of the African dance circle that always moves in a counterclockwise direction, and I realized I had found a

Figure 2.2. Gladys Crampton with her painting *Eternal Dancer*. Photo courtesy of author.

piece of art that represented the theme of my life as the "Eternal Dancer." I knew it was my painting, and I eventually bought it, paying by installments after graduating and getting my first tenure-track university position. Today, *Eternal Dancer* hangs in my home in Sacramento, and every day reminds me of the wisdom, vision, and artistic genius of my late Auntie Gladys Crampton.

The life that I created in Hawai'i was motivated by obtaining my PhD degree, and my continuing dance career supported that goal. But these women, as my Honolulu friends, also allowed me to achieve that goal, graciously facilitating my living in Honolulu while attending classes at the university. My dance classes on both islands and my Honolulu hosts facilitated my two-island lifestyle, enabling me to earn my doctorate that led to my second career as an academic. As Katherine Dunham always said, "One does not do things alone"; I began to comprehend her statement from the supportive village I created through dance in Honolulu.

Dancing, Choreographing, and Directing *Middle Passage*

I also continued to learn that Dunham lesson by collaborating with a few Black artist-friends on the Big Island, who helped me create another incarnation of *The Evolution of Black Dance.* Per my usual modus operandi, in 1995 I began juggling several balls in the multi-career air at once—researching, writing, administrating, producing, choreographing, and dancing—through my work on this new iteration of old production. This time I included live music and gave it a new name: *Middle Passage: The Beat of the African American Journey.* The written script for *Middle Passage* was based on my older versions as far back as 1974 in Bay Area schools. The production had expanded at the University of Ghana in 1976 and developed further once I had founded Everybody's Creative Arts Center in Oakland during the 1980s. *Middle Passage* became my way of teaching the islands about Black culture while earning the income I needed to support my doctoral work without a steady job.

Hence, I had two decades of performing the various eras of Black history through dance. The performance always started with African dance that traveled to the US to become re-envisioned slave plantation dances and continued with US cultural transformation in the 1920s Jazz Age with the Charleston, advancing through the decades to the rock and roll 1950s with the twist dance craze, and ending with the contemporary dance era of the period in which the story was being produced. As most people in the islands knew very little about the cultural history of African Americans, I knew this kind of "edutainment" was needed and could easily get booked into schools and various venues.

The main problem with producing my Black history performance in Hawai'i was I didn't have trained dancers. So, instead I used who were available: an abundance of musicians. Kimathi was enthusiastic about being a part of *Middle Passage* because it gave him an opportunity to perform as a musician, playing his bass guitar and percussion instruments. Two other Black musicians filled out the four-member roster of *Middle Passage*: saxophonist Ramu Khensu-Ra, originally from the Bay Area, and Reggae McGowan, a

Figure 2.3. Performers in *Middle Passage: The Beat of the African American Journey* (*left to right*: Ramu Khensu-Ra, the author, Reggae McGowan; *seated*, Kimathi Asante). Photo courtesy of author.

master drummer who had lived in Hawai'i for many years and accompanied my dance classes on the Big Island and in Honolulu. I decided to focus on a fifty-minute to one-hour scripted show that could easily be booked into the schools on several islands. With these three male musicians and me as the sole female dancer-actor, I started creating what was publicized as "The story of the joyous, mournful, and courageous history of African peoples in the United States," and we eventually performed the lecture-demonstration on all four major islands.

I incorporated all my cultural, historical, and experiential knowledge as researcher and artist into *Middle Passage*. The production encompassed the cultural gamut, from Yoruba chants to the plantation Ring Shout, and from the 1930s "Shorty George" dance of the Savoy Ballroom to hip-hop dance with the then popular "running man" step. I utilized the music of my live musicians everywhere possible within the different historical eras, and that aural focus proved to be powerful. Live music allowed musical interludes, without dance, as representations of a particular historical period. For example, after the opening Yoruba chant that invoked Esu-Elegbara, the deity of the crossroads, along with the Ghanaian *kpanlogo* dance that Khensu-Ra and I performed to Reggae's drumming, all three musicians segued into playing an avant-garde jazz interlude.

This musical interlude invoked disjointed chaos, representing the horror of the journey of the transatlantic slave trade, or Middle Passage. Kimathi composed the music that began with a rhythmic bass riff overlaid with Reggae's conga drum rhythms, while Khensu-Ra added saxophone sounds of screams and moans. This musical break invoked the horrific trauma of the trans-Atlantic trade; music, rather than dance, conveyed the tragic transition in the African-to-African American story. During this musical interval, I was offstage changing my costume from African dress to a colonial-type costume typical of an enslaved woman made of a long skirt, ragged blouse, and head tie. As the music softened, I walked back on stage to deliver my scripted lines about the quintessential cultural shift ending in slavery:

> But the rich cultures of ritual, music, dance, and reverence for the gods was not to last. The white man came from Portugal, France, England, Germany, and Belgium to partake of the fertile land and its treasures— and the greatest treasure of all was the people themselves. Strong, Black, able to withstand intense tropical heat, and a long history of Indigenous agricultural techniques. The perfect free labor for the triangular trade between Africa, Europe, and the Americas.

Khensu-Ra then added:

The Middle Passage, the long journey across the Atlantic, was to be the journey of history, the history to change the world, to enslave an entire "race," but also to bring the spirit and the rhythms of those people to the entire world!

Even with only four performers, the live music along with the script, based on twenty years of research and theatrical experience, made *Middle Passage* a powerful statement, particularly in the Hawaiian Islands. My main directorial task was coaching the musicians to be convincing actors with their parts in the scripted narrative throughout the production. I worked with them on their theatrical delivery, and they eventually brought affective meaning through their portrayals that the history demanded. *Middle Passage: The Beat of the African American Journey* became a resounding success throughout the Hawaiian Islands.

My work with UH-Manoa's College of Continuing Education that produced the 1994 African American Visions program became instrumental in my multi-island bookings of *Middle Passage*. My production became the perfect follow-up to that two-week high-profile Black culture project, and Dean Victor Kobayashi helped me book eleven performances on several of the islands from February 1995 to June 1996. I also utilized my nonprofit organization Black Choreographers Moving (BCM), Inc. to contract with the Summer Sessions office. We started the tour, interestingly enough, at the Women's Community Correctional Center on Oahu, and continued with performances in public schools from fourth through twelfth grades on Oahu, Kaua'i, our own island of Hawai'i, and even the smaller island of Moloka'i. I also booked several larger public venues on my own, such as the prestigious Honolulu Academy of the Arts as well as the grassroots Akebono Theatre in our hometown of Pahoa.

Everywhere we performed, children and adults alike appreciated learning about Black history in this theatrical way. Many audience members bombarded us after our show with how much they had learned as well as how much Black history paralleled the Native Hawaiian plight. It was very fulfilling to know that my *Middle Passage* production was bringing such needed understanding about our Black cultural history. I realized this was yet another manifestation of my life's mission: to tell my ancestral story through dance theater.

By 1997, I had expanded *Middle Passage: The Beat of the African American Journey* into a full two-hour production, adding several Honolulu artists to the three Big Island musicians. With this expanded full-evening spectacle, I booked a Black History Month Tour throughout the island. The tour started in late January at the University of Hawai'i-Hilo's main stage, where I had produced Katherine Dunham in 1994 when we arrived in Hawai'i three years earlier. Our tour continued to two of the army bases on Oahu—Schofield Barracks and Fort Shafter—where there were large Black military audiences. Continuing on Oahu, we then performed at Leeward Community College, co-sponsored by the East-West Center in conjunction with my BCM, Inc., and ended the tour at the large Maui Arts and Culture Center. I was using my honed arts administration skills to spread the good word about Black culture throughout Hawai'i.

For the larger production of *Middle Passage,* I added two major Honolulu artists: drummer Jan Jeffries, a Philadelphia transplant who accompanied my UH-Manoa dance classes, and singer Azure McCall, known as "Hawaii's Empress of Jazz." These two consummate female artists brought a gender balance to the show and diversified the artistic expertise of this version of *Middle Passage,* designed to appeal to a general public audience in larger theaters. I was able to use Azure's powerfully soulful voice in song interludes like "Motherless Child" in the slave plantation section, as well as her sassy jazz rendition of "Sweet Georgia Brown" in the 1930s Savoy jazz swing section. On that latter song, I also added Jan Jeffries's tap dance expertise, incorporating her improvised tap solo accompanied by her own playing of the snare drums. Several of the venues paid a considerable fee for this two-hour production of *Middle Passage,* allowing me to hire more drummers like Michael Wall of Dara Dara and my best dance students Janette Cross, Leena Graves, and Ryoko Sato. This expanded version of the show received many accolades from our audiences, and on each island we toured, the Black culture theme lured many long-term African American islanders who had not partaken in their culture for decades. My life's mission was being actualized yet again in new ways in Hawai'i with *Middle Passage: The Beat of the African American Journey.*

Adding My Voice to Hawaii's Modern Dance

Besides creating, performing, and producing my own original theatrical production, I also participated in the organized modern dance scene in Hawai'i. One of my major choreographic works created during the seven years we lived in the islands was *Oshun, Goddess of Love.* This dance piece synthesized Yoruba spirituality and African dance through a contemporary dance sensibility. Oshun is the goddess of love, fertility, sweetness, and coquettishness, and represents beauty, joy, fertility, and fresh-water rivers. Oshun is also the

Figure 2.4. Author dancing *Oshun, Goddess of Love,* Hilo, Hawai'i, 1996. Photo: Eva Lee–Tea Hawai'i.

patron saint of the dance, making her a natural subject for choreography. One of her Yoruba praise names is *Yeye Jo,* Mother of Dance. I first created it as a solo for myself to represent all of Oshun's attributes through her traditional signature movements within the Cuban *orisa* dance tradition through a modern dance lens. My costume was a floor-length wide gold shirt (Oshun's colors are yellow, gold, and orange), with a matching gold head wrap and leotard. Around my waist I wore a cowrie belt that I had bought twenty years earlier in Ghana, with hanging cowrie seashells flaring outward when I turned.

The Oshun solo dance was first performed as a piece at a contemporary dance concert for the Big Island Dance Council at the East Hawai'i Cultural Center. The Hilo concert was produced by Eva Lee, a powerhouse choreographer-dancer at the center of the Big Island dance scene. But the Oshun solo was destined to become the centerpiece in a larger group work. That work, *Oshun, Goddess of Love,* premiered on Oahu at the 18th Annual Dance Festival at Leeward Community College (LLC) Theatre on April 26 and 27, 1996. I set group dance sections on my advanced students of varying ethnicities—Janette Cross (Japanese/African American), Norbert Larsen (white American),

Ryoko Sato (Japanese), and Andrea Torres (Brazilian). I based the group choreography on traditional African dances—Guinean *Kuku* and *Soli*—along with Dunham Technique, all of which they had learned in my classes.

With my choreography based in Cuban and African traditions, framed by a modern dance structure, *Oshun, Goddess of Love* stood out from the typical traditional modern dance or modern Hawaiian hula presented by my fellow choreographers on the LLC performance. The other choreographers were from LLC's own dance department, UH-Manoa's dance department, and Punahou School. Few contemporary dances accompanied by recorded music can effectively follow choreography with live African drumming. Hence, *Oshun* was positioned as the finale of the nine dances presented in the festival. Kola Robinson, an African American drummer from New York, trained in Cuban and African drumming styles, led an ensemble of drummers who galvanized the audience and gave my choreography the authenticity required.

The choreographic structure of *Oshun, Goddess of Love* consisted of five sections and revealed how traditional African societies renew themselves through invoking spiritual forces while transferring cultural knowledge to successive generations through initiation into adulthood.

Oshun, Goddess of Love became a big hit in Honolulu, and in the audience program I wrote: "Oshun is the deity of love, rivers, fertility, and all things sweet in the Yoruba spiritual pantheon of Nigeria. Her laugh is both the joy and the irony in life." At the end of the dance, I always bellowed out a loud symbolic Oshun laugh and threw gold dust into the air, as the lights slowly faded on Oshun's laughter and falling gold flakes (see book cover).

In this manner, I continued my dance and choreographic career as I earned my doctorate. I persisted with my own Black theatrical production that supported me and other Black artists in Hawai'i, taking *The Evolution of Black Dance* to new heights. At the same time, I developed my creative choreography in relation to my spiritual path with my best dance students. Even while the scholar was developing, the perpetual artist in me lingered and even flourished. Yet, I was not satisfied with only those accomplishments. I had to immerse myself in the dance culture that was all around me. I had to learn and perform hula.

3

Dancing in Hawai'i

Performing Hula and a Hip-Hop Doctorate

Ho'okoana—she who achieves and performs
Hawaiian name bestowed on author by Kumu Hula Ehulani Stephany

While continuing my dance career with *Middle Passage,* I was also studying, and eventually performing, hula. As a trained dance ethnologist and a protégé of Katherine Dunham, I could not ignore the danced-based Indigenous culture where I lived. Soon after I arrived on the Big Island, I joined Ehulani Stephany's *Halau Hula Kama Kani Hali' Ala O Puna* (The Returning Fragrant Winds of Puna). We had met in Richard Koob's Kalani Honua–generated "Appreciating the World's Cultures through Hawaii's Heritage" lecture-demonstration. For that production I had to learn some hula to perform during the Hawaiian section of our lecture-demonstration, and as a result I started attending Ehulani's weekly hula classes almost as soon as we arrived in the islands. Kumu Ehulani's halau was not the most well-known hula school in East Hawai'i, but she was very disciplined about developing a strong, authentic approach for *all* people who wanted to participate in Hawaiian cultural traditions. Our halau had all races and ethnicities, with me representing the *popolo*-Black side of the halau's multicultural profile. Richard and Delton would occasionally come to the class, but Lily Chan and I became religious about attending Ehulani's Monday night hula classes.

Ehulani, about my age, was a typical "local" Hawaiian, birthed with at least five ethnic mixtures—Hawaiian, Chinese, Filipino, Irish, and other—as she used to joke. Her name, Ehulani (heavenly redhead), refers to her maintaining a red hue to her hair. On her website she states that she started her own dance school in 1991, a mere three years before I arrived.[1] So, I arrived in Puna at a time when she was just beginning to build her school's reputation, and I like to think that my sincerity about my hula studies helped in her establishing the disciplined school for which she is now known. She taught us hula *kahiko* (ancient hula) and hula *auana* (modern hula), as well as *oli* (traditional chants) and lei-making.

Hula is truly a multilayered discipline consisting of several components comprising the complex spiritual tradition of Native Hawai'i. On her website, Ehulani's visionary goal states, "Expose the world to the beauty and majesty (sovereignty) of Hawaiian culture and be a guiding light in traditional hula, promoting its practice as a spiritual discipline." Although Ehulani became my personal friend, it was her emphasis on the spiritual aspects of the tradition that most attracted me, expecting reverence to Native Hawaiian culture through the discipline and practice of hula. I wrote in my journal about my experience of rehearsing and performing in my first hula show in December 1994.

> *Ehulani asked me to be a part of the hula show for the senior citizens at Nani Mau Gardens this past Tuesday. Intense rehearsals set me on a path of refining movement and steps. There is an exactitude with which each symbolic motion, representing the mele (song), must be done. Each motion is precise in displacing space—angles of arms, focus of eyes, and, of course, the rhythm of the steps—and is exact in a way that allows the spirit to flow through precise representation of sentiment. When the movements are done correctly, my soul relates to the mana (spirit) in the meaning that flows from the dance.*

What made hula so different from other dance traditions I had previously studied was the making of crafts integral to complete knowledge. It was necessary to learn how to make one's musical instruments, costumes, and leis of flora and fauna worn during the dance. I not only had to become skilled at the dances that visually represented specific *mele* and *oli* about beautiful Hawaiian name places or the great Hawaiian *ali'i* (royals), such as Hawaii's original King Kamehameha, King David Kalākaua, the Merrie Monarch, or Hawaii's last monarch, Queen Lili'uokulani, but I also had to know where to find specific vines, leaves, and flowers on the aina, as well as how to use them for making leis that had to be worn while I danced. In this way I became more in tune with the earth than I ever had been living in the urban mainland.

One example was making the hand rattle that one plays while dancing certain hulas. During one rehearsal, Ehulani announced that we were to make our own *uli'uli,* the feathered rattle musical instrument. This meant we had to sew each feather on by hand, and there were hundreds of them; I looked at her incredulously and said, "Ehulani, I'm working on a PhD, I can't possibly take on this time-intensive project." Her only response was, "All you have to do is when you get in bed each night, sew five feathers onto the frame, and you'll be surprised at how fast it will go." I followed her advice, and today I have my beautiful hand-made *uli'uli* as well as my doctorate. I learned a new kind of discipline from studying the complex and multilayered art of hula.

As I grew in my execution of hula movements as well as Native Hawaiian knowledge, Ehulani incorporated me into her performing ensemble, and I became even more aware of important Hawaiian landmarks and history. Toward the end of 1996, right after my fiftieth birthday, she got an invitation from the Kalapana O' Hana Association to have our halau perform for a *ho'olaulea* (festival) fundraiser. The occasion was the commemoration of the relocation of the historically famous Star of the Sea Painted Church to a location on Highway 130, not far from our home. It was built in 1930 by Father Evarist Gielen, a Belgian missionary, and has become a National Registry Historic Site, with beautiful hand-painted interior walls by Gielen. The *ho'olaulea* was to commemorate the church being saved from the Kilauea volcano lava flowing in the direction of its old location.

Our halau's performance was particularly significant to me because Ehulani gave me my first hula kahiko solo, "Moloka'i," and I was nervous. It is one thing to perform my new dance form with a *group,* but, as any dancer knows, a solo does not allow one to hide in the group movement dynamics. Adding to my unease was the reality that there was another hula halau performing at the festival as well, with seasoned hula practitioners who knew that particular hula I was to perform, and they would be intensely scrutinizing me. On the positive side, as I began performing "Moloka'i," a misty rain started falling, which I interpreted as a blessing from heaven, and felt honored to be dancing for the new location of the famous painted church.

I had recently returned from a mainland trip to see friends and family and teach some dance classes in Oakland. While there, I celebrated my fiftieth birthday by cutting my hair into a short natural Afro again, as I had done in my twenties. When I returned to the Big Island, Ehulani was taken aback because it did not represent her image of a hula dancer. Hawaiians prefer long flowing hair (albeit kinky-curly like the original Hawaiians) when performing. Before cutting it, I had usually worn my hair in braids to my shoulders, which gave the illusion of length. I simply told Ehulani I was an African American Elder and this was my culture, and therefore she had to accept my new short-cropped coiffure. The majority local Hawaiian audience must have accepted me and my hairstyle because after the halau's performance, several Native Hawaiians congratulated me. We all left our leis of *kauna'oa* vines, picked in that same Kalapana area, at the head of the altar of the church, and my short Afro hairdo was never mentioned again.

Comparative Research of Hawaiians and African Americans

Hula, in fact, was not that difficult for me to learn because many movements are similar to African dance, particularly Central African Congolese styles. Hawaiian hula is always done with bent knees (*aiha'a*), like African dance styles; although the torso is usually held in a more relaxed erect position and not bent toward the earth as in many African dances. The biggest similarity are the various Hawaiian hip rotations, like *'ami* (hip circles), *'ami kuku* (hip circles going down and up in threes), and *'ami 'oniu* (figure eights). These are akin to the hip rotations in *zebola* and *ngoma bakongo,* danced in the Republic of the Congo. When I first began studying with Ehulani, she was initially surprised at how quickly I was able to execute the hip movements, and at one rehearsal she gave me permission to show the similarities between hula and Congolese dance. All the halau members were fascinated to learn about how cultures so geographically far apart could be so similar in dance styles. I explained it this way: the human body is obviously the same worldwide, and dance cultures that remain connected to an earth-based worldview will use the human instrument in similar ways to imitate nature and its rhythms.

I used this perceived similarity between African dance cultures with the new Hawaiian dance culture I was embracing as an impetus to conduct some comparative scholarly research. Along with my movement analysis, I also investigated the historical parallels between African Americans and Hawaiians from the perspective of "the politics of the body" through the oppression endured by both groups. As a result, during my doctoral study in Hawai'i, I wrote an unpublished essay, "The Politics of the Body: A History of Cultural Resistance through Dance by Hawaiians and African Americans," which was presented at two scholarly conferences—the Popular Culture Association and the Congress on Research in Dance (CORD). I started the presentation, using Adrienne Kaeppler's work on hula and that of Robert Farris Thompson from the standpoint of the body:

> Viewing the general stance for Hawaiian hula and many African dance styles, a bent-knee position is observed. Anthropologist Adrienne Kaeppler, in her book *Hula Pahu*, discusses the *ai'ha'a* bent-knee position as a foundation for ancient Hawaiian dance derived from the sacred ritual movements that were distinguished from the secular *hula*."[2]
>
> Similarly, African art historian Robert Farris Thompson discusses the use of the bent-knee stance in many African cultures' signature dance styles, which he calls the "get-down" quality. He notes that, "a performer or a group of performers assume a deeply inflected, virtually crouching position, thus moving in proximity to the level of the earth;

[this] is important in Africa and found in a number of societies of the western and central portions of the continent.[3]

My article, "The Politics of the Body," established the *corporeal* bodily parallels between African and Hawaiian dance that, at the time, was a relatively new scholarly comparison.

But the primary purpose of my essay and presentations was to demonstrate the similar historical politics of repression of the dance and culture of African descendants in the United States and that of Hawaiians in the Sandwich Islands, as Hawaiʻi was earlier called. The majority of the essay took the following tone:

> The outlawing of African drumming and gatherings among slaves in the southern colonies in 1740 and the banning of the hula among Hawaiians in 1830 were prime examples of the threat of dance and music to the power of 18th- and 19th-century Euro-American hegemony. Hula, under the stern and scrutinizing eyes of early New England Calvinist missionaries, became a "lascivious" act that could not be tolerated in the Euro-American "civilizing" project in Hawaiʻi.[4]
>
> Indeed, the history of European domination of the "Third World" has been based not only on military and political power, but also on cultural erosion brought about through the tactics of divide and conquer, the commercialization of symbols of the subordinated culture, and the enactment of specific laws banning particular overt cultural practices.[5]

In my scholarly presentation I compared Hawaiian resistance and complicity through hula in the face of culture change to African American's history of regaining a sense of cultural integrity through several historical reassessments of their African roots. I concluded my presentation by emphasizing my concept of the "politics of the body" regarding the two cultural groups.

> The *politics of the body* is an intricate web of the dominant culture's hegemony and subordinate culture's oppositional strategies. As Hawaiians and African Americans continue their renaissances of cultural rediscovery through their dance, they encountered a similar struggle for regaining cultural identity. Both Hawaiians and African Americans view dance and music as one of the keys to self-identity and, as Katherine Dunham says, as a way of potentially saving themselves.[6]

My research for writing "The Politics of the Body" helped me make political connections between African Americans and Native Hawaiians historically as well as in contemporary times while I was living in Hawai'i. The modern-day Hawaiian sovereignty movement held frequent protest marches and sit-ins in front of the Hawai'i State Capitol building on Beretania Street in Honolulu. Native Hawaiian oli and hula were often used in these public protests, emphasizing the centrality of the traditional culture of the islands that remains alive, despite the decades of the appropriating tourist industry. During my research I also discovered a 1980s article written by Professor Haunani-Kay Trask documenting meetings between 1970s Hawaiian sovereignty activists and Black militant activists from the Bay Area.[7] When I started my research, I knew nothing about specific Black activists from my home area being in dialogue with Hawaiian militants while both groups were trying to form resistance movements.

The obvious link between African Americans and Native Hawaiians regarding their mutual history of oppression was also dramatized while I was living in Hawai'i in the late 1990s, albeit from a more middle-class perspective. On January 16, 1998, I participated in an event called "The Queen and Dr. King" held at Honolulu Hale. This theatrical program was a joint venture of the Dr. Martin Luther King Jr. Holiday Coalition, a Honolulu Black organization, and the Hawaiian Sacred Times and Sacred Places organization. The two groups jointly produced the well-attended event to celebrate Martin Luther King's holiday, then only in its fifteenth year as an annual national holiday.

This important public occasion brought African Americans and Native Hawaiians together, and was executive produced by longtime Honolulu civil rights activist Marsha Joyner. To represent Hawaiian culture, Joyner got the Royal Hawaiian Band and the Kamehameha Schools Choir to perform. Representing African American culture, Honolulu Black musicians and singers performed James Weldon Johnson's Negro National Anthem, and I performed a solo dance while also premiering an African American history slideshow I had assembled. The centerpiece of the entire event was a theatrical production written by Joyner that revealed parallels between the last Hawaiian monarch, the dethroned Queen Lili'uokulani, and Reverend King, both of whom chose nonviolence in facing their oppressors. Marsha Joyner's audience program read, "They were people of peace whose lives were notably lacking in peace." The Queen & Dr. King was an original narrated musical performance that documented the two groups' common struggle for dignity and human rights, and I was proud to be a part of it.

Performance as Research through Hula

Since arriving in Hawai'i and positioning myself in academia and the modern and hula dance scenes, I became aware of the concept of "performance as research," allowing me to utilize my dancing and my observations within the performance arena as a tool of my academic investigations. Living on the Hilo side of the Big Island was indeed advantageous for growing my knowledge base of Indigenous Hawaiian culture. Hula halaus from the other islands come to pay tribute to the Kilauea active volcano ruled by the powerful fire goddess Pele at her Halemaumau crater. My halau made several trips to perform oli to the goddess and to leave *ho'o kapu* (ti leaf packet offerings) at the edge of the crater. It is said that if the goddess shows one favor, the winds will blow one's sacred packet offerings into the pit. In a half hour I could drive from our home in Leilani Estates to Volcano National Park, the home of the active Kilauea volcano. I realized I lived in the heart of Native Hawaiian mythology and culture.[8]

But nothing gives Hilo and East Hawai'i cultural prestige like the annual Merrie Monarch Hula Festival. This weeklong hula festival is held in the month of April in Hilo, with all the major hula halaus arriving from around the islands to compete. The festival's name honors King David Kalākaua, called the "Merrie Monarch" for his patronage of Hawaiian arts and the restoration of many Hawaiian cultural traditions during his nineteenth-century reign, including the hula. Today, Hawaii's main hula halaus train and prepare choreography all year for the competition while producing travel fundraisers to send their best dancers to compete in Hilo's Merrie Monarch festival. Although our halau never competed, we did participate in several ancillary events preceding and during the annual April Merrie Monarch Festival.

On April 5, 1998, after four years of hula training alongside my friend and hula sister Lily Chan-Harris (Ululani), I underwent *hula uniki* (hula graduation). Kimathi, several of my African Americans friends, and the rest of our halau *haumana* (members) and their friends were in attendance as our audience at Hawai'i Volcanoes National Park to witness the occasion. I had called my family in California to make them aware of my hula uniki, which had become as important as getting my doctorate. Some family members responded with well wishes: my father called me that very morning, my sister Brenda left a message of congratulations on my phone, and I talked to my mother the day before. I had a warm fuzzy feeling when she wished me success. It felt like my family, and, by extension, my ancestors were physically with me on the day of my hula uniki. Even before that day Ehulani Stephany had bestowed a Hawaiian name on me: *Ho'oko'ana* (she who achieves and performs). *Ho'oko ku* means to achieve, while *hana* means to perform well. I was honored that my kumu hula recognized my hard work and gave me such an appropriate and meaningful name.

Ululani and I had to master four *hula kahiko* and four *hula auana,* with the two dance styles taking place at two different locations within the park. The ancient hula performance happened at the sacred Pa Hula Platform created by the Hawaiian elder Mary Kawena Pukui for the sole purpose of preserving hula kahiko. That location gave our ancient hula performance a serious tone. For the modern hula auana that followed, we performed in the picnic camp area of Bird Park, and afterward hosted a potluck lunch with all of our friends who had come to witness our uniki.

After arriving in Hawaiʻi Volcanoes National Park that morning, we first had to pay homage to Pele for allowing us to be on her sacred Kilauea slope by offering a prayer at Halemaumau. All of us—Kumu Ehulani, Ululani, and Butch, our drummer accompanist who was also performing his uniki as a musician, and me—said the *E Hoʻo Mai* meditation chant with which we always started our weekly hula practice. We then placed our prepared *hoʻo kapu* at the crater's edge and were grateful to see the wind quickly blow them into the crater. When we arrived at the hula platform area, the other halau members serving as our *lima kokua* (helper-attendants) helped us dress with the costumes that we ourselves had sewn and ink-stamped with ancient Hawaiian symbols. Our neck leis and *kupeʻe* (ankle and wrist leis) were made from braided *palapalai* fern, prevalent in the Volcanoes Park area. Our crown lei, or *lei poʻo,* were made from *lehua* blossoms from the *ohia* tree, sacred to Pele. All leis had been made the day before in a marathon session of preparations for this sacred day of uniki.

As we stood at the entrance to the Pa Hula Platform chanting the *oli kahea* (chant for permission to enter), Ehulani, Butch, and the other musicians played the *ipu* (musical gourd) kneeling on the opposite side of the platform. Ehulani chanted the answer chant, giving us permission to enter the platform with the *hula kaʻi,* or entrance hula. I felt the *mana* and danced in the lowest *aihaʻa* I could manage at my age. Our first hula was "Pua Ana Kamakani," a *hula noho* (seated hula on the knees, which I could never execute now), performed with *ili ili* (stone rocks) that we had gathered on a halau excursion to the ocean.

Our second hula was "O' Lilu'o Kalani," which praised the last reigning monarch of Hawaiʻi and felt so powerful that it seemed as though the Queen Liliʻuokulani herself was there witnessing her honorific hula. Our third hula, "Ke Haʻa La Puna," one of my favorites, is a hula in homage to Madame Pele herself. I danced with my personally made *uliʻuli* rattle that had taken a year

Figure 3.1. The author (*right*) and Ululani (Lily Chan-Harris) perform hula *noho* during hula *uniki* in Volcano National Park, 1998. Photo courtesy of author.

to complete and felt personally powerful. The final hula kahiko of our uniki performance was "Holo Ana O'Kalakaua" for the Merrie Monarch himself. Kumu Hula Ehulani Stephany had taught us well, and even with a few minor mistakes, I realized I had been taught hula the *pono* (righteous) way, which she had insisted must be maintained even in the midst of continual modern-day cultural change. I wrote in my journal, *"I danced the sacred dance in praise of the gods and the ancestors of Hawai'i. I danced for Mother Earth herself."*

Our halau and audience members then made the transition to Bird Park, about a mile lower down the mountain, for the secular hula auana part of our uniki. While hula kahiko is about the spirit, hula auana is about the heart, and together they are the breadth and depth of life for hula practitioners. One is supposed to smile while performing auana, and initially I responded to this dictate the way I did when I was told to do the same in ballet class: I felt it was phony and insincere to always plaster on a smile. Hula auana, however, allowed me to find the *heart* chakra that allowed a sincere inner smile; I discovered how to transcend the gestures and steps to extend my heart through each movement, gladly projecting my heart through the various auana dances we performed that afternoon: "Koali," "Palisa," "Aia La O Pele," and "Green Rose Hula."

Ululani and I danced beautifully together for our friends, family, and hula *ohana* (family). As we danced to the melodic meles sung by Ehulani and Butch, my hula sister and I flowed in unity with *aloha* exuding throughout our bodies. Our audience appreciated that our uniki performances allowed them to value hula at a new level. I directly experienced what Miss Dunham meant about dance and cultural patterns: "The emotional life of any community is clearly legible in its art forms, and because the dance seeks continuously to capture moments of life in a fusion of time, space, and motion, the dance is at a given moment the most accurate chronicler of culture pattern."[9] My uniki performances allowed me to embody the patterns of Hawaiian culture, and I was grateful.

After our auana performance, Ehulani made a concluding speech acknowledging our dedication, perseverance, and hard work, revealing that she had started with fifteen uniki students and ended with we three who had the discipline to go through the rigors of hula to graduate—Butch, Ululani, and Hoʻokoʻana. I felt that now I had truly become *Hoʻokoʻana,* she who achieves and performs. Kumu Hula Ehulani Stephany even mentioned that I accomplished uniki while I was working on my PhD, which brought tears to my eyes as my hula accomplishment truly hit me. I felt a little like what Katherine Dunham must have felt back in the 1930s in Haiti as a new initiate from another culture having survived the *lave tet* (head cleansing) ceremony in vodou. My hula uniki was a major cross-cultural accomplishment. The day ended with all of us—my husband and friends with my halau sisters and brothers and their families—sharing a meal at the picnic tables on a bright sunny day. I had accomplished my hula graduation, and it was now time to redouble my efforts to achieve the academic one.

Staying Connected to the Mainland and Developing My Scholarship

Even with my busy life in the islands—working on my doctorate, performing hula, and touring my *Middle Passage* production, Kimathi and I tried to stay connected to family and the cultural changes on the US mainland. While living in the middle of the Pacific, halfway between the continental US and the Asia Pacific Rim, I wanted to remain knowledgeable about the developments and shifts particularly in dance and African American Studies. So I occasionally traveled to various dance conferences and returned several times to the Bay Area to see my family and dance community.

My first trip back was in January 1995 to serve on the old Expansion Arts panel for the National Endowment for the Arts (NEA) in Washington, DC, and as a dance panelist at the International Association for Blacks in Dance (IABD) in Philadelphia. Coming from tropical Hawaiʻi and landing in cold twenty-degree Washington, DC, weather was a shock; however, being surrounded by Black folks again made me aware of how much I missed being in a Black environment.

Sitting at the conference table at the NEA, I recognized how much the conservative policies of President Bill Clinton's second term, as he compromised with a majority Republican Congress, was affecting the arts. Being at the federal government's only arts-funding agency reminded me of the continual struggle in the US to convince the government of the vital importance of the arts and the political pendulum underlying that lack of support. This was another reason to make a transition from the arts to the humanities—from dance to academia, although the humanities were being funded only slightly higher than the arts. I had always joked that I was a triple minority: Black, a woman, and a dancer.

Arriving in Philadelphia for the IABD conference, I entered the second leg of my mainland journey. As I was riding the bus through Germantown to visit my dance colleague Brenda Dixon Gottschild, I had my spirit renewed being surrounded by Black folks chatting and laughing on the bus. The conference itself reinforced my relationship to Black dance: I reconnected to my dance sister Cleo Parker Robinson, who was on the Executive Committee of IABD, and reestablished my relationships with the other major Black divas of major regional dance companies: Founder of IABD and host of that year's conference Joan Myers Brown of PHILADANCO, the late Jeraldyne Blunden (1940–1999) of Dayton Contemporary Dance Company, Ann Williams of Dallas Black Dance Theatre, Cleo Parker Robinson of Cleo Parker Robinson Dance in Denver, and Lula Washington of Lula Washington Dance Theatre in Los Angeles. But this conference also became a coda to what I had discovered at the NEA Expansion Arts Program: these artistic directors were feeling the lack of federal funding the most.

I felt at home at the IABD conference, mingling with all of the Black dance legends, like choreographer Donald McKayle, ballerina Janet Collins, modern dancer Carmen de Lavallade, and African dancer Chuck Davis. I was hobnobbing with all the Black dance scholar-activists like Brenda Dixon Gottschild, Katrina Hazzard-Donald, the late Kariamu Welch (1949–2021), and Marta Vega. Being in Philadelphia at IABD allowed me to reconnect to my Black dance roots while living in my Hawaiian paradise and working on my doctorate.

Another noteworthy trip back to the US mainland was in October 1997 when I returned to Oakland for CitiCentre Dance Theatre's twentieth anniversary. Twenty years after I had returned from Ghana fired up to create a multicultural arts institution, my nonprofit organization, which had started as Everybody's Creative Arts Center (ECAC) and morphed into CitiCentre Dance Theatre (CDT), was still going strong, making me extremely proud.

On October 26, nearly two hundred guests celebrated the twentieth anniversary occasion at Oakland Chinatown's Silver Dragon Restaurant on Webster and Eighth Streets, not far from the Alice Arts Center, now the Malonga Casquelourd Center for the Arts. Fania Davis, sister to Angela Davis and one of the original members of the ECAC founding committee, was then President of the Board of Directors, and she billed the event as both an anniversary and awards ceremony.

My long-term Dunham mentor, Ruth Beckford, was prominent at the twentieth anniversary celebration. She gave her newly established Extraordinary People in the Field of Dance Awards to key pioneers in the Oakland dance community. Miss Beckford bestowed the Ruth Beckford Award on Fua Dia Congo, Zak Diouf, and Naomi Ghedo-Diouf of the Diamano Coura West African Dance Company; Ron Guidi, artistic director of the Oakland Ballet; C.K. Ladzekpo of the African Music and Dance Ensemble; her protégé Debo-

Figure 3.2. Ruth Beckford Extraordinary People in the Field of Dance awardees, 1997. (*Standing left to right*: C. K. Ladzekpo, Ron Guidi, Naomi Ghedo-Diouf, Zak Diouf, and Malonga Casquelourd. *Seated left to right*: Deborah Vaughan, the author, Ruth Beckford.) Photo courtesy of author.

rah Vaughan of Dimensions Dance Theater, and me as founder and former artistic director of CDT.

The anniversary had been three years in the planning, led by a group of volunteers headed by long-term ECAC/CDT dance student Leona Hodges. The community dedication I saw upon my return told me how much the Oakland Black dance community valued and depended upon the cultural institution I had founded. CDT continued to flourish and grow because it continued to fulfill a need in the East Bay for an African-based dance center—a safe space for people who wanted to dance in blackness. I felt a little like what Katherine Dunham must have felt whenever she returned to East St. Louis, her city that she had changed through Black dance.

As I sat at the VIP table with my mother Tenola beside me, I was extremely proud of the dance institution I had founded, particularly because it was maintained by the very community for which it was established. The organization represented the critical relationship between individual initiative and inspired collective communal work for socio-cultural justice and change. An artist like myself, with a vision, could start an arts initiative, but it takes the collective community being served to achieve the longevity of institutionalization, and I couldn't have been prouder. Even though I was now living in Hawai'i, the Africanist-focused dance organization I had created after my sojourn in Ghana continued to flourish and serve Oakland's arts community.

I was receiving validation for my community activism as a dance leader in Oakland, as well as for my dance career in the Bay Area, since my early twenties, and my mother was there to witness it.

Figure 3.3. Author with her mother, Tenola Hall, at the twentieth anniversary of CitiCentre Dance Theatre, Oakland, California, 1997. Photo courtesy of author.

Kimathi and I also tried to stay connected to our families while living in Hawai'i. We not only returned to the mainland but had them visit us in the islands. I brought my niece Anjelica, the daughter of my sister Brenda, to stay with us on the Big Island during several of her summer vacations, allowing me to practice being mother to a young girl for a change. In July 1996, Kimathi's family visited us from Ohio for the first time, giving us another excuse to host another one of our "Afro-Hawaiian Luaus" that we had become well known for in our new community. His mother Betty, sister Susan, and her husband and daughter Kyra all crowded into our small two-bedroom home. They enjoyed our traditional Hawaiian luau, complete with food cooked in an underground *imu* pit, and hula and African dance performances. It was an enriching cross-cultural experience that our mainland family thoroughly enjoyed. It was a celebratory family party where we shared with them the unique joys of our new natural and cultural environment.

On the Road to Earning My Doctorate

By 1997 I had completed the American Studies department's core courses and electives and became a PhD candidate. This qualified me to be hired as a lecturer to teach the department's lower-division courses to undergraduates. The undergraduate courses I taught gave me lecture experience and also qualified me for a tuition waiver, thereby giving me income and free time to write my dissertation. In fall 1997 I began teaching The American Experience and Diversity in American Life.

I had learned the American Studies interdisciplinary approach to representing the complexity of the United States and was anxious to test my academic teaching ability in the particular multicultural mix that is Hawai'i. For Diversity in American Life, I took a literature approach, contrasting Native American, local Hawaiian, and African American novels to teach undergraduates about American cultural diversity. Susan Power's *The Grass Dancer* (1994), about Sioux heritage with their grass dance as a metaphor for historic oppression and contemporary aspirations, was perfect for my emphasis on the importance of dance in native cultures. Toni Morrison's classic *Song of Solomon* (1977), which unravels the Great Migration of African Americans northward, was my course's Black cultural unit. Her central character, Milkman, traces his roots back to the South to find "his people" and, in the process, himself.

My third novel was a hit with my students. It was Lois-Ann Yamanaka's short stories about the mixing of Hawaii's ethnic groups into a "local" culture through a Japanese-Hawaiian lens in her *Wild Meat and the Bully Burgers*

(1996). She utilizes a humorous use of local pidgin English familiar to my students with which they could really identify. That novel helped the students interrogate the underpinnings of their own contemporary lives in Hawai'i. The course became my first strictly humanities-based teaching experience that allowed me to focus on literature as a socio-cultural teaching tool.

Learning about US multiculturalism through literature was a useful device, and the students responded very positively to the course's methodology. All three novels grappled with the complexities and ambiguities of identity, a conscious collective past with ever-present ancestors, along with the layered personal unconscious. Coming to terms with these multifaceted forces of identity was particularly important in the latter nineties when we were first realizing how much the internet and the World Wide Web was influencing national and global social dynamics.

We were still in a time of innocence, where personal identity was far less complex. Then there were no smartphones, Facebook, Instagram, TikTok, Twitter, Snapchat, Tinder, artificial intelligence, or streaming platforms; nor were we plagued with the dark web, online conspiracy theories, identity theft, sexting, social media trolling, and cyberbullying. In the latter nineties we could never have imagined how much more complex our world was destined to become with increasing technology. And for Black folks, the term *Afrofuturism* was little known, then an elitist term bantered about by only a few hip New York cultural pundits and academics.

My growing personal scholarship was bolstered by UH-Manoa occasionally presenting African and African American scholar and intellectuals who stimulated my critical thinking about our contemporary times in relation to the past. One such occasion was in October 1997 when Ngugi wa Thiong'o, distinguished Kenyan novelist, playwright, and essayist, gave a brilliant talk as a part of the university's Distinguished Lecturer Series, and I encouraged my students to attend as an extra credit assignment.[10] His talk, "Native Languages and the Politics of De-Colonization," made astute connections between African languages and the Hawaiian language that were both spoken before any European language was ever uttered in their Indigenous locales. He argued that language, as a system of communication, created a vital connection between Indigenous peoples and their values, which is critical in shifting postcolonial power relations in the world.

This was a particularly important message in Hawai'i during the late 1990s when the Hawaiian sovereignty movement was growing stronger. Gaining speaking proficiency in the Native Hawaiian language was a part of the growing identity politics in the islands. Thiong'o emphasized that "language produces a community, as the primary seed of the culture," and this was the provocative message that pro-sovereignty professors like the late Haunani-Kay Trask wanted to emphasize at the university, as her Hawaiian Studies department stressed Hawaiian language classes, like most of the other universities throughout the islands.

The following February, prison political activist, author, professor, and my friend Angela Davis came to UH-Manoa. It was a part of the same Distinguished Scholar Series, co-sponsored by the Center for Hawaiian Studies along with the university's African American Curriculum Task Force directed by my friend Dr. Kathryn Waddell Takara. Having Takara's task force as a co-sponsor was an important statement given the marginal status of African Americans at UH-Manoa, even after the 1994 African American Visions project. Angela Davis was then professor in the History of Consciousness Department at UC Santa Cruz, and spoke about a concept that had only recently begun circulating in public discourse, but today is ubiquitous in social justice analysis: the Prison Industrial Complex. Of course, Angela drew a capacity audience at the Campus Center Ballroom for her talk entitled "Racism in the Criminal Justice System."

Her lecture had particular resonance in Hawai'i at the time because of a raging public debate about a potential new prison for the state's growing incarcerated population in the Ka'u district on the Big Island. A *Honolulu Weekly* article about Angela's university appearance emphasized her argument about how the US "over-criminalized drugs, and as a result are imprisoning record numbers of young blacks who are guilty only of self-medicating."[11] The racist perspective undergirding Black criminalization and illegal drug use was not really exposed until twenty years later, when in 2019 opioid addiction among white suburbanites became an epidemic. The public discourse for that crisis focused instead on physical and mental health rather than criminality. Angela, like Ngugi the previous year, brought a critical comparative understanding of the oppression of people of color, which was important for interrogating the power relations among ethnic groups in Hawai'i.

The following day Takara's task force sponsored a reception for Angela Davis at the Center for Hawaiian Studies. I opened the reception with a dance performance with live drumming, led by African American musician Sango Muyiwa, with whom I occasionally worked in Honolulu. I performed Yoruba *orisa* dances, designed to invoke two of the seven main African deities—Elegua, god of the crossroads, and Yemonja, goddess of the ocean, an obvious important natural force in the islands. I sang songs for the two African gods and performed their traditional dances, beginning with Elegua to bless the opening of the reception, and then Yemonja for her cleansing waters.

But I also made sure to honor the Hawaiian spirits. Ever aware of the host culture, I paid homage to the Hawaiian spirits by chanting the "Hawaiian Oli Oli" I learned in my hula studies on the Big Island. As I chanted the last *oli* note, Sango began the opening prayer to the deity of the crossroads, creating a powerful instant of the two cultural traditions communicating in the same sacred moment. As soon as we finished, Angela jumped to her feet and rushed to hug me. Angela Davis's heartfelt acknowledgment of my dance to the orisas in Hawai'i will forever be etched in my historical memory. I felt like the orisas came to tell Angela that they were blessing her so she could continue to carry the baton of justice for the long-distance marathon.

Hip-Hop as My Dissertation Subject

In between my performance obligations and attending graduate classes, in 1998 I began intense research for my doctoral dissertation. After finishing my last class, I began to write the proposal for my dissertation, the next step in the arduous PhD process. Helbling, as a Harlem Renaissance scholar, was himself in the throes of writing his most well-known book, *The Harlem Renaissance: The One and the Many*, published in 1999, the year I would graduate. When I joined the department, he had confessed he knew little about dance and performance, except for their effects on jazz music in the 1920s and 1930s. So I was really on my own in formulating my topic. Since I had entered American Studies with the idea to research the influence of African American performance on American society in general, I proceeded to construct a dissertation proposal on the historical influence of Black dance and music. That dissertation eventually became *African Aesthetics, American Culture: Hip Hop in the Global Era.*

Even though hip-hop culture was becoming more influential through rap music in the 1980s and the early 1990s before we moved to Hawai'i, being a baby boomer who was weaned on the Black Arts Movement in the late sixties San Francisco Bay Area, I knew little about hip-hop culture. Everyone knew about the West Coast rapper Tupac Shakur, and I had heard the names of Digital Underground and the Oakland rapper Too Short, but I had little interest in "what those kids were doing." But an innocent life coincident can often be the trigger for an entirely new research trajectory. Kimathi's teaching at Pahoa High School and my observation about how much mainland US urban Black culture was affecting local youth in our rural area of Hawai'i at his school forced me to realize I was witnessing a rich and influential cultural phenomenon deserving of in-depth investigation. The beginning paragraph of my first published book after graduation, *The Africanist Aesthetic in Global Hip-Hop: Power Moves* (2007) was a revision of my eventual dissertation, and it captured the pivotal movement when I made the decision to write about hip-hop culture's effect on American culture and the globe:

> "There's hip-hop in Hawai'i?" I blurted out, as I drove my ex-husband into the parking lot of the only high school in the rural area where he taught. "I mean, I figured it was in Honolulu," I continued in amazement, "but I just didn't think that these kids in the country were into rap." His answer was simple: "They live in the world too; they watch MTV." This verbal exchange was prompted by a high school student who pulled into the parking lot alongside us, with a gangsta rap of Master P pumping loudly out of his car stereo, while he leaned coolly in his backward-turned cap and sunglasses. Having moved from Oakland, California, to the small village of Pahoa on the Big Island of Hawai'i four years earlier, this young local Hawaiian with his rap music and cool attitude, for me, was like a déjà vu experience.[12]

The globalization of hip-hop culture, therefore, became my dissertation topic: how Black urban youth culture—hip-hop—was now affecting youth identity around the world.

If I was going to do justice to my newfound subject, I had to quickly learn the history and foundational issues of hip-hop youth culture. I had to acquire a lot of information quickly. As some of my Big Island Black friends had children who were teenagers and young adults, whom I knew were into hip-hop culture and rap music, I convinced a cadre of those young men, who called themselves "hip-hop heads" in the vernacular, to make me several mixtape music cassettes. They assembled rap classics, like Sugar Hill Gang's "Rapper's Delight," N.W.A.'s "Fuck Tha Police," Cyprus Hill's "Insane in the Membrane," Public Enemy's "Fight the Power," Geto Boys' *We Can't be Stopped*, Yo-Yo's *Make Way for the Motherlode*, Bone Thugs-N-Harmony's *E. 1999 Eternal*, Dr. Dre's "Nuthin' But a 'G' Thang," and others. I began to "woodshed," consuming the music, taking notes, and asking my young crew about slang meanings and general hip-hop lore. They were impressed that an "old woman" like me really took their culture as seriously as they did and were always willing to supply the hip-hop background information I needed. When I emerged from these intense youth cultural sessions, I wasn't a hip-hop aficionado by any means, but I could hold my own with the average rap music enthusiast.

I also began to read some of the early hip-hop scholarship that became critical to my dissertation. I devoured Trisha Rose's *Black Noise, Rap Music and Black Culture in Contemporary America,* published in 1994 as a revision of her own PhD dissertation. That book is the classic "go-to" for early New

York hip-hop history and analysis. William Eric Perkins's anthology *Droppin' Science: Critical Essays on Rap Music and Hip-Hop Culture* (1996) provided an important overview of the four hip-hop elements—deejaying, rapping, breaking, and writing or graffiti art—as well as sociological, gender, regional, and beginning perspectives on globalization of the youth culture.

As I dove deep into the existing hip-hop research and writing, journalist Nelson George published *Hip Hop America* in 1999 from his seminal New York insider perspective. In 1985 George had already coedited *Fresh: Hip Hop Don't Stop,* which captured the formative mid-1980s hip-hop in New York. That book included description and analysis of what the media started calling breakdance, which was a chapter by the late dance theorist Sally Banes (1950–2020). In 1998, the renowned rapper Chuck D of Public Enemy authored an insider perspective in his *Fight the Power: Rap, Race, and Reality,* providing an important global perspective from the group's world tours produced by Def Jam Records. In this way, I synthesized research and the consumption of rap music to begin writing my dissertation on hip-hop as the current phase of the US appropriation of Black culture.

I realized I had been in the thick of controversial stances and alternative cultural perspectives since I decided to make dance and Black culture the foundation of my career. Hip-hop scholarship was now becoming an extension of my lifelong cultural rebellion, with a contemporary youth culture signifier. Back then in the late nineties I had to find my unique contribution to the inchoate field of Hip-Hop Studies to finish my dissertation and earn my doctorate, which would become the ticket to my future.

My approach to writing my dissertation was blending hip-hop academic and journalistic scholarship with texts focused in African American and Cultural Studies. This created a rapprochement of disciplines that revealed insights about the burgeoning American youth culture and its multiple contexts, including youth identity representation, urban sociology, and capitalism's ubiquitous cultural appropriation. For example, I devoured Fredric Jameson's classic *Postmodernism, or The Cultural Logic of Late Capitalism* (1992), which became a large part of my economic analysis in my fourth chapter, "'It's All About the Benjamins': Hip-Hop as a Sign of the New Millennium Times." In hindsight, I was tuning into an Afrofuturism as we approached the twenty-first century, and I predicted hip-hop would play a seminal role in how that future would manifest, posing a counternarrative to the continuing "Fear of a Black Planet," as Public Enemy rapped. That future is now, and hip-hop is the most consumed popular music on the planet. I was recognizing the past slipping into the present while the future was ever-looming.

My primary argument was that hip-hop culture had become the quintessential sign of the times and was then becoming central to this current stage of *late* capitalism. I maintained that global capital circulation depends on the shifting definitions of "cool" in popular culture to function, and hip-hop had become the new postmodern sign of "cool" driving worldwide capitalism, particularly since the advent of the "gangsta" rap genre at the beginning of the nineties. One of my overarching contentions was that although hip-hop was in cahoots with free enterprise entrepreneurship, it also retained a counter-hegemonic resistive element. I called this seemingly contradictory identity of the youth culture the "complicity and resistance in hip-hop."

To prove this perceived dialectic, I established a major comparative study of youth consumers of hip-hop, as well as interviews with important Hawai'i hip-hop professional artists. I designed and conducted a comparative study between students at nearby Pahoa High School and Oakland's Castlemont High School, in the heart of East Oakland as the city's Black ghetto. Also, I conducted nightclub research in Honolulu, interviewing several internationally competing breakdancers, like TeN (Justin Alladin) in Honolulu and Jason Frasco in Hilo, as well as Strategy (David Comer), a dancer with the Hawai'i chapter of the Rock Steady Crew. The co-founder of that international hip-hop dance organization, Crazy Legs (Richard Colon) from the Bronx, fortunately for me, came to the Big Island to teach a b-boy (breakdance) workshop, and I was able to interview him while he was in Hilo. Kutmaster Spaz (Derrick Kamohoali'i Bulatao), one of Honolulu's most well-known hip-hop deejays, became an important inroad into understanding Honolulu's unique rap and deejaying scene.

My sociological study comparing the two high school groups was an important empirical component in my overall qualitative analyses about global hip-hop. Funded by the Hawai'i Committee for the Humanities, I was able to spend time in classrooms in both schools video-taping group interviews with teenagers engaged with the same youth culture thousands of miles apart. I recorded those differences in both my dissertation and the *Power Moves* book:

> At Castlemont High School the black youth interviewed also placed rap music high on the list of their musical preferences yet had a much more sophisticated understanding and desire for other forms of Black-originated musical styles. R&B, soul, and funk oldies but goodies and even jazz were listed as important to their lives. In contrast, when I asked the Hawaiian youth about R&B, the majority said they rarely listened to it. Particularly for Hawaiian male students, R&B was considered too

palatable and bland and not "hardcore" enough. Pahoa High youth represent hip-hop's global consumer market. As such, they are entering the continuum of Black music exportation at a certain historical juncture where *ghettocentricity* and the thug image are central. Hip-hop youth in Hawai'i are reflective of current marketplace emphasis, while Black hip-hop youth in mainland urban areas have an added familial culture that puts them in immediate proximity to predecessor music forms that invoke their ancestors.[13]

Yet, I also found that hip-hop professional artists in Hawai'i had a similar response as the Oakland Black youths. This led me to conclude that artists in the global sphere, even though removed from urban Black America, do their background homework and become knowledgeable about rap's derivative sampling approach from previous Black musical styles. Thus, in my dissertation research I was able to utilize my contacts and insider status in Oakland in my research on the globalization of hip-hop, with Hawai'i as a case study.

I benefited from how much the internet had expanded because I could also conduct global research online, corresponding with hip-hop practitioners in different international locations. My dissertation, and subsequent first book, compares hip-hop in England, France, Russia, and Japan, as well as Hawai'i. My guiding hypothesis evolved into the following premise: anywhere hip-hop is located, it must be steeped in an Africanist aesthetic to be identified as that specific youth-oriented subculture.

Through my long-term research into what comprised the Africanist aesthetic in *dance,* which I used in the many incarnations of *The Evolution of Black Dance,* I was able to delineate those performance patterns as they appeared in hip-hop culture in rap and deejaying, not only hip-hop dance styles. I also theorized about how one recognizes the aesthetic, even when it was glossed with in another international language or music tradition.

My dissertation committee members were impressed with my analyses and findings and gave me important feedback in the process of my writing. With Helbling's help, I was able to situate the ascendancy of gangsta rap within the long-standing American cultural ethos of the *outlaw as hero,* from icons like Jesse James as a nineteenth-century outlaw bank and train robber during the later part of America's "manifest destiny" westward movement to 1920s Chicago prohibition mobster Al Capone. Tying this thesis into the long-standing influence of Black performance in the US was supported and furthered by the brilliant insights of my long-term friend VèVè Clark from UC Berkeley, the off-campus "outside" member of my committee who sharpened my growing critical perspectives.[14]

My defense presentation was scheduled for October 25, 1999, in Moore Hall, the home of the Department of American Studies. My committee was assembled—Mark Helbling, David Stannard, David Bertelson, and Kathryn Takara, with VèVè Clark participating over the phone. Departmental rules said that the public could also attend, so Gladys Crampton was present as well. Kathryn picked her up and drove Gladys to campus for the event, and I felt blessed that my elder auntie would be in attendance on this auspicious day.

The dissertation defense proceedings followed typical protocol. At the end of the doctoral grilling on the text and my concepts, I left the room. When I returned they all greeted me as "Dr. Osumare." They noted that not only was I graduating with a solid 4.0 grade point average, but moreover they had never had a student go through their doctoral program in the record time of four years. I again joked, "Well, I figured I had to hurry up and graduate to be eligible for a tenure-track job, before it's time for me to retire." Part of me was not joking; I was one month away from my fifty-third birthday, but I had accomplished my goal of fully making the transition from dancer-artist to academic-scholar.

On December 19, 1999, I walked across the commencement stage at the University of Hawai'i at Manoa and received my doctoral diploma, the first graduation I had attended since George Washington High School in 1965. Mark Helbling was there to help University President Kenneth P. Mortimer place the doctoral hood over my head at the moment of conferring the degree, and I did indulge myself with a little self-pride. VèVè told me, "I've had a lot of my old friends try to go back to school to get their graduate degree, but you have actually done it." Kimathi had flown with me from the Big Island and was sitting in the audience; after the ceremony, as he put many flower leis over my graduation gown, he told me that he didn't really believe it until he saw me walking across the stage. Three months earlier we had celebrated our twenty-first wedding anniversary, and more than anyone he knew what it had taken for me to accomplish this life transition. That night my friend and dance student Amy Kogut gave me a graduation party at her home, and friends like Kathryn Takara, Adela Chu, Dhira DiBiase, and my drummers Reggae and Michael Wall, partied with us into the night.

Developing Hip-Hop Studies and Finding a Tenure-Track Job

When I reached the dissertation-writing stage in my doctoral program, I began applying for university teaching positions in California and Ohio, the two states where Kimathi and I had family. It was unwritten policy that the

University of Hawaiʻi did not normally hire its recent graduates as faculty, so I always knew we would have to move back to the mainland to start my tenure-track academic career. Although I had taught at Stanford University for twelve years, becoming a legit professor on the tenure track would be a new beginning in academia, and Kimathi agreed to move to wherever I got a job offer as assistant professor. We began adjusting to eventually leaving "paradise" to live nearer our kinfolk.

Of course, I mostly got rejection letters for the positions for which I applied in American Studies, Ethnic Studies, Performance Studies, and Dance. I did make the "short list" for a couple of institutions but was not selected, including the University of California, Riverside, where I had taught for the Department of Dance as a visiting professor in Spring 1999. Even though rejection letters are standard while one completes their dissertation, each was a bit disheartening. But with a myriad of life examples that the universe supports my efforts, I had faith that eventually the right position would find me.

While I was waiting for a university job offer, I was hired in another visiting professorship position as lecturer in the familiar Department of African American Studies at University of California, Berkeley. Through VèVè's pull, I had gotten the temporary position for the Spring 2000 semester to teach the first accredited class on hip-hop culture, a course I called "Power Moves: Hip Hop Culture & Sociology." I was also hired to teach a Haitian/Dunham class in the Dance department. I hired my favorite Haitian drummer, the late Zeke Nealy, and together we showed the students the power of Dunham Technique and Caribbean dance and rhythms. The UC Berkeley appointment allowed me to combine my familiar role as dance educator with the new function of academic.

I moved in with my mother in San Francisco, the family house in which I had never really lived. I had left home right after high school in 1965, the same year my stepfather moved our family into that house, as the family became one of the first Black homeowning families in the Westwood District near SF City College. My temporary UC Berkeley position allowed me to stay with Mom and commute to the East Bay twice weekly.

The hip-hop course, in the slang of the time, was "off the hook," with 150 students enrolled and a waiting list of another fifty more. The enrollment numbers qualified me to hire three teaching assistants to help manage the course and grade papers. VèVè recommended some of her best graduate students as my TAs. I had never taught a hip-hop course before, let alone a class of that size; but I felt up to the challenge and dove into it with all my newly acquired expertise in the subject. Caribbeanist scholar Percy Hintzen was Chair of the department at the time, and he gave me all the support I needed to teach my first academic hip-hop course. Glen Robertson, my old friend from high school who had become the technical coordinator for the department, helped me teach my class in a multimedia manner with video and internet access that a course on hip-hop culture required.

I was testing my hip-hop research on 150 young students at UC Berkeley who knew far more about hip-hop culture on the ground than I ever would. But I faked it well and depended upon my young Teaching Assistants: Quamè Patton, a deejay and now lecturer in the UC Berkeley African American Studies department; Ayize Jama-Everett, now a published science fiction and speculative fiction writer; and Michael Barnes, a current-day radio deejay and sociology lecturer at Cal State Long Beach. They were invaluable in filling in my many knowledge gaps regarding this youth culture that I had chosen as my research area. They lived it; I was only studying it.

The course took on the revolutionary Bay Area character as word about my hip-hop class traveled. The class was filled with youthful practitioners of hip-hop, from freshmen to graduate students, the latter of whom could not even receive credit for my undergraduate class but wanted to be a part of this groundbreaking event: UC Berkeley's first accredited hip-hop course. I had accomplished b-boys and recognized Bay Area emcees, and once the news spread into the Bay Area's radical community, I got requests to speak from many well-known personalities, such as David Hilliard and Bobby Seale, living legends from the revolutionary Black Panther days. Coming from the sixties' revolutionary era myself, I should have expected that broader attention to my UC Berkeley hip-hop course, but I was still humbled nonetheless. Although most of those potential speakers did not actually materialize, their requests dramatized the original mandate of African American and Ethnic Studies: to bridge academia and community activism. Hip-hop as an academic subject is actually reviving the purpose of Black Studies because students of all ethnicities are inspired by the relevancy that hip-hop brings to their education in relation to their lived experiences.

One revolutionary celebrity who did come to speak at my UC Berkeley course was the late Afeni Shakur (1947–2016), mother of the famous slain West Coast rapper Tupac Shakur. On Friday, March 10, 2000, the subject of Tupac's classic rap, "Dear Mama," Afeni Shakur, walked into my class, having been invited by Ayize who happened to be a family member. She walked into the large lecture hall after I had already begun the class and stood in the back listening to my lecture. Then Afeni, a slight, dark-skinned woman, came down front onto the platform where I was teaching. I immediately stopped talking and walked over to greet her; we instantly embraced and looked into each other's eyes, and I simply said, "Welcome, thank you for coming."

The class that Afeni Shakur attended reinforced my belief in what I call "the grand choreography of life." The unit I was teaching was appropriately on hip-hop and capitalism, and when Ms. Shakur began to speak to the class, she started by reinforcing my argument: "I am so glad to hear your professor talking to you about hip-hop as a business because, believe me, it is. I am in the midst of so much of the legality of the business around my son's legacy. Learn as much as you can about the business of hip-hop, and don't be naïve." That simple statement from the mother of one of the greatest nineties rappers was an important validation of my approach to the developing discipline of Hip-Hop Studies I could have ever gotten.

Afeni challenged the cult of personality trend in hip-hop, and I recorded more of her personal statements to my students in my journal: *"Afeni Shakur encouraged us to not look at Tupac for what we wanted him to be, but to look at him for who he was. She said, 'He was the product of who I am, my mother, her mother, and her mother before that who was an enslaved human being. He was the product of all that history. Sometimes it is not the breath of life that sustains you but keeping the integrity of who you are.'"* Such was the tenor of my first hip-hop class in academia, reflecting on the new Black culture phenomenon while invoking the ancestral spirit at the same time. Such is the meaning of the Ghanaian Sankofa bird symbol: looking backward to move forward.

Many of my students went on to make hip-hop culture the vibrant and all-pervasive youth culture it is today. One of them is the noted hip-hop filmmaker Eli Jacobs-Fantauzzi, who was then a budding artist who used my course to hone his writing skills for a film he was working on about hip-hop in Ghana. In an oral presentation he showed excerpts of his award-winning film *Home-Grown: HipLife in Ghana,* produced by his own Clenched Fist Productions. His film today is one of the notable documentaries on hip-hop in West Africa.

Teaching about the socio-cultural dynamics of the burgeoning hip-hop youth culture necessitated using its artistic elements in my teaching methodology for the course. At the end of the Spring 2000 semester, I concluded the course with a big open mic, allowing b-boys, emcees, and deejays taking the course to "throw down" in what became a historic culminating last class that was documented in the *San Francisco Chronicle*. A 2000 news article captured the groundbreaking innovative nature of Power Moves: Hip-Hop Culture & Sociology at UC Berkeley. The article read in part:

> Using a 3-inch-thick reader of essays and news articles and the text *Droppin' Science: Critical Essays on Rap Music and Hip Hop Culture,* Osumare has led her class through an investigation of the history, aesthetics, urban context, economics, and institutional policing of hip hop

in the United States. For good measure, she also included the globalization of hip-hop, which has taken over the youth culture almost everywhere.[15]

I was re-entering academia as a cutting edge scholar, positioning myself within the *suspect* subject of hip-hop that was causing much controversy in the media and in communities, both Black and white. My rebellious, independent nature had me again on the challenging side of my new profession, advancing the argument that hip-hop youth culture was worth scholarly attention and advancing the burgeoning field of Hip-Hop Studies.

Transitioning from Hawai'i to Ohio

Finally, among my myriad of job applications to universities in California and Ohio, I was offered a tenure-track position at Bowling Green State University (BGSU), near Toledo, in Northwest Ohio. An academic unit called the School of Human Movement, Sport, and Leisure Studies (HMSLS) appointed me Assistant Professor of Dance. HMSLS was split between the Kinesiology Division, in which the Dance Program was situated, and the division of Sports Management, Tourism, and Leisure Studies. Although this was a rare academic configuration for a dance position to be housed, it actually followed the old university model of dance as physical education; hence, dance in kinesiology rather than a part of an arts department coupled with theater or music. HMSLS viewed my credentials—a PhD in American Studies, a master's degree in dance ethnology, and a BA in Dance and Theater Arts—as providing a scholarly image that would potentially enhance the image of the Dance Program. I accepted the position at BGSU because Kimathi and I would be a two-and-half-hour drive from his family in Columbus. Toledo is situated one hour south of Detroit and forty-five minutes from the college town of Ann Arbor, Michigan, which are both more culturally active. We began to prepare to leave Hawai'i after our six-and-a-half-year sojourn in the islands.

Although I was tentative about living in the Midwest, this was going to be the first time I would be consistently closer to my in-laws, and I was looking forward to a closer familial connection with them after all our years of marriage. We dismantled our home, packed a twenty-cubic-foot container to ship across the Pacific, cleaned and rented the house to a fellow teacher-friend of Kimathi's at Pahoa High, and sold the car. We couldn't leave Hawai'i without having one more Afro-Hawaiian luau at the house with our friends to say goodbye. We bid *a hui hou* (until we meet again) to all the people who had become our supportive community in East Hawai'i. Our move was going to be another major transition for me.

We left Leilani Estates in early July 2000. As we were walking away from our home of the last seven years for the last time, we turned to look back at the one-acre plot of land with its lush rainforest surrounding the modest little house that we had made into a home, and we breathed deeply. This is where we had brought together the African American and Hawaiian communities in Puna, and we knew this was the end of an era. Although I had been working hard as usual on "my mission," running back and forth between the mainland and the islands, Hawai'i had also given us time to relax and renew our personal commitment to each other. Now, I was making the transition from PhD graduate to Assistant Professor of Dance at Bowling Green State University. Kimathi was supporting my next career move while moving closer to his family. We were both looking forward to our new life in Toledo, Ohio.

4

Dancing in Ohio and Nigeria

Until the lion tells his side of the story, the tale of the hunt will always glorify the hunter.

Zimbabwean Proverb

There's nothing enlightening about shrinking so that other people won't feel insecure around you. We were born to manifest the glory of God that is within us.

Marianne Williamson, *A Return to Love*

As we moved from Hawaiʻi back to the mainland for my first tenure-track position, it finally sank in that I was becoming an academic scholar as a second career. I had studied for my PhD during the last four years at the University of Hawaiʻi at Manoa, and two years before that started my graduate studies at the master's level at SF State University. As I reflected on this transition, I realized that my entire artistic life had been focused on Black history through popular dance and culture. Contemplating my past artistic focus allowed me to clearly see I could flip my bifurcated life script to now emphasize the *humanities* of performance. I remembered what Katherine Dunham had reinforced in me: dance is a way of life, with many dimensions beyond the stage or studio.

I often use quotation marks around the word "dancing" in this memoir, referring to my research and writing about dance and performance during this latter part of my life—dancing from the stage to the page. My career transition occurred at a strategic time when my body was beginning to feel a lifetime of overuse. I began to feel the pains of osteoarthritis and a loss of cartilage in my knees, prompting me eventually to have double knee replacement surgery; but that was still years in the future. In the year 2000, knee braces became my friends, giving me extra support while I continued to perform and teach. Later, when my physical incapacity to dance began, I always embraced Katherine Dunham's concept of "dancing." Starting in her eighties, when she needed to use a wheelchair, people would often ask her about when she stopped dancing. Miss Dunham would simply answer, "NEVER!"

As I aged, I began to recognize how I was using the principles of dance—

rhythm, shape, space, and dynamics—while interacting with every aspect of my life in the world. I began to comprehend how knowing what to say at the right time (rhythm), in the right way (shape and dynamics), and in the correct place (space) is what life is all about. I started fully grasping how to create the grand *choreography* of life itself. As osteoarthritis established itself fully in my knees, based both on heredity (my mother suffered from it) and a lifetime of overuse in teaching, rehearsing, and performing dance, I knew I had found another way to "dance."

Ohio, Bowling Green State University, and Hip-Hop Scholarship

Kimathi and I arrived in Toledo, Ohio, in early August 2000. We rented a townhouse on Sylvania Avenue, near the border of the Sylvania suburb in Lucas County. Interestingly enough, I found out later this area had historically been a site of the Underground Railroad during slavery. Bowling Green is twenty-five miles from Toledo, necessitating a half-hour commute to the campus. This was my first time living in the Midwest, so-called heartland America, and I was interested to know how "the independent one" would fare in *this* area of the United States.

Kimathi's four sisters—Rosemary, Cathy, Pauline, and Susan—prepared me with both physical and psychic armor. They gave me a couple of warm coats to brave the severe winter months as well as a psychological warning: "You know this is not California, don't you? Brace yourself for some in-your-face racism." I realized this was how Black folks had historically survived the pre–civil rights US apartheid system: sharing cautionary survival tactics. We still have to utilize similar tactics today, in what I call the "Afro-Present," where sometimes it can still be life-and-death serious. I proceeded into my Midwest sojourn being duly warned.

I had an immediate indication of their warning about Ohio's brand of racism at the turn of the millennium, when I attended Bowling Green State University's (BGSU) summer picnic for new faculty at the university president's home. As I had not done any research on BGSU's administration, it was a complete surprise to find out that the president of BGSU was a Black man, Dr. Sidney Ribeau, a Communication Studies scholar. As I understand it, he had been a token Black candidate for the position, with a white candidate as the first choice. However, the university's primary *intended* candidate for the job dropped out at the last moment for a better position elsewhere, leaving Ribeau as the next candidate in line for the job. Even within entrenched systemic racism, tokenism can backfire, and the grand choreography of the Afro-Present can often contain seminal victories.

Just as I had noted in my job application, I brought researched-based *scholarship* to the Dance Program of the Kinesiology Division of the School of Human Movement, Sport, and Leisure Studies (HMSLS) of BGSU. Their published job description for the assistant professor of dance position had said, "MFA in dance required, doctorate preferred"; and so there I was, armed with my eclectic dance background, a master's degree in dance ethnology, and my newly minted PhD in American Studies. I had emphasized my strength in "socio-cultural analyses in relation to dance and performance" in my application, but there were few lecture-based courses in the dance curriculum. I taught studio jazz dance classes as well as Dunham Technique within my modern dance classes; I also created an undergraduate lecture course in the Division of Kinesiology in order to teach my hip-hop curriculum that I had developed during my one semester at UC Berkeley. I also wanted to teach at the graduate level in HMSLS, and devised a graduate course based in aesthetic theory within the context of sport. I had gained the academic acumen to quickly adapt to the educational context in which I found myself to get the most experience out of my first tenure-track job.

My Hip-Hop Culture and Sociology course was a predictable hit with the students, but equally an expected controversy in a conservative university in heartland America. I first taught the course in the 2001 summer session, and students from all over the campus flocked to the course. But one day, I got a phone call in my office from the head of HMSLS, telling me that the Office of the President needed a copy of my course syllabus. Apparently, some donor to the university had become incensed that there was a course on hip-hop at BGSU and complained to President Ribeau. I forwarded my well-designed syllabus to the head of my academic unit, complete with its timeline of scholarly readings, and she could pass it up the academic chain of command. I had anticipated this scrutiny of my hip-hop course at BGSU and was prepared, making sure my approach to Hip-Hop Studies was grounded in solid academic theory. Once I sent my syllabus as an email attachment, I never heard any more about it. The course syllabus for Hip-Hop Culture and Sociology stood the rigors of academic scrutiny, and I knew that President Ribeau was glad he did not have to enter into an academic censorship issue, especially with a Black faculty member.

My hip-hop course was such an anomaly that the local Bowling Green newspaper, the *Sentinel-Tribune,* interviewed me and ran a story on the class.

At first glance the scene in Eppler Center 223 [classroom] does not look to be anywhere in the vicinity of the cutting edge . . . The professor

Halifu Osumare is discussing the key texts in the discipline the students are studying, and she asks the students to respond to a reading complete with the scholarly apparatus of footnotes and citations . . . Welcome to "Power Moves: Hip-Hop Culture and Sociology," a summer session course being offered at Bowling Green State University.[1]

Students interviewed for the article emphasized they were a part of the hip-hop generation and felt validated to finally have a legitimate academic course on their youth culture. Ironically, the campus was the home of the first Popular Culture Studies major and department in the country. The Department of Popular Culture, founded by Ray Browne (1922–2009) in 1973, is still today the only US university department offering a BA and MA solely in the discipline of popular culture.

Browne was in working retirement when I got to Bowling Green, but we had several conversations, and he was supportive of my situating hip-hop within the developed academic discipline of popular culture. He was also the founding editor of the *Journal of Popular Culture* and the *Journal of American Culture and Comparative Cultures,* both of which were official publications of the Popular Culture and American Culture Association. He published one of my first journal articles on hip-hop—"Beat Streets in the Global Hood: Connective Marginalities of the Hip Hop Globe"—in the Spring and Summer 2001 issue of the latter journal. This article was an excerpt of a chapter in my dissertation, and its publication added my voice to the burgeoning field of Hip-Hop Studies. Its theme was an explanation of why hip-hop had become so quickly international from a grassroots US urban street culture. My argument was a counternarrative to the usual top-down American cultural and economic imperialism analysis. It articulated my theory of "connective marginality" that became influential, positioning me as a new voice in hip-hop scholarship.

In the article I compare England, France, Japan, and Russia, showing how the elements of hip-hop culture, as it traveled globally, aided youths in speaking truth to power in their particular countries. I argued that youths felt marginalized in four areas: *class* inequality in terms of second-class citizenship; *historical oppression* of groups experiencing hundreds of years of systematic subjugation; *culture* in the African diaspora, where African-based cultural expressions are viewed globally as inferior to European-based cultural forms; and *youth* itself as a marginalized status in the ever-dominant adult social world. Hip-hop culture's elements of rap, deejaying, dance, and graffiti art offer global youth populations a voice to articulate their own worldviews, as well as grievances lodged in these four areas of marginality. This paradigm, I argued, connected international youth culturally into a growing Global Hip-Hop Nation (GHHN).

One example I used for the marginality of class was the French rap group NTM, consisting of North African Arabs who felt discriminated against in Paris and throughout France. My research had revealed that second- and third-generation North African Arabs were descendants of colonial immigrants living in ghettoized *les banlieues* (suburban Parisian ghettos with high-rise housing projects) and are bound by their lower-class ethnic status.

As I was transforming my dissertation into my first publishable hip-hop book in Toledo, the 2005 Parisian riots broke out, and I analyzed NTM's lyrics, recorded ten years earlier about inevitable street retribution, which presaged the contemporary riots, just as N.W.A.'s and Ice T's lyrics about poverty and abusive police relations had predicted the Los Angeles Riots of 1992. I made clear the connection between the maltreatment of US Blacks and the internationally disenfranchised. I eventually published *The Africanist Aesthetic in Global Hip-Hop: Power Move* in 2007 with a major New York international academic publisher, Palgrave Macmillan. Since then, graduate students around the world have used it as a basic text of hip-hop's internationalization, particularly drawn to my concept of "connective marginality."

Hip-Hop Studies was growing all around me, with many universities convening entire conferences on the subject, and academic associations forming hip-hop panels during their annual conferences. The nearby University of Michigan (UM) in Ann Arbor, for example, convened "The Hip-Hop Paradigm: Mapping and Transcending its Boundaries" conference in March 2001, in which I presented a paper. The Hip-Hop and Cultural Studies Collective, a group of graduate students researching hip-hop at UM, organized the conference. Being from the baby boom generation I knew it was my *ancestors* who led me to this provocative academic field. If I was starting this new career in my early fifties, I would need to advance quickly to make my mark in academia. Hip-hop became a facilitating shortcut for my academic advancement as I situated myself in a brand-new field at the center of contemporary social controversy. I always listen to my ancestors' subtle, and not so subtle, life nudges.

My Dance Scholarship and Critique of the Dance Field

As I was becoming a hip-hop scholar, I simultaneously used my new skills to further analyze the dance field. As a part of college dance's national structure, our BGSU Dance Program hosted the American College Dance Festival's (ACDF) Northeastern regional conference. Deborah Tell, our program's director, and Tammy Starr, the only other professor of dance besides me, organized our region's ACDF convocation, and all three of us were involved in designing the 2001 regional ACDF conference. After the weeklong conference for hundreds of student dancers and university dance instructors was over, I reflected on the event in my journal: *Our ACDF conference represented where modern dance has developed in the academy. From the Bennington years of Graham, Holm, Weidman, and Humphrey to now is about sixty years, not a long time in the scope of the development of an art form, but time enough for cultural entrenchment. "There are too many modern classes, and not enough 'specialty' classes that we can take at our schools," was one of the main evaluative comments by students from our post-conference survey. Students thought the lack of diversity in the dance curriculum needed improvement. At the beginning of the 21st century, modern dance has become a hegemonic force in the concert dance world.*

I began to assess where I was in relation to the dance field that had nurtured me since my undergraduate years in the late 1960s. I viewed myself as a representative of "the edges" of the discipline, having focused on the *Africanist* contributions in dance and established my own dance institution in Oakland—Everybody's Creative Arts Centre/CitiCentre Dance Theatre. I had built an infrastructure around my own artistic, cultural, and aesthetic choices, rather than relying on the modern dance establishment in the Bay Area.

However, since the advent of so-called postmodern dance in the 1970s, dancers emerging from that genre at the turn of the century also viewed themselves as "edgy," and not mainstream. The postmodern movement in dance, which challenged mainstream modern dance and its founders, solidified itself as a new contemporary dance movement by the early 1980s, with annual events like Brooklyn Academy of Music's Next Wave Festival. From eschewing formal dance technique and privileging a pedestrian-driven back-to-basics movement focus in the 1970s, to the gradual reintroduction of dance narrative and even actual text by the 1980s,[2] postmodern dance had become entrenched within academic dance departments' curricula. It had now become the mainstream itself, not the edge.

The shift in what was considered the dance mainstream is what I most recognized at our regional ACDF conference at BGSU in March 2001. Continuing my thoughts on this subject, I wrote an essay in my journal called "The Hegemony of Modern Dance." The essence of that journal entry read: *Although many modern teachers and artists think of themselves as edgy, few realize how mainstream they have become. Release Technique, as the growing style of the "New Dance" postmodern era, has become the center. Coming a close second is the quirky, hip-hop inspired modern explorations, using popping and locking. It is not that these styles are not interesting, but they have become part of mainstream modern dance that seems to still buy into the high-low art dichotomy, even as they delve into the popular.*

I see myself representing the continually marginalized African American modern dance called the Dunham Technique. Not one of the university teachers who brought their students to ACDF took or observed my class. Most of them had heard of Dunham, to whom they probably devote a short marginal section of their syllabus called "Black Dance History." But few, if any, know anything about her technique or are even interested.

I would later follow this line of analysis in a book chapter I published, questioning what was really "postmodern" by using the purely hip-hop dance aesthetic of Philadelphia choreographer Rennie Harris. I interrogated his street dance aesthetic exhibited by his Rennie Harris Puremovement company in "The Dance Archaeology of Rennie Harris: Hip-Hop or Postmodern?" published in the 2009 anthology *Ballroom, Boogie, Shimmy Sham, Shake: A Social and Popular Dance Reader,* edited by dance scholar Julie Malnig. The chapter appeared in a section of the book called "Theatricalizations of Social Dance Forms"; however, I was actually challenging mainstream dance's perceptions of its own origins, not merely showing how hip-hop as a street dance form had arrived on the high art proscenium stage. I complicated the argument about what is postmodern dance with:

> Given this typology of postmodern dance characteristics, Rennie Harris's aesthetic becomes quintessentially postmodern at the turn of the twenty-first century. Although Harris may not have been aware of the convolutions of the shifting postmodern concert dance scene at the beginning of his company's career, his natural instincts as a creative artist, coming of age in the hip-hop era, fit naturally into these explorations.[3]

Brenda Dixon Gottschild had already challenged the postmodern dance establishment thirteen years earlier. In her *Digging the Africanist Aesthetic in American Performance: Dance and Other Contexts* (1996), with her chapter "Barefoot and Hot, Sneakered and Cool: Africanist Subtexts in Modern and Postmodern Dance," she analyzed their lack of *proper sourcing* of the postmodern aesthetic:

> The fact that postmodern culture exists inside of, around, and on top of Africanist cultures is a fact of intertextuality, not merely parallel development. The problem is that the chroniclers of postmodern performance have credited sources from the European historical avant-

garde . . . They have not given credence to the Africanist aesthetic as a pervasive subtext in postmodern performance.[4]

When I stepped onto the dance scholarship stage with my critique of the discipline and my newly acquired knowledge of hip-hop culture, the groundwork had already been laid by Gottschild. My critique was *continuing* the challenge to the dance mainstream initiated by her.

Certified Dunham Instructor and Teaching and Performing Hula in East St. Louis

My experience with the Katherine Dunham dance legacy reached a crescendo in July 2001 when I went to the Annual Dunham Seminar in East St. Louis and became an officially Certified Dunham Instructor. Miss Dunham had asked Albirda Rose, my friend whom she had appointed the director of Dunham Certification, to inform me that she wanted me to become a certified instructor. I had avoided taking on that status because it meant becoming involved with the inevitable "politics" within the East St. Louis Dunham scene. I had purposefully remained on the periphery of the people surrounding her in East St. Louis. After producing the 1989 Dunham Stanford Residency and the 1994 Dunham Hawai'i Residency, my dedication to Miss Dunham and her legacy was apparent, and I felt I did not need the outward validation of certification. But when I heard Miss Dunham said *she* wanted to sign my certificate, I knew it was my *personal* call from the master. I had already written the required Dunham history/theory essay exam and sent a video tape of my teaching while I was still living in Hawai'i, but the Certification Committee Albirda had formed asked that as my final requirement I teach a class on-site during the seminar for observation.

Miss Dunham, at ninety-two years old, was in rare form at the 2001 Dunham Technique Seminar. She taught her master classes each week, demonstrating to the drummers what she wanted rhythmically and giving us her continual pearls of wisdom: "Honesty in motion is what we're after," "Always use the energy of the drums, even when you're standing waiting to go across the floor," "Feel the *reason* to change a movement in choreography," and the unforgettable, "We have more access to the danger around us, but less protection; knowledge of Self is the only protection." These gems of dance and human insight were a part of the incomparable Dunham experience, and I was proud to become a certified carrier of her holistic approach to the art of dance and living—Dunham Technique as "A Way of Life."

While I was in St. Louis that year, Miss Dunham insisted I teach and perform hula, as my newly acquired dance form from my seven years of living in Hawai'i and dancing with Kumu Ehulani Stephany's halau. During one of her master classes, she coaxed me to the front to teach a few of the basic steps of hula to students attending from all over the country and from abroad. She was demonstrating through me that Dunham Technique's foundation is an anthropological approach to dance, and the Dunham dancer must avail herself to all available dance cultures. At the closing Seminar Showcase, I performed *Ke Ha'a La Puna,* my favorite Pele dance with my *uli'uli* rattle, dressed in full regalia from my hula *uniki* (chapter 3). As I was performing the sacred *hula kahiko* for the East St. Louis packed auditorium, I felt I was carrying on the tradition of one of Miss Dunham's central theories, intercultural communication. I was embodying Hawaiian culture, showing its deep reverence for its powerful volcano goddess, and as I bowed after the performance, I noticed Miss Dunham's wry smile. I knew I was truly dancing the Dunham legacy.

After the 2001 seminar, Miss Dunham had Jeanelle Stovall, her administrative assistant, establish a weeklong hula workshop for me at the Children's Workshop next to the Dunham Museum in East St. Louis. I was hired to offer a five-day program at the Dunham Children's Workshop I called "Hawaiian Ecology through Hula," which fulfilled a national grant that Jeanelle had obtained. I designed the workshop to focus on dance in relation to the environment. What better dance form than Hawaiian hula to create a series of classes

Figure 4.1. Author before performing hula *Ke Ha'a La Puna* at Dunham Seminar, 2001. Photo courtesy of author.

that merged dance with knowledge about the ecology of the local flora and fauna? Jeanelle had written me during my transition from Hawai'i to Ohio about conceiving dance classes with an ecological focus. My "Hawaiian Ecology through Hula" proposal was perfect to fulfill the grant, and I taught the workshop July 2–6, 2001. Los Angeles dance scholar Catherine "Scoti" Scott was also hired as my assistant for the project to help organize twelve young East St. Louis African American girls for that hula dance workshop.

The problem was East St. Louis was *not* Hawai'i; the beauty of the land in the islands that inspire so many hulas was not found in the trash, debris, and neglected fields of poverty-stricken East St. Louis. Teaching the potent relationship between dance and the land was not going to be an easy task. I saw my "Hawaiian Ecology through Hula" workshop as a continuation of the East St. Louis creative experience that Katherine Dunham first established in the late sixties—the Performing Arts Training Center. But the obstacles she faced are still a part of the city. The community is still economically devastated, streets are trashed and buckled, and buildings are abandoned and gutted.

The crumbling Katherine Dunham buildings reflected the East St. Louis surrounding context, except for her important redeeming elements: hope, optimism, and vision supplied by the dogged tenacity of Miss Dunham and Jeanelle Stovall with their small staff. Just as Miss Dunham's spirit in East St. Louis did, we prevailed, and the hula workshop was a resounding success. The twelve young Black girls, ages six through thirteen—Rhonda, Alvia, Briel, Ashley, Gabriel, and others—learned personal discipline, their own personal Black beauty, and the way to find beauty in their environment.

My methodology for success with the Children's Workshop was emphasizing "hula discipline" that I had learned. I stressed discipline as the key to accomplishing any goals while emphasizing that one could find beauty in the face of seeming ugliness. The girls learned the ability to tell their story with dance through cooperating with each other while performing each task at hand. For example, one day we took an excursion into the community, walking through fields of weeds. I showed them that even in an overgrown, junky, abandoned field where people had thrown trash, there was beauty to be found among the growing "volunteer" weeds, and we picked those weeds to make their leis for our culminating performance. They were amazed to find this "beauty" in what they thought was only "ugliness," and they began to understand nature in a different way.

We had a final performance for their families and community members on the outdoor platform stage behind the Dunham Museum. They danced *Nawiliwili,* about a beautiful bay on the Big Island. They wore wrapped Hawaiian cloth, head leis (*lei po'o*), and wrist leis (*kupe'e*) that they had made themselves from the excursion into the field of weeds. The children received and appreciated the human qualities that I taught them through hula. They shone like true ghetto princesses—like flowers in a field of weeds, hope in the midst of despair. My "Hawaiian Ecology through Hula" became another link in the long chain of arts projects generated by Miss Dunham's philosophy of Socialization Through the Arts.

After the 2001 Dunham Seminar and my hula workshop in East St. Louis, I went to San Francisco to see my mother and sisters. During my return to the Bay, Albirda Rose was conducting the Dunham Certification Workshop at SF State University, and as a newly minted Certified Instructor I helped evaluate seven dance educators who were candidates for certification. Albirda had institutionalized certification by establishing the Institute for Dunham Technique Certification (IDTC), encouraged and sanctioned by Miss Dunham.

One of the requirements for Dunham certification that Albirda established early on in the process was a history-theory essay exam covering the history of the Dunham dance legacy and her articulated theories and philosophies underlying the technique. In that 2001 Certification Workshop at SF State, I suggested the candidates view the newly premiered dance documentary *Free to Dance: The African American Presence in Modern Dance* by filmmaker Dave Lacy.[5] I advised that the second of the three parts of the film would aid their understanding of Dunham intellectually, as a major portion of the second hour is devoted to Dunham's legacy, encompassing her Caribbean dance research and the trials and tribulations of touring the Katherine Dunham Dance Company. I am one of the dance scholars appearing in the film, reflecting on her contributions to the field of dance. It was timely that *Free to Dance* premiered in 2001 because it could help in preparing dance educators who were serious about Dunham certification.

The 9/11 Tragedy and Continuing Hip-Hop Scholarship

When I returned home to Kimathi in Ohio that summer, I was also happy for our reunion. I began to prepare for my Fall 2001 courses, but little did I know that one of the greatest tragedies in United States history was about to occur. The catastrophe of what we now call "9/11" or "September 11" happened when three planes, commandeered by Middle Eastern terrorists, struck three different US locations simultaneously, with the most visually devastating being planes flying directly into the Twin Towers of the World Trade Center in New York City.

When the planes struck the towers, I was teaching my graduate course Aesthetics and Sport. I didn't find out about the tragedy until *after* class, and most faculty used the next few days to help students process their thoughts and feelings within the classroom structure. My dance classes became lessons in human connection through movement improvisations. I used my Dunham class to focus on spirituality, allowing students to connect to their internal selves. The next class meeting of Aesthetics and Sport became an open discussion of the tragedy in all its ramifications: human loss, race, xenophobia, Middle Eastern people and scapegoating, gender and the issue of the draft for men and women, US media and the perpetual news loop, our own programming as Americans, and of course, the US's role in the Middle East.

The first "National Day of Remembrance" was established within one month of the tragic events of 9/11 with a prayer vigil at St. Paul's Cathedral in Washington, DC. I watched the event on television, prayed for the families of the victims, and let myself weep. I asked myself why I was crying. My answer to myself was, for the pain of those immediately affected, for the pain of the entire human race living with the flaws of the human condition itself. I also wept for the social hierarchies and racial and religious divisions that we have created among ourselves as human beings. I thought about my role as a teacher and leader, and in one of my dance classes, I taught the Liberian *Fanga,* a dance of peace and welcome to strangers. This was my duty as a dance educator, to use movement as a healing antidote to hate.

A month and half after the 9/11 tragedy the Congress on Research in Dance (CORD) conference was happening at New York University, and I was scheduled to fly to New York City, only two weeks after domestic airline flights were reinstated in the country. I was to present my recently written academic paper "Global Breakdancing and the Intercultural Body" at the 2001 CORD conference with its theme of "Transmigratory Moves: Dance in Global Circulation." I remember the apprehension I had boarding the plane to New York in October 2001.

While in New York at the CORD conference, I visited Miss Dunham, who had moved there from East St. Louis. She was staying in a beautiful apartment building for the elderly in Midtown Manhattan near Central Park, and we had great talks in her bedroom, with all her spiritual crystals spread out around her, as well as the continually looping television news stories on CNN in the background. She expressed a desire to move to Harlem: "I feel I have something to offer and something to learn. There are many things happening there, but a common purpose is what's necessary. Perhaps I can help with finding that purpose." This was the way Miss Dunham always thought—what could she do to facilitate a "common purpose." She always saw herself as a catalyst for change, and I always wanted to spend time with her because I felt the same purpose. I intuited I was indeed carrying on her legacy, whether in my dance activism or my scholarship. I made some attempts to see if I could aid her move to Harlem, but it never came about. Miss Dunham had already done her work, and I believe given the spiritual heights she had attained, she could now accomplish anything from *any* spatial point.

My paper "Global Breakdancing and the Intercultural Body" was very well received at the CORD conference, where many of the major voices in dance scholarship had gathered. Brenda Dixon Gottschild was there, as well as the social activist Yogi, Becky Thompson, and even the feminist political activist Bettina Aptheker. I met the distinguished dance scholar Barbara Browning, Chair of the entire 2001 conference and a faculty member in Performance Studies at NYU. It was from this meeting with Browning that I was invited to submit a complete essay version of my paper to the *Dance Research Journal* (*DRJ*) for a featured section in the Winter 2002 issue on dance and globalism.

Barbara Browning captured the multiple theoretical lenses that I used in my article, as I began to view breakdancing—b-boying, b-girling—as a global force. In her introduction to our section of that DRJ journal issue, she had this to say about my article:

> Osumare performed her fieldwork in Hawai'i—which is, of course, a part of the United States but also remains in cultural dialogue with other parts of the Asian Pacific . . . Osumare draws out both aspects: the appropriative (with a caveat about who is profiting from this global spread of the hip hop aesthetic) and the indigenizing (in which performance techniques of black resistance come to serve local purposes). She also looks back at references to Asian culture within African American communities, citing, for example, Bruce Lee, who held iconic status as a figure of resistance within many black communities.[6]

This was an accurate assessment of my work on breakdance at that point and reflected my fieldwork and speculative thinking about Hawai'i as my main site of field study at that point.

One of the main concepts that I asserted was the "salutary aspects of global breakdancing," alluding to the possibility of a *positive* appropriation possible from the inevitable circulation of breaking. "In the process of conducting my research, a salutary embodied intertext was revealed to me that I call the 'Intercultural Body.' I explored the Intercultural Body as a tangible result of the globalization of American pop culture in general and hip-hop subculture in particular."[7] My theory was based on feminist rhetoric scholar Judith Butler's concept of *performativity,* in that globally circulating Black-Latino hip-hop dance coalesces with inherited local cultural moves of Indigenous performativity to create an embodied *intercultural* dialogue in each adept dancer. It is important for me to position my hypothesizing in the reality of the body and people's lived experiences as my inheritance from dancing myself. My concept of the Intercultural Body argues for the possibility of a healthy cultural appropriation in the inevitable globalization of American pop culture.

Black "Power Moves" and Capitalist Technology

Article by article, book chapter by book chapter, I grew as a Hip-Hop Studies scholar, analyzing both the music and the dance as a part of the current-day trajectory of Black performance—hip-hop—globalized in a whole new way during the late capitalist cyberspace age. Black people and the perception of blackness are at the core of hip-hop's internationalization, and capitalism thrives on the latest "cool" trending moves of Black youth. Using hip-hop lingo, I called the youth culture's insinuation into the global capital marketplace "power moves."

Today, social media has upped the ante of the game altogether; one has only to view the pervasive use of TikTok, released in 2016 as a video-sharing social networking service by Chinese company ByteDance. As digital studies professor André Brock Jr. perceives, "Black digital practice has become hypervisible to mainstream white culture and the world through positive, negative, and political performances of Black cultural aesthetics and, more recently social media activism."[8] Throughout the first and second decades of this century, Black culture created a *power move* into the defining elements of globalization and late capitalism, with hip-hop aesthetics at the center of that commanding influence. These international dimensions are at the center of the larger possibilities of an Afrofuture never imagined before.

As I grew as a Hip-Hop Studies scholar, I grappled with those issues. I articulated how this "new" Black youth culture, since my initial mission of representing my culture through dance in my various iterations of *The Evolution of Black Dance,* had become increasingly more complex. All-pervasive cultural appropriation and its effects on Black culture itself, grew exponentially more multifaceted as hip-hop "blew up" globally into a multi-billion-dollar industry. The tools I gained from my graduate training, along with my long personal history in Black dance and performance, gave me the intellectual tools to grapple with these intricacies as a practitioner-theorist, as an artist-scholar.

Surviving Ohio

Living in Toledo, Ohio, turned out not to be the best experience of my life. Having been nurtured by the SF/Oakland Bay Area's cosmopolitan multiculturalism, with the iconic Golden Gate Bridge opening to the vast Pacific Ocean and the Asian Pacific Rim, geographically the bland cornfields of Ohio were not engaging. The closest I could get to a body of water was Lake Erie, which I did often, but it was not the Pacific. The flat cornfield landscape in between the small Midwest Ohio towns and the big cities like Cleveland, Columbus, and Cincinnati, left *me* flat; I was used to the Sierra Mountains and the hilly terrain of Northern California's Pacific Highway 1 coastline, and more recently the warm Pacific waters and multiethnic Hawai'i.

Socially, I was used to an environment informed by a global and politically activist culture endemic to the San Francisco Bay Area. This was definitely not the cultural milieu of Ohio. Besides feeling culturally isolated, I found few friends in Toledo, Black or otherwise, with whom I could really relate. I did meet three Black sisters with whom I formed friendships: History Professor Lillian Ashcraft-Eason (as well as her late husband Dr. Djisovi Eason), an American Studies graduate student Ramona Bell, and Toledo jazz singer Ramona Collins. That was it. I used to say, "The sixties revolution must have flown over Toledo and landed in nearby Detroit." Michigan, just across the border of Northwest Ohio, allowed me some relief. Driving to Detroit, one hour north, and occasionally to Ann Arbor, a college town that reminded me of Berkeley, became my survival mechanisms. I went to Detroit frequently, and often crossed the Detroit River into Windsor, Ontario, to have lunch, just to get outside of the US for a few hours. Before the 9/11 tragedy, one did not even need a passport to enter Canada.

Detroit nurtured a vital and active hip-hop culture. My most memorable hip-hop event was at a club featuring New York's DJ Premier and Philadelphia's DJ Jazzy Jeff, two of the best East Coast deejays. Experiencing their deejay sets in Detroit was one of my nurturing cultural events, allowing me to witness the new technique of computerized deejaying, with turntables used only for improvisatory scratching. It was rewarding to know that the new deejay technology had not replaced the age-old Africanist aesthetic of call and response, which remained at the cultural center of their music sets, creating a human ritual with the audience that was ancient. Indeed, hip-hop deejays, through their use of continually advancing computerized technology, were naturally leading the youth culture into an Afrofuture imaginary.

Another crucially sustaining Detroit experience was Black dance. My friend Penny Godboldo, former dance professor at Marygrove College, produced a lecture-demonstration with the famous Motown choreographer Cholly Atkins (1913–2003). On November 3, 2001, I witnessed one of the most *elegant* dancer-choreographers of the twentieth century. Mr. Atkins demonstrated the grace and soul that had given Motown singers their rhythmic movement style and sophistication. As a former tap dancer and partner to Honi Coles in the famous Coles & Atkins team, the eighty-eight-year old Cholly Atkins still had the articulate classiness for which he was known. He ended his lecture-demonstration about his Motown years by teaching the audience members his original choreography to Aretha Franklin's iconic hit, "Respect," originally recorded by Otis Redding. I discovered the Atkins choreography had a complicated time signature with 7s thrown in with the usual 4s and 8s, for good measure; it was fun learning his choreography from the master himself. Afterward, he signed a copy of his memoir published that year that I bought, *Class Act: The Jazz Life of Choreographer Cholly Atkins,* written with Black dance historian Jacqui Malone. Urban Detroit culture enriched my Midwest experience, giving me cultural experiences to which I could connect.

I also made another personal connection while teaching at BGSU. I became very close with a young female graduate student in her mid-twenties, Erica Washington, whom I began to call "my daughter." Not having children myself, finding this kind of nurturing relationship with a young woman was a unique and welcome experience. Erica was enrolled in BGSU's College of Musical Arts' Music History Graduate Program and was interested in African drumming and dance. She wanted to find her own cultural roots by moving beyond her classical musical training in clarinet and music history. She began coming to some of my dance classes accompanied by master Ghanaian drummer and BGSU student Habib Iddrisu. First becoming my dance student, Erica and I began spending more personal time and developed a mother-daughter relationship.

Her background was of a Black girl growing up in Washington, DC, who had been "rescued" from her environment and sent to a boarding school in the South. Noticed for her scholastic aptitude in middle school, Erica convinced her mother to allow her to attend boarding school in Mississippi that afforded her a chance at success. As the cost to attend the school was based on family income, a Washington, DC, city politician paid her tuition and costs. She eventually graduated from Bethune-Cookman University in Music Education and arrived at BGSU for her graduate education. It was during this period that I became her "adopted" mother.

Erica and I grew close, providing each other the missing familial relationship that each of us seemed to need. Our mother-daughter relationship gave me a chance to "practice" my mothering skills, which came rather naturally for me at her young woman stage of life. As we grew closer, Erica even went to New York with me in August 2002 to a special Dunham Institute event sponsored by the New York City Board of Education, where I was hired as humanities scholar. However, as our relationship grew, Kimathi thought of her only as my close friend, not accepting the mother-daughter relationship. As our marriage began to deteriorate, Erica would become even more important in my life.

Erica's interest in African culture developed along predictable lines. On several summer study-abroad trips to the Republic of Benin and to Ghana, she gained more knowledge of the cultures and their traditional spirituality. After one of her West Africa trips, she asked me to give her an African name. After a little research I bestowed upon her the name of Bolade Chinue, "Honor has arrived in God's Own Blessings." Her new name was meant to invoke a sense of honor for her biological family in Washington, DC, through her natural spiritual nature. As a very religious person, Erica went to a church almost every Sunday in Toledo that was affiliated with the Full Gospel Fellowship while her interest in African religion was simultaneously growing.

The trajectory of her life eventually had her returning home. She got to know her family again, and became very close to her mother while reconnecting with her twin brother Eric, who had been disabled in a shooting. She continues to work to bring honor to her family, eventually becoming a Yoruba priest, now with the name Iya Osundara Sangoronti.

Toledo, for Kimathi, was an entirely different experience. Having grown up in Columbus, he was used to Midwest culture; even though he was adjusting to the northwestern region of Ohio, he was now back on his home turf and close to his family. After briefly teaching in the Toledo Public Schools, he got a job as the principal of a Toledo charter elementary school that was a part of the statewide charter school system. I was proud of his accomplishment, for he now had the chance to develop a school curriculum that reflected what he thought elementary education should be.

He and a few family members considered having a big family reunion in Springfield, Ohio, where he was born, and I set about helping him organize the July 2002 reunion. His mother Betty's siblings, his aunts and uncle, came from all over the country, allowing me to meet Betty's older sister Joan Crosswhite from Los Angeles, her Aunt Carol who also lived in Columbus, and her brother Jake, who came from Colorado. The reunion took place in a large Springfield park with rental cabins where each family could have their own accommodations. Before the reunion began Kimathi and I arrived early to make sure that everything was in place, and I insisted on using *my* growing African spirituality to have a private libation ceremony. I wanted to ask his ancestors to bless his first family reunion. Kimathi was not a believer in African spiritual traditions and reluctantly agreed, halfway participating in my heartfelt pre-reunion ancestral ceremony.

Regarding my own family, my paternal grandmother, Ethel Wallace, died on September 12, 2002, at age ninety-seven. I had visited her many times as an adult, and I had witnessed this "rock of a woman," as my father called her, grow in her Christian faith until her spiritual life had become her whole existence. I intuited she was ready to make her transition and wrote in my journal while in Bay City, Texas, at her funeral: *My grandmother arrived in this town as a sharecropper on the Heaverson Farm, and left an honored elder by one and all. You could have sent her a letter addressed to "Mama Ethel, Bay City, Texas" without a street address, and it would have been delivered. Ethel Green Wallace, the steadfast, loving, solid-as-a-rock mother-figure, who had unwavering faith in God the Creator, is now a revered ancestor.* I realized that the roots she pulled from the ground as a cotton-picking sharecropper became the *roots* that kept me grounded as I traveled throughout the world.

Challenging Midwest Dance Culture and Shifting Dance Education

On the job front, looking back at my time in the BGSU's Dance Program, I realize I was a cultural anomaly in a fairly narrow-minded Midwest dance scene. My incongruity came to a crescendo in the Spring 2003 semester, when a group of five dance majors, who were taking my Dance History and Jazz Dance III courses, complained about my teaching. They first went to the director of our Dance Program and were sent to the Chair of the Kinesiology Division. The head of our Dance Program did not want to deal with this minefield and referred them to her boss to lodge their formal complaint against me. Their grievance was: I had "inappropriate course content in my lecture class and was insensitive and humiliating in my studio classes." This situation threw me off guard because I thought I was doing a fairly good job. I knew my dance classes were challenging, and I could be occasionally "old school" in my teaching approach, the way Ruth Beckford had taught me as a young student in San Francisco (chapter 1, *DinB*). However, I felt I mitigated that old-school approach with a more jovial, nurturing side.

I realized the key problem really was that I was shaking their core beliefs about concert dance as a field itself. Underlying their grievance was that modern concert dance was basically "white," with a smattering of people of color contributing from the periphery. The text for my dance history course was the then *new* revisionist history on dance history from a strongly multicultural perspective, *Moving History/Dancing Cultures: A Dance History Reader,* just published in 2001 by Wesleyan University Press and edited by Ann Dils and Ann Cooper Albright. Dils and Albright were attempting to move the dance field into an era of rethinking its history and representation of itself, like many other disciplines in academia had been engaged since the 1970s. I was inspired to use this next wave text, and assumed my 2003 students would be delighted to learn a different perspective on their discipline's historical formation.

I couldn't have been more wrong in my thinking about where twenty-first-century white Ohio dance students were in their readiness for a revisionist history perspective on the discipline. Chapters like Jane Desmond's "Dancing Out the Difference: Cultural Imperialism and Ruth St. Denis's *Radha* of 1906," Ananya Chatterjea's "Chandralekha: Negotiating the Female Body and Movement in Cultural/Political Signification," Brenda Dixon Gottschild's "Stripping the Emperor: The Africanist Presence in American Concert Dance," and Ann Cooper Albright's "Embodying History: Epic Narrative and Cultural Identity in African American Dance" all in tandem confused their previous notions of concert dance. My approach to dance history was forcing them to rethink dance in terms of cultural politics and identity, positioning dance right in the midst of the American cultural wars, and they could not handle the challenge. They began to find fault with all of my classes, including my studio technique classes, driving them to report me to my university superiors.

But I had been hired *because* of my scholarly approach to dance, as well as to bring more racial diversity to the thirty-member faculty in the School of Human Movement, Sport, and Leisure Studies (HMSLS). There was only one other Black person in the entire unit, along with a couple of Asians. I had made only a few connections among the HMSLS faculty, like Professor Nancy Spencer in the Sport Management Division who wrote about race in the world of tennis, particularly the then growing phenomenon of Venus and Serena Williams. When our Division Chair asked for a meeting in her office about the students' complaint, she quietly listened to my perspective. Then she revealed to me, "I realized that their lack of knowledge of the changing representation of dance was the problem, and I asked them, 'What makes you think you know what should be taught in Dance History; have you taken it before? We hired Professor Osumare for her scholarly background and stand behind her teaching.'" My colleague, the Chair of the Kinesiology Division, thankfully understood the dynamics of cultural racism at play in the students' challenge to my teaching and supported me. Nothing more was mentioned about the students' complaint against me, and I finished the semester with those students barely speaking to me outside the normal classroom interaction. Needless to say, I continued with my revisionist dance history approach, and they simply had to deal with it.

I had disturbed the dance students' neat little (white) vision of what the dance discipline was supposed to be. From their perspective, I was bombarding them with challenging new racial, cultural, and gender perspectives on the field that made them extremely uncomfortable. This scenario reinforced what I already knew: dance in academia is a conservative field that clings to its "whitewashed" past and is slow to change with the times. This is why, similar to music departments immersed in western European music, the curricula of dance departments in the US continue its (white) modern dance curriculum bolstered by European ballet. Jazz has traditionally been the popular *stepchild* of the triad, but never considered a *core* part of the curriculum, nor rarely taught from its Africanist roots perspective. Now that hip-hop is taught in every community studio in the country, dance departments were forced to incorporate the street-oriented dance to attract university students who are, in fact, the hip-hop generation.

Yet, except for a few pockets around the country, until now, there has been no serious commitment to a diverse dance curriculum, nor a rethinking of dance from a substantive multicultural perspective. As dance education theorist Nyama McCarthy-Brown notes, "Dance educators have the power to nurture and support students' connection to their kinesthetic cultural heritage in addition to Western dance or other dance forms; one does not have to displace the other."[9] And Takiyah Nur Amin echoes McCarthy-Brown's observations with, ". . . as dance educators, we have to do more than disrupt this kind of faulty thinking that disregards one's own cultural experience in favor of something deemed of higher value."[10] Now in the third decade of the twenty-first century, dance conferences and think tanks are convening to discuss "decolonizing dance education" and "anti-racism in the dance field." But I ask, is it really indicating a significant change in dance education, or are they merely trendy buzz terms culled from the Black Lives Matter times? Is dance in higher education really changing? The fact remains that dance departments in the United States are Eurocentric, and a *substantive* inclusive dance curriculum is yet to be established.

Spiritual Initiation and the Big Breakup

In 2003 a major shift happened in my personal life: I became a Yoruba-Lucumi Priestess. Since the late 1980s I had been flirting with Yoruba spirituality, one of the primary African religions that survived slavery and had become entrenched in Cuban, Puerto Rican, Haitian, and Brazilian cultures. Since the first Cuban *santería* and *lucumi* priests came to cities like New York and Miami in the 1950s, the religion has grown in the United States. I had actually conducted a study of its practitioners in the Oakland-San Francisco Bay Area in the early nineties for the City of Oakland Cultural Affairs Department and had found approximately three thousand adherents in my local Bay Area at that time. I documented how widespread nationally the Yoruba religion had become at the end of the twentieth century.

I had learned all I could intellectually about the cosmological belief system of my African ancestors through reading and attending *bembes* (ceremonies celebrating the *orisas* or saints). Before moving to Hawai'i I had already undergone several steps leading toward priesthood, but had not felt ready to take the serious plunge into the Yoruba initiation itself. But in 2003, I had saved up the money to become initiated to Oya, the orisa of the Winds of Change and Keeper of the Ancestors. During my studies and initial spiritual steps, I realized that this force of nature called Oya had been with me from the beginning of my life. Deciding to fully commit to this spiritual tradition would allow me fuller awareness of the energy that was "on my head" and was already a part of my inner spirit. As a warrior deity, Oya was at the center of my independent, rebellious spirit that informed my life choices. Hence, I was initiated to Oya by the Oakland *ile* (religious house), Ile Orunmila Oshun, headed by the famous writer and my friend Luisah Teish, whose priest name is Yeye Oshunmiwa Fagembola Fatunmise.

Although Kimathi was not that supportive of my initiation, I knew this had to be the next step in my spiritual growth. He never wholeheartedly objected to my *studying* Yoruba traditions, but viewed the belief system with skepticism. However, I hoped that my spiritual elevation would eventually enhance our relationship when I returned to Toledo. I left home in June of 2003, going first to Hawai'i to relax and meditate before my big spiritual transition. Reflecting on this major life decision, I could not shake the feeling of lack of support from my husband for my spiritual transition. I had a sickening feeling that Kimathi and I were breaking up after twenty-five years of marriage. I knew I had put my career—my mission—first throughout our marriage, but that mission had helped us both accomplish so much together for the arts in the Bay Area and Hawai'i. We had become the symbol of a Black couple that survived and thrived with love and community commitment. I pushed my sick feeling aside and prayed that my actual initiation would eliminate the overpowering feeling of loss that was overcoming me.

I arrived in San Francisco on June 19, 2003, and went straight to my mother's house to prepare for my initiation that was to take place in Oakland. Surprisingly, my family was very supportive, even though they had no conception of the Yoruba religion in which I was involved. In Galveston, my birthplace, I attended my grandmother's Baptist church, but growing up in San Francisco, I became Catholic. My mother was a devout practitioner and very involved in her neighborhood Catholic church. So I used the Catholic saints to explain the concept of the orisas to her. African traditional religions in the Americas had survived by syncretizing the orisa deities, or forces of nature, with the saints of the Catholic church. For example, my orisa, Oya, had been associated with St. Theresa, a saint who was associated with the cemetery like Oya, keeper of the ancestral dead. In this way I explained my belief system to my mother. Mom Tenola and my sister Pat took me shopping one day to help me purchase the new white clothes I had to wear during my eight days of initiation seclusion, as well as for the next twelve months for the mandatory "year of whites." Unlike me they enjoyed shopping, and our shopping excursion became a female ritual, allowing me to have fun and feel extremely supported by my family. I called Kimathi each day to tell him what I was doing, trying to keep him a part of my process.

The initiation, or *Ocha* (eight days), was a very elaborate process, and even more so for orisa Oya. Initiation for the deity of the keeper of the ancestors required nine days of cemetery rituals before the main eight ceremonial days started. Yeye Oshun Miya assigned an ile member to accompany me to the cemeteries for prayer to attune my sensibilities to the ancestral spirits. Susheel Bibbs, originally from St. Louis, became my *ajibona,* or helper, during that pre-initiation period. Susheel is a former concert opera singer who became a writer and actress, performing her own original one-woman theater show while teaching communications classes in the engineering department at UC Berkeley. Each day Susheel and I visited a different Bay Area cemetery, some of which had my own deceased relatives interned. I actually found my maternal aunt Effie Mae Boudreau's unmarked grave and got my family to collectively purchase a proper marked gravestone during this process.

One of the most poignant grave ceremonies during the nine days was the ninth and last day, when I ended the cemetery visits at the new gravesite of my long-term Congolese dance friend Malonga Casquelourd. Malonga was recently killed in a freak car accident on June 15, 2003. I had attended his funeral on June 24 at the Acts Full Gospel Church of God in Christ in Oakland, right before I started the initiation process on July 1. When I revisited his gravesite, I sang the *Kutumbele* song he had taught me in his Congolese dance class at SF State during my master's graduate work. I felt his spirit strongly as I sang the Congolese song over his still fresh grave. The song ends with a line that says "true *wealth* is spiritual," and I was honored to chant those words over my dear friend's grave. The pre-initiation ceremony rituals prepared me for the powerful mantle of Oya, the keeper of the ancestors. Those nine days of cemetery rituals bound Susheel and I closely, binding us as lifelong friends.

During the eight days of actual initiation, I went into the process as Halifu Osumare and came out as *Oyadamilola,* "Oya Gives Me Wealth." Suffice it to say, my initiation was spiritually much greater than any mind-altering LSD drug trip I experienced during my Haight-Ashbury 1960s hippie years. Through my Yoruba initiation, I found my spiritual path that continues to guide my destiny today, and I am forever grateful. Yeye Luisah Teish brought the late Nigerian Yoruba Priest Baba Bolu Fatunmise (1947–2018) to perform the sacred part of ritual. Baba Bolu was a man around my age from Ile-Ife, Nigeria, then living in Atlanta with his own ile. He was a highly respected *babalawo,* or diviner, and had recently initiated Yeye Oshun Miwa into Ifa, the divination part of the tradition, as a female babalawo, or *Iyanifa.* I would be initiated by an ordained Nigeria babalawo as my spiritual father, but with a Cuban Lucumi priestess as my spiritual mother.

Having Baba Bolu perform the actual initiation generated an eclectic community gathering for my July 13, 2003, *ocha bembe,* the public celebration of a newly initiated Yoruba priest. On that day I was presented to the gathered community as Oyadamilola, a child of Oya. Nigerian babalawos and lucumi priests came together on the occasion in a way that rarely happens. Baba Afolabi Epega, the Nigerian babalawo who wrote *The Sacred Ifa Oracle,* one of the main translations of the sacred parables, or *odus,* underlying the Yoruba religion, was present. Well-respected Oya priestess Iya Oyafunmike Ogunlano from the South Carolina traditional Oyotunji Village, also known for her starring role in the 1993 indie film *Sankofa,* was flown in to be the main Oya priestess during my ocha. My entire initiation process brought together the disparate parts of the sacred tradition created by the transatlantic slave trade, and I felt this was in keeping with my life's trajectory. My initiation served as a bridge across time and space, and I felt blessed.

I was now fifty-six years old and entering my year as *Iyawo* (a priest in training), wearing all white from head to toe for twelve months. After my eight days of initiation, I left the ile to stay a few days at my mother's house to *stabilize* myself in the world again. I reflected one morning lying alone in my mother's bed with my maternal grandmother Alberta's picture hanging above my head. My energy had definitely shifted, had been refocused. I felt more "seated" in orisa than ever before and grounded in spirit.

But I knew the true test was how I would deal with the thought of Kimathi and I separating. When I started the trip in Honolulu, I felt him seriously questioning our future together, and my heart felt like it was tearing apart. But now when I thought of him not being able to continue this journey with me, I was not as devastated. I knew then I could deal with a breakup emotionally because I was more stabilized spiritually. When we talked on the phone after I left Ile Orunmila Oshun, he said, "This was your choice, and we'll just have to see how it works for the both of us." A divination I received during my initiation had actually given me guidelines for dealing with my husband as an Oya wife, and I was ready to return to Ohio and show him that my Yoruba initiation could indeed strengthen our marriage.

Returning to Kimathi in Toledo in early August, several weeks before our twenty-fifth wedding anniversary, I knew I had a challenge: maintaining my spiritual discipline as an Iyawo while bringing my husband along on this journey with me. I could see clearly that Kimathi was struggling with being married to a strong woman who had dominated much of our life choices together: founding CitiCentre Dance Theatre/Everybody's Creative Arts Center, *Evolution of Black Dance* and Hawaii's *Middle Passage* productions, the actual move to Toledo for my job at BGSU, and now my becoming a priest. He wanted to *lead* now, but my dressed-in-all-white appearance, with my head always wrapped, was a constant reminder to him that my life choices were still dominating the marriage. Although it was not in my nature to *play* the dutiful wife, I knew I could support him with his job as the principal of his school. I was also clear that if our marriage was to survive this obvious crisis, it also depended upon him growing spiritually.

For our twenty-fifth anniversary I made a special effort to make it as special as I could. That evening we went to dinner at one of our favorite Toledo restaurants, but things were not lighthearted, and I continued to pray for love to prevail. Within twenty-four hours of our twenty-fifth anniversary our marriage crashed.

I had a suspicion that a teacher at his school, with whom he had become friends, was attracted to him, but I naively trusted him implicitly and could not conceive of him cheating on me. But I should have because that is exactly what had been happening for quite a while. He had been having an affair with the teacher, a married Latina with her own school-aged children. She called him at 8:00 a.m. the day after our wedding anniversary, and that was it. He said, "I just don't feel the spark anymore, and I don't want to keep hurting you." But what he didn't say was that he had to explore a relationship with his other woman. In *that* relationship he felt he was the leader, thereby enhancing his sense of manhood. I began to realize he was actually going through a male mid-life crisis.

I began to understand what he had been doing even before I left for Hawai'i, and my premonitions during my trip were messages from spirit preparing me for this life crisis. My six weeks away for my initiation gave them time to solidify their relationship, and he basically made his decision by the time I arrived home. He felt guilty when I returned and faked his way through the sham of the twenty-fifth anniversary, but finally had to stop living the lie; he had to leave me. This entire breakup scenario flashed before me: Kimathi was now going to be with a woman who was in a lesser professional position and who looked up to *him*. But he didn't realize what I perceived as her controlling manipulative nature, and from my perspective she was actually leading him. Turning one's back on a twenty-five-year marriage, for a man, usually means another woman is involved, a younger woman, and she was about ten years his junior. I found myself in a classic case of the love triangle.

The man who was the love of my life, who co-founded Everybody's Creative Arts Center with me in 1977, performed with me in countless productions over the decades, created community with me in our new life in Hawai'i, and moved with me back to his home state of Ohio, left me, and I was emotionally devastated. When I divined to Oya, she told me emphatically that it was ordained that he had to go, and that was it! I would have felt much worse had I not undergone my recent spiritual elevation. My initiation fortified my spirit, giving me the inner strength to carry on without completely falling apart emotionally.

I survived this emotionally devastating period of my life with the help of my friends. Erica moved in with me, allowing us to bond even closer as mother and daughter. Ironically, she had gotten a teaching position at his school and was privy to Kimathi's growing personal relationship at work, including how the students were talking about the obvious affair going on between their principal and one of their teachers. But that was not my concern, and I chose a non-vindictive approach to the breakup. My focus was on healing myself, and having Erica's daughterly love around me in my home definitely helped. My ajibona, Susheel Bibbs, also aided my recovery; she called every day to ask me how I was doing. I felt love in the midst of my emotion devastation, and I slowly began to heal.

Trip to Nigeria with Baba Bolu

Baba Bolu Fatunmise informed members of Ile Orunmila Oshun that he was organizing a trip to Nigeria for his American initiates and friends. Even though I was still an Iyawo with one more month in whites, I really wanted to go to Nigeria again. A journey to the source of my religion to experience the sacred shrines with a well-respected babalawo was a journey I could not pass up. As she had never been to Africa before, Susheel also wanted to go, as well as Iya Fakayode, another priest in our ile who had been initiated as Iyanifa by Baba Bolu. The three of us left San Francisco together on June 3, 2004, for Atlanta, where we got our connecting Delta Airlines flight to Paris, France, and then on to Lagos, Nigeria. After a grueling eleven-hour flight, we met Baba Bolu at Lagos's Murtala Muhammed International Airport with his assistants and were thankfully ushered past the usual intense Lagos airport tourist hustle.

Baba Bolu had arrived in Nigeria a few days earlier than our West Coast contingent, and had brought one of his Atlanta initiates, Ifabanke, a Haitian woman living in the US. She made four women making the pilgrimage to Yorubaland. Baba Bolu's driver took us directly to his home in the ancient sacred city of Ile-Ife, dating back to 500 BC. The two-and-half-hour drive from the congested commercial bustle of Lagos, Nigeria's largest coastal city, to Ile-Ife was indeed an ordeal.

The Yoruba believe Ile-Ife is the place where humankind was born, and it's considered sacred as the royal seat of the Yoruba state. It is where the Ooni of Ife, the High Chief of the Yoruba resides, as well as the Araba, the highest babalawo priest. Hence, when Baba Bolu Fatunmise, himself a respected babalawo, comes home, he is sequestered in a kind of royal "bubble," with, as Tupac Shakur raps, "all eyes on me." In turn, we as his American guests were automatically situated in that same royal arena. Susheel, Iya Fakayode, Ifabanke, and I found ourselves in the center of an imperial reality that rendered us very visible, beyond the usual visibility of foreign tourist. Everyone in Ile-Ife knew that four American women had arrived in their sacred town and were guests of the respected priest Baba Bolu Fatunmise.

Our "celebrity" also made us targets, and during our first night in Ile-Ife we immediately realized we were also in negative crosshairs. Susheel and I shared a bedroom right across the hall from Fakayode and Ifabanke's room. Our two rooms were a few yards away from Baba Bolu's larger bedroom in another corridor of his relatively large home, situated in a gated compound. Just after Susheel and I changed into our bed clothes for much-needed sleep, we heard loud noises outside our bedroom door. Screaming voices bellowed in Yoruba in the hallway along with rumbling sounds of a fight in the corridor. I remember asking Susheel, "Should we go out there to see what's going on?" and she answered, "No, it sounds like Baba Bolu has it under control, and we might distract his bodyguards who seem to be handling whatever it is." So we decided to push our luggage and furniture against the door to barricade ourselves in our bedroom from any potential danger. After the noise and scuffling subsided, we opened the door to discover Fakayode and Ifabanke's door wide open, revealing a ransacked room with their belongings strewn across the hallway. Baba Bolu was standing in the hallway in his bed clothes, holding his head and being aided by his three bodyguard assistants. When he saw Susheel and me, he asked, "Did they break into your room?" We answered in the negative, and he replied, "It was the *ebo;* thank God."

We were quickly informed that seven young men had broken into Bolu's house with a battering ram, creating a gaping hole in his bedroom wall, to steal money and valuables. Large homes of the rich are always situated within gated compounds, and if they had tried to enter through the front, the thieves would have had to break the gate and immediately tackle the guards stationed at the front just for that purpose. Therefore, the interlopers devised a plan to enter the home from the side, knowing exactly where Bolu's bedroom would be. All of Baba's money and jewelry were stolen, he had been thrown to the floor, and his outnumbered bodyguards overtaken. The thieves had also broken into our fellow travelers' room and taken their passports, money, and jewelry. After the thieves left the compound, they immediately re-entered to return Fakayode and Ifabanke's *elekes* (sacred orisa necklaces). Their leader, who had been waiting in the getaway car, knew the difference between elekes and regular jewelry and ordered his minions to bring them back into the house. The Yoruba belief system is ubiquitous in Nigeria, particularly in Ile-Ife, and the outlaws did not want to immediately incur the wrath of orisa. But they did not realize that in violating a highly respected priest like Baba Bolu, they already had.

What Baba Bolu meant when he said, "It was the ebo," was that a sacred sacrifice had been offered to orisa for *my* safety as a recently initiated priest. An ebo is an offering to spirit in exchange for blessings. He pronounced the ebo as the reason why the thieves *had not* broken into Susheel's and my room, even though it was directly across from the other women's room they did enter. An ebo can be as simple as a plate of orisa's favorite food and drink or as complex as a blood sacrifice of an animal. In this case, a goat had been sacrificed before my arrival in Nigeria.

It is customary before a long-distance trip to divine about safety, and Susheel had done just that about her first trip to Africa. In her divination, my orisa Oya had "spoken," revealing the trip could bring "turbulence and disharmony, and even the possibility of death." This disturbed Susheel enough that she took the issue to priestess Ohen Imene (our friend Nedra Williams), and she got the same divination results, where Oya warned about danger on the trip. Nedra instructed Susheel to tell Baba Bolu about the two divinations and the negative predictions. Once Baba Bolu was informed, he said he could also "make ebo" for our safety. Money was sent to him in Nigeria, and he performed the protection ebo for our safe journey and stay in Nigeria. I was only told about these divinations in a perfunctory manner, as they were protecting me in my delicate Iyawo state.

When the violent armed robbery happened our very first night in Ile-Ife and Susheel and I were the only ones spared, it was as if our room became invisible. The story now sounds like something out of an otherworldly futuristic television series so prevalent today. But it was Afrofuturism in real time because when the intersection of the world of spirit and the world of the living collide, unexplainable things can occur. This real-life Nigerian story in Ile-Ife became my immediate and overt validation of the potency of the spiritual path into which I had been initiated. There was no other logical explanation for why the thugs had not broken into our bedroom. I was completely untouched, remaining safe and unviolated.

The crime and violation became *the* talk of the town of Ile-Ife. If we Americans were not already in the spotlight, we were now completely front and center in the town. We four Americans, the violent offense committed against us, and Baba Bolu were on the lips of every market woman, vendor, and office worker in this famous town of a half million people. The news also reached the Yoruba chief, the Ooni of Ife,[11] and his palace staff. Baba Bolu had planned to take us to pay respects to the Yoruba high chief, but now the Ooni himself summoned us all to his palace. However, before we made the excursion to the royal palace, practical matters took precedent: Iya Fakayode and Ifabanke had to go to the American embassy to report their stolen passports as well as to wire home for more money.

But the most powerful aftermath of the notorious transgressive robbery happened the very next morning: a major meeting of the region's highest babalawos took place in the living room of Baba Bolu. A violation of one was a violation of them all, and Baba had lost a considerable amount of money. He had remained calm, and Susheel and I gave him money as the only ones who didn't lose finances during the crime. The gathered priests discussed their plan of action about what was to be done spiritually. Also, one of the convocation of babalawos was the actual Chief of Police, allowing us to understand how the religious and civil officials are intertwined in that city; the Police Chief immediately stationed two armed policemen outside our compound. Another layer of personal protection was the famous Ibeji (twins) priests, known as the Ejiogbe Twins, who pledged to travel with Baba for the remainder of our trip as his spiritual bodyguards. From that day, the Ejiogbe Twins escorted Baba Bolu everywhere we went. Suffice it to say, within the six weeks I was in Nigeria, five out of the seven criminals had already been apprehended.

The following day the Ooni of Ife summoned Baba Bolu and his American contingent to the palace. The Ooni was much beloved by the Yoruba people as their high king, and when he summons someone, one immediately goes. The late Oba Sijuade Okunade (1930–2015) had ascended the throne in 1980. He was a descendant of the Ogboru ruling house, and took the name of Olubuse II after his grandfather Ooni Sijuwade Adelekan Olubuse I. We arrived at the palace one early afternoon, walking down a long outdoor corridor with fenced-in exotic-looking ostriches. We were greeted by the Ooni's palace attendants to whom Baba Bolu conversed in Yoruba, giving all the obligatory praises to the house. After introductory protocols we were led into the opulent throne room where more palace attendants were seated along one side, with Ooni Olubuse II seated on a raised dais awaiting our entrance. Baba Bolu immediately bent down to *kunle* (prostrate on the floor) before the Ooni, giving the obligatory praise to the high Yoruba king. He then introduced each of his American guests in protocol order: Iya Fakayode as the oldest Ifa priest, Iya Ifabanke who was in Nigeria to receive Ifa, Susheel, and finally me, the Iyawo still in my new initiate whites. Each woman knelt in order in front of the high chief.

The Ooni wanted us to know that the "Big Violation," as I call it, did not represent who the Yoruba people are, and he apologized on behalf of his people. I was impressed that the secular head of Yorubaland felt obligated to apologize directly to us, allowing me to further grasp Baba Bolu's stature in the city of Ile-Ife. The Ooni then welcomed us to the sacred center of the Yoruba ethnic group and invited us to return to the palace for a luncheon he wanted to have prepared in our honor. The crime that we had immediately experienced in his city, and from which I had been miraculously protected, had become the impetus for our experiencing Yoruba hospitality and recognition from their high chief. A few days later the four of us returned with Baba Bolu for the royal luncheon. Although the Ooni did not attend, we were treated to a delicious lunch in our honor and served with the royal gold-plated silverware. We had become royal celebrities within one week of arriving in Nigeria, a completely different experience than my first trip to the country in 1976, twenty-eight years earlier (chapter 5, *DinB*).

Another defining experience Baba Bolu gave us in Ile-Ife was a visit to the main Obatala Shrine. Obatala is the deity of the highest ethical behavior, who sits at the right side of Olodumare (The Creator) and fashions the body of each human being, into which Olodumare blows the breath of life. As such, Obatala guides practitioners to good character (*iwa pele*) and is known as the "Deity of the White Cloth," denoting his high spiritual position. Baba Bolu as well as Iya Fakayode had been originally initiated for Obatala. Also, Obatala is "my father," residing next to Oya. Hence, our pilgrimage to the deity's main shrine was particularly meaningful to all of us.

Baba Bolu had arranged for the principal Obatala priest maintaining the sacred shrine to open for a private gathering just for us to experience the deity's home; such was the power and respect of my spiritual father. At Baba's own original initiation years ago, it was divined that Baba Adebolu Fatunmise was to be "a babalawo of the world." As a traditional Yoruba priest now living in Atlanta, he was fulfilling his purpose abroad while continuing to be honored at home. His prestige opened the main Obatala Shrine to his American initiates, whom he had initiated into the Yoruba religion. He was fulfilling his destiny as babalawo of the world, and we had become a part of him fulfilling that calling.

When we arrived at the entrance to the shrine, we were met by the head priestess, Iyalorisha Awoyemi. Her presence commanded attention and respect, but her demeanor was humble. She was the first woman we met in Yorubaland who truly demonstrated *female* spiritual power. Dressed in a white lace flowing *grand bubu* with a matching *gele* (head wrap) and carrying a white feather fan, she welcomed us into the inner courtyard of the Obatala Shrine. The main Obatala priest, Babalorisha Obalela, was calmly seated in the doorway to the sacred altar where the orisa's accoutrements reside. We were led to kunle before him and give our greetings and gratitude for being allowed to have this special gathering at the Obatala Shrine. I had brought a special offering of a white painted *shakere* (beaded gourd percussion instrument) that had been made by my friend Baba Igbinlade, an American Yoruba priest, for the purpose of offering it at the Obatala Shrine. He had instructed me that if we visited the shrine on our trip to please give the special gourd as an offering. When I presented it to Iya Awoyemi, she graciously accepted and whispered to me, "You will never regret becoming an Iyalorisha." I received her personal pronouncement to me as another blessing.

Our time at the Obatala Shrine, on a very hot day, was spent enjoying traditional drumming and singing for orisa Obatala by drummers seated in a shaded area of the courtyard. We, the visitors, complemented them by dancing a subtle two-step to their infectious rhythms. The courtyard was an open-air oval shape surrounded by covered areas for shade, allowing us to avoid the ninety-degree humid sun. We all sat on mats on the ground in the shade until we were called to dance to the drummers' rhythms in the open sunny area. Our entourage were all dressed in white, as was most of the shrine members attending our special gathering. We all felt the subtle *peaceful* power of Obatala, the orisa of the white cloth. It was a day I will always remember.

We never went anywhere in Yorubaland without Baba, and as the Gwaniyi

Figure 4.2. Author in Ile-Ife, Nigeria, 2004. (*Left to right*: Alaba Fatunmise [Mama Bunmi], the author, Baba Bolu Fatunmise, Eji Ogbe Twins [*background*], Iya Fabanke.) Photo courtesy of author.

of Ile-Ife, his celebrity inured us. Although we were mostly seen as *oyinbo* (white foreigners), Baba's notoriety elevated our status and allowed us more of an insider view of the culture. Besides his self-appointed bodyguards, the Ejiogbe Twins, Baba's sons—Bunmi, Tunji, Bolu Jr., and Laide—as well as his nephews Sheyi, Akin Aiyo, Sanjo, and Elias would also accompany us throughout the town. They also accompanied us when we went to stay at Baba's second home in Oṣogbo, another important Yoruba town famous for its Osun River and Osun Shrine. In Oṣogbo we met his first wife, Mama Bunmi (Alaba Fatunmise), mother to his first-and-second born sons. The entire family treated us kindly because we were the initiates of Baba Bolu, and he made sure we were comfortable, with familiar food made by a cook, Oshun Funmilayo, he hired just for us. Besides Nigerian food, we had pancakes, American cereal, and fresh fruit and vegetables each day. We were treated royally, and this special treatment mitigated the beginning experience of the "Big Violation," making the trip an overall positive experience.

Toward the end of my five weeks in Nigeria, I asked Baba to permit me to make a side trip beyond Ile-Ife and Oṣogbo to Kwara State outside of Yorubaland in southwestern Nigeria. I wanted to travel to the town of Jebba to experience the Niger River. Jebba, situated at the head of the Niger, is populated predominantly by Muslim Nupe people. As a priestess of Oya, I really wanted to experience her sacred waterway—the Niger—for which Nigeria itself is named. I desired to pay homage to my orisa by making a pilgrimage to her sacred river about which I had heard so much folklore. I stayed longer in Nigeria so I could have this experience. Susheel and Iya Fakayode had returned to the US after three weeks, but Ifabanke and I remained in Nigeria for two more weeks.

However, my desire to experience Oya's Niger River revealed a difference between the branches of the Yoruba belief system. When I asked Baba Bolu if he could arrange the trip for me, he was reluctant. Although the Cuban Lucumi branch of the Yoruba religion positions the Niger as sacred to Oya, the Nigerian tradition does not *unanimously* hold that belief. Baba felt I would be wasting my money to hire a car and driver to make an excursion to the river that he did not believe was actually sacred to Oya. But I was so insistent on making my pilgrimage to the river that he acquiesced and made arrangements for my one-day trip to Jebba with a chauffeur and two male escorts, which included his nephew Seyi.

One morning in early July, before leaving Nigeria, we drove off from Osogbo, the capital of Osun State, for Jebba in a black Toyota Corolla. Jebba is in Kwara State, and is culturally both Yoruba and Nupe, with a population of about 22,000 people. It was a hot sunny day, and my Yoruba male escorts were jovial and informative, giving me many tourist facts as we drove through the various towns and villages. Seyi and I had become good friends, with me often assuming the role of his aunt. He asked curious questions about the US and was very inquisitive about Black popular culture and hip-hop in particular. As we drove through Ogbomosho, and then to Ilorin, a fairly large city and the capital of Kwara State, we exchanged information about our two countries.

Arriving in Jebba was unimpressive, for it seemed like any other small town in Nigeria; but when we arrived at the Niger River on its outskirts, I knew why I had made this three-hour journey. The river is very wide and much larger than the Osun River with which I was familiar. What I discovered was that Oya's river was extremely calm, and its vast calmness immediately impressed me. In fact, the Niger River is the principal river of West Africa and the third largest on the continent. It extends some 2,600 miles from the Guinea Highlands, running through Mali, Niger, Benin, and Nigeria, and ending in the Niger Delta at the Gulf of Guinea in the Atlantic Ocean. I had reached one of the great rivers of Africa, and my orisa, Oya, was the patron deity of its flowing currents.

The Nupe and Yoruba people at Jebba are the keepers of the lore of Oya and the river. In fact, Oya is originally considered a Nupe deity. Anthropologist Judith Gleason (1929–2012) tells of the river's origin in relation to Oya this way:

> According to Ifa, the Niger River was produced in the following manner. The King of the Nupe . . . consulted the oracle in time of war. How might he prevent invasion? Ifa replied that the besieged king should procure a length of black cloth and appoint a virgin to tear it. The king's choice fell upon his own daughter. Summoned by the elders . . . the young woman took up the black cloth. *O-ya*—"She tore"—it. Then she flung the two pieces on the ground, whereupon, before the wondering eyes of the assembled Nupe, the cloth turned into black water, which spread out and began to flow protectively around the nucleus of the kingdom, now an island. Though the Nupe eventually transferred their capital to the mainland, Jebba Island remains in the midst of the Niger.[12]

The problem with this story is that the Nupe do not use Ifa divination, and the few Nupe elders who still live on Jebba Island do not know it. As Gleason says, "It is a Yoruba story, projected, as we would say, upon the Nupe. It is a story of a foreign princess from a bordering kingdom, which presumably the Yoruba themselves were preparing to invade."[13] Although the Yoruba could not conquer the Nupe, the princess "could be brought across," along with her black-cloth power. Indeed, the Nupe princess, who turned into Oya in the projected folklore, became a quintessential part of the Yoruba pantheon and synonymous with the vast river. The competition between the Nupe and Yoruba embedded in the folklore, which I suspected was also the source of Baba Bolu's initial reticence, only amused me. I was focused on the spiritual connection I deeply felt with orisa Oya that the river represented.

Upon arriving at the Niger River that day, I did not see Jebba Island, but I did experience the river's power as I paid homage to Oya. The chauffer parked the car on a nearby dirt road, and we walked the rest of the way to the river's bank. My three male escorts stayed back, resting on a small nearby hillside, allowing me to approach the river by myself. As I stood near the flowing calm waters, I was surprised at the peace I felt. Oya is associated with natural disasters like tornadoes and hurricanes and is perceived mostly as a warrior goddess. Yet her river is calm and peaceful. I felt the tranquil power of my patron deity—my mother—in a way that I did not expect, allowing me to experience the serenity within her strength, and I understood Oya's so-called devastations were more about pushing humans to transform ourselves for human evolution.

Sitting on a rock at the shore, I then proceeded to make ebo, preparing an offering of a hard shell coconut over which I poured honey and palm oil. Praying over my humble gift, I then cast the coconut into the flowing, slightly green waters. I watched it float away, immediately caught in the river currents; Oya accepted my ebo, and I felt blessed. I then stepped into the water and reached down below the shallow riverbank and pulled up a rock. It was a half-inch thick and light brown in color, laden with flecks of sparkles throughout. Interestingly enough, the rock had a similar shape to the continent of Africa, becoming my gift from the goddess, and today it sits on her shrine in my home.

The pilgrimage to the River Niger was one of my last experiences in Nigeria before returning to the reality of my transitional life in Ohio. Ending my Iya-wo year in whites in the original home of the Yoruba orisas with their sacred shrines was exactly what I needed for my healing. Even with the "Big Violation" that started my trip, the entire Nigerian experience, including meeting the Ooni of Ife, experiencing the Obatala Shrine, and paying homage to Oya at the Niger River was healing. The trip to Nigeria spiritually fortified me to return to Toledo and the looming divorce. I left Lagos on Delta Airlines on July 8, 2004, and retraced my itinerary back through Paris to New York, and finally to San Francisco. I was to go through the formal coming-out-of-my-year-of-whites ceremony in Oakland at Ile Orunmila Oshun with Iya Fagembola before returning to Toledo to begin the Fall 2004 semester at BGSU.

Returning to BGSU and the Divorce

Returning to my teaching schedule at BGSU, I created a routine that was another link in my emotional healing process. I'm sure teaching dance classes in white jazz pants and leotards while wearing a white headwrap for every class seemed a bit peculiar to my students and colleagues, but they quickly got accustomed to my new look.

At the end of the Fall 2004 semester, I decided to have my Dunham Technique students send a Christmas gift to Miss Dunham: a video of them performing Dunham Technique along with selected Dunham term paper essays I had assigned. This gesture from my BGSU class reassured her that the younger generation was indeed learning her technique and philosophy of dance, and Miss Dunham was truly appreciative. She sent me a special thank you note that I shared with my students. These kinds of job-related activities helped me focus on giving to others rather than thinking about my personal life transition.

During that same semester, on November 16, 2004, Kimathi and I met at the Lucas County Courthouse in downtown Toledo and went through the perfunctory legal hearing to obtain our no-contest divorce. As a part of the divorce proceedings, I also changed my legal name from "Janis Miller Williams" back to "Janis Miller," ridding myself of his surname. As it was a no-contest divorce with no quibbling over assets, we took the option of a marriage dissolution, which is cheaper than a regular divorce. Kimathi knew ending our marriage was *his* choice, and he gave everything to me.

"Incompatibility," the judge pronounced as the reason for the divorce, and it was over in ten minutes. As we walked out of the courthouse on that dreary fall day in Toledo, I looked him in the eyes and said, "You know this has been your choice, so I hope you are happy." He looked back at me and simply said, "I know, and I am truly sorry." At that moment, all those years of joy, sorrow, laughter, tears, and more importantly, many great mutually transformative community accomplishments came flooding back between us. Then we parted and went our separate ways.

I moved forward with confidence into my new life as a single woman while still healing the deep wound of separation and the end of a twenty-five-year marriage. I had lost a husband, but gained an adopted "daughter" and the awesome friendship of my ajibona Susheel. Of course, continuing contact with Ile Orunmila Oshun and Iya Fagembola was also crucial in surviving the separation and divorce. I also had visited Baba Bolu Fatunmise in Atlanta right before the divorce and had received spiritual fortification from him as well. I kept hearing the famous words attributed to Nelson Mandela in my head that had been circulating around the internet: "Our deepest fear is not that we are inadequate; our deepest fear is that we are powerful beyond measure." But the part of the aphorism that loomed large in my head was: "Your playing small doesn't serve the world. There's nothing enlightening about shrinking so that other people won't feel insecure around you. We were born to manifest the glory of God that is within us." I arrived at the realization that I was correctly living out my life's destiny.

On further research, I discovered that wise adage, which is an epigraph for this chapter, originally came from Marianne Williamson's *A Return to Love* (1992). I could not have *diminished* myself to make Kimathi feel better about himself. I had felt a little guilty that I had spent so much time away from him pursuing my mission, my purpose. But once I truly comprehended that I had done nothing wrong, my healing became easier and I moved forward with Oya fully on my head.

I returned to the Bay Area that December and spent the Christmas/Kwanzaa season in San Francisco with my family and friends. I was amazed at the support they all gave me after the divorce. I appreciated my sisters even more: Brenda's assuredness, Pat's sensitivity, Tenola's emotional probing for my true feelings, and Tracey's openness. Mama was the loving grand matriarch as usual and assured me that I had a wonderful life ahead of me. Erica came to visit me in San Francisco and bonded beautifully with my family, and they accepted her as my adopted daughter. Amazingly, I had naturally slipped into "motherhood," advising her in both small and large matters.

Thankfully, at the year's closing bembe at Ile Orunmila Oshun, a message from Oya came during our ceremony: "Prepare for royalty. We can all be kings and queens." For me, it was a message from spirit to rise and take my rightful place. My spiritual revitalization began almost immediately because before I returned to Toledo, I visited Baba Bolu in Atlanta again. He performed a spiritual renewal ceremony for me, known in the tradition as a head cleaning or rogation, and he assured me that he was preparing me for a glorious 2005.

Transitioning Back to Northern California

I had finished my Iyawo year and was out of whites, and just as Baba Bolu predicted, 2005 did indeed bring me an abundant new life. Toledo, and Ohio in general, represented cultural blandness for me, and it now also symbolized the death of my marriage. I longed for a geographical and cultural change. I re-entered the online job market, focusing on trying to get a university appointment anywhere in Northern California. I desperately wanted to leave the Midwest and live in my home area again. During my job-hunting, an opening came at University of California, Davis (UCD) in their African American and African Studies (AAS) Program, for which I applied. UC Davis, only a twenty-minute drive west of Sacramento and a little over a one-hour drive to Oakland, would put me right where I wanted to be.

Applying for the UCD assistant professorship, I worked hard on my application and cover letter, trying to "choreograph" a much-needed geographic shift. I made sure that my five years at BGSU would count toward eventual tenure; at my age I could not start over from the beginning. As eligibility for tenure usually happens in one's seventh year, I was getting close to that academic milestone. I did make the "shortlist" out of over one hundred applicants and was invited to campus for an in-person interview. They provided accommodations in a Davis hotel, and Susheel joined me the night before my interview. We prayed to Oya together, and I readied myself for my job interview the next day.

The faculty of AAS were impressive, with Africans, West Indians, and African Americans all working together with notable scholarship in African religion, African literature, South American anthropology, the Black church, and Black film and television. My expertise could add Black performance through hip-hop and dance studies to their teaching and research mix. My research lecture for the job was on global hip-hop, "Hip-Hop in the African Diaspora: Cuban *Raperos* and Brazilian *Favelas,*" comparing Cuban and Brazilian hip-hop. I was also required to give a teaching presentation to students in an actual classroom, and I chose to prepare my lesson presentation on African American representation on television, called "From *The Cosby Show* to *Yo, MTV Raps.*" Lastly, I had to have an "exit interview" with the director of the program, Professor Jacob Olupona, a noted African religion scholar now at Harvard University. We had a productive talk beyond the job requirements, discussing current issues of Nigerian politics and culture, and I left campus feeling positive about my UC Davis interview performance.

Teaching at UC Davis meant I would be closer to my family and my Bay Area community, as well as moving academically out of dance and into Africana studies. My friend Linda Goodrich, living in Sacramento with her new husband John Roberts, was teaching dance at California State University, Sacramento. My old Bay Area colleague Bobbie Wynn, now Bobbie Bolden, was living in Davis, having just retired from the UC Davis Department of Dance and Theatre. I went to lunch with them while I was in Davis and recognized the support network they would provide if I got the job. Linda said, "We need you back here," which was another omen that the Sacramento area was where I was meant to be.

On June 12, 2005, I got a call from the African American and African Studies Program at UC Davis offering me the position. That phone call changed my life! Everything I had accomplished since my master's degree in 1993 to my PhD in 1999, from my tenure-track position at BGSU to my growing hip-hop scholarship and publications had paid off. Career-wise, I was moving from dance to African American Studies, emphasizing the other side of my bifurcated research agenda. Now I was truly flipping the script from performance to the humanities, and I was ready. During this transition period in my life, I realized both my academic and spiritual work had born fruit. California was my destiny, and I was now going back home.

5

"Dancing" in Sacramento and Davis

There's a future past what we think is the end.
Camille A. Brown, choreographer-director

The move from Ohio back to Northern California was a much-needed transition that absolutely shaped the next phase of my life. Soon after I finished my last spring semester at Bowling Green State University (BGSU) in early May 2005, I flew to the Bay Area to look for a place to live. I stayed with Mama in San Francisco while looking for rentals in Sacramento. My friend Susheel, who had been renting in SF for years while teaching at UC Berkeley, decided to ride with me to Sacramento, as she was interested in the Sacramento real estate market for a potential house to buy. Real estate agent and friend Brenda Jew Waters met us in Sacramento to show her a few houses. I kept wondering why I was getting involved with Susheel's home buying, when I just wanted to *rent* a house near the highway for an easy commute to my new UC Davis job.

I got my answer almost immediately. Susheel and I fell in love with the third house Brenda showed us in the Roble district off of Del Paso Road, which is close to Highway 80 connecting to Davis. The two-story house had three bedrooms, two and a half baths, lots of light, and even a patio pool and a hot tub. Susheel immediately announced she wanted to consider buying it if I would move in with her as a renter, allowing her to afford the initial mortgage. She *did* buy the house, and I agreed to rent from her and share the entire house. After finding the perfect living situation in Sacramento, I returned to Toledo to teach summer session and then packed to move back to Northern California after eleven years of living in Hawai'i and Ohio.

In late June, on a warm sunny day I left Toledo on Interstate 475, literally yelling a symbolic scream of freedom out of my car window as I drove out of town. I went to Columbus to see my (ex) in-laws before flying back to California. My sisters-in-law had been my friends for over twenty-five years, and that did not stop with my divorcing their brother. Cathy wanted to buy my car, so I first drove it to her house, and then visited Mama Betty and her other daughters for a few days. The only communication I had with Kimathi was regarding the home we still owned together in Hawai'i. Then on July 1, 2005, I happily flew to San Francisco and my new life. My journal entry read: *Driving out of Toledo was liberating. I felt like I was being released from a very complex dream (nightmare?).* Indeed, I *was* leaving one of the darkest periods of my life in the Midwest and returning to the light of my "California dreaming," where I belonged.

Oya Fun Mi Laiyo (Oya brings me joy) was a part of the *odus* (parables) divined from Ifa regarding my move to Sacramento. As we moved into our new house in Sacramento, Susheel and I chanted that phrase together, for we felt that Oya had given us this perfect new home. I wrote: *Ever since our trip to Nigeria last year, Susheel and I were brought together to quicken our spiritual development and to live abundantly in an undeniably tangible way.* Although the Yoruba have a pantheon of gods, like Oya, they believe each deity is a different *face* of Olodumare, the Supreme Being. Philosopher E. Bolayi Idowu explains it this way: "As far as they [the Yoruba] are concerned, the full responsibility of all the affairs of life belongs to the Deity [Olodumare]; their own part in the matter is to do as they are ordered through the priests and diviners whom they believe to be the interpreters of the will of the Deity."[1] Following our divination reading, we felt all of the pieces of our lives had fallen into place: from driving to Sacramento together to quickly finding her beautiful home that I could share, as well as her finances converging perfectly to buy our new home. Now, each of us could start a new life.

Susheel's beloved mother had passed in 2003 and she was still grieving from that loss, so moving out of her small rental apartment in SF to a beautiful home in Sacramento with a pool was a blessing to her, as well as to me. She generously gave me the master bedroom with its own bath and took the smaller bedroom with an adjacent room that became her office. I converted the upstairs overhang above the living room into my own office, making the house perfect for two busy professional women.

Bolade (Erica), who had moved back to her family in Washington, DC, while she continued to work on her master's thesis at BGSU, came to visit me for her July birthday, and it was a wonderful reunion. She was a twenty-nine-year old young Black woman whom I had taken under my wing to fill in some gaps missed by not having been fully nurtured by her birth mother, and we were continuing our mother-daughter relationship.

In early September, before my first quarter at UC Davis, members of the New York dance company Urban Bush Women (UBW) performed in Sacramento at the Guild Theater in Oak Park, one of Sacramento's Black communities. UBW is a women's dance collective founded in 1984 by my friend Jawole Willa Jo Zollar, who had performed in my Black Choreographers Moving Toward the 21st Century project in the late eighties in San Francisco. The well-established UBW New York company performing in Sacramento let me know that my newly adopted city was becoming more of a cultural center.

The Guild Theater was a part of a complex of buildings that Kevin Johnson, former NBA basketball player for the Cleveland Cavaliers and the Phoenix Suns, had built. Having grown up in Oak Park, Johnson renovated several buildings in his home area after retiring from his basketball career, creating the Guild Theater, Underground Books, 40 Acres Art Gallery (and eventually his Fixins Soul Kitchen restaurant), a small coffee shop, and even an old-school barber shop, all between Thirty-fourth and Thirty-fifth Streets at Broadway. Little did we know then that Johnson would become mayor of Sacramento for two terms in 2008. His renovated complex of buildings became an important renewal of Black culture in California's capital city, and UBW's performance was just one of many world-class artists and authors who would appear at his two-hundred-seat capacity Guild Theater.

Urban Bush Women's performance of *Hair Party* was danced by four touring members of the company exploring the multiple lenses of race, personal identity, Black beauty standards, and US history through dance. Per Urban Bush Women's modus operandi, they engaged the audience in dialogue after the performance. Four years prior to Chris Rock's *Good Hair* documentary, Urban Bush Women's *Hair Party* allowed me to feel the Sacramento community's growing consciousness from its previous reputation as a "cow town" untouched by the Black revolution. Black, white, and Latinx audience members communed openly in a therapeutic mode, telling their own stories while celebrating individual and collective issues around cultural racism and hair. As dance scholar Nadine George-Graves notes, "Through a postmodern bending of styles and juxtaposition of choreography, music, text, history, culture, and spirituality, the members of the [UBW] company challenge their audiences to reimage society and renounce old definitions of black dance, and indeed, black identity."[2] And UBW did just that in their 2005 Sacramento performance. Even though it was not the Bay Area, in Sacramento I felt I was finally back home in a cultural environment that made sense to me.

Joining the Faculty of UC Davis and Earning Tenure

As I began setting up my office in Hart Hall on the UCD campus, I was becoming acclimated to Sacramento and Davis, as well as renewing my relationship with the Bay Area. The UCD faculty members were supportive, encouraging me not to take on too many service committee assignments, but to focus instead on getting my first book published. As UCD is a Research 1 university, publishing was absolutely the most important component of my appointment and would almost ensure tenure. Finishing revising my dissertation on global hip-hop and the Africanist aesthetic into a publishable book would position me for tenure evaluation in the 2006–2007 school year. Everything was being arranged for my success: I was given my initial Fall Quarter off from teaching to get to know the UCD campus culture, enabling me to concentrate on my book manuscript. I gladly used my free time to work hard on what was to become *The Africanist Aesthetic in Global Hip-Hop* and finished a first draft for several publishers' review.

Starting to teach in the winter quarter at UC Davis allowed me to use some of my own published writings. I taught a lower-division course, AAS 051: The History of Black Dance, using my very first published journal article, "Aesthetic of the Cool Revisited: The Ancestral Dance Link in the African Diaspora." Teaching outside the dance studio in a lecture hall was now becoming familiar territory. And I was no longer bound by Midwest conservatism, but now encircled in West Coast liberalism that was more my style. My lecture teaching methods were maturing, as I allowed what I called "ancestral voices" to guide me. I taught my students about great Black dance artists, such as Asadata Dafora, Pearl Primus, and Alvin Ailey, all ancestors, along with the current legacy of the great Katherine Dunham and the challenging younger Black choreographers like Bill T. Jones, Jawole Willa Jo Zollar, and Bebe Miller. But I also taught them about the place of dance and music historically in Black societies among the regular folk and how we used our performance legacy as a tool of surviving the devastations of slavery and Jim Crow segregation.

UC Davis has a world-class arts presenter on campus with the Robert and Margrit Mondavi Center for the Performing Arts and its state-of-the art theater venue. At the end of January 2006, the Mondavi Center presented the Children of Uganda, a touring company of Ugandan youths who were orphaned by the AIDS crisis in Africa. The dance company of young people had become performing dance and music ambassadors for their country. I not only made attending the performance mandatory for my students in my Black dance lecture course, but the Mondavi Center asked me to serve as the facilitator for the curtain talk with the audience after the performance.

With this invitation, the UCD campus was immediately utilizing my Black dance expertise, allowing me to serve as a kind of cultural bridge to introduce the campus to African dance culture while making sure the young Ugandan performers knew they were welcomed and appreciated. During the curtain talk on stage that night I told the Children of Uganda, "You are doing such an important thing for us; you are teaching us how to be human beings," and they answered en masse, "Thank you." Their rhythmic dancing, drumming, and singing were so open, joyous, and human, I perceived that they were allowing the largely white audience to witness how much "Black lives matter," before that became the trending protest slogan. That night when I returned home to Sacramento, I stayed up late writing in my journal about my relationship with particular African countries important to my life's journey:

I have had a special relationship with Africa for most of my adult life, from Ghana that gave me my personal liberation to Nigeria that has fortified me spiritually. In Malawi I established my direct professional relationship with an African dance company on the continent. I know how and what to communicate with my African brothers and sisters. This little girl from Galveston, Texas, has grown to become a US cultural ambassador to the continent of her African ancestors. I hope I am making my egun (ancestors) proud.

When I went up for tenure in 2006, *The Africanist Aesthetic in Global Hip-Hop: Power Moves* was "in press," just in time for the review process. The highly regarded international academic publisher Palgrave Macmillan had accepted it for publication. Although I had to submit it to the tenure committee in manuscript form, Palgrave's letter of acceptance for publication accompanying the manuscript sealed the deal for a successful tenure review. My 2005 teaching evaluations from UCD students were very high, and, along with a few teaching evaluations from my five years at BGSU, all cinched my promotion to associate professor in July 2007.

I had to acknowledge that dancing, choreographing, or even teaching dance were not going to be my sustaining work, even as they served as the foundation of my knowledge. My past career as dancer and choreographer was essential to my embodied knowledge of performance and Black culture. But at sixty years old my first book publication was appearing in print,[3] and that achievement was responsible for me earning tenure. Given the *logocentric* nature of Western society, it was obvious that the recording of my vision of Black performance in written analysis, not dancing, was going to provide the stability for my elder years.

Dunham Technique and My Purpose

Around that same time, I bought a copy of Ruth Beckford's 1967 PBS television show of one of her Dunham Technique classes in which I appeared as a student at age twenty (chapter 1, *DinB*). The old black-and-white kinescope tape by Bay Area PBS affiliate, KQED, had been converted to DVD and distributed by Insight Media as "African-Haitian Dance Class: Dunham Technique," and is now on YouTube.[4] It was a revelation watching myself forty years earlier performing Miss B's strenuous Dunham barre with my peers Yvonne Daniel, Naima Gwen Lewis, Shirley Brown, Deborah Vaughan, and others. Observing the skinny young woman with her short Afro hairdo before she went off to live in Europe to follow her destiny, I realized I was viewing my very beginnings in the field of dance, and now forty years later I was the prodigal daughter returned to my Northern California roots. The video of the 1967 dance class also reinforced how Dunham Technique was my foundation. Although Miss Dunham had evolved the technique and I saw several exercises that have been modified when I studied with her during her evolutionary 1980s period at her annual Dunham Seminars in East St. Louis, Miss B's 1960s Afro-Haitian classes were undeniably my beginning in Dunham Technique.

In 1988, as Miss Dunham was approaching her eightieth birthday, she began emphasizing a holistic consciousness through the body, evolving her technique to its *fourth* generation with a concerted spiritual component. Katherine Dunham was often called a renaissance woman, and this was nowhere more evident than in her holistic inner mindfulness that became the hallmark of Dunham Technique. She had been a *vodou* priestess through her lifelong love of Haiti, and in her later years she became a practicing Buddhist. The latter tradition had found its way into her *new* emphasis on breathing and *chakra* energy work in relation to body alignment. In doing so, she began encouraging the Dunham dancer to focus on higher consciousness. When I rediscovered Dunham Technique in the late eighties, I felt I had come full circle, as she was now emphasizing the technique even more as a way of life. I had been all over the world studying and performing various dance techniques, only to come back "home" to Miss Dunham's holistic approach to dance. Her technique had been my initial awakening to the possibilities of dance, and now at the feet of the master, I was experiencing it anew as *embodied* consciousness.

Viewing Miss Beckford's old dance video brought back a flood of memories that allowed me to mentally synthesize my entire life. Watching me as a twenty-year-old, moving in her black leotards and fifty pounds lighter, I contemplated the wealth of knowledge I had gained through dancing, choreographing, and organizing community through dance. I had explored different societies and cultures far beyond the Bay Area—Scandinavia, Morocco, Ghana, Boston, New York, Hawai'i. I had started my own dance company in Copenhagen, founded an enduring cultural institution in Oakland, and created a national initiative in San Francisco, Los Angeles, and San Diego. The many roles I had played and the great artists I had met in my long performance trajectory—my dancing life—all came flooding back. I recognized my unique convergence of interests and accomplishments that constituted who I had become at that point. At the end of my UC Davis History of Black Dance course, a student came up to me and said, "Thank you for being passionate about what you do," and I answered, "I love what I do." She ended the exchange with, "It shows." I had mastered the symbiotic relationship between practice and theory and had synthesized them as my teaching approach in the classroom. I also realized how necessary and, unfortunately, rare it is to make a living through one's sense of purpose. I felt blessed.

Katherine Dunham Joins the Ancestors and the Northern California Dunham Legacy

By late spring of 2006, another major event happened that affected me and the entire dance world: Katherine Dunham decided to make her transition into the world of the ancestors. She passed on Sunday, May 21, 2006, one month before her ninety-seventh birthday. I frame her death as a *decision* because she once told me about a near-death experience that she had when I visited her at her East St. Louis home on North Tenth Street (now called Katherine Dunham Way): "Halifu, I felt my heart stop the other night, and I had to go inside and do some very deep breathing to bring myself back. I still have some things I need to do." As she told me this very matter-of-factly, I looked at her incredulously, and she simply proceeded to teach me a new breathing exercise (which I still do today); this anecdote reveals the spiritual power Katherine Dunham had attained in her later years. Hence, the Grand Dame of Dance finally *decided* to lay down her mantle. Before she left us on this plane, she passed on her great legacy, and all her protégés who spent time with her, like me, consumed as much of that great legacy as we could. At the time of her transition, we all knew it was now our turn to carry on that Dunham mantle.

Presciently, a year earlier Ruth Beckford had formed a group of us Bay Area protégés into the Northern California Dunham Legacy Committee. She planned to hold a Katherine Dunham June 2006 ninety-seventh birthday celebration with three days of classes and performances in Oakland at Laney College. Our organizational preparations for her birthday celebration positioned our group to hold the first memorial celebration of Katherine Dunham's transition. There would be several Dunham memorials in New York, Detroit, and East St. Louis/St. Louis, but our June 8–10, 2006, "Celebrating the Dunham Legacy" Memorial at Laney College in Oakland, California, was the first.

Dunham obituaries appeared immediately in the news throughout the country. Jack Anderson's *New York Times* notice read, "In the late 1930s she founded the nation's first self-supporting black modern dance troupe that visited more than 50 countries on six continents. Her achievements came at a time of racial discrimination which she fought against, refusing to return to segregated theaters in the South."[5] The *Chicago Sun-Times* read, "Katherine Dunham—dancer, choreographer, teacher, cultural anthropologist and social activist—was on the scene long before there was an Alvin Ailey American Dance Theater, before there was 'The Lion King,' and before there were such artists as Garth Fagan, Donald Byrd, Ronald K. Brown and many others."[6] The *Washington Post* paid tribute to her with, "In her unparalleled career in dance, where she educated the world about the power of African dance as found throughout the diaspora, Dunham mixed academic research and showbiz flair."[7] And our own Brenda Payton, staff writer with the now defunct *Oakland Tribune* and former dancer and board member with my CitiCentre Dance Theater, wrote, "Her legacy is monumental, and thrives in the Bay Area, which has the greatest concentration of teachers of the Dunham Technique in the country."[8] Payton's article appropriately chronicled our three-day Oakland memorial tribute to Katherine Dunham.

"Celebrating the Dunham Legacy," convened by Ruth Beckford's Northern California Legacy Committee, was an impeccably produced three-day event that would have made Miss Dunham proud. Thursday, June 8, was the free "Opening Ceremony" in the Laney College Theater, and Miss Beckford used it to pay tribute to her great dance mentor and friend. The event was also recognition of the Bay Area Dunham legacy that Miss Beckford had single-handedly created starting in the 1960s with all of we protégés. Friday, June 9, and part of Saturday, June 10, were the actual Dunham Technique classes taught by Director of the Certification Albirda Rose and the late Alicia Pierce as one of the first certified instructors. Keith Williams and Ruby Streate from the East St. Louis area taught advanced Dunham Technique and Dunham choreography respectively. The major concert on Saturday evening, "The Showcase," featured performances inspired by Dunham Technique, including Deborah Vaughan's Dimensions Dance Theater, a choreographic work by Keith Williams, and more.

To organize such a comprehensive three-day Dunham memorial, our meetings for the intended ninety-seventh birthday celebration started in late July 2005, right after I had moved to Sacramento. We usually had our monthly meetings at Lynn Coles's home in the Oakland hills, who was then Chair of the Laney College Dance Department. Initially, it was dancer and Beckford protégé Carolyn Himes who first suggested a Dunham birthday celebration and convinced Beckford to convene her protégé to plan such a project. To participate I had to organize my monthly drives to the Bay Area to see my

Figure 5.1. Northern California Dunham Legacy Committee, Oakland, CA, 2006. (*Standing left to right*: Shirley Brown, Alicia Pierce, Carolyn Himes, Lynn Coles, Deborah Vaughan, Andrea Lee, Colette Eloi; *Seated left to right*: Albirda Rose, Ruth Beckford, the author, Wendy Kelly, Linda Tregle.) Photo courtesy of author.

family around the Dunham Legacy Committee's meetings. Our Dunham legacy group consisted of Shirley Brown, Wendy Kelley, Andrea Lee, Linda Tregle, Deborah Vaughan, Albirda Rose, Lynn Coles as chairperson, Colette Eloi as secretary, and Carolyn Himes as treasurer, with Ruth Beckford as honorary chair. Due to Miss Beckford's impeccable organizational skills, we became systematically prepared as an ad hoc committee with a written mission statement that partially read, "To bring attention to Miss Katherine Dunham and to pay homage and respect to her work . . . [we] also recognize that many are not aware of the history of the importance of the work of Miss Dunham. Therefore, it is imperative that the legacy be passed on to current and future generations . . ."

The free Thursday, June 8, "Opening Ceremony" became the memorial centerpiece of the weekend. We opened the ceremony solemnly with a multicultural spiritual invocation in keeping with Miss Dunham's religious eclecticism: I, as a Yoruba priestess, poured traditional African libation while chanting a Yoruba ancestor prayer; Albirda Rose, as an ordained minister, said a Christian prayer; and my former dance student Soyinka Rahim, as a Buddhist practitioner, chanted the Nam Myōhō Renge Kyō prayer as she rang a power-

Figure 5.2. Author performs Yoruba libation at Katherine Dunham's Memorial, Laney College Theater, Oakland, California, July 8, 2006. Photo: Alan Kimara Dixon.

ful Buddhist bell. This multidimensional spiritual invocation was performed in front of a projected image of Miss Dunham's in her 1983 Kennedy Center Honors attire with her Lifetime Achievement metal. Our opening Dunham memorial ceremony created a hushed oneness; one could have heard a pin drop in the theater.

After our spiritual invocation, Lynn Coles, as Chair of Laney's Dance Department, welcomed the full capacity audience. Miss Beckford's requested me to deliver a formal Dunham biographical summary, which I titled "Who is Katherine Dunham?," and I was honored to do so. My prepared Dunham introduction brought everyone in attendance onto the same page, both veteran Dunham followers and those new to her dance legacy. I finished my speech to a roaring applause with, "Although Miss Dunham wanted to be cremated, she had always said her tombstone should read, 'She Tried.' But toward the end of her life, she had begun to say that it should read, 'She did it!'"

Then the *event* of the evening happened: a screening of a videotaped personal message from Miss Dunham specifically addressing the event. Because of Miss Dunham's advanced age, Ruth Beckford never wanted her to actually travel to her planned public ninety-seventh birthday celebration. Therefore, early on in our organizing, Beckford arranged for a videographer to tape Miss Dunham in her New York apartment. This obviously turned out to be a wise decision, as the film short, "Katherine Dunham's Personal Greeting to the

Northern California Dunham Legacy Group," became a recording of Miss Dunham thanking the audience for attending her birthday event, *one month after she had died*. The video captured her continuing vitality while sitting up in bed as she offered her sincere gratitude for everyone's continuing support, and particularly the Northern California Legacy Committee. The audience vividly witnessed Katherine Dunham's elegant graciousness projected onto the big theater screen, filmed just a few months before her transition. There was not a dry eye in the audience.

After the memorial part of the Opening Ceremony, the event progressed into presentations on Dunham's career and technique. The late Dr. VèVè A. Clark had edited a film short of archival footage called "Dunham in Holly-wood," showing excerpts from Dunham's dance sequences in the 1943 *Stormy Weather,* explored in the introduction, and the 1955 film called *Mambo*. The latter was an Italian movie featuring a Dunham Technique class that includes her company members. In the film, the leading lady, played by Silvano Mangano, finds new self-confidence and becomes self-empowered by joining Miss Dunham's dance class. It was instructive to see how Miss Dunham used movies to showcase the power of her dance oeuvre to a wider audience. Following the film screening, Albirda Rose and Alicia Pierce offered a Dunham Technique lecture-demonstration performed by their SF State dancers, along with Albirda's troupe of middle school students, The Village Dancers.

The finale of the opening Dunham event was Miss Beckford's "Legacy Tree" that visually showcased all of her protégés from her Afro-Haitian Dunham Technique classes since the 1960s. All her former female students (there were no men) came from all over the country to be introduced on stage, altogether forming what she called the "Northern California Dunham Legacy Tree." Naima Gwen Lewis came from Atlanta, the late Elendar Barnes and Mary Vivian came from New York, as well as others who had scattered around the US, joining with us former Beckford acolytes still living in Northern California. Ruth Beckford, then eighty-one years old, sat downstage center on her walker that she used to aid her entrance on stage. We had submitted our current biographies to Miss Beckford, from which she read, allowing the audience to know what accomplished women—educators, PhDs and EdDs, and directors of this and that—she had help create through Dunham Technique. Miss B, as we called her, wanted to prove to the audience that Dunham Technique was not only about dance, but it was a socializing tool that develops productive citizens as leaders in the world—one of the Dunham theories, Socialization Through the Arts. As I have said elsewhere, "The socialization process occurs at both the individual and community levels: an individual's productive and effective work within his/her own community environment produces a cohesive, uplifting, functional society."[9] This is exactly how the late Ruth Beckford (1925–2019) saw her work with us, her living "Legacy Tree" of accomplished women.

Miss B definitely wanted us to *look* the part for her Dunham legacy demonstration. Each of us had been instructed to wear long African dresses or ball gowns and was given our particular spots to occupy on the stage (like beauty queens in a pageant). As she read our names, titles, and accomplishments, we walked onto the stage, came downstage to briefly stand next to her, and then took our assigned stage positions. Her message about her Legacy Tree in the audience program stated, "My goal was to inspire them to have a high sense of self, to pursue higher education and follow their passion, to be courageous and free spirits." By the end, the stage was filled with beautiful Black women in our fifties and sixties, decked out in our colorful finery. Ruth Beckford then announced, "Ladies and Gentlemen, the Dunham Legacy Tree in full bloom." I wish I could have been in the audience to see it myself.

The ending Saturday Showcase on June 10 consisted of Dunham-inspired choreography that culminated in what was called Miss Dunham's "Living Birthday Card." Dance works presented by Lynn Coles, Keith Williams, and Deborah Vaughan's Dimensions Dance Theater were enthusiastically received. But the featured dance work was conceived by Carolyn Himes and di-

Figure 5.3. Ninety-seven dancers perform the sacred Haitian dance *Yanvalu* for Katherine Dunham's Memorial, June 10, 2006, Laney College Theater. Photo: Alan Kimara Dixon.

rected by Haitian American Colette Eloi: ninety-seven *yanvalu* dancers—one dancer for every year of Katherine Dunham's life—from age eight to eighty years old, all dancing in a circle around drummers led by the late Zeke Nealy (1948–2021). The dance represented Miss Dunham's patron lwa, *Damballa,* the Haitian serpent deity representing the benevolent healing circle of life. It was truly a sight to behold and an even more intense experience. In hindsight, the dance ritual was an example of my definition of Afrofuturism—invoking the continuity of the past in the present to *perform* the prospective future possibilities. As the elders danced yanvalu with the youth, the endurance of the ancient healing dance connecting past, present, and future was imparted.

I personally *had* to dance in this once-in-a-lifetime experience that would surely go down in history as Katherine Dunham's *tribute* yanvalu dance at her first memorial celebration. This was the dance she had brought to the US from Haiti, representing so many levels of her message to the world: form and function, intercultural communication, and embodied spirit personified.

Personal Transitions and Meeting My Future Husband

While meeting the demands of my new faculty position, going through the tenure process, and adjusting to a new city, I began to think about dating again as a part of my healing process from the divorce. I needed to mostly be alone for a while in order to mend properly, and I welcomed the solitary period beginning when we separated in 2003. But I also knew that I was not meant to be alone, and that another mate would eventually enter my life. I joined Match.com, but I also knew I really wasn't ready to *trust* any man, continually asking myself, "How could I not have seen through the man I was sleeping with every night for all those years?"

After a few dead-end dates, eventually a man did come into my Match folder who seemed interesting enough to start serious email communications. Gene Howell, a divorcé himself with two grown sons, was a visual artist and poet who had lived in Oakland all his life. We had engaging and enjoyable email conversations about the Oakland Black arts scene. He was a full-time employee at a large telecommunications company, but had been a visual artist all his life, working in oils, acrylics, and mixed media; and he exhibited his work. Online he was intelligent, funny, and engaging, and from his home page photo was not a bad "looker": tall and dark-skinned with a shaven head and deep penetrating eyes. When I told him all I had accomplished in Oakland in the dance community for many years, he told me he knew the Alice Arts Center and had been to Dimensions Dance Theater concerts, and wondered why *we* had never met before.

Then he sent an email telling me he had found someone with whom he was going to pursue a love relationship. He then pronounced the all-important words: "I just want you to know because I am strictly a one-woman man." I emailed him back that I wished him well and hoped his new relationship worked out for him. After getting off the computer, I told Susheel, "It's so good to know that there are honest, truthful men still left in the world. He didn't have to tell me about his relationship, but he did. I really wish him well."

After a few more disastrous dates, I had decided to stop online dating altogether. But at a Sacramento "Sister Circle Gathering" that Susheel and I had joined, one of the women suggested I try BlackPeopleMeet.com. She assessed that this particular dating site would narrow my field and told me she had found some interesting *Black* men on it. I followed her advice, and to my amazement found Gene Howell again six months after our last online meeting. I immediately asked him what happened to his relationship, and he simply said, "It didn't work out." We both marveled that we had found each other again in cyberspace and decided it was time to finally meet physically. I kept hearing his words in my head, "I am a one-woman man," and knew I could trust him. I agreed to meet him if he drove to Sacramento for a restaurant meeting.

But there was a glitch in my ensuing meeting with Gene. My sixtieth birthday was approaching, and I had scheduled my big Oakland dance legacy celebration at the Alice Arts Center, newly renamed Malonga Casquelourd Center for the Arts. My November 18, 2006, birthday event was titled "Claiming Eldership: Sixty & Still Sexy," taking place on the third-floor studio and lobby one week before my actual birthday, which, as usual, fell on Thanksgiving weekend. The byline for my birthday event flyer read, "The Founder of CitiCentre Dance Theatre, Black Choreographers Moving Toward the 21st Century, and community dance activism." I felt my first meeting with Gene should not be a big public event about *me;* I wanted our first encounter to be a one-on-one focus on *us* so we could get to know each other without distraction. As we continued to communicate by phone, I purposely did not inform him of my impending community birthday bash. And just like for my 1978 wedding (chapter 6, *DinB*), I proceeded to convene a committee of my girlfriends, with Susheel at the helm, to help me organize such a public event.

"Claiming Eldership: Sixty & Still Sexy" was a great celebration with all my old friends and colleagues in the Oakland dance community, including Madame Ruth Beckford. The party featured performances by several artists, including my godson Lance "Derique" McGee, who had been born to my oldest San Francisco friend, Dr. Sandra McGee, when she was just fifteen years old. As he adeptly performed a hambone routine, I remembered Sandra and our fun-loving time as kids playing on the streets of San Francisco's lower Fillmore district. Now her grown son was performing hambone as a professional New Vaudevillian Clown for my sixtieth birthday party. Being back home allowed me these connecting experiences across my entire life span.

I was also happy to have my family with me that night: Mama and all my sisters—Pat, Tenola, Tracey and her husband Torben, as well as Brenda and her husband Frank Dawson who came up from Los Angeles. My father Leroy did not come because he felt a little ill that night, but he was there in spirit. What a night! My birthday celebration let me know my wealth of friends and family who love me and demonstrated that my dance legacy was still lodged securely in the Oakland Bay Area. I had truly come full circle in my life's journey and was now back home!

After my public birthday celebration, I invited Gene to meet me at Rio City Café, my favorite eatery on the Sacramento River in the capitol city's Old Town. It was the very next Saturday, on my *actual* birthday weekend, and he drove an hour and a half from Oakland. I arrived first and sat on a bench outside the restaurant on an unusually warm November afternoon, anxiously waiting his arrival. Then, a tall dark handsome man approached me with a unique lumbering walk; as a choreographer, I first notice people's body language and gait. Gene looked straight at me with a slight smile, and we immediately embraced and went inside Rio City for our first date.

As we began our lunch, I was unusually nervous because I had lied about my age on my online profile, putting it back by eight years. Being a dancer who had kept myself well-preserved, I could pass for fifty-two years old. But I knew that most men in their sixties and seventies are usually dealing with a few health problems, and felt I needed a younger man to match my health profile. To set the record straight, I immediately let Gene know about the lie, telling him that we were meeting on my actual sixtieth birthday weekend. He looked at me incredulously, so I took out my driver's license to prove it. He told me that he was fifty-four years old, and that if I had *not* lied about my real age, I would not have appeared in his online matches; his limit for a mate was fifty-eight years old. After my big reveal, the only thing he asked me was, "Did you lie about anything else?" I answered, "No, everything else was the truth." My immediate truth telling during our first meeting in 2006 was way before today's notorious misrepresentation and fake identities rampant with online dating sites, called *catfishing,* to attract people. As a lack of truthfulness was the main downfall of my marriage, I wanted to start this potential new love relationship at a level of complete honesty.

Gene and I proceeded to have a great lunch overlooking the beautiful flowing Sacramento River, with an engaging and fluid conversation to match, and ended up spending most of the day together. After lunch we went to the nearby Railroad Museum in Old Town (he is a train buff from childhood), and later drove to Undergrounds Books in Oak Park (he loves books and reads voraciously). Underground Books is a part of Kevin Johnson's business complex, allowing me to introduce him to *Black* Sacramento. I loved every minute of our time together, finding out we had a lot in common. Before he left to drive back to Oakland, he gave me a present of one of his small acrylic paintings he had brought with him; I was very surprised he would give me one of his *original* art works as a gift on our very first date. Then, as we were about to part, he asked, "Can I kiss you?" But before I could answer, he was moving closer, and I simply said, "Do you have to ask?"

Gene and I talked by phone every day after our perfect first date, and he came back to Sacramento the following weekend for us to attend a jazz concert at the Mondavi Center that featured saxophonist Ravi Coltrane (John Coltrane's son) and veteran drummer Roy Haynes. I wrote in my journal about our fast-growing relationship:

> *I only asked for some fun dates, and now Gene has come full-blown with all the right qualifications: intellect, sensuality, sensitivity, kindness, calm-centeredness, patience, love of music, painting, and all the arts, as well as a love of Black history and culture. Now, after only one week of meeting each other physically, he emailed me that his second job is "to make you happy." One part of me says hold on and slow down, because slow and methodical wins the race. Yet there is no denying what he calls, "our strong union." We both went ahead and took down our profiles from BlackPeopleMeet.com.*

Our relationship grew quickly, and I got to know his family almost immediately. His full name is Doyle Gene Howell, named after his father, from whom he was estranged. Although he grew up in a two-parent household like me, he identified with his mother Frankie Mae Howell as his most influential parent. When I met her, she was unfortunately suffering from Alzheimer's disease, although still somewhat coherent. I could hold simple conversations with her when we first went to visit, and she always told me, "You're so pretty." After her divorce from Gene's father, her partner over the past forty years was James Rich, a saint of a man who meticulously cared for her in their Oakland Fruitvale District home, where Gene had grown up; Rich, as we called him, saw to Frankie Mae's every need and was completely dedicated to her. I could also see that Frankie loved Gene, as she perked up every time we came over to visit. As Alzheimer's patients can be obstinate, Gene could always get her to eat, even when Rich couldn't.

Mama Frankie had been a self-made Black woman who went back to school to get her high school diploma and even took a few junior college courses. She was also a Black memorabilia buff, and Gene told me that they would have heated debates about the political correctness of her mammy figures and watermelon-holding, bug-eyed Black figurines. I knew from these acquired bits of their history that he had gotten his intellect and strong Black consciousness from his mother, and I wished I had known her before Alzheimer's had taken her full mind and power. His flirting with Black Panther ideology and his paintings of Malcolm X, Huey Newton, and Eldridge and Kathleen Cleaver had garnered him recognition as a young artist while still at Oakland High School. Gene has a bachelor's degree in information technology from the University of San Francisco, and as we continued to get to know each other, I found that we were compatible on so many levels. He even had interest in learning more about my Yoruba belief system, and I began to feel I had found my new mate.

Another life-changing event happened around the same time I began dating Gene: I left my religious house, Ile Orunmila Oshun. For several years, tension had been building between the elder priestesses and me in the spiritual sanctuary that had initiated me a Yoruba priest. Their two main complaints about me and my priesthood is that I had not gotten enough training living in Ohio, and more to the point, I was not humble enough to them as my spiritual elders. Most of the women in the ile were younger than I, and some felt that I did not defer enough to them because I was *chronologically* older. But I was now living in Northern California and able to go to the ile to do spiritual training and attend more ceremonies.

After trying to discuss the issue with Yeye Luisah Teish and getting nowhere, I finally had to divine to Oya. My mother orisa told me to leave the ile! The odu that came from my Oya divination said that leaving my spiritual house would actually bring me peace of mind and would elevate my *ori* (spirit). I remembered how I felt when Kimathi left our home in 2003, prompting my revelation that sometimes one has to leave that which one loves the most. Oya was telling me that my ultimate contract to which I had to be true was with Olodumare and my own ori. I had to follow my own head.

The final validation of my decision to leave Ile Orunmila Oshun was receiving a phone call from Baba Bolu. He called to wish me a happy birthday (his birthday was a day before mine, so he always remembered). He told me he had seen the split coming and was not surprised. There was an ensuing formal ceremony to "excommunicate" me from the ile, where I had to give up my *elekes* (spiritual orisa beads) that the elders had made for me over the years. Although it was a difficult ritual in which to partake, I knew I was doing the right thing for my spiritual path, and I left my ile that evening with a heavy heart but a light spirit.

Leaving my spiritual community was another step in my growing closer to Gene. I had given him an orientation to the Yoruba belief system, and he understood the seriousness of my leaving. We had begun spending nights at each other's homes—he coming to Sacramento for a day or two, and my staying with him at his West Oakland home other days. After I left the ile that fateful evening, I went to the nearby Emeryville Bay to be silent. I looked out at San Francisco across the water and thought about how many times I had visited the Pacific Ocean at different times in my life, mentally pouring my questions, joys, and heartaches into the lapping waves. Once I felt better, I drove to Gene's house, and he embraced me and said, "Don't worry; I'm here for you." I had found my man!

The *Power Moves* Book Takes Me Back to Hawai'i

After the momentous year of 2006—continuing to process my divorce, Miss Dunham's passing, leaving my spiritual family, and meeting Gene—2007 became a rebirth. *The Africanist Aesthetic in Global Hip-Hop: Power Moves* was published by Palgrave Macmillan in January of that year, and I was ecstatic to have my first academic book in print and on the market.

Gene rejoiced in my success as much as I did, going with me to all my promotional book readings in the Bay Area. In fact, his oldest son, Anyi Malik Howell, a then twenty-three-year-old stand-up comedian whose day gig was working for the nonprofit Bay Area organization Youth Radio, helped me make a television PSA announcement for an upcoming Hawai'i book tour I had arranged. Gene had read parts of the book and would often engage me in discussions about one chapter or another. In terms of hip-hop, he claimed interest only in its so-called golden age, which includes groups like Public Enemy, X-Clan, and Arrested Development. Other than those early groups, he had the typical baby boomer attitude toward hip-hop in general: "it wasn't really music" like his beloved Isley Brothers, The Temptations, and Luther Vandross. But I worked to shift his attitude by turning him on to Lauryn Hill, The Roots, and Mos Def (now Yasiin Bey).

The Hawaiian book tour was an important part of my book promotion as well as a chance to share my previous island life with Gene. I had decided that since the *Power Moves* book (as I called it) was an extension of my dissertation that had been researched in Hawai'i, I should start a book tour in the islands. Gene had never been to Hawai'i and decided he would take vacation time from his job and accompany me. On March 20, 2007, we left together for the islands. I still owned the house in Leilani Estates on the Big Island, and Hawai'i will always hold a special place in my heart as my second home. I was looking forward to sharing it with the new love of my life.

The tour was important because I was able to reconnect with my Hawai'i hip-hop artists who had introduced the youth culture to me and gave me the perspectives I needed to write about hip-hop. In Honolulu I did a reading at a Borders bookstore (the now defunct major book chain) with Kutmaster Spaz (Derrick Kamohoali'i Bulatao), my deejay friend who demonstrated some of his turntable wizardry as a part of my reading event. I had written extensively about him in my third chapter, "Props to the Local Boyz: Hip-Hop Culture in Hawai'i":

> Like the master drummer of an African village, Kutmaster Spaz's ability to create community with his rhythmic turntable antics and emcee skills in the hip-hop club is a source of pride to him as master deejay. "That's where I get my energy from: the crowd. The response is everything to me. Whatever the crowd wants, I give them. If they want dancing, if they want me rapping, deejaying; whatever they want I give it to them. I want the crowd to be interactive with whatever I'm doing on stage."[10]

As I argue in *Power Moves,* to be hip-hop one must engage the Africanist aesthetic despite one's own cultural origins.

In attendance at that Honolulu book reading were two very important people who had helped me achieve my degree from University of Hawai'i' at Manoa: my dissertation chair, Dr. Mark Helbling, and my Honolulu painter-friend Auntie Gladys Crampton (chapter 2). After the reading, during a brief chat at the bookstore, I received an important validation from Helbling, as I had included American Studies theoretical perspectives in my reading. I utilized a balanced approach between theory and practice as the bookends of how I represent hip-hop culture, and Kutmaster's performance had brilliantly demonstrated the *practice* of the culture, validating my written theoretical perspectives. Auntie Gladys's presence meant a lot because she had been one of my main Hawai'i "cheerleaders," having come to my dissertation defense presentation on campus. Gene and I had gone to pick her up at her Ke'eaumouku apartment and brought her with us to the Borders reading. We took her to lunch afterward, where she praised my accomplishments. She also let me know that she approved of Gene, and given her psychic abilities as a wise sage, her personal endorsement meant a lot.

After Honolulu, Gene and I flew to the Big Island for a book reading at Borders Hilo. The Big Island was the home of one of the biggest rap groups in the islands, Sudden Rush. I had written extensively about them in *Power Moves,* and I got two members of the trio to appear with me at the Hilo book reading: Don Ke'ala Kawa'auhau (Da Rappa Nui) and Shane Vincent (Da Waterman). Sudden Rush promotes Hawaiian sovereignty in relation to the US, and I wrote about one of their tracks, "True Hawaiian," in *Power Moves:* "They position the political hegemony of the *haole* (white) plutocracy in the Pacific that eventually led to the overthrow of the Hawaiian monarchy as a part of the past 500 years of general displacement of people of color."[11] Sudden Rush understood their oppression as Native Hawaiians in relation to African Americans' and Native Americans' political persecution as well. "True Hawaiian" was recorded on their second album, *Ku'e!!* (to oppose or resist), and on it they articulate my concept of "connective marginality": *They tell us that we're equal / But if you look at history, we're just another sequel.*

I was proud to have their non-commercial approach to hip-hop as a part of my Big Island reading. Don and Shane met Gene and me at Borders in Hilo and set up a boom box with their beats to give my book reading audience a sample of some of their famous raps in between my reading excerpts from *Power Moves.* Of course, I read from my chapter 3, where I discuss their relationship with the active sovereignty protest movement, making the entire event a big hit. We had a good crowd because the event had gotten good publicity, including radio announcements and the television PSAs Gene's son Anyi had made.

The trip to the Big Island was a chance for me to reconnect with my Black sister friends as well as my hula community. Kathy Crayton-Shay invited a few of the sisters over to her Ainaloa home, and we had a reminiscing potluck gathering. We also had lunch with my kumu hula, Ehulani Stephany, and my hula sister Lily Chan-Harris (chapter 2), and they too approved of Gene. They had only known me with Kimathi, but now Gene, because of his kind and gentle manner, was endearing himself to my extended Hawai'i family. Although he had not traveled much outside of the continental US, he was open to new cultures and was very well read. His quiet enthusiasm allowed him to embrace the uniqueness of the islands, and he fit right in. When we went to my favorite black sand beach in Hilo, he watched me swim from the shore, and later told me he wanted me to teach him to swim. We were growing closer through our first travel experience together.

Becoming the "Hip-Hop Professor"

I began to use *Power Moves* as one of my texts for a popular UC Davis course I developed: AAS 181, Hip-Hop in Urban America. This title was more succinct and "catchy" than my original "Power Moves: Hip-Hop Culture and Sociology," created for my UC Berkeley teaching position in 2000. I was now using my own published text to teach a course in my chosen research area.

Of course my hip-hop class really resonated with my students as the hip-hop generation. I remember one male student using a section from chapter 1, "Dope Rhymes: *Nommo* and the Power of the Word," for his oral assignment, and was surprised at the degree to which he understood its nuanced analysis. He articulated my concept of the "improvisatory self" in relationship to *nommo* as an ancient African aesthetic, which links the wordplay of contemporary hip-hop emcees to that of the Western African *griots* or historians. I knew my book had done its job of making these cultural connections clear and relevant. I was witnessing the effect my written text could have on readers' perceptions of the subject, themselves, and the world. I realized how my new career could reach even more people and potentially have an even greater effect than my dance and choreography.

News of my hip-hop course content and teaching methods quickly traveled throughout the campus, earning me the colloquial title "The Hip-Hop Professor." The Black sorority Delta Sigma Theta, Lambda Xi Chapter at UC Davis gave me an award: "Outstanding Faculty of 2007." I was humbled that my passion and teaching abilities were being recognized so soon by students. My position in African American and African Studies was becoming what I began calling "my dream job," and I realized all Oya had proclaimed for me was coming true.

I also began giving campus readings of *Power Moves* on campus that furthered my reputation as the hip-hop professor. I positioned various contentious hip-hop themes in the national public discourse as the subjects of those readings. In fall 2007, I gave a talk for the Women's Resources and Research Center called "Women, Gender, and Hip-Hop." Their publicity for the event read, "Professor Osumare will explore how hip-hop is a sign of the postmodern times and what this means for the imaging of women today." I discovered various ways of locating my book within the many controversies hip-hop was engendering, which mirrored agendas of different campus groups. By embracing hip-hop's controversial nature, I used my research to address social issues, like the representation of women in rap lyrics, to expand my scholarly reputation. On that particular subject, I purposely concentrated on the early *proactive* women of hip-hop, like Queen Latifah, MC Lyte, and Salt 'N Peppa, who always projected a strong womanist perspective that formed a counternarrative to hip-hop being primarily a male genre.

Starting each UC Davis school year in September, there is an African American & African Fall Welcome, and in 2007 I was asked to start the proceedings on campus with a Yoruba libation. With this invitation, my spiritual and academic lives were intersecting in performing the libation because my campus colleagues were also recognizing my expertise as *spiritual* leader. I was honored to invoke the sacred ancestors right after our department's Student Affairs Coordinator and my friend John Ortiz-Hutson welcomed Black students, staff, and faculty to the new school year. I felt like I was now a part of the campus Black community in a very integral way, and they were recognizing the fullness of who I was becoming.

That same September, I also wrote a poem that captured the *choreography* of the different levels of my life in a way that came to me in an unusual gendered way:

I Am Woman

Who Am I?
How can this be answered?
I am Woman
Of the Niger
Of the Mississippi
Of the Pacific
I am Woman
Laced in white
Of Spirit and efun
Perfumed in nag champa
Natty dreads weaving their Medusa tentacles
Into space like a labyrinth of meditative wonder

Spanning and spawning eons of time and space
Africa, Europe, the South Pacific
From the arches of Andalusia
To the souks of Marrakech
From Rainy Hilo Bay
to Akosombo Dam
From the plains of Navrongo
To the River Oshun
And from Lake Malawi
To the beaches of Galveston

I am Woman
Worlds of space and time
Black & Blue
Crowned with Violet rays of Illumination

And the blushed Reds of Passion
Insights of Loving and Caring
Wet and fertile
Yet embraced in Intellect and knowledge
Intuition & Spirit

Who Am I?
How can this be answered?
I am
Soul, Flesh, Mind, & Heart
I am Woman

My sense of womanhood had always been innate, without much direct emphasis on feminism or womanism. So I was a bit surprised when this poem about my essence was birthed in this manner. I had choreographed *Feminine Trinity* in 1981 (chapter 6, *DinB*), about the multidimensionality I associate with being a woman. But this poem came pouring out wholesale, without much editing, allowing me to process the different stages of my life from the Bay Area to Europe and from Africa to Polynesia. Like poetry succinctly does, *I Am Woman* allowed me to envision who I had become as a strong sixty-one-year-old female.

Family, Friends, and Gene

After taking a trip to New York and visiting the famous African Burial Grounds near Wall Street, Gene and I ended the year with several gatherings with my family, allowing them to get to know him as my new life partner. Thanksgiving dinner that year at Mom's in San Francisco was warm and fuzzy, and included Susheel; but Erica did not fly in for her usual holiday visit that year. My sister Tenola was not present either, for she had become estranged from the family. As someone battling alcoholism for years, she was in a period of being on the "outs" with the family, and we all prayed for her to seek treatment yet again and return to us. Our Thanksgiving dinner was harmonious and flowing with my mother, my father Leroy (who came over for special occasions), my sisters (including Brenda from Los Angeles), and my nieces Theresa and Anjelica, and now with Gene.

That San Francisco trip was made even more special because two days later I arranged for the family to go to the Orpheum Theatre in downtown San Francisco to see a touring production of Alice Walker's 1982 Pulitzer Prize–winning *The Color Purple.* It was particularly poignant for my family members, as one of its messages is that true human connection of family never dies. Because of Tenola's estrangement from us, it became an important message for my family to experience.

One of the members of my *extended* family, VèVè Clark, whom I considered my "big sister," died around that same time of complications from diabetes. She was my friend who had pierced my second and third holes in my ears during my twenties, and she was my sister who had brilliantly guided me through my theoretical perspectives and the writing of my dissertation in my fifties. She had now joined the ancestors at only sixty-two years old. I was glad I had saved her voice message on my cell phone congratulating me on publishing *Power Moves;* I listened to it repeatedly, savoring the friendly and sisterly lilt of her voice lauding my scholarly accomplishment. Her taking the time to leave that phone message had meant a lot. I remembered the one time she had come to Hawai'i during my dissertation writing process, and had met with my dissertation chair, Mark Helbling. They had spontaneously started speaking in fluent French (VèVè spoke several languages, including Haitian Creole). As I grieved her death, all these personal memories came flooding back.

Dr. VèVè Amasasa Clark's memorial was held on December 14, 2007, at University of California, Berkeley, in Barrows Hall, the home of the African American Studies Department, where she spent most of her time on campus. Organized by Sara Johnson, who had coedited VèVè's last book, the seminal Dunham anthology *Kaiso! Writing and About Katherine Dunham,* in 2005, the memorial was attended by an impressive array of national Black intelligentsia and local community members. I was very proud to conduct the opening ancestor libation and chant the Yoruba Mojuba prayer, allowing the memorial to begin in an appropriate African cultural mode. The memorial testimonies of friends and collogues that followed were like a praise song of laughter and tears that testified to VèVè's vast intellectual influence and the personal loving care she took with students and colleagues alike. The *San Francisco Chronicle* had this to say about her academic emphasis:

In 1991, Professor Clark returned to UC Berkeley, where she earned praise for coining the phrase "diaspora literacy" in a paper titled "Developing Diaspora Literature and Marasa Consciousness." She defined the term as "the ability to understand multilayered meanings of stories, words, and folk saying in African diaspora communities through the knowledge and lived experiences of the community members' cultures," the university said in a statement. . . . She was very interested in Haiti and dance and spent time researching and working as an archivist for choreographer Katherine Dunham.[12]

Gene had been a part of an annual art exhibit called The Art of Living Black for several years before he met me, and in 2008 he became a *featured* artist in their annual exhibition of Bay Area artists. Held at the Richmond Art Center during Black History Month in Richmond, CA, at that time, it was a non-juried show of up to fifty Black visual artists in all media, from oil, acrylic, and pastel paintings to sculpture and ceramics. He was also a featured artist that year in one of the smaller *satellite* exhibits called "Distinctive Visions," where he could show a few more pieces of his art than the limit of one in the larger exhibit, sharing that smaller exhibit with artists Constance Terrell and Atiba Sylvia Thomas at the San Pablo Arts Gallery in Richmond.

Gene chose eight of his mixed media pieces, one of which included his photo transfer work called "Black and Blue Labor." It showed a group of Black laborers, dressed in overalls and work clothes standing on a bridge, looking stoically into the camera. The technique of photo transfer is the application of a photographic image onto a surface; Gene had taken the photo of workers and adhered it to a canvas and then proceeded to work his magic, transforming the black-and-white photo into a painting highlighted with gray, black, and blue acrylic paint. I saw the piece as a statement about his family and ancestors who worked hard all their lives building a nation that didn't fully appreciate their labor. The stoicism on the laborers' unsmiling faces said, "This is our fate; we have no choice, but we hold our heads high."

Another of Gene's photo transfer pieces in the "Distinctive Visions" exhibit was "The Wind Conjures Halifu." I had shown him many of my old photos as a dancer in my twenties, thirties, and forties, so he could get a sense of who I had been as a performing artist. He fell in love with one of my early photos taken at the first Everybody's Creative Arts Center venue in Oakland (chapter 6, *DinB*). Photographer Bill Santos had taken a series of photos of me in a long black shirt and flesh-colored leotard. Gene had picked the one with my arms lifted upward above my head. My face was in profile with a short afro hairdo and a regal demeanor. My arms in the photo appear like wings, making the entire moving image very bird-like. Gene took that dance photo and positioned it as symbolic of Oya. He had listened to my stories about my orisa—The Spirit of the Winds of Change—and created a sense of the moving wind throughout the painting. He knew that Oya's number is nine, so he drew nine black and white clothespin-looking figures (he called them "hovering ancestors") at the far left side of the painting, with a white spiral figure between "the ancestors" and my dancing figure. In the lower right bottom of the art piece, he glued an actual seashell, with a Chinese-fortune-cookie-type paper emerging from it, reading "caste your fate to the wind."

When I first saw "The Wind Conjures Halifu" I was in absolute awe. I could not believe the symbolism with which he had transformed my old dance photo and situated it within the essence of my spiritual path. It was then I realized how much Gene truly "got me." Everything was there: the spirit of Oya, my ancestors, the spiral (one of my favorite symbols), and the seashell that symbolically brought it all together. I was speechless, sensing the love that had gone into this painting featuring me as dancer of the winds of change. Throughout his life Gene had relegated his talent to a hobby, working full-time to raise his sons Anyi and Armand as a divorced father with joint custody. But experiencing "The Wind Conjures Halifu" I wondered what he could have done if instead he had made art his profession. He obviously had the talent and vision of a fine artist.

The very next year, The Art of Living Black awarded him the featured artist position in the *main* show at the Richmond Art Center. "The Wind Conjures Halifu" became a highlighted piece in his wall of works in the main exhibit hall. Many viewers talked about that piece in particular at the opening reception of the 2009 exhibit. Many visual artists are inspired by the moving body, just as Gene was by my photo that inspired his "The Wind Conjures Halifu." The mutual inspiration between the fields of art and artists is the reason most of my friends are artists of all genres. We understand each other, easily seeing the multidimensions of the social and natural worlds. Over thirty years after the original dance photo was taken, it had now become a featured work of art through Gene Howell's visionary creativity.

Black Dance Classics

In February 2008 my choreographer friend Linda Goodrich had the annual season of her dance company, Sacramento Black Art of Dance (S/BAD). As Professor of Dance in the Department of Theater and Dance, she had started S/BAD in 1992 after moving from Oakland, where we had co-founded CitiCentre Dance Theatre (chapter 6, *DinB*). She established S/BAD on the aesthetic foundation of Dunham Technique and had created a strong semi-professional student dance company, single-handedly establishing a Black modern dance tradition in California's capital city. As I have said, Linda was one of the reasons I wanted to move to Sacramento when I applied for the faculty position at UC Davis. So it was an honor to attend the sixteenth anniversary concert of S/BAD, which her company dancers dedicated to her with the title "Testimony—A Tribute to Dr. Linda S. Goodrich: Educator, Mother, Artist."

The main choreographers of that 2007 concert were alumnae of S/BAD who had returned to Sacramento State to choreograph on the current young students to pay tribute to their dance mentor. Linda's young choreographers Sheila Coleman, Nzinga Woods, Shani Alford, Jurusha Woods, and Associate Artistic Director Nathan Jones, among others, all came together to choreograph for her tribute concert. The concert was a true "testimony" to their love and appreciation for Linda, who had given so much to them and the university campus. I was very happy to witness her Sacramento legacy that established professional-standard Dunham-style dance, which was built on the work she had done with me in Oakland.

The large tribute concert contained sixteen different pieces, ending with Linda's signature work, *Ancestral Memories,* to music by the jazz fusion group Yellowjackets. She had premiered that piece in 1992 at the inaugural concert of her company, and as she reflected, "it was my way of initiating S/BAD into the Sacramento community."[13] Her choreographic inspiration grew from the Yellowjacket's 1987 hit "Wildlife" "because it makes musical references to the African diaspora, i.e., West Africa, Brazilian Capoeira, and Cuba." These diasporic musical references, to Linda, naturally dictated a Dunhamesque approach to the choreography for seven dancers in earth-tone leotards. *Ancestral Memories* became her signature statement about what Black concert dance meant to her. Like Dunham, Goodrich was trying to articulate what Joanna Dee Das calls "a politics of diaspora."[14]

After seeing S/BAD as a student semi-professional company, I went to the UC Davis Mondavi Center for the Performing Arts a few months later in early 2008 to see the company considered the pinnacle of Black dance, The Alvin Ailey American Dance Theater, during their fiftieth anniversary tour. I have been a follower of the Ailey company throughout their long tenure in the dance world and particularly when they toured to the Bay Area, but also when I saw them at their City Center home when I lived and danced in New York in 1972 (chapter 3, *DinB*). I had also flown to New York back in 1987 to see Ailey's full-evening reconstruction of fourteen of Katherine Dunham's choreographic works called "The Magic of Katherine Dunham." I had also written and published an article in a local periodical about Ailey's passing in 1989. So I particularly wanted to see the internationally reputed dance company of the Black tradition during the auspicious time of their half-century mark.

Luckily that night I was able to witness, for the umpteenth time, Ailey's signature work, *Revelations,* and was looking forward to assessing how the piece held up over time when performed by a younger generation of dancers who could be my grandchildren. After all, I had seen the late great Consuelo Atlas perform "Fix Me Jesus," Judith Jamison's undulation as the lady with the umbrella in "Wade in the Water," and the transfixing Dudley Moore in "I Wanna Be Ready." So, these younger dancers had something to prove to me.

Had they been trained enough and *lived* enough to take up the great mantle of *Revelations?* Back home after the dance concert I was not able to sleep and ended up writing this long passage in my journal:

Dance, at its best, is a dialogue between technical skill and dramatic passion, between athleticism and intrinsic meaning. Tonight, at the Mondavi Center on UCD's campus I saw the Alvin Ailey American Dance Theater after several years. Now fifty years old, I have been able to witness the company and their signature work Revelations *over decades. As I watched the young dancers perform the familiar choreography and movements that I know so well, I got an illumination about the forces at work in a great classic dance.*

Revelations is a masterwork. What makes it such is the choreography, both movements and overall structure. The opening "I've Been 'Buked" and "Fix Me Jesus," for examples, are structured beautifully in relation to the exquisite musical arrangement, allowing Ailey's intent to come through every time, even if the dancers don't truly "get it." That's the mark of a great work: the choreographer's intent is so well crafted into the very fabric of the dance that its effect is often independent from the performers.

The other dimension of master choreography is its music, and if the dancers truly embody the deep meaning of the work and the spirit of an oppressed but spiritual people, which is etched into the music and the movements themselves, then magic will happen. Magic did not happen in the performance tonight. We often think a dance is as good as its dancers, but the original intent in a masterwork should shine through no matter. In this manner, Revelations *came through loud and clear on the UC Davis Mondavi stage, and Alvin Ailey's spirit and vision was ever present.*

When one has seen the original dancers, who worked directly with Ailey, to whom he personally transferred his "blood memories," there is simply no substitute. I saw the young dancer performing "I Wanna Be Ready" as a dance, not as his very soul, as Dudley Moore did. When one has witnessed George Faison, Clyde Thompson, and John Parks attack the fierce men's tour-de-force trio of "Sinner Man," then one sees the young men performing tonight that were adequate technically, but their portrayal of the plight of Black men running for their lives while trying to find their personal salvation left something to be desired.

Revelations is the kind of dance that carries the DNA of the race, and yet represents all oppressed people's plight. It represents the best of Ailey's blood memories that connect African Americans to the human race. The choreography is a seminal moment in the telling of the Black American story, which serves as the central narrative—connective marginality—of the human experience in our times.

But the 1960 Revelation is nearly as old as the fifty-year-old company, and unfortunately our youth are losing the deep empathetic connection to the past, even though the past is present—the past is indeed prologue. I left the theater feeling rewarded that the dance itself stood on solid ground—Ailey's message is even stronger than the messengers.

Experiencing *Revelations* again at UC Davis was an important juncture in my understanding of dance by a Black choreographer telling his people's spiritual story of resilience. It allowed me to understand the nature of the art of dance itself and how a work can live on through the generations as a classic. Thomas DeFrantz's introduction to his *Dancing Revelations: Alvin Ailey's Embodiment of African American Culture* (2004) had already validated my perceptions four years earlier:

> As my title suggests, I propose that Ailey encoded aspects of African American life and culture in concert dance. These "aspects"—aesthetic imperatives termed "Africanism" by cultural theorists—flourish in the movements of dancers Ailey worked with; they are also embedded within the very choreography Ailey made. They emerge in the compositional strategies, choices of music, structuring of performance, casting, and approach to company operations.[15]

Thankfully, because of our "aesthetic imperatives," often initiated as "blood memories" pushing our choreographic and organizational choices, a classic like *Revelations* can live on forever, transcending the dancers.

Fulbright Fellowship to Ghana

In March 2008, I got one of the most important emails that I have ever received: "On behalf of the J. William Fulbright Foreign Scholarship Board (FSB), I am pleased to congratulate you on your selection as a Fulbright scholar grantee to Ghana," read the email from the Chair of FSB. I had been praying for, invoking, and conjuring up this Fulbright fellowship for several years, and it had finally happened. I first applied to the Fulbright Scholar Program six years earlier when I was in graduate school at University of Hawaiʻi; and then again after I had become a PhD. The saying "third time is a charm" became true for me after publishing *Power Moves* and receiving a tenure-track university appointment.

My Fulbright application was reinforced with important Ghana endorsements. I had written recommendations from some of the most prominent Ghanaian scholars: the late ethnomusicologist Dr. Kwabena Nketia (1922–2019) and the late choreographer/dance scholar Nii Yartey (1946–2015). The crux of the application was to teach in the Department of Dance Studies at University of Ghana, Legon, and I emphasized my familiarity with the continent of Africa that highlighted my previous self-funded 1976 research trip to Ghana (chapter 5, *DinB*) and my USIS 1990 appointment in Malawi (chapter 6, *DinB*). I also centralized my concept of the "Africanist aesthetic" throughout the diaspora and my published book on global hip-hop. The entire proposal was called "African American and Ghanaian Cultures in Dialogue," written for the Fulbright Lecturing/Research program, proposing to teach dance lecture courses in the Dance Studies Department and simultaneously conduct fieldwork on the effects of hip-hop culture on the youth in the capital city of Accra.

I was absolutely elated that I could now study the influence of US hip-hop in Ghana, thirty-two years after I had first visited the country.

One can accept the Fulbright for a full year or a half year. I chose the half-year program so I would not be away from Gene for so long. Thinking practically, a half year would also allow me to take the Fall Quarter off from teaching and not lose part of my regular university salary. One opportunity afforded faculty on the quarterly configuration of the school year, as opposed to the semester system, is it allows one to use one quarter for research by teaching my required four yearly courses in the other two quarters. I conducted my Fulbright fellowship in Fall 2008, permitting me to return to UC Davis for Winter and Spring Quarter teaching. Most importantly, the Fulbright would facilitate in-depth research to focus my second book on hip-hop in Africa, at that point a timely subject with few scholarly texts.

It did not escape me that my return to Ghana represented the completion of a large life cycle. When Gene heard the news, he immediately announced he would take one month of his earned vacation time from his job to go with me as his first trip to Africa. I performed a sacred duty by introducing him to our Motherland as an African American. He had the usual fears and trepidations of the unknown, but he also had a personal resolve that he was meant to go to Africa as a possible turning point in his life; I knew it absolutely would be.

I was to be one of 120 Americans selected to represent the US through the Fulbright Program for Africa. Administered by the Bureau of Educational Cultural Affairs of the US Department of State with the assistance of the Council for International Exchange of Scholars (CIES), the CIES became the hands-on organization that held an annual Pre-Departure Orientation for all Fulbright scholars at the Washington, DC CityCenter. Preparations for my Fulbright fellowship were well planned and executed. And while in Washington, DC, I met with my "daughter" Bolade (Erica), after not seeing her for two years.

Within a week of returning to Sacramento, I was contacted via email by the US Embassy in Accra, Ghana. I was to be given the title of Senior Lecturer based on the University of Ghana's British-based academic system, and I would be housed at what was called "the Fulbright House," a two-bedroom apartment in a compound on the outskirts of the Legon campus. The email was from the Ghana-based Cultural Affairs Specialist Nii Sarpei Nunoo, and he also informed me of the practical details of my arrival in Ghana: he would meet Gene and me at the airport upon our August arrival to take us to our campus accommodations. I was happy to receive this important logistic information from Mr. Nunoo, letting me know that everything was organized for my Ghana Fulbright fellowship. I felt like a pampered celebrity, like my 1990 US Information Service-sponsored residency in Malawi with their national dance company. The 2008 Fulbright was definitely going to be different from my previous 1976 Ghana trip, when I was "winging it" on my own at every step.

I contacted the Head of the Department of Dance Studies Mr. Oh! Nii Sowah, who has an MFA in dance from UC Irvine, and he advised me that the department needed me to bolster their graduate program. We decided I would teach a dance anthropology course to their master's degree students to help them formulate their required thesis topics, usually centered on various Ghanaian dance festivals and rituals, as well as providing theoretical and methodological models for fieldwork. I also suggested an undergraduate course in US Black dance history based on my UC Davis AAS 51 History of Black Dance course. These pre-fellowship email exchanges were important in shaping both the personal and professional aspects of my soon-to-be Fulbright fellowship. Gene and I were excited to be making our first international trip together, and he was anxiously anticipating going to Africa for the first time as a Black man. A new adventure awaited us!

6

Hip-Hoping Back to Ghana

New genres are created in response to changes in social experience such that the existing genres no longer provide an adequate means to speak to it.
Karin Barber, Foreword, *Popular Culture in Africa*

Sankofa—Go Back and Get It.
Ghanaian Adinkra Symbol

Gene and I were solidified as a couple by the time I got my Fulbright fellowship for Ghana. We had been together for a year and half and recognized that our relationship was real and solid. He had enough accumulated vacation days to take off from his job for a month to help me re-establish myself in Ghana for my Fulbright residency. I was returning to my West African home, thirty-two years after my first Ghanaian sojourn, and Gene would experience the Motherland for the first time. I knew that first month would be another point of connection between us, as his experiencing the African continent for the first time would bring us even closer together.

On August 10, 2008, Gene and I flew Delta Airlines from San Francisco to Atlanta, and then Atlanta to New York, where we boarded the final flight to Accra. But it was not a trip without travel issues: we waited inside the plane for three hours on the tarmac in New York before taking off for Accra. Having a drink to pass the time, we joked about the three months the Middle Passage slave voyages took to reach the "New World": if our ancestors endured that grueling inhumane journey for that long, surely we could endure these few hours before our ten-hour flight *back* to Africa.

When we arrived at Kotoka International Airport in Accra as planned, the representative of the American Embassy, Nii Sarpei Nunoo, a pleasant and competent middle-aged Ga man, was there waiting to move us through customs. He efficiently escorted us through the airport paperwork and into his car, driving us to the Fulbright House on the University of Ghana's campus, and I noticed the short distance through the familiar streets of Accra had become more bustling with an increased number of cars on the road. The Fulbright House was a spacious furnished apartment with a large kitchen, living room, two bedrooms, and one bath. However, it was not clean, and we immediately decided to buy cleaning supplies the next day to make it comfortable for us. It was definitely luxurious compared to my accommodations in South Legon thirty-two years earlier. I felt privileged having everything practically arranged for us as a Fulbright scholar.

Changes and Similarities in Ghana

As the first week flew by, I was not surprised how so many cultural memories came flooding back, facilitating my immediate adjustment. My journal read: *The lilting tenor of my voice immediately came back when I speak to Ghanaians to make myself more understood. Reciprocately, I immediately understood the local Ghanaian English accent; while Gene is continually asking, "What did he say?" Amazingly, I also remembered certain place names, as well as certain landmark sights, like the entrance to the University of Ghana, Legon with its majestic fan palms was very familiar. Old memories return, even after three decades.*

I also noted the *cultural* shifts as well as the similarities over time in Accra. Much had remained the same, like the many poor people, the "hawkers," selling everything from bananas to toilet paper on the roads, but other products were new, like cell phones and sim cards. Everybody had a cellular flip phone and were constantly buying phone minutes for the new mobile phone service that did not exist during my last visit. As a non-credit-based society, buying time was how people maintained their cell phone service. I remembered that time in 1976 when I had to schedule a week in advance to make a call to Kimathi in California, only to be sequestered in a small booth listening to static during most of our conversation (chapter 5, *DinB*). Some things had definitely changed in my West African home!

Communications technology had also shifted Africans' connections to each other and the rest of the world, allowing them to leap-frog over landline phone infrastructure, ubiquitously available in the West, and moved directly to personal mobile phones. Moreover, they had the Global System for Mobile Communication (GSM) platform, so once they bought their minutes, they could call *anywhere* in the world, whereas in the US our cellular service is based on the Code Division Multiple Access (CDMA) system, limiting our calls only within the country. Experiencing the new cellular technology in Ghana made me realized how much US capitalism limits our global access. Therefore, I bought a Ghanaian cell phone with a GSM SIM card and called home to California anytime I wanted. I saw firsthand André Brock Jr.'s concept of "a Black techno and cybercultural matrix," where the theoretical frame of "CTDA (Critical Technocultural Discourse Analysis) prioritizes the belief systems of marginalized and underrepresented groups' conceptions of self with respect to their technology use."[1] In other words, the so-called digital divide between the West and the Global South was being bridged through Africans' ontological sense of collectivity, all through the new communication technology offering them maximum access to each other.

Another difference was that most of the *tro-tros* (local public transport) were now minivans instead of covered flat-bed trucks with wooden benches. Ghana had become "modern," with many more cars on the road, creating crawling traffic jams, like in Lagos. But most noticeably were the preponderance of high-rise buildings, designer shops, as well as the new Accra Mall with its supermarket, where we shopped for food to stock the Fulbright House and our cleaning supplies to make it presentable. Global consumerism had arrived in Accra.

Western consumerism was shifting every aspect of Ghanaian life, but what was most interesting for me was observing Gene's first impressions of Ghana. When we went to the Accra Mall, the young women were now mostly dressed in jeans and wore hair weaves as opposed to traditional dress and braids. Both sexes were hanging out in front of the cool designer store, ironically called "Identity," near the mall's entrance. Gene's first impressions of the new Accra Mall was a comparison to the one he grew up with in Oakland: "There is little difference between this and the Eastmont Mall, except there is no police harassing the youth." He was comparing the Ghanaian mall scene with the African American mall scenes in the East Oakland ghetto; the difference for him was the lack of surveillance of young Black people in Africa, where "Black" people are the majority, as opposed to the perpetual scrutiny of US Blacks by white police in public spaces.

I eventually analyzed Ghana's significant technological and cultural changes had been superimposed on old traditional customs. The country's economic development obviously demanded more Western-type stores, ushering in an emerging global consumer culture. But right off the main highway in the nearby market town of Madina, most of the people still shopped in the town's outdoor market and continued to live in relative poverty while cooking outside their shacks on coal pots. This is the reality of much of the Global South—the ancient traditions exists alongside the Western "modern," with increasing levels of commodity goods that augment the socioeconomic juxtaposition between the haves and have nots.

I also perceived that hip-hop culture was at the center of this cultural shift and immediately saw the implications of my research I had come to conduct. Global youth pop culture was having a major impact on Ghanaian society and, by extrapolation, African cultures in general. I wrote in my journal regarding this discovery: *While I am here, I will try to identify and expose how hip-hop has played a part in these Ghanaian cultural changes. A gamut of pop music is on the radio from Lil Wayne's "Lollipop" to local rap in English but with local beats, and to hiplife sounds in Indigenous language with highlife rhythms. It's all here, and I have already identified a grad student, Terry Ofosu, who is working on Ghanaian pop culture who can help me make inroads into the Accra hip-hop scene.*

Visiting the W.E.B. DuBois Centre in Accra

Our first week was spent just being tourists and getting the Fulbright House livable. I wanted Gene to see some of Accra's sites before the semester started and the beginning of the teaching part of my fellowship; after all, he was only going to be with me for one month. The highlight of that first free week was our visit to the DuBois Center, where W.E.B. DuBois and his wife Shirley Graham DuBois lived the last years of their lives in Ghana. The facility is on 1 Circular Road in the Cantonments district, just a few meters from the US Embassy, and is formally called The W.E.B. DuBois Centre for Pan African Culture. I had read that DuBois, disillusioned with the US in the last years of his life, had expatriated to Ghana in 1961 when his passport was reissued after becoming one of the victims of 1950s McCarthyism. DuBois had met President Kwame Nkrumah during the 1945 Pan African Conference held in Manchester, England, and Nkrumah, upon hearing that DuBois was free to travel again, invited him to live in Ghana. He was given what became the DuBois Centre, a compound of structures with his main living quarters as the current museum. The DuBois Centre is living proof of how close Nkrumah was to the African American plight as well as his pan-African vision for building Black unity not only in Africa, but throughout the African diaspora.

As Gene and I walked onto the grounds, I felt his awe as a strong Black nationalist who considered DuBois a hero. As we stepped across the threshold into the greeting foyer of the DuBois museum, I knew we were going to experience, to quote VèVè Clark, an important *lieux de memoire* (sites of memory). We paused outside on the manicured lawn to get a groundskeeper to take a picture of us with the bronze stature of DuBois' head. It sits on a commemorative marble pedestal that reads, "William Edward B. DuBois, 1868–1963."

As we entered, it was like going back in time. My journal entry reads: *DuBois' office had his desk and library with its original copy of* The Souls of Black

Figure 6.1. Author with Gene Howell next to the tribute bronze head at the entrance to the W.E.B. DuBois Centre in Accra, Ghana, 2008. Photo courtesy of author.

Folk *and one of his novels,* Darkwater. *It was a humbling feeling to see these actual artifacts of the great man about whom I have studied.* It indeed was an awe-inspiring experience to peer back in time when Ghana was the fledgling first independent African country, when Nkrumah and DuBois, as one of the pillars of the early US Civil Rights Movement, were united and collaborating on the future of the Black world.

The DuBois Centre is a lesson in Black and world history. Photos representing those seminal times lined its walls. A large portrait of DuBois honoring his then 140th birthday (1868–2008) was central. Also included were photos of Nkrumah's and DuBois' meetings, one of which was with Shirley DuBois in formal dress at a state dinner. There was a photo of DuBois with Mao Zedong, the then President of the People's Republic of China, taken on one of DuBois' visits to China. We felt like we were in a time machine that had deposited us in the middle of the Cold War when the world lined up either behind the Western Bloc and the so-called free world or the Communist Bloc with Russia and China. Nkrumah and DuBois were at the center of that historic global conflict, which would eventually cause the demise of Nkrumah, with Ghana's 1966 coup that overthrew him. But during our 2008 tour of the DuBois Centre, historically none of that had taken place yet, and we were in the world of DuBois in Ghana during the Civil Rights Movement and before the 1963 March on Washington. We were catapulted back to the time in Ghana when Nkrumah was trying to unite Africa while playing the US and the Communist Bloc against each other, taking money from both sides in his nation-building efforts.

The highlight of our visit to the DuBois Centre was actually much quieter and more meditative: sitting in the small mausoleum house with the DuBois couple's remains. His coffin is displayed beside a pedestal with her cremation urn in a room lined with carved Asante stools. I said the egun prayer and thanked him for his many contributions to the advancement of our people and the world. Our docent, Belinda, took pictures of Gene and me sitting on stools contemplating DuBois' life, and I felt a reverence that reminded me of my own sense of purpose—my mission. Like DuBois, who bridged Africa and African America, I too have worked to bring these two geo-political/cultural areas of the Black world together, or at least offer a better understanding of each other.

My approach is popular culture and dance, while DuBois' method was political organizing and literature. I can in no way compare my impact with that of the great W.E.B. DuBois; however, meditating in his mausoleum, I did feel a resonance between our international visions for the Black world. I was in Ghana to research that cultural and artistic connection between Africa and African America via hip-hop. Visiting the W.E.B. DuBois Centre for Pan African Culture was indeed the right note for Gene and me to start our Ghanaian trip.

While at the DuBois Centre we met Joss, a producer-choreographer who directed the Afrique Dance Theatre in Accra. He invited us to return the following Sunday for a performance by his company. He obviously saw us as important Black Americans who might be able to help promote the company, as he announced the performance would be exclusively for us. We exchanged numbers, and, like clockwork, on Sunday morning he called to invite us to return to the DuBois Centre for a 3:00 p.m. private concert. I was surprised that he had followed through because hustling Americans is a "profession" in most African metropolitan areas. Gene said, "Well, I wonder how much this is gonna cost."

We arrived a half hour early to the small amphitheater in the rear of the DuBois Centre, containing an outdoor concrete thrust stage with an area in front for folding chair seating. Joss, a well-built medium brown man about thirty-five years old, was setting up drums, which I identified as an Ewe drum set. Surprised I knew the drums, he greeted us by holding out two hands, the right hand to shake while cupping that elbow with his left hand, all the while slightly dipping in his knees; this is the traditional respectful African greeting of elders. He had arranged two regal-looking cane chairs as our guests-of-honor seats, as we were indeed, as promised, the only two invited guests. However, never once was there any talk of us *paying* for this honor. I began to feel like my West African ancestors were using this performance to greet us royally.

While Joss and his ten dancers were setting up for our exclusive performance, Gene and I wandered around the back part of the DuBois grounds that we hadn't focused on the previous week. In the far corner there were two large buildings: the African Diaspora Conference Center and the Marcus Garvey Guest House.[2] The former building holds international conference meetings, while the latter provides accommodations for traveling conferees. The names of the buildings on the DuBois Centre grounds indicates Nkrumah's Pan-African vision, and I was very proud that Gene got to experience Ghana's first president's Pan-African vision in my West African home of Ghana.

When we finished our grounds tour, we went back over to the stage area and took our regal seats. Joss's Afrique Dance Theatre's private concert was a lively and authentic Ghanaian cultural performance with Ewe and Dagomba dances. His name, Joss, indicates that he was a Northerner, where the Ghana-

Figure 6.2. Author dances *Bamaya* with the Afrique Dance Theatre of Ghana. Photo courtesy of author.

ian dance, *Bamaya,* originates (chapter 5, *DinB*); and Bamaya was, indeed, the dance with which the company ended that afternoon. Bamaya was one of my favorite Ghanaian dances I had learned during my 1976 visit, and to show my Ghanaian dance knowledge, I jumped on stage, dressed in my tradition African cloth and headwrap, and performed the hip-swiveling dance with the young men. Because the dance requires a fan, a female dancer on the sideline quickly handed me one, and as I joyously performed Bamaya, all the company members started hailing my performance.

Our performance visually testified to the fact that I not only understood the dances they were performing for us, but I could dance with them. My dancing with the Afrique Dance Theatre became the grand finale that Joss had not expected. Gene was so impressed with the professionalism of the company, he gave each of the ten performers a twenty-dollar bill, which at that time was the equivalent of fifty dollars in Ghanaian *cedis,* a lot of money in 2008 for Ghanaian dancers. My dancing and the cultural exchange made me feel like I had truly arrived back in my West African home.

Touring Ghana and the Slave Castles

During Gene's stay in Ghana, I wanted him to see more of the country besides the university campus and metropolitan Greater Accra, so we took two trips to other parts of the country. Our first trip was to visit my friend Harriet Kaufman and her Jamaican husband Mike, who had changed his name to the Ghanaian name of Kweku. Harriet was my African American sister-friend who lived in Hawai'i during my sojourn on the Big Island (chapter 2). She and Kweku had moved to Ghana and bought land even before I had left the islands. They had built an impressive homestead on a hill overlooking the Volta River in the Eastern Region, outside of the small town of Atimpoku. It took several tro-tro rides from Accra and a taxi from Atimpoku across the Adombe Bridge, Ghana's largest suspension bridge, to arrive at their compound grounds. They had built their home and the beginnings of several small structures for an eventually bed-and-breakfast facility they planned.

I was not surprised at Harriet and Kweku's pioneering spirit because this was exactly the back-to-the-land spirit they exhibited in Hawai'i. We disembarked from the taxi at the bottom of their hill at a structure that was to serve as their office-library for the B&B. Kweku was building his own structures using hired Ewe workers in the area. Beautiful tropical flora and fauna, including Hawaiian plants, lined their terraced landscaping, leading up to their circular home at the top of the hill. As we sat outside on their lanai overlooking the Volta River on our first night, we peered into the clear, star-filled sky, without city lights, and shared our perspectives as diasporans returned "home." As African diasporans gathered in the Motherland, we felt at peace discussing our various journeys to arrive at this point in Africa. Yet, being on the continent, our perspectives are always ambivalent, as we never stop being considered foreigners. In Ghana, we are always *obruni* (white foreigner) while simultaneously trying to approach some form of "quasi-Africanness" on our way to learning the Indigenous languages.

Harriet and Kweku had many stories about their diasporan Ghanaian experiences regarding being recognized as Africans. Their stories about adjusting to their local Ghanaian community while trying to be accepted prompted me to write in my journal: *Ghanaians' perception(s) of us and ours of them constantly shift and remain a divide separating us, while blood and cultural imaginary, in equal portions, continue to bind us to each other. We come "home" trying to make this land ours again. But is that ever really possible? As Saidiya Hartman says about Ghanaians' perception of this issue in* Lose Your Mother, *"No matter how big strangers' eyes are, they cannot see." But I am here to establish a dialogue between Ghanaians and African Americans through popular culture as my Fulbright proposal said, and I will try to succeed. Perhaps all I can really do is establish a small forum of exchange, such as in my classroom at Legon and during my fieldwork interviews. But we continue the arduous task of establishing communication across the Black Atlantic.*

The next morning, before the heat of the day, Kweku arranged for us to take a canoe ride on the Volta River to view the Akosombo Dam, a hydroelectric facility that supplies electricity to Ghana and the surrounding countries of Togo and Benin. The dam was Nkrumah's last major infrastructure project before the big coup that dethroned him in 1966. That morning we arrived at a small village around 9:00 a.m. on the shore of the Volta River, and Kweku and Harriet spoke in a combination of English and Twi to a local canoer who was to take us on our morning journey down the river's tranquil waters. The four of us and our tour guide climbed into the carved-out canoe, and he rowed us up the peaceful river toward the dam. Along the way, we saw friendly Ghanaian fisherman in their canoes and passed small villages along the shore with waving friendly people. The common river experience created a camaraderie between us and canoeing fishermen who always cordially spoke, making us feel welcome as we approached the great Akosombo Dam that had pushed Ghana into the modern world. After our canoe trip we arrived back at Harriet and Kweku's to get their car and drive to the Akosombo Hotel for lunch. We dined on the patio restaurant overlooking a majestic view of the dam while eating fresh tilapia from the river and my favorite spicy fried plantain called *kelewele*. The entire trip allowed me to reconnect with my homesteading friends in Ghana as well as experience one of the great infrastructure accomplishments on the African continent.

Our second August trip was to the Cape Coast area in the Central Region, with its famous slave castles, an obligatory tourist voyage for African diasporans. But "Obruni!" was the first word I heard as we walked into St. George's Castle in Elmina, a famous town because it hosts the first slave castle built on the Gulf of Guinea by the Portuguese. As Gene and I were walking into the fifteenth-century monument to pay homage to our ancestors who had been enslaved there awaiting the inhumane voyage across the Atlantic, a Ghanaian woman in traditional cloth exiting the castle called me "White" in a casual off-handed way. The incident became a seminal example of what African Americans face, particularly those of us with light brown skin, when journeying to Africa, revealing the ultimate irony of our historical position, even in the twenty-first century. My "race" incident walking into the slave castle represents the perfect paragon of the nocturnal conversation we had on Harriet and Kweku's balcony overlooking the Volta River a few nights earlier.

As we entered the former slave castle, I was dressed in a white traditional African *lapa* and top, which I had made for me in Oṣogbo, Nigeria, during my Iyawo year (chapter 4); I was feeling spiritually humble, wearing my priestly *elekes,* and particularly sensitive because the historical experience in which we were about to engage. As we walked across the draw bridge entrance into Elmina Castle and I heard the dreaded word "Obruni" yelled at me, my response to the Ghanaian woman was automatic and just as loudly accusatory: "I am not white; I am a Black American, and my grandmother was your color." Surprisingly, she immediately apologized and said she understood that I was her sister. As we work through the repercussions of our tragic slave history that we share, perhaps these are the kinds of encounters that need to happen as a part of the ongoing dialogue between Africans and African Americans across the Black Atlantic.

Thankfully, the encounter did not thwart our intentions for coming to the slave castle. I proceeded to give my reverential homage to my ancestors— praying, singing, and sprinkling *efun* (Yoruba cleansing white chalk) on the dungeon floors. Gene said he felt anger when we entered the men's dungeon, as he touched the encrusted brown walls where the enslaved males had been kept. Sensing the degradation of human life that had transpired in those dungeons, I simply felt an intense sadness. When we came to the Door of No Return, where slave ships had awaited our ancestors' embarkment, I felt some of the sorrow, confusion, and bafflement they most certainly experienced.

We then ascended stairs to the roof of the castle to look out over Elmina town, intensely feeling the whole sordid history as I viewed the small St. Jago

Figure 6.3. Author standing on the balcony of Elmina Castle overlooking Elmina town and St. Jago Castle. Photo: Gene Howell.

Castle on a nearby hill, built by the Dutch as a military fort to protect the more important St. George Elmina Castle, housing their lucrative "cargo" for sale in the Americas. I suddenly felt the history of the original purpose of these trading monuments that also held tons of gold for shipment out of the Gold Coast, Ghana's original name before independence. Human slaves had eventually become even more rewarding than the pillaged gold and ivory, as the Western world built its wealth on the precious natural resources and human beings of Africa.

After we left Elmina, we traveled about eight miles to Cape Coast Castle, the largest of the over forty slave monuments lining the Ghanaian coastline, and the site of the movie *Sankofa* I screened at UC Davis (chapter 4). As we were entering, Gene verbally objected to the entrance fee that was charged, saying he was a descendant of those enslaved in the castle and, therefore, should not have to pay; the entrance fees *are* actually structured on whether one is a Ghanaian, European, American, etc. Then, pushing his point about getting the gate attendant to recognize who we were, Gene asked, "Can we at least get a discount?" Of course, none of his arguments made any difference, but Gene felt obligated to make them anyway and voice his objection to the castle administration for not recognizing African diasporans. After paying our entrance fee, we proceeded toward the museum, but not before stopping to observe the old rusted-out canons dotting the edge of the large courtyard that once guarded the coast from other European rivals. Cape Coast Castle was built by the Swedes in the 1650s, some 175 years after the Portuguese had built Elmina Castle, but it was soon taken over by the British in 1662. Even before formal colonialism began, Africa was a continent in continual play among greedy rival European nations, and the canons remain as visual reminders of the necessary weapons used to defend their coastal African territories.

The Cape Coast Castle museum exhibit focuses on the ominous shackles and chains that were the tools of enslavement. However, there was also an exhibition that acknowledged famous descendants of those enslaved Africans, like W.E.B. DuBois and Marcus Garvey. The display of famous African diasporans displayed our resilience in full view and indicated the necessary Black Atlantic dialogue of which the Cape Coast administration was obviously aware.

That Black Atlantic dialogue was highlighted in sharp global relief when President Barack Obama and his family visited Cape Coast Castle in July 2009 during his first term. His campaign for the presidency was happening during my Fulbright fellowship, and Ghanaians were extremely interested and excited about the potential of him becoming the leader of the most powerful nation in the world. However, by the time Barack and Michelle, along with their two daughters and Michelle's mother Mrs. Marian Robinson, visited Ghana, I was back home in Sacramento. From the reports of their two-hour tour of Cape Coast Castle in 2009, President Obama stood in that same canon-filled courtyard to deliver his presidential, but personal, response to the experience of the slave castle: "It is reminiscent of the trip that I took to Buchenwald. It reminds us of the capacity of human beings to commit great evil . . . It is particularly important for Malia and Sasha, who are growing up in such a blessed way, [to know] that history can take very cruel turns."[3] The image of a Black US president, standing in the historic Cape Coast courtyard with his Black family was a powerful symbol of the ongoing Black Atlantic dialogue, and will forever be etched in history.

The Ghanaian press focused on an even more personal note from the point of view of First Lady Michelle Obama and her mother, as direct descendants of American slaves because they can personally trace their lineage to Ghana. Michelle Obama apparently discussed her direct ancestral connection to Ghana to the then Minster of Parliament Hon. Fritz Baffour, their guide for their Cape Coast Castle tour. Her second great-grandfather had passed down the family story that "the last point they arrived at before being shipped to Virginia was the British Cape Coast Castle." Hon. Fritz Baffour also revealed that the mother-in-law Mrs. Robinson was the most emotional during the tour. Baffour publicized his perception of the Obama's Cape Coast Castle experience: ". . . even though the Obamas were unable to locate the exact part of Ghana or West Africa their ancestor came from; the Obama family was visibly touched in body language during the tour."[4]

The Black Atlantic dialogue continues even now in Ghana. On December 2, 2019, 126 African Americans and Afro-Caribbeans, in colorful traditional dress, became dual citizens of Ghana in a special ceremony conducted by current President Akufo-Addo. Our friends Harriet and Kweku were among them. The dual citizenship ceremony was a part of what was known as "The Year of Return," celebrating four hundred years since a British man-of-war ship landed in Jamestown, Virginia, in 1619, marking the first Africans enslaved on what became the United States of America. The 126 Black people taking part in the ceremony, many of whom had been long-term residents of Ghana, took the oath of citizenship administered by a Ghanaian judge at the Jubilee House, the seat of government, before shaking hands with Akufo-Addo. This symbolic act sealed a relationship first made by Kwame Nkrumah and W.E.B. DuBois at the beginning of the country's independence. The past is absolutely prologue, and the Afrofuture is awaiting.

Gene left Ghana to return to Oakland on the morning of September 5, 2008. I was so happy that he had come to help me get established for my Fulbright research, and that I was able to introduce him to Ghana. From his masculine point of view, he told me he particularly wanted all the men in my social and work sphere to know that I had a man, and that if they "tried anything" with me, he would only be a plane ride away. Indeed, after he left, every time friends and colleagues saw me, they always asked, "How is Mr. Gene?" He had not only established an atmosphere for me to feel safer, but our month together in Ghana became another milestone in solidifying our relationship. He promised to call me every day, which he did about 7:00 a.m., Ghana time, each morning. When I got back to the Fulbright House after seeing him off, I had to record that moment in my journal: *Gene left this morning, and when he went up the escalator at the beginning of the airport security check, he didn't look back. That is the way I must conduct this next phase of my Fulbright residency: don't look back; move forward with why I am here.*

Teaching Dance Studies While Conducting Hiplife Research

Gene had also helped me solve several practical problems, like tracking down a new power cord for my Apple computer after discovering my worst nightmare: I had left mine at home. He also helped me purchase a television set and a VCR to watch popular TV shows to observe American popular culture's and hip-hop's influence on Ghanaian culture, which became crucial to my research.

Starting to teach, I met with my undergraduate and graduate classes and got integrated into the Department of Dance Studies in the School of Performing Arts. This administrative configuration was also a change from thirty-two years ago, as dance, music, and drama were previously all under one academic unit, The School of Music, Dance, and Drama. The Fall 2008 semester started with controversy, as there was a teachers' strike for back pay, bringing confusion to the beginning of the fall semester. This was nothing unusual because, like in many developing countries, the University of Ghana was always claiming budget deficits and lack of funds.

Eventually I did start teaching my "History of Black Dance" course to twenty Ghanaian undergraduates and a graduate course on dance ethnology to eight graduate students twice weekly. My undergrads were "diploma students," meaning they were enrolled to receive a certificate to teach Ghanaian dance in the public schools. They had a superficial knowledge of how African American dance related to them and no understanding of dance history in the US. My graduate students already had a bachelor's degree in dance, and each was trying to figure out how to research and write about a particular dance festival or ritual related to their own Ghanaian ethnic group for their master's thesis. To them, I first had to convey a basic understanding of anthropology as a discipline with its socio-cultural principles in relation to dance. My anthropology training, along with invoking the spirit of Katherine Dunham, aided in this teaching goal.

I quickly discovered the books and files I had shipped over through the US Embassy were my saving grace, as there were few up-to-date resources in Balme Library on campus. For the grad course I assembled a dance ethnology reader of photocopied essays and book chapters. Some of the beginning articles consisted of Judith Lynne Hanna's introduction in *To Dance is Human* (1987), Deidra Sklar's "Five Premises of Culturally Sensitive Approach to Dance" (2001), and my own "Katherine Dunham, A Pioneer of Postmodern Anthropology," published in *Kaiso! Writings by and About Katherine Dunham* (2005). I did the same for the undergraduate dance history course, using a photocopied reader, consisting of my "'Aesthetic of the Cool' Revisited: the

Ancestral Dance Link in the African Diaspora" (1993), Brenda Dixon Gott-schild's chapter "First Premises of an Africanist Aesthetic" in her *Digging the Africanist Presence in American Performance* (1996), and excerpts of Jacqui Malone's *Steppin' on the Blues: The Visible Rhythms of African American Dance* (1996). All of these texts were new to the students, and they appreciated being exposed to this level of dance analysis.

One of my graduate students, dancer-choreographer Terry Ofosu (men-tioned earlier), was focused on Ghanaian popular dance as his research area, and I quickly became aware that he would be a perfect Ghanaian "cultural broker," the anthropological term for an informant who has a foot in both cultures, the researcher's and the culture under study. Terry had been to the US and was very knowledgeable about the influence of African American cul-ture—dance, style, dress, music—on Ghana. His tentative thesis title was "The Synthesis of Popular Dance and Choreography: Dance Aesthetics and Cur-rent Trends." Although his focus was on popular dance, as one cannot sepa-rate dance from music in African cultures, his knowledge base was in both disciplines. Terry began to select key hiplife musicians—Tic Tac, Okyeame Kwame, Reggie Rockstone, and others—whom I needed to interview for my research. He helped obtain their contact information and made introductions of me and my research to them.

From watching pop culture television, I also knew I needed to research the recording, television, and radio industries. I wrote in my journal: *It is excit-ing to begin this phase of my research. Ghana follows the trend of the West with several reality shows, talent shows like* Gang Starz, *and hip-hop music video shows. My teaching about ethnographic research and about African American dance should dovetail quite nicely with my own research into Accra's popular hip-hop scene.*

Before I started interviewing hiplife artists, I needed to get a sense of the general club scene in Greater Accra and observe the continuum of popular music hangouts to assess where the local hiplife music scene fit at that point, as it was a relatively new genre starting in the mid-90s. I began near the cam-pus in East Legon with a restaurant-bar called Chez Afrique that featured live highlife and reggae bands. Chez Afrique, owned by African American Michael Williams and his Asante wife, Afua Frimpong, had operated since 1998. Besides being an entrepreneur, Michael was also an educator at the Aya Centre, an organization established to enhance the experience of groups and associations visiting Ghana. Nkrumah's legacy of making the country friendly to African diasporans after Ghana's independence had established a tradition for it being a "user-friendly" West African country for Americans. Michael's long-term residency in Ghana as an expatriate who had recently gotten his "right of abode card," as well as being married to a Ghanaian, all allowed him to legally own a well-known business. Chez Afrique was indeed a popular weekend "watering hole," always packed with Ghanaians and a few African Americans.

Known as a highlife club that also includes reggae, dancehall, and Afrobeat sounds, Chez Afrique always featured *live* music, which was one of its drawing cards every weekend. Young musicians played the well-established, danceable highlife sound that had long ago established the Ghanaian cultural template of combining African rhythms with Western musical instrumentation, starting as early as World War I. In my eventual 2012 book resulting from this Fulbright residency, *The Hiplife in Ghana,* I explore this cross-cultural dimension of highlife music:

> Highlife, as the worldwide-acknowledged Ghanaian pop music, is central to the birthing of the three generations of hiplifers. Ghanaians had already mastered the indigenization of Western music through a hundred years of highlife music and its precursors . . . The British might have brought their pompous upper class "high life" style displayed in waltzes, foxtrots, ragtimes, and ballroom dance music, but it was the adapted African rhythms of Caribbean calypso and US jazz that ultimately intrigued Ghanaians to evolve the rhythmic dance music with lyrics of social commentary that would eventually become known as highlife music.[5]

No matter how old highlife music is, it always generates new contemporary sounds and continues to be very popular among young and middle-aged people at Chez Afrique. They crowd the dance floor in between eating contemporary Ghanaian food and drinking from the bar situated in the center of the dance floor. A constant flow of patrons perform their rhythmic shuffles and torso isolations to the infectious rhythmic music and Indigenous lyrics.

But there was an obvious generational difference between Chez Afrique and the hiplife-oriented clubs in the heart of Accra. Nightclubs in Accra proper almost all have *recorded* music played by a deejay, with a mix of hiplife and African dancehall that draw a younger crowd. For example, Duplex Nightclub in Osu, in the heart of the Ga ethnic group district, was very popular at the time. Deejays played a mix of the latest hiplife music, and Ghanaian twentysomethings flocked to the crowded dance floor every Saturday night. In 2008, one could hear the "Granpapa" of hiplife, Reggie Rockstone's "Ese Wara" featuring dancehall singer Batman Samini; Obrafuor's classic "Pae Mu Ka"; Tic Tac's classic "Kangaroo," popular among Ghana's Black Star soccer team; and Okyeame Kwame's "Woso" that blasted in most taxis I rode that year. All these popular 2008 hiplife hits kept the patrons on the dance floor; but the clubs also played American soul and R&B music, as well as some hip-hop from Jay-Z, Biggie Smalls, and Tupac Shakur.

I found that the hiplife music movement had "indigenized" hip-hop and, thereby, created an entirely new form of popular music by using highlife as its local reference point. Even though young Ghanaians had obviously gone through the imitation phase of hip-hop when it first went international, young Ghanaians had consciously chosen to use their own popular music as their cultural locus. As I said in *The Hiplife in Ghana:* "Just as James Brown, Chic, Kool and the Gang, and Parliament Funkadelic were the typical samples from soul, R&B, and funk music genres in the United States, young Ghanaian musicians began to use Mac Tontoh and Osibisa samples at the beginning of the development of the new hiplife sound."[6] This phenomenon of hybridization was exactly what I had come to Ghana to explore, and I found it in Accra's dance clubs.

I began working with Terry Ofosu more intensely, and he became invaluable in helping me find the right agents, spokespersons, and representatives of the artists I needed to interview. I also needed to talk to the producers and agents themselves, those who made hiplife popular as a *business* and a new West African genre of music. I had several interviews with concert producer Panji Anoff, a Ghanaian who had started with Reggie Rockstone in London during the early exploration of hip-hop and highlife. I also interviewed music producer Abraham Ohene Djan who owned the influential OM Studios that produced artists' videos and albums.

Another angle to my research was the television industry that promoted shows with hiplife music. Iso Paeley was a television producer at TV3, a Ghanaian station that focuses on popular culture, and I dubbed it the "Ghanaian MTV." Paeley is actually a Liberian who had moved to Ghana in 1993 and quickly advanced within the Ghanaian television industry, making his mark with the popular talent competition show *Gang Starz,* similar to *American Idol.* He got me a studio pass to view a live broadcast, and I was able to observe firsthand how much African American music and style had influenced the young competing artists. I also observed the surrounding audience members' familiarity with Black American music, going back to the '70s and '80s.

During my interview with Iso Paeley, the history of Ghana's relationship with touring African American hip-hop artists was also revealed. Iso discussed an infamous October 2006 Jay-Z concert at the Accra International Conference Centre, where Ghanaian hiplife musicians Batman Samini, Reggie Rockstone, and Obrafuor were opening acts for the international hip-hop star. However, when I interviewed Rockstone, he was not positive about his experience with Jay-Z's appearance in Ghana; he felt Jay-Z was unapproachable and did not mingle with the Ghanaian artists who had helped him bridge his hip-hop performance with the young Ghanaian audience. Again, the ongoing conflictual Black Atlantic dialogue reared its complicated head.

Researching the Complex Dynamics of Hiplife Music

I began to focus my Fulbright research on *how* to penetrate that Black Atlantic interchange to even deeper complexities of the cultural negotiation between Africans and African Americans. Ghanaian hiplife music offers an intriguing representation of this complex interchange as an entirely new musical genre. Hiplife researcher Jesse Shipley explains the continuing intricacy embedded within the two-way cultural exchange:

> Diasporic signs in Africa provide a kind of promise; a debt is incurred that promises future connection. As the story of inversion in which African American visitors swap clothes and hairstyles with their Ghanaian hosts shows, from a Ghanaian perspective, exchanges with diasporic people are a form of cosmopolitan appropriation that embody debates about continuities and disjunctures among black people . . . Diasporic styles stand in for newness that is also familiar. Evading the intractable, dialogic relationship between black and white, diasporic blackness allows youths to fashion new public voices.[7]

It was exactly these "new public voices" that I was trying to reveal during the research part of my Fulbright fellowship. As Karin Barber's epigraph beginning this chapter says, ". . . new genres are created in response to changes in social experience,"[8] and the globalization of hip-hop has indeed created changes in social experience internationally.

One tool of any researcher is the interview instrument: developing the right questions and asking them in the right way, at the right time. The process becomes like the music itself; to create a hit, one must have just the right lyrics composed to address just the right topic and supported by just the right melody and rhythmic timing. I had to focus on crafting my questions: 1) How do you see the "origin question": Did the aesthetic components of hip-hop start in Africa or America? 2) How do you see appropriation of hip-hop in Ghanaian hiplife, and what is the continuing role of highlife in the music? 3) How do you experience the economics and business of hip-hop in Ghana? Is it mainly for money, or do the artists emphasize finding their individual voice? 4) Hip-hop in the US has been accused of misogyny; does this anti-women issue exist for hiplife in Ghana as well? What is the place of women rappers here? 5) What is the influence of the telecommunications companies in Ghana that use hiplife culture to gain customers? How do cell phones play a role in hiplife music's growth? 6) Where is hiplife now in its development, fifteen years after it started? Is it still growing, or is it dying? These were the complex, meaty questions I cultivated to penetrate the cultural, gender, economic, and historical complexity of the Black Atlantic dialogue that had fashioned hiplife music in Ghana.

One of the hiplife musicians, Obour (Bice Obour Osei-Kufuor), was very involved in shaping the discourse around the music. He had a holistic sense of the various stages of the music as it had evolved to that point. Obour is considered second generation, entering the hiplife music scene just as the Ghana Music Awards started in 2000, which helped institutionalize the hiplife music genre. Obour was voted Artist of the Year by that organization in 2002, and was not only considered a credible artist, but also a youth activist. Early in his career he promoted youth literacy and empowerment of Ghanaian girls and women through education, as well as youth participation in electoral politics. His prominence in establishing a discourse for youth and music in Ghana continued to grow after my Fulbright, allowing him to become the first hiplife artist to be elected to the presidency of the Musicians Union of Ghana (MUSIGA).

In my interview with Obour he laid out his perspective on an evolutionary sequencing of hiplife's development since the mid-nineties. Reggie Rockstone was arguably considered the "founder" of hiplife when he returned from London in 1994 and started rapping in Twi, when most were still imitating American rap. During that same period, there was also a trio of emcees, VIP (Vision in Progress)—consisting of Lazzy, Prodigal, and Promzy—experimenting with using Indigenous languages in their raps. They hailed from the Accra ghetto of Nima in the Osu district and came to prominence during the mid-nineties. Reggie dropped his first album *Maaka Maka* in 1997, and VIP released their first album *Biibiibo* in 1998. All the subsequent hiplife artists emerged from that mid-to-late nineties period.

Obour's comprehension of the evolution of the new music form became important for my understanding of the development of the entire hiplife movement. During a December 2008 interview, right before I left Ghana, he explained his authoritative conception of five stages of hiplife that explained the continual Black Atlantic aesthetic negotiation. I simplified those five phases and summarized them into three distinct eras: 1) Imitation—hip-hop rhythms with local dialects for lyrics, exemplified by the first generation with Rockstone; 2) Adaptation—hip-hop mixed with some local highlife beats and local dialects as the first experimentation with highlife pop music; and 3) Indigenization—traditional highlife rhythms and Indigenous languages and also using traditional lyrics alluding to local Akan proverbs. These three phases allowed me to understand hiplife's evolution over the fifteen years before my research.

Obour's own collaborative album with the elder highlife musician A. B. Crentsil, *Best of the Lifes: Highlife and Hiplife,* is a perfect example of a young hiplife musician consciously including the *original* Ghanaian pop music by joining forces with a respected highlife musician. In *The Hiplife in Ghana,* I explore how Obour and Crentsil mixed their two generational musics and styles: "Although the two self-presentations show distinctive generational differences, the album's music makes a definite statement about hiplife's strong allegiance to highlife as its parental music form."[9]

I became friendly with a popular hiplife artist, Okyeame Kwame (Kwame Nsiah Appau), during my Fulbright residency. I interviewed him multiple times, and once he even brought his crew to my Fulbright apartment to meet his "American Mom." I was drawn to his driving ambition as well as his genuine connection with his people. I perceived he was using his celebrity, like Obour, to raise the awareness of Ghanaians to several current issues, including promoting Ghanaians' connection to their own *traditional* culture and rhythms.

Key sociological differences between hiplife and hip-hop emerged during my research. Okyeame Kwame, for example, comes from a middle-class family and is a college graduate. His background made me aware of a key component of most Ghanaian hiplife artists that diverges from American hip-hoppers: schools, rather than the streets, is where many Ghanaians hone their rap "chops." It becomes the site where young aspiring Ghanaian hiplife artists connect and find the agency to enter the growing global hip-hop genre. This is a direct contradiction of the US stereotype of the music being bred only in the ghetto by poor school dropouts headed toward incarceration. Ghana provides just the opposite scenario: upper middle-class youth with education could more easily access global Western values and were also fluent in the all-important English language. Hiplife artists like Okyeame Kwame use their music to also enlighten Ghanaian youth to critique their social norms. In his case, Okyeame reminded his youthful fans of the power of their own Indigenous culture as opposed to strict imitation of American values.

I was able to observe Okyeame Kwame use his unique personal agency in concert at the International Conference Center in Accra in November 2008 as a part of Joy 99.7 FM Radio's "Nite of the All-Stars." He had become a popular artist two years earlier with his first solo album *Bohye Ba.* But it was his second album *M'awensem* (Poetry), which had dropped that year under his One Mic Entertainment label (an obvious allusion to Nas's famous line), that pushed him to the top of the Ghanaian pop music charts. As mentioned before, his hit song "Woso" was ubiquitous on the radio and in the streets, and he was enjoying his newfound celebrity, becoming one of the featured artists at the annual radio Joy 99.7 concert. I arrived early with my video camera in tow to see the entire show. The remix version of "Woso," with his inclusion of Ghanaian R&B singer Riche, was the finale of the entire event that also included other major hiplife artists.

What made Okyeame Kwame's performance so unique was his dramatic stage production of a Ghanaian Asante (Ashanti) cultural scene, complete with traditional *kete* drumming and *fontomfrom* dancing. I recorded its unique blending of Ghanaian tradition with African American hip-hop in *The Hiplife in Ghana,* and it's worth including a lengthy description of the staged cultural counternarrative:

> He entered the stage as an Ashanti chief in traditional *kente* cloth wearing an Akan gold crown, while being carried on a chief's palanquin (carved boat-like conveyance reserved for high-ranking chiefs) on the shoulders of several young men in traditional African draped cloth. On the opposite side of the proscenium a battery of young drummers, also in traditional cloth, were seated at Ashanti *kete* drums. He shocked the audience at the hiplife concert with this highly unusual traditional Ghanaian cultural stage entrance, one with which the youths were quite familiar but usually associated [only] with their elders.
>
> In one deft stroke he brought traditional Ashanti culture to the contemporary popular culture stage. As he was lowered to the stage floor and stepped out of the palanquin, Kwame began the traditional stately and regal *fontomfrom* warrior dance along with another male dancer who was an obvious expert. The Ashanti *fontomfrom* dance with its strong rhythmic leg kicks is embedded with meaningful hand gestures about battle strategies and prowess in war. The dance and drumming is normally performed at royal occasions at the chief's palace or during solemn ceremonies like funerals; here Okyeame Kwame had transformed the dance's purpose to re-orient young Ghanaians, many of whom eschew traditional culture in favor of Western youth pop culture. At an annual hiplife music event, Okyeame Kwame's performance had succeeded at this point in replicating a traditional Ashanti royal ceremony without any references to hiplife or hip-hop.[10]

With the dominance of Western hip-hop and its association with global modernity, the significance of Okyeame Kwame's positioning of traditional Asante culture and values on the hiplife stage that night cannot be overstated.

The traditional Asante performance did not end with the traditional *fontomfrom* dance. "The performance continued with a demonstration of the correlation between traditional drum language and rapping. After throwing off his *kente* cloth at the end of the dance, Kwame moved stage left to the drummers and began to rap specific Twi phrases that they replicated with their *kete* rhythms . . . This cultural call and response is exactly what occurs at Asante state events, with the traditional linguist, or *okyeame* [pronounced oh-chee-A-máy], chanting the praises of the chief and offering proverbs to the people by which to live, accompanied by the traditional drum language."[11] The youth at the performance that evening got a strong reinforcement of the traditional culture, from which they had begun to turn away in favor of American pop culture.

When the performance eventually transitioned into the hiplife deejayed mix of "Woso," Okyeame Kwame had reinforced the lesson of reverence to his own tradition Ghanaian culture. He had lived up to his assumed hiplife name and became the linguist for his generation. He revealed an important lesson to the youth gathered that night for a contemporary music event: the "new" is based on the "old"; hip-hop rap is a current representation of an ancient tradition coming from their families' culture. The intertextual transition from the traditional to the contemporary happened as the tempo of Kwame's speech-drum dialogue increased to a rapid-fire pace, and the deejay, stationed upstage center, began to overdub hip-hop beats on top of the drumming, which provided a smooth segue into the synthesized looped beats of "Woso"'s hiplife sound, signaling male and female dancers to emerge on stage performing choreographed hip-hop dance and b-boy moves.

In the entire performance Kwame took the chance to not merely appropriate or signify on "traditional political orators," but to actually *replicate* their performance, complete with traditional dress and drum-speech culture of Ghana. His bold performance allowed contemporary hiplife youths to experience one of the *sources* of hip-hop's aesthetics in Ghanaian tradition. My hiplife research in Accra was providing me an overview of the global dynamics at play in hip-hop's internationalization, with both its negotiated adoption and its re-inscription for local purposes.

"The Arc of Mutual Inspiration"

Out of this engaging research grew my concept of "The Arc of Mutual Inspiration," which became the primary concept of my second book. It illuminates the naturally occurring cultural relationship between Africa and its diaspora, and became my conceptual lens through which I viewed hip-hop on the continent. The construct explains the circle of musical and dance influences from Africa to its diaspora and back again, validated by the Sankofa bird symbol. Absorbing the work of artists like Reggie Rockstone as one of the originators of hiplife, Obour as the sociopolitical rapper, and Okyeame Kwame's direct cultural synthesis all helped me understand how the cultural priorities and rhythms of Africa, revised in the US, had returned home through hip-hop.

My growing theoretical foundation was reinforced through long intellectual conversations with key informants who knew the Ghanaian music business well. Analyses from producers B. B. Menson and Panji Anoff, as well as my cultural broker Terry Ofosu, became my foundation into how hip-hop had become *indigenized* in Ghana through a localization process that carried the society's social, political, and economic contexts. This process produced a whole new genre of music using rhymes and metaphors in local languages like Twi, Ga, Hausa, and Ewe, mixed with guitar-based highlife musical phrasings,

Figure 6.4. Asante Sankofa Bird symbol of Ghana.

as well as incorporating well-known *anansesem* traditional proverbs of the Asante. These revelations would eventually find their way into *The Hiplife in Ghana: West African Indigenization of Hip-Hop*.

The arc of mutual inspiration, like the Sankofa bird, draws strength from looking historically backward to the past for grounding in the present. But sankofa also carries "the egg"—the seed—to the future. My research led me to artists who intuited how the sankofa process could work through today's hiplife music to enlighten the youth. The past, dialoguing with the present, points toward an Afrofuture that is still unfolding.

Working with ASWAD and Teaching the National Dance Company

Shortly after Gene left, I was asked to join the Association for the Study of Worldwide African Diaspora (ASWAD) by my friend Dr. Abena Busia, Ghanaian scholar and daughter of the late Dr. Kofi Abrefa Busia, one of Ghana's early prime ministers. She was a professor of literature and women's studies at Rutgers University and is now the Ghanaian ambassador to Brazil. We had a long history, as I had hosted her at Stanford University in a reading of one of her books of poetry back in 1989. As an Oxford-educated, well-known feminist scholar, she was then president of ASWAD, which was planning its 2009 bi-annual conference in Accra. Abena had assembled a planning committee consisting of a who's who cadre of Ghanaians, West Africans, and diasporan literati living in Ghana at the time, and I felt privileged to be counted among them. Being a bi-annual conference, it had convened in Barbados in 2007 and Rio de Janeiro in 2005. Our committee was planning the first time an ASWAD conference would happen on the African continent, and Abena was calling in all of her favors from her Ghanaian friends and colleagues to make that conference an auspicious occasion of ASWAD "coming home" to its defining continent.

ASWAD is a worldwide organization uniting "international scholars seeking to further our understanding of the African diaspora, that is, the dispersal of people of African descent throughout the world."[12] I felt right at home on such a committee. I considered ASWAD as an important academic component of the continuing Pan-African movement, with a strong multi-disciplinary approach, to which I could contribute as both an academic and artist. My working on the ASWAD 2008 planning committee moved me into a new phase of my Fulbright residency as I was meeting people of like mind, spirit, and profession.

I definitely moved into the second phase of my Fulbright fellowship in Ghana when I was invited to teach Dunham Dance Technique classes to the resident dance company at the National Theatre in Accra. I met the then Director of the National Dance Company, David Amoo, and had spent time with him and his family in Accra. He was excited to have his young dancers learn a well-known dance technique for their warm-ups before their daily rehearsals. I felt like what Katherine Dunham must have experienced when she was commissioned by President Léopold Senghor to work with the National Ballet of Senegal. But my work with Ghana's National Dance Company would be far less complicated than Dunham's was in her 1964 Senegalese residency.

In the sixties, when African nations were first negotiating their postcolonial identity, national dance companies became a tool to help solidify their various ethnic groups into one national voice. Senghor's National Ballet of Senegal and Keita Fodèba's Les Ballets Africains in Guinea established the template for such a postcolonial effort through dance and music. Touring African dance companies were perceived as a primary means of establishing the newly independent West African countries' *cultural* right to be a part of the global world.

However, in the 1960s, there were complications regarding how to choreographically represent pre- and postcolonial identities. Dance historian Joanna Dee Das has analyzed Dunham's mindset in working with the Senegalese company in the mid-sixties: "Her ideas were rooted in romanticized notions of Africa's greater connection to nature and spirituality. Instead of seeing dynamic cultural exchange occurring within Africa itself, she viewed Africa as one of the primary sources for cultural creolization in places such as the Caribbean."[13] One's sociopolitical era indeed contextualizes one's art and often shapes one's aesthetic approach. In 2008 I had no such romanticized essentialist notion of Africa and its dance. Now in the twenty-first century, I saw African dance companies as having a vast range of traditional and contemporary themes and movement methodologies, with many cosmopolitan creative African choreographers. I simply felt privileged to bring Miss Dunham's solidly codified technique as *one* dance approach to the National Dance Company of Ghana, which could add to their aesthetic toolbox.

I had worked with the late Nii Yartey, the well-known choreographer and dance theorist of Ghanaian contemporary African dance. Having many dance leadership roles on both sides of the Atlantic, he was at the forefront of the development of dance theater and contemporary African dance in Ghana. He had been an associate professor of dance in the US, Head of the Department of Dance Studies at Legon, and Artistic Director (1976–1993) of the Ghana Dance Ensemble (GDE), the original national dance company started at UG Legon as a part of African studies in the 1960s (chapter 5, *DinB*). He had also started his own contemporary dance ensemble, Noyam Dance Company, to explore his creative form of contemporary African dance.

Francis Nii Yartey had also been the Artistic Director of the National Dance Company at the National Theatre from 1993 to 2006, having just stepped down a few years before my Fulbright residency. As I said about him in *Dancing in Blackness,* "His contribution to contemporary African dance became a third phase of development of the GDE, which he called, 'observation and research . . . used to form the basis of work to inspire the present and the future.'"[14] His observation and research became a part of what Yartey calls Ghana's movement toward "experimentation" that allowed for the GDE's repertoire to be "relevant to the contemporary world."[15]

When I started my dance classes with Ghana's National Dance Company in 2008, I was ready to train those taut Black bodies in the strengthening aspects of Dunham Technique, making them ready for whatever kind of choreography David Amoo and his artistic colleagues deemed appropriate. Hence, when I approached the national dance company with a six-week workshop in Katherine Dunham Technique, they were already working in the contemporary African choreographic vein. David Amoo had taken over the company after Nii Yartey stepped down and was continuing in his footsteps.

Even before Gene left, Amoo had invited us to see the company in rehearsal. We arrived one afternoon at the National Theatre, a beautiful architectural structure built by the Chinese in 1992, in the Victoriaborg district of Accra. After viewing the magnificent lobby with its dramatic fontomfrom drumlike pillars, we were escorted to a second-floor large studio with excellent sprung hardwood floors. David Amoo greeted us and introduced the dancers in the company, young men and women numbering about thirty members strong. After our formal introductions, Gene and I watched a rehearsal of a Ga-oriented piece that utilized traditional movements choreographed into a contemporary composition, with the dancers also playing traditional gourd instruments. I was impressed, and afterward the dancers excitedly expressed their strong desire to learn Dunham Technique.

David and I immediately worked out an agreement for the six-week Dunham workshop. As the company administration did not have a large budget to really compensate me for teaching, they offered instead to pay for my taxi transportation during the six-week period from the campus to the theater, and I agreed. After all, I was being paid handsomely through my Fulbright fellowship, and I considered it an honor to work directly with some of the best trained concert dancers in the country. Each week I arrived at the National Theatre and entered the second-floor large studio, I was greeted by an enthusiastic group of dancers and musicians, who voraciously grew in their understanding of Dunham Technique each week, easily retaining what we had done the previous week and allowing me to build a strong Dunham choreographic progression.

The dancers took to Dunham Technique like fish to water. They easily understood the natural swings of Dunham fall/recovery and facilely accomplished the grand pliés with hip rotations. Their quadricep thigh strength was amazing during hinges into the floor, and every technical movement sequence I offered was consumed ravenously, like they were eating delicious food of which they could not get enough. Of course, the center floor isolation sequence was natural for them. Dunham was the American dance artist who had codified African-based torso articulations central to all Africanist dance styles, allowing for sophisticated polyrhythmic movement. The Ghanaian dancers smiled as they embodied what they already knew naturally in their Asante, Ga, and Ewe dances, but now broken down in each part of their facile Black torsos in detail.

I developed Dunham movement progressions across the floor, adding new sequences each week that accumulated into a choreographed dance by the last week. There were always four to six live drummers accompanying my classes, and they composed a specific repeatable rhythmic musical composition, which also included an excellent flautist, for the dance I created. At the end of my last class, the Ghana National Dance Company performed my Dunham choreography for a small audience in the studio. At the very end, David Amoo rushed up to present me with a special piece of kente cloth as a parting gift, and there were lots of hugs and *midase* (thank yous). My six-week Dunham dance workshop provided me a rewarding dance experience with Ghanaian dance professionals, who equally appreciated what I had given them.

Testing My Traditional Ghanaian Dance

One evening I was invited to an award ceremony and social event on campus at Legon Hall. Dr. June DeGraff-Hanson, a Ghanaian scientist teaching in the US and who was also staying at the Fulbright compound, asked me to accompany her to the event. Her late father had been the headmaster of Legon Hall for many years, the first dormitory built at UG, and she was asked to accept his posthumous award at the event called "Honoring of Distinguished Alumni and Fellows of Legon Hall." June was becoming a good friend as a fellow Fulbright scholar visiting her Ghanaian home. Her invitation to the event again positioned me in a who's who university event, allowing me to mingle with the higher university echelon. She introduced me to some of the oldest remaining first-generation scholars on campus, who came out of Ghana's missionary school period and who would have been Nkrumah's contemporaries.

It was at this Legon Hall event that I was presented to the then Vice-Chancellor of the university, Professor Clifford Nii Boe Tagoe. Vice-Chancellor Tagoe complimented me on the traditional African attire I was wearing, an outfit I had made by a campus tailor. He and I immediately launched into a discussion of the upcoming US elections and candidate Barack Obama. I felt comfortable with him and was candid about my politics, as most Africans hoped Obama would win the election. I told him of my long-term connection to the Legon campus, going back thirty-two years as a young Black American; I was feeling like I really fit in again.

The high point of that evening event at Legon Hall was my dancing *adowa* to drumming by the Ghana Dance Ensemble. The drummers played kete drums after the speeches and the formal unveiling of the commemorative plaque that contained June's father's name. As adowa is an individual dance, their playing was for anyone who wanted to enter the outdoor courtyard open area to dance. June knew I was familiar with Ghanaian traditional dance and kept encouraging me to get up and "show my stuff," knowing all eyes would be on me. I recorded that event in my journal:

> *Adowa that I had learned 32 years ago immediately came back to me. I could "hear" the rhythms and drum messages and knew exactly where to place my feet within the beats. I felt extremely comfortable with my movements and my transitions from one repetitive sequence to the next. I created a "story," and everyone felt it. The only other person on the floor was a young man who began to dance adowa with me. I had not forgotten any of my Ghanaian dance ability; my muscles and spirit memory took over and I was again dancing like at the Asante funeral in the village of Kaasi decades ago.* (Chapter 5, *DinB*)

Afterward, the elders all congratulated me, admitting they could not have done what I had just done. Ghanaian academic types are not always adept in their traditional dances, and in some small way, I had spoken a Ghanaian language through my body, transcending some of their cultural knowledge.

Dance, as part of the soul of culture, held me in good stead and allowed me to become a part of making the award event special. The current Artistic Director of the UG's Ghana Dance Ensemble, Ben Okri, introduced himself and complimented my dance. I was establishing a place of honor through my dance, and I knew I was truly home. My Ghanian dance knowledge was imparted to me long ago by the best elder Asante cultural masters, Prof. Albert Mawere Opoku and Auntie Grace Numah. I felt they were reaching out from *orun*—the ancestral realm—and blessing me with their grace, and I was grateful.

Reconnecting with My 1976 Ghanaian Family

On a personal level, I suppose it was inevitable that I would reconnect with Fargos, my 1976 Ghanaian escort and boyfriend. Our "reunion" was not direct, but through his family, his brother and children. Asu Atiso, or Fargos as everyone called him, had passed in 2003, but it seems preordained that I reunited with him through his family. He had latched on to me at the very beginning of my 1976 Ghana sojourn, introduced me to his Christian Village home near the Legon campus, and accompanied me to Togo and Nigeria. In many ways he was like my guardian angel, generally taking care of me as a young Black American woman alone in West Africa for the first time (chapter 5, *DinB*).

Two weeks after Gene left, my connection to his family occurred through a miraculous chance meeting with his brother, whom I had not known before. One day I took a taxi from the Legon campus to Accra for several errands, and while negotiating with the driver to make several stops, I found him to be genuinely friendly and cooperative. The next day he was again at the front of campus waiting for passengers, and we recognized each other. I hired him again to take me to the American Embassy in Accra. That taxi driver turned out to be Fargos's brother named Christian, and it was during the second taxi ride that we made the connection. He said, "My name is Christian," and I responded, "Oh, just like the village." He quickly answered back with, "Oh, do you know that village?" and I rejoined with, "Yes, I know a family there by the name of Atiso." Then, as if time stood still, the conversation stopped. Christian revealed, "My name is Atiso; did you know my brother Fargos?" At that moment we both realized we had made a familial connection, and another of my life circles was made.

Once Christian and I made our personal discovery, he decided to stay with me throughout my day's activities and announced he would be my driver free of charge. As he drove me to the embassy and then the Accra Mall, we talked about Fargos, and he informed me he had died through "juju" and his illness could not be diagnosed; he had mysteriously gotten sick, rapidly declined, and died. One hears about those types of deaths in Ghana due to spiritual hexes. As I thought about the details of his death, I surmised that Fargos, being a hustler, had probably crossed the wrong person. But, as life would have it, I had a chance to now reconnect with his family and get to know his progeny, who represented the best of what he had accomplished while he was alive.

After we finished my errands, Christian asked if I wanted to go to the village, and I immediately said, "Yes, of course." The village itself was more crowded, and the Atiso family house had grown larger with new additions, and now even had electricity. Thirty-two years ago, I had lived in that house for a month with kerosene lamps for night light and no running water. As I sat in what was now the living room of the old compound, twenty-first-century culture intruded into our day on their wide-screen television: we watched a show with the American girl group, The Pussycat Dolls, sexually gyrating. I had another major indication that cultural change had indeed come even to my old Christian Village.

Getting to know Fargos's four children was an interesting process that allowed me an up-close-and-personal overview of Ghana's changes. I remembered his oldest son, Kudjo, whom I had carried on my back in the village as a two-year old. But Fargos had continued producing children after my time, and I met his younger son Kwashi and his youngest daughter Antoinette; he also had an older daughter, Carol, who lived in another village. Kudjo, as the eldest, had updated their Christian Village living quarters, and made it very neat and comfortable. But I could see they were still poor and struggling to keep up with "modern" standards. I realized the Atiso family was a microcosm of the changes in Ghana over the last thirty years. Even with more infrastructure and prosperity, there is still a lot of rampant poverty.

But, for a few hours that day, the Atiso family and I transcended all the educational and economic differences between us and reveled in the *spiritual* wealth of their culture, as we watched the lavish two-day funeral they gave their father/brother on a VHS video tape they showed me. While watching the video of the funeral, I knew Fargos's spirit had been pleased by the second-day cultural performances by village dance companies he himself had managed. I remembered the first time he had encouraged me to dance at a Sunday Ewe *agbadza* social dance and play rattle with the musicians in the village. He was proud of his Ewe traditions and had encouraged me to participate with his people. Now, thirty-two years later I was back in Christian Village with his family remembering his unique spirit. Fargos's children—Kudjo, Kwashi, Antoinette, and Carol—now approaching middle age with their own families, have become my Ghanaian family. We saw each other several times a month while I was on my Fulbright, and we have stayed in touch ever since my return to the US through Skype and direct messaging, taking advantage of the new technology that allows the whole world to instantly connect.

Waga Hip Hop 8 Festival in Ouagadougou

During my Fulbright fellowship I heard about an annual hip-hop festival in Burkina Faso, the Francophone country at Ghana's northern border, and I knew I had to go. Because of its proximity, I figured traveling would be fairly easy. I wanted to widen my view of hip-hop's effect on West Africa besides Ghana; plus, I was anxious to practice my French language skills again. I had packed a bag the night before my big campus lecture at IAS and was prepared to journey alone to Ouagadougou right after the lecture.

But traveling in Africa is not always the easiest and most straightforward endeavor. I first had to get to the Main Transport Yard in Accra for the STC Bus to Kumasi, where I then had to change to the Ouagadougou bus in another station. Once in Kumasi, trying to get a straight answer as to where the other bus station was for the Upper Region was a chore in itself. After conquering that task and walking a half mile with bags in hand through bustling Kumasi crowds, I arrived at the right bus station, only to find out that the bus to Ouagadougou was about to leave within minutes, so I had to rush. I couldn't wait to get on the second bus to sleep.

The next morning, we arrived at the border town of Pago in Ghana's Upper East Region, where we had to go through customs. I was greeted by a huge archway that read: "Goodbye & Safe Journey"; Burkina Faso was just on the other side of that arch. After customs checked our passports and visas, we boarded the bus again and were off to Ouagadougou, the capital of Burkina Faso. We arrived in the late morning of October 17, and I went straight to the official festival hotel, the Ran Hotel Somketa. It was a pleasant hotel with amenities of a small refrigerator, air conditioning, and even a minibar in the rooms. I also noticed that the employees at the hotel's front desk were not patient with my stumbling French language attempts, just like they weren't in Paris back in 1969 during my European sojourn (chapter 2, *DinB*). The thought occurred that the French must export their snobbish intolerance along with their culture.

French-speaking Burkina Faso was very different than English-speaking Ghana. The first thing I noticed was there were far less cars, with more people riding motor scooters to get around the city, which I found environmentally better. I immediately recorded some of these differences in my journal:

Francophone Africa is quite different from Anglophone Africa. The French West Africans seems far more cosmopolitan due to the kind of colonialization attributed to the French: "La Civiltrise"—The Civilizer—was the concept where the French saw themselves offering Africans a civilizing process by becoming "French." This was the "carrot" they extended to Africans as an incentive to what they perceived as actually becoming fully "human." But of course, "La Civiltrise" was a doubled-edge sword: they were given French status, and therefore accorded individuality, but had to give up their intrinsic Africanness. This meant there was a closer social relationship between the French colonizers and their African subjects in Senegal, Guinea, Congo, Niger, etc., than that of the British in Ghana, Nigeria, Gambia, Sierra Leone, and Liberia. The British followed a system of Indirect Rule, where the chiefs of different regions reported to the English governors of each colony, with little cultural interaction between the British and the Africans.

Hence, I was anxious to see how the difference between Francophone and Anglophone Africa manifested in hip-hop and young African people in the twenty-first century, from both the artist and audience perspectives.

The hotel lobby was bustling with hip-hop-styled young people from throughout Africa and Europe. Luckily, I met Ghanaian music producer Panji Anoff, whom I had already interviewed. Sharing a cool drink in the hotel restaurant, he gave me an orientation to the festival as well as an invitation to the sound check for that evening's main performance. He was traveling as the manager of one of Ghana's well-known emcees, King Ayisoba (Albert Apozori), who was to perform that evening with some Francophone hip-hop artists. The evening's performance was to be one of the largest concerts of the festival, held at the nearby outdoor Centre Culturel Français (CCF) amphitheater, now the Institut Français.

After attending that first concerts on October 17, I realized the emphasis of the festival's hip-hop music was definitely on *indigenization,* including rap songs in local languages and French, as well as the use of live traditional African instruments. There was a full battery of *djembe* drums (the ubiquitous West African drum originally from the Senegal, Guinea, and Mali region), a melodic *balaphon* (forerunner to the Western xylophone), and the *mbira* (thumb piano), representing familiar traditional Francophone African instrumentation. This told me that "La Civiltrise" had not truly been successful, and today's Francophone youth were creating their own counternarrative by embracing their Africanness through hip-hop. Two perfect examples of African self-empowerment through popular culture were singers Fredy Massamba from Congo-Brazzaville and Awa Sissao from Ouagadougou. Massamba's combination of rap and singing in French and Lingala mixed seamlessly with the French and Moré melodies of female singer Sissao; and her sonorous voice reminded me of Miriam Makeba and Oumou Sangare. Although French was the official language of the festival, becoming the linguistic link between the myriad of participating African ethnic groups, their Indigenous languages were always a part of their musical performances. When Massamba and Sissao sang the infectious opening song "Mama Africa," we needed no translation for that central theme of Waga Hip Hop 8.

Ayisoba, as the only Ghanaian artist, was a primary icon of the indigenization of hip-hop on the concert. I wrote about his unique style and approach to his music:

> King Ayisoba added an important Indigenous element to "Mama Africa." Ayisoba's stage dress, a vastly different semiotic style marker, was in stark contrast to the contemporary hip-hop look of the other musicians on stage. His costume of a loin cloth, off-the-shoulder animal skin cape, and traditional sandals, while carrying his ubiquitous "ancestor" stick, provided a visual time warp that took the audience to an Africa that is not usually represented in contemporary African music . . . King Ayisoba's persona is one of complete indigeneity without any allusions to Western culture—a "roots man" persona.[16]

His complete traditional look, wearing few clothes, surprised me because during his sound check, the dreadlocked Ayisoba wore the traditional woven smock-*batakari* of Northern Ghana while carrying his ancestor stick. The image of his half naked dress on stage took the audience into another African era.

I rode back to Ghana on the same bus with Panji and King Ayisoba and was able to query Panji about Ayisoba's unique style as well as how he first joined the contemporary hip-hop movement. Panji revealed that, "Ayisoba has three registers that he sings in: a whisper, low, and high. The high register is what he used to talk to the animals when he was a cow herder near Bolgatanga."[17] He also informed me of the depths of Ayisoba's reverence for his Frafra culture, particularly about his ubiquitous ancestor stick that was given to him by his grandfather and always accompanied him. I had witnessed his fans' appreciation of his affective "roots man" approach to hiplife music, which I took as an affirmation of the importance of Indigenous African identity at the core of Ayisoba's persona. He has joined contemporary hip-hop on his own terms, using a primal *nommo* force he retains from his ancestors.[18] Even though his musical style has been subsumed within hiplife in Accra, his people obviously appreciate his embrace of his cultural roots, mapping their Upper Region culture onto Ghanaian popular culture. My trip to Waga Hip Hop festival reinforced my growing notion that an indigenization process was most assuredly the contemporary trend of African hip-hop.

While in Ouagadougou I scored an interview with the director of the festival. Umané Culture was the producing organization of the annual Waga Hip Hop festival that started in 1997. On the last day of the 2008 festival, I interviewed Ali Diallo, the director. I elicited the help of Senegalese graduate student, Jenny Fatou M'Baye, who spoke English and French, to be my translator for the interview, as Diallo did not speak English and my French is, at best, middle school level. Through Jenny, he laid out the festival history, informing me that even though the hip-hop events had drawn larger crowds each year and had recognition from the international press, the Burkina Faso government had not given any funds to Umané Culture. The organization's tenacity spoke to the empowering entrepreneurship in hip-hop globally. Collective agency is at the heart of this youth culture with near-fanatical belief in their right to be and grow. For Diallo and his crew, their tenacity showed the importance the Ouagadougou festival had become to the young artists and their fans across West and Central Africa.

Diallo also explained the concept behind the image on the official festival poster: a drawing of a Black woman's head with a huge Afro coiffure. They wanted to have a strong female emcee/singer focus in this 2008 festival. He said Umané Culture recognized hip-hop's male-oriented image, and past Waga Hip Hop festivals seemed to invisibilize female rappers. He explained, "the only way to rectify this was to *feature* women, and there are a lot of female rappers throughout Africa."[19] I realized the festival I was attending was a proactive initiative to promote women in African popular music and hip-hop. "Several of the festival's concerts featured all female singers . . . This was not a token opening [night] gesture of the festival; the concentration on female emcees and singers continued on the third and fourth days of the festival with Alif, one of the early female hip-hop groups from Sénégal, and Youmali from Burkina Faso."[20] This proactive feminist stance spoke to the evolving consciousness of these African hip-hop organizers. They wanted to address long-standing issues like sexism within the global youth culture. If indigenization, self-empowered entrepreneurial tenacity, and a counternarrative to sexism was the future of global hip-hop, then the Afrofuture had promise for substantive changes to entrenched social norms such as male domination. Returning to Ghana I was optimistic about continuing my hip-hop research after experiencing the youth culture's wider effect on Africa.

Experiencing the Election of Barack Obama in Ghana

The entire continent of Africa was ecstatic about the possibility of a Black man becoming president of the most powerful nation in the world. The fact that Barack Hussein Obama was the son of an African—a Kenyan—made that possibility even sweeter for my African brothers and sisters in Ghana. All during my 2008 sojourn, the street hawkers were selling Barack Obama election campaign memorabilia. I remember the road hustlers rushing over to my taxi at stop lights and thrusting small American flags superimposed with Obama's face into my window. News talk shows on television discussed the ramifications of an African becoming head of the United States of America. I didn't know whether Black America or Africa was more excited, but I knew the upcoming election was becoming a world phenomenon.

For me to cast my vote in Ghana, I had to go into Accra two weeks before election day to the American Embassy in Accra with my passport. I stood in line with other Americans to cast my ballot at a makeshift voting booth arranged for US expatriates. I felt particularly proud when I entered the embassy, with which I was already familiar; I had several interviews with key US Embassy staff regarding my research. When I cast my vote for Obama, I was acutely aware of its historic meaning, made even more poignant by my being in Africa. My journal read: *November 4, 2008, will go down in history. It is the day a Black man will become president of the most powerful nation in the world—the United States of America. Barack Obama is destined to begin to illuminate the 400 years of the degradation of people of African descent worldwide. People here in Ghana are poised to celebrate just like in the US.*

With a seven-hour difference between Ghana and California, I had to stay up into the early morning waiting for the election results on November 4. Ghanaian television talk shows assembled both Ghanaians and African Americans news commentators, university professors, and NGO heads to pontificate all night about the possible election results and the meaning of Obama having a good chance of becoming president. The moment the election results hit the airwaves, the African and African American men on the show I was watching all broke down on camera, allowing tears to publicly roll down their faces. At the moment of Obama's victory, there was a brief moment of unity throughout Africa and its diaspora, and I witnessed it in those Black men's televised teary faces on Ghanaian television.

When President Barack Obama's victory rally in Chicago's Grant Park was broadcast, with Michelle and their daughters standing by his side, there was not a dry eye in Ghana. His powerful acceptance message transversed thousands of miles, borders, and ethnicities: "If there is anyone out there who still doubts that America is a place where all things are possible, who still wonders if the dream of our founders is alive in our time, who still questions the power of our democracy, tonight is your answer." In 2008 those words traveled around the world instantaneously, and I received them in my living room at the Fulbright House on the campus of the University of Ghana, and I cried too. Gene called me as usual around 7:00 a.m. Ghana time, midnight his time, and we celebrated our collective victory together by phone.

I slept in late the next morning, and when I did rise around 11:00 a.m. I knew I had to organize a celebration at the Department of Dance Studies. I called an elated Oh! Nii Sowah and said, "We have to gather all our dance students and the Ghana Dance Ensemble with the drummers to have a celebration for this momentous world event." Oh! Nii immediately agreed, and I told him I would be at the department at one o'clock, ready to party. By the time I arrived, some of the dancers and drummers had already gathered, but more were needed. Exercising my authority as an elder, I told one of the young female dancers to bring more people to celebrate. As she went off to gather more dancers, the drummers started to play, a sure attraction of more people to the grassy courtyard in the middle of the surrounding departmental classrooms.

The drums did it! As the drummers started their Obama victory rhythm, we began to have an African diaspora dance party numbering thirty dancers and drummers in front of the Department of Dance Studies. Oh! Nii had printed sheets of paper plastered with Obama's campaign slogan in large letters, "YES WE CAN," and distributed them to a few of the revelers. I told the drummers to play *kpanlogo,* the ubiquitous Ga party rhythm that was my signature Ghanaian dance I taught in many US workshops back home. All the dancers fell into kpanlogo movement variations, each taking turns leading the dancing group. Terry Ofosu, my assistant, had worn an American flag shirt, symbolically celebrating a "new America," and I wore my white T-shirt with President Obama's photo emblazoned on the front, as we all danced for our collective victory.

Then I felt we had to dance something *specifically* African American. I told everyone, "OK, y'all, we gonna dance the Electric Slide." I gave the drummers the tempo and told them to play whatever they felt. I led a raucous Electric Slide line dance as we chanted, "Yes, we can, and yes, we did" to the infectious party rhythm. I'm sure it was the only Obama victory party on the Legon campus that day, which was appropriate, as we were the Department of Dance Studies. My 2008 Ghanaian trip was positioning me on a whole new level: I was no longer a young *student* of Ghanaian dance culture as I had been in 1976; I was now an elder *disseminator* of the culture. I had assumed my place as the catalyst and gathered my Ghanaian family together to celebrate our *world* victory: a Black man—Barack Obama—was president of the United States of America.

Figure 6.5. Oh! Nii Sowah, then head of the Department of Dance Studies, and author celebrate President Obama's victory, University of Ghana, Legon, 2008. Photo courtesy of author.

Finishing Dance Courses and Presenting Dunham Technique

I taught my last dance lecture classes in early November, with students who seemingly appreciated my intellectually rigorous courses. I finished the Black Dance History course with my article "Global Breakdancing and the Intercultural Body," explored in chapter 3. I had two colleagues come in as visiting lecturers on hip-hop dance from both sides of the Atlantic: Terry Ofosu gave the young diploma students his assessment of Ghana's adaptation of hip-hop dance and their general popular dance history in Ghana, while my African American friend, Adia Tamar Whitaker, who was visiting Ghana, gave the students her perspectives on the global transference of hip-hop dance. Being a part of the hip-hop generation as well as a dance student from my alma mater, SF State University, she was able to relate to the students from the same generational perspective. Adia went on to form Àṣẹ Dance Theatre Collective, a major New York neo-folkloric performance ensemble specializing in African diaspora material.

To end my Fulbright teaching assignment, I used my students to present a major lecture-demonstration on Dunham Technique on November 13, 2008. "Lecture-Demonstration: Dunham Dance Technique, The Anthropological Model" took place in the Performance Hall, the same venue I had presented my Ghanaian version of "The Evolution of Black Dance" thirty-two years earlier (chapter 5, *DinB*). My dancers were four grad students—Fabiola, Aristides, Afriye, and my one African American student, Eleanor,—as well as three of my undergraduates, Priscilla, Lesley, and Ernest. I used three drummers, Kwaku, Reginald, and Godson. My dance students and the drummers were extremely excited to present a Western dance technique containing elements of their traditional dance, and wanted to demonstrate how an Africanist approach to movement was a worldwide codified concert dance technique.

The presentation drew a packed audience, with all the professors of the Department of Dance Studies present, as well as the late Professor Kwabena Nketia, then ninety years old, as the esteemed elder and founder of the entire School of Performing Arts at Legon. My Ghanaian colleagues comprehended the importance of an institutionalization of an Africanist aesthetic in dance. They also appreciated learning more about Dunham Technique specifically, as they had heard much about it but had not seen a demonstration of it.

I choreographed a beginning Dunham Technique demonstration with formal entrances and exits by the dancers. The program consisted of fall and re-

Figure 6.6. Author (*standing center*) with dancers and drummers after Dunham lecture-demonstration; Professor Kwabena Nketia far right, University of Ghana, 2008. Photo courtesy of author.

covery, flatback, plié hip rotations, as well as torso isolations and progressions across the floor. The drummers provided lively accompanying rhythms they had arranged in advance. The lecture-demonstration was interspersed with my prepared oral description and contextual interludes, which informed the audience about components of Katherine Dunham's life and technique. I emphasized her concept of the integration of mind, body, and spirit that renders the dance technique holistic.

I was particularly proud to have Professor Nketia present to observe my evolution as an artist and educator, as he had witnessed my "Evolution" presentation on the same stage thirty-two years earlier. The presentation offered me a culminating sense of the entire Fulbright residency. It conveyed my accumulated knowledge now as a respected scholar, artist-educator, and Elder, and brought me full circle in my West African home.

Ending the Fulbright Fellowship

After finishing my teaching assignment at the university, I was free to continue my hiplife research during my last month of the Fulbright fellowship. That period allowed me to review my fieldnotes and interviews to discern where I might have gaps in my understanding of the hiplife music and cultural scene in Accra. I appreciated this concentrated research time, as my attention was divided during the previous five months, juggling teaching obligations. I wanted to leave with enough insights to write a substantive book on the dynamics of the relatively new hiplife music scene in the country. I knew the literature on African hip-hop was sparse compared to other areas of the globe, and I realized my hiplife research could provide more focus on the global youth culture in this part of the world.

Luckily, during December a major hip-hop/hiplife concert took place produced by Zain (K.S.C.), a new telecommunications company moving into the Ghanaian cell phone market. Hiplife artists had become a major economic pawn among competitive telecom companies scrambling for the lucrative West African market, and the Zain 026 Experience concert provided the perfect opportunity for me to study this economic aspect of the growing Ghanaian hiplife business. As the first act didn't start until 9:00 p.m., four hours after the advertised time, I was grateful the hiplife artists, whom I wanted to see, were the beginning warm-up acts. The experience was made even worse by the glass barriers that cordoned off each tiered-price seating area, and even lined the entire field, rendering us completely separated from the artists. The concert was a complete disaster, giving me a sense of how the telecommunication companies in Africa were exploiting African pop music artists.

I conceptualized that telecommunications companies in Africa were, in fact, implementing a twenty-first-century neoliberal colonialism that was ultimately detrimental to the artists they were exploiting. This insight became the basis for my chapter in *The Hiplife in Ghana* I called "'Society of the Spectacle': Hiplife and Corporate Recolonization." The Zain concert experience served as proof of the neoliberal economic situation Ghanaian hiplife finds itself in.

On November 27 I gave myself a treat and checked into the Labadi Beach Hotel in Accra on the Atlantic coastline for my sixty-second birthday. The Fulbright House had been adequate for most of my fellowship, except for the nuisance of a major water shortage on the campus. But I wanted to make *this* birthday special, and staying at one of the best hotels in Accra on the scenic Atlantic coast was my present to myself. The Fulbright had allowed me to return to Ghana, which I considered one of the seminal *liberation* sites of my life's journey, and I had earned enough academic "credits" to have the US government pay for my big return. As I relaxed on the beachfront in a hotel lounge chair looking out at the Atlantic Ocean, I was compelled to journal about Ghana's past in relation to my current research:

> *I see the Atlantic as the transporter that took my ancestors away after they walked through the Door of No Return; the Atlantic that eats away at some of their bones who didn't make the journey lying deep at the ocean's bottom; the Atlantic that brought Caribbean sailors, returning with various rhythms called calypso, gombay, and rumba; the Atlantic that brought the Europeans with their greed, thirst for power, global commerce, and their culture: their grand balls with waltzes that attracted poor Ghanaians peering at their "highlife" and began imitating this new white upper class with their own music and dance versions. Today, the same Atlantic Ocean currents bring a mixed bag of new influences and change called hip-hop.*

That day on Labadi Beach I felt I had returned to the Motherland changed, but also the same; I still had the same humility, allowing me to know I still had much to learn about West African culture, even though I was now considered a knowledgeable Elder. I was still a student willing to learn all that Ghana was willing to teach me, and I gave thanks for my West African home.

I reflected deeply on what I had come to Ghana for this time and what I had received, as well as projecting myself into my own personal Afrofuture. I remembered my trip to Burkina Faso to witness Waga Hip Hop 8, the Francophone-oriented hip-hop festival in Ouagadougou. This experience had given me a wider vision of hip-hop in Africa in which to position the specific niche of hiplife in my future book. I knew I would be able to eventually return to lecture on Ghana's hiplife music culture and hopefully bring copies of my newly published book on the subject. I had accomplished what I had come to Ghana for during my half-year Fulbright fellowship, and I was now ready to return home and to Gene.

7

Becoming a Public Intellectual and Celebrating Blackness

Aspiration is realization, and this truth is not recognizable by logic, but by actual experience.

Sengai, Zen Buddhist Monk (1750–1837)

Returning to my teaching position at University of California, Davis (UCD), I had only a three-week transition to get ready for the Winter quarter. Although I had little concentrated time to personally reflect upon my six-month Ghana Fulbright residency, I did give a university-wide talk I called "The Ghanaian-African American Experience," which was very well received by students and faculty alike. And at the end of the quarter the late UCD Chancellor Larry Vanderhoef held a reception in honor of Fulbright scholars at the official chancellor's home, and this became my first time at the abode of the head of the university. The Fulbright was helping me penetrate the upper echelons of university administration.

I gained a new professional confidence, which I not only attributed to my academic training, but also to my teaching and performing dance. Dancing allows one a great sense of embodied assurance through self-presentation that I was now using in the lecture classroom. The moment I walked into the room, I was aware that I was naturally on stage, and I "performed" accordingly, trying to put my students at ease as much as possible. My teaching assistant for that quarter, Education graduate student Lorraine Wilkins, told me how much she enjoyed my teaching style; I was becoming a role model for the next generation of Black graduate students. I knew students responded when you give something of yourself with the lesson delivery, which, in turn, helps them connect to the knowledge you are trying to impart. Part of my teaching philosophy became "be myself" as I transitioned from artist to scholar.

Personal Life Changes

The year 2009 brought major changes in my personal life. My sister Tenola, my mother's fourth daughter to whom she gave her own name, passed from chronic alcoholism and severe liver damage at age fifty-four, on March 27, 2009. We were not shocked, for when she passed, she had been back at the family home with Mom only a few months, after being homeless on the street. Even though she had been a brilliant professional office manager for several corporations and was an empathetic person with a big heart, Tenola had always been Mama's troubled child. She had inherited the disease of alcoholism from her father, my stepfather Herman; but she had pushed alcoholism much further, and eventually could not hold down a job. Now my mother was burying her child, and Tenola's daughter Theresa was burying her mother much earlier than she should have.

To cope with Tenola's death, I focused on remembering the good times I had with my sister. Six years earlier, she had been the only family member present at my *ocha bembe* for my initiation into the Yoruba priesthood; her presence at that important transition in my life showed me her beautiful supportive heart. I remembered going to a SF Alcoholics Anonymous meeting with her to return the support and feeling like she could beat her disease; but in the end she could not. Brenda, Tracey, and I took it hard, but no one took it as hard as Pat, who was only eleven months older than Tenola. They grew up almost like twins, strongly connected to each other mentally and emotionally. I held Pat's hand at the funeral and could feel the deep emotional grief lodged in her heart. All we sisters took responsibility for a different task around the funeral arrangements, and mine was placing the obituary in the newspaper. Part of what I published read: "She was a graduate of Lowell High School and became a much sought after executive assistant for several prominent corporations, including Chevron, Chiron, and FiberGen." We laid our beloved sister, Tenola Yvonne Hall Bennett, to rest on April 3, 2009.

Life taketh and life giveth! That same year, Tenola's daughter Theresa and her husband Jonah Tice had a baby girl on December 10, the day after Theresa's birthday. Ada Mae was a beautiful girl that became my mother Tenola's first great-grandchild. Mine is a family with few offsprings, so it feels like a miracle when a new child comes into the family. I wished Tenola could have seen her grandchild Ada Mae, but I felt she was looking down and smiling.

Also, that year several real estate transactions changed my life. Kimathi and I finally sold the house in Hawai'i in May 2009, after having it on the market for two years. The economy had gone bust in 2008 with the Great Recession, a major national catastrophe that beset the Obama administration just as he took charge of the country. I had lost $10,000 in my retirement account while in Ghana, and we ended up having to sell the Hawai'i house for less than it was worth; that's how bad the economy was. But most importantly, the house sale finally severed all ties between Kimathi and me. We no longer had to negotiate our continuing mutual home ownership, which had become the only remaining link between us.

I took my part of the sale money and put a hefty down payment on the first house bought solely by myself. Luckily, due to the economic market downturn, what I had loss on the Hawai'i home sale I got back as a buyer.

I purchased my new home in Sacramento's Natomas Park neighborhood, just a few miles from my living quarters with Susheel, at a cost much less than the previous owners had paid. Luckily, Susheel was retiring and got a good retirement package from UC Berkeley, allowing my move to not become a financial burden on her. Selling and buying in 2009 gave me a bird's-eye view of the real estate market and the effects of the subprime loan abuses that ushered regular middle-class folks like me into a mild Depression. The Obama administration immediately had a major financial crisis to deal with, including bailing out the big banks and the entire automobile industry. Personally, I used my Yoruba practice to negotiate the financial adversity. Both Esu, the deity of the crossroads, and Oya, the winds of change, helped me make the right moves at the right time to end up on the winning end with my new home in Natomas Park.

The two-story, 2,700-square-foot home, built in 2003, was a real blessing, and I felt like Oya had led me to it. Gene helped me move in and slowly began to set up homestead with me. When I placed my 35" × 35" painting of "Eternal Dancer" by my Auntie Gladys Crampton (chapter 2) on the upstairs hallway wall, I knew I had moved into *my* home. Six weeks later we had a housewarming along with my birthday celebration at my new home, with many loving friends and family members celebrating with us. I had made a new life with a new home, a dream job, and a loving and supportive mate.

Still living and working in Oakland, Gene had assisted me with the big move, helping me pack, set up the new household, and even purchase many of the new appliances I needed. Now that I had my own home, he stayed in Sacramento longer, only leaving to be at work by 7:30 a.m. He got used to driving up and down Interstate 80 with a two-city lifestyle. Luckily, he reached his landmark thirtieth-year retirement mark with the telecom company in August 2009 and retired right before his fifty-seventh birthday. I marveled at the discipline it took him to work in a non-management job in corporate America that long, although I knew I could have never done it.

My career destiny in the arts and education had led me down a completely different path, but now Gene and my different life trajectories had converged. After his formal retirement, Gene stayed in Sacramento for longer periods, leaving his West Oakland property to his long-term tenant who lived in his larger front house. We became a live-in couple, making a life together in Sacramento—he as a retiree and I as a working university professor climbing the academic ladder.

Combining Dance, Hip-Hop, and African American Studies

Dance always remained central to my identity and career. Even when I expanded my research agenda into hip-hop music and culture and taught general African American Studies courses at UC Davis, I continued teaching dance, attending dance conferences, and writing about Black choreographers.

The Dance South LA festival, in which I participated on a panel in 2009, became an occasion to keep one foot in the dance field. The Los Angeles event took place at the Nate Holden Performing Arts Center on West Washington Blvd., and was organized by my old friend James Burks, who worked for the City of Los Angeles Department of Cultural Affairs (chapter 6, *DinB*). The conference focused on enhancing the dance scene of the South LA region and included many of the city's dance movers and shakers, like dance ethnologist Allegra Fuller Snyder and my old colleagues Lula Washington and Linda Yehudin, the co-founder and artistic director of Viver Brazil. Also participating was the great legendary LA dancer Carmen de Lavallade, who started with Alvin Ailey in the Lester Horton Dance Company, as well as noted hip-hop dancer-choreographer Rennie Harris. When the great late choreographer Donald McKayle (1930–2018) came to one of the evening concerts, we all bowed down.

The conference had both a concert and street dance focus, and I contributed my knowledge on both sides of that assumed dichotomy at the conference. I gave a formal presentation on *The Africanist Aesthetic in Global Hip-Hop: Power Moves* and sold copies at a book signing. I also participated on the "International Influences of Hip-Hop" panel, where I offered my hiplife research from the Ghana Fulbright fellowship. At my *Power Moves* book signing, I was honored to have Carmen de Lavallade come to my talk and I gifted her a copy. At the evening performance, the then seventy-eight-year-old Carmen de Lavallade performed her famous "The Creation" by James Weldon Johnson, becoming, for me, the highlight of the entire conference. Carmen de Lavallade's dance was a true testament to the power of a great dance artist performing at every life stage, and she lit up the stage.

Back on the UC Davis campus, ten days later on May 13, I organized and convened an academic panel called "The Meanings of Obama," exploring the historic election of Barack Obama from various scholarly perspectives. We had a standing-room-only audience in our campus Memorial Union venue. Besides myself, I gathered three faculty members from across the UCD campus to investigate Obama from their respective disciplinary viewpoints. Sociologist Nicki King, of the Human and Community Development department, presented his history in the rough and tumble history of Chicago politics in relation to the Black community; and historian Lisa Materson explored Obama across the entire trajectory of his career from state representative to US senator and his presidential campaign. Folklorist Patricia Turner from our department, who focuses on racial dynamics in folklore and popular culture, showed slides of Obama quilts made by Black quilters as excerpts of her then recently published *Crafted Lives: Stories and Studies of African-American Quilters.*

I concluded the academic event with a PowerPoint presentation I called "Barack Obama as a Hip-Hop Generation Pop Icon." I focused on his cool demeanor style, his music playlist, and his use of hip-hop allusions during his campaign. "The Meaning of Obama" became an assembly of scholars exploring Barack Obama from political history to his pop culture breakthroughs, demonstrating the layered meanings of Obama as the first Black president of the United States.

Toggling back and forth between academics and dance, I finished the 2009 spring quarter in Denver at Cleo Parker Robinsons' fifteenth Annual International Summer Dance Institute. Since his retirement Gene started traveling with me to various dance and academic commitments to see more of the country. He began to immerse himself in what I was contributing to the world of dance and academia. In Denver, I taught Dunham Technique to Cleo's company members on a daily basis as well as in the summer youth program. Since I had brought her company to my Black Choreographers Moving Toward the 21st Century in 1989 (chapter 6, *DinB*), as well as our co-producing the 1994 Dunham in Hawai'i Residency (chapter 2), we had remained close. I call her the grand dame of Rocky Mountain dance, for she has built a company, school, and dance institution in Denver—Cleo Parker Robinson Dance—on a vision and a prayer since the early 1970s, and that now exceeds the Denver Ballet. When one says "dance" in Denver, one says "Cleo Parker Robinson."

Two weeks after the Denver dance experience, I was in the St. Louis, Missouri/Edwardsville, Illinois area for our annual Dunham Certification Workshop followed by the Dunham Technique Seminar. Held at Southern Illinois University Edwardsville (SIUE) about twenty-five miles from St. Louis, the Institute of Dunham Technique Certification was then working with the East

St. Louis–based Katherine Dunham Centers for the Arts and Humanities (KDCAH) to present a joint summer workshop for our teacher training and their community dance classes. Albirda and I, along with other certified instructors, held the teacher certification component July 20–24, teaching the chosen certification candidates in Dunham Technique, pedagogy methods, and basic history and theory of the Dunham legacy. My niche had become the history-theory classes, positioning Dunham scholarship as an important component of the training alongside the technique and pedagogy training. As such, I became the chair of the Academic Subcommittee of Certification and, during this period, began to standardize the teaching of her theories of Form and Function, Intercultural Communication, and Socialization Through the Arts.

We stayed in dormitories on the SIUE campus, and luckily our studios and classrooms were air-conditioned, protecting us from the hot, humid Southern Illinois summer. The majority of our classes were held in Katherine Dunham Hall, the home of the campus's Department of Theater and Dance. However, SIUE's dance curriculum had nothing to do with Dunham Technique or legacy, only giving lip service to the Dunham name because she had taught at the university for several years. This was exactly the lack of substantive recognition of the Dunham dance legacy in the larger dance education world that precipitated our certification organization and annual dance seminar.

The annual Dunham Seminar of community dance classes started immediately after we finished the certification workshop, and our candidates for certification were expected to attend to build their required two thousand hours of training in the technique. Ruby Streate, Keith Williams, Theo Jamison, Penny Godboldo, and Rachel Tavernier were the anchor Master Teachers and Certified Instructors teaching the technique classes. Along with Dr. Glory Van Scott, the former Dunham company member who taught a children's theater workshop, we had now become the next generation of trained elder Dunham dancers since the passing of the Master Teachers of the Dunham company—Walter Nicks, Tommy Gomez, Lucille Ellis, and Talley Beatty—and those who were still around, like Vanoye Aikens, who were too elderly to attend anymore.

After also teaching my Dunham history-theory classes for the seminar, I left the SIUE campus for St. Louis to see a huge Dunham exhibit. The exhibit itself, "Katherine Dunham Beyond the Dance," was a massive exhibition by the Missouri History Museum honoring Dunham's life and career, featuring numerous costumes, accessories, paper-mâché theater props and masks, as well as examples of Haitian and African folk art from her collection. The name of the exhibit indicated that the exhibit's scope was "beyond" her famous dance career to also showcase Dunham's anthropological research, global activism, and enduring legacy. It also focused on her work in the St. Louis area after disbanding her company in the mid-sixties. The enormous visual displays encompassed several rooms and was difficult to consume in one visit.

Promoting the exhibition were several ancillary educational events, one of which was the Katherine Dunham Symposium, in which I was the keynote speaker. The afternoon symposium happened in the Missouri History Museum's Lee Auditorium adjacent to the exhibit. My presentation was a reprise of my "Katherine Dunham's Anthropological Model" PowerPoint, emphasizing her Caribbean research inspiring her dance technique and her concept of Form and Function. I focused on how her form and function concept in dance borrows from early anthropology functionalist theory and how she applied it to dance as a social system.

To bring her theory to life I also included a dance demonstration of Dunham Technique. Before leaving Sacramento, my friend Linda Goodrich allowed me to work with four of her Sacramento Black Art of Dance dancers—Nzinga Woods, Michael Smith, Shani Alford, and Angela Dee Alforque. I had set the basic choreography on them back in Sacramento, which included fall and recovery, plié hip rotations, Dunham walks, prances, triplets, the rocking horse, and ending with a short Caribbean-inspired choreographic piece. The dance demonstration took my symposium presentation beyond a history-theory lesson to a dance experience of the Dunham oeuvre, vividly demonstrating how theory and practice work in tandem. "Katherine Dunham's Anthropological Model" revealed the brilliance of dancing the Dunham legacy—how art and scholarship can enhance each other to penetrate the human condition.

Rounding out the symposium, after my lecture-demonstration was a panel of Dunham Certified Instructors. The panelists joining me were Keith Williams, a well-known St. Louis Dunham teacher who was certified along with me by Miss Dunham in 2001; the late Theo Jamison, who became one of Miss Dunham's main teachers and demonstrators at the East St. Louis Performing Arts Training Center; and Ruby Streate, the East St. Louis Master Teacher who was the repository of Dunham choreography and director of the annual seminar. Also joining us on the panel was a white dancer from St. Louis, Sarah Burke, a student of Miss Dunham's and owner of the City Studio Dance Center, where we had held previous annual seminars. The panel consisted of personal anecdotal stories of our time with Miss Dunham and remembrances of the evolution of Dunham Technique. We also revealed the financial and organizational struggles to keep the KDCAH organization going in East St.

Louis. The Dunham Symposium at the Missouri History Museum became an important and informative event. It not only contextualized the Dunham exhibit but illuminated Miss Dunham's profound influence on the St. Louis area.

I continued my hip-hop scholarship the next year in 2010 with several university presentations, including the April "Triggering Change 2: Hip-Hop, Community Engagement & Sites of Empowerment" conference at Hampshire College in Amherst, MA. Several of the attending educators were using my *Power Moves* book in their courses, and many of their students brought me the book to be autographed. I was surprised I was becoming a recognized hip-hop author by students of the culture; but I realized the acknowledgment validated my choice to become a hip-hop scholar in the first place.

I gave the keynote address, "Health, Wealth, Knowledge, Prosperity: Hip-Hop Sites of Empowerment," anchoring the weekend of discussions about hip-hop activism and alternative hip-hop education. I took the audience on a journey through various educational, artistic, and political sites of various hip-hop initiatives and programs throughout the country. Using Public Enemy's famous song, my basic message was "don't believe the hype" about the deleterious effects of commercial hip-hop culture because the on-the-ground youth culture was, in reality, creating dynamic new relationships with education from elementary school to higher education. Moreover, many community programs were engaging youth's creativity while attracting them away from drugs and violence.

The conference's special guest artist was one of the original Rock Steady Crew dancers, Popmaster Fabel (Jorge Pabon), who "dropped science" about hip-hop dance in the South Bronx during the early days. He and I became the Elders at the conference, holding up the art and academic ends, and it was a joy having lively discussions with him about the culture. That hip-hop conference convinced me that I was becoming an authority in the growing academic field of Hip-Hop Studies.

As my reputation grew as a hip-hop scholar, along with my already established credentials in dance, university dance departments exploring the new youth culture also had me as a keynote speaker at their conferences. The Department of Dance in the Claire Trevor School of the Arts at UC Irvine (UCI) invited me to keynote their October 2011 "Hip-Hopracy: Hip-Hop and the University Imagination" two-day conference. It was the brainchild of Dr. Sheron Ama Wray, a Black dance professor who was going up for tenure at the time. The department was the home of the renowned Donald McKayle, and he attended most of the conference activities. Sheron, as I call her, had taken UCI students to Ghana the previous year to "examine the cultural axis between Africa and North America." Her conference mission on the publicity flyer stated: "This research now brings the focus back to the USA. Hip Hop is a form of dance that comes out of the African-American experience, with roots traceable from the continent of Africa to the now diverse ethnicities that practice hip hop as a part of the American family."

Sheron's Ghana Project, as the basis of the Hip-Hopracy conference (I loved the play of words in the conference title), was taking research of Black Atlantic movement connections to a new level. As a Black Britisher with a PhD from the University of Surrey, she views the US from somewhat of an outsider perspective while simultaneously being on the "inside," particularly through her work in jazz improvisation. She has developed a theory and practice called Embodiology that she calls "a neo-African approach to contemporary dance improvisation," discussed further in chapter 8. Under her organization, the entire academic conference subtext became a new approach to the Afrofuture.

My keynote address in Winifred Smith Hall on the afternoon of October 26 was called "Global Hip-Hop Appropriation and the Academy." It set the tone for the two-day conference by illuminating what I called the "quagmire of dance in the liberal arts college." I argued that dance is usually viewed in the academy as a non-knowledge-producing discipline. I also suggested hip-hop dance was a potential saving grace from that quagmire in the age of globalization of the American youth culture defining world popular culture. Hip-hop dance had the potential of revitalizing staid ballet and modern dance curricula by collaborating with the humanities to explore how dance represents embodied knowledge of continually shifting national identities.

I used Sheron Wray's conference to argue how important it is for the academy to recognize how crucial the discipline of dance is for comprehending the totality of hip-hop youth culture, instead of only analyzing rap lyrics as hip-hop's identity. Although hip-hop music had become ubiquitously synonymous with the youth culture, breaking, popping, locking, and house dance forms deserved to be investigated and comprehended. I examined how the youth culture had become co-opted by the capitalist marketplace through the music, while the dance, though also vital in hip-hop's global commercialization, had remained, for the most part, in the hands of communities and creative individuals.

This socioeconomic state of affairs provides the opportunity for dance departments, like UC Irvine's, to help define hip-hop dance's aesthetic dynamics, challenges, and future possibilities. The dance is definitively a part of an Afrofuture that must be explored. That artistic and curricular point was driven home by the inclusion of noted Philadelphia hip-hop dancer-choreographer Raphael Xavier, a former dancer in Rennie Harris Puremovement company, who presented knowledge-based workshops and choreography during the two-day academic hip-hop dance conference. I was proud to be a part of this conference that brought together so many aspects of my own approach to dance and hip-hop.

Finishing Fieldwork in Ghana

However, I still felt I needed more interviews with Ghanaian artists to solidify my perspectives for my new hiplife book I was writing. Hence, in September 2010 Gene and I returned to Ghana for a follow-up, one-month research trip. Upon arrival, we both adjusted much quicker to the cultural shift. Ghana had become my West African home, and I was comfortable being in a social environment surrounded by mostly Black people. Personally, with all the people we knew, from academics to artists, it was easy to fit in and immediately start my work.

We stayed in the East Legon district at Catters Hostel located at the Shiashie intersection, not far from the campus. This location put us right in the mix of urban Accra rather than the rarefied environment of the UH-Legon campus. As soon as we stepped outside onto Lagos Avenue, taxi drivers started honking at the sight of my light brown skin, which equates in their minds as dollars. Being near the Legon campus, the Accra Mall, and Accra proper made it relatively easy to travel to interviews, club dates, and concerts. Also, we were right around the corner from Chez Afrique, Michael Williams's restaurant and club (chapter 5), where we would often meet my Atiso Ghanaian family, who had changed their surname to Ahadzi.

From my previous six-month Fulbright research, I had gotten to know the main players in the hiplife music scene. I hired Terry Ofosu as my formal research assistant to introduce me to any new artists I needed to interview to flesh out my research. I had already contacted Reggie Rockstone, so he knew to expect me. He granted me two extra interviews at his home, which allowed me to fill in the gaps of his seminal origin story, as well as his perspective on the development of hiplife in Ghana. Terry insisted I meet two third-generation artists who were big on the scene in 2010: Trigmatic and Sarkodie, the latter of which Akon, the famous Senegalese American singer, had recently signed to his Konvict Entertainment label. Terry felt they would both give me a stronger sense of the various splinter genres emerging within this newer generation of hiplife musicians.

I decided to add a gender and women's dimension to my research, which I had not consciously done before. Even though there were a few women involved in what was then called Afro-Pop, a derivative of hiplife, artists like Mzbel (Nana Akua Amoah), Eazzy (Mildred Ashong), and Mimi (Wilhelmina Abu-Andani) were making waves negotiating various female brands, like the Western-oriented "Sex Siren" as well as the Indigenous "African Diva." An extensive 2010 interview with Mimi and a brief encounter with Eazzy gave me some insights into how female artists saw themselves in Ghanaian pop music.

I also began to identify what I called the "global-local problematic," the synthesis of inherited American hip-hop with one's local Indigenous identity, in relation to hiplife female emcees and singers. This would add an entirely new dimension to my profiles of the ubiquitous Ghanaian male hiplife artist. With new gender and globalization perspectives, I now felt ready to begin pulling together the bits and pieces of my research into what would become *The Hiplife in Ghana.*

Bringing Artists to UC Davis: Blitz, Ntozake, Rennie

Throughout my eleven years teaching at University of California, Davis, I combined my teaching and administrative skills by bringing various artists and scholars to campus that advanced my scholarship. The week of May 22, 2010, I created and produced "Spreading the Word: Hip-Hop in Ghana & the US," two hip-hop events on campus for the annual Black Family Week. That Wednesday I screened the hiplife documentary *HomeGrown: HipLife in Ghana,* a recognized film on hiplife music by my old UC Berkeley student Eli Jacobs-Fantauzzi (chapter 2). His film showcases the hiplife music movement in Ghana through the lens of Vision in Progress, one of the first-generation hiplife groups in Accra. In the film, Eli follows the three-member group, who hail from Accra's Nima district, over a ten-year period.

Preceding the film screening, I gave a PowerPoint presentation on Ghana's hiplife music, growing out of my 2008 Fulbright research. The combination of my slides and the *Homegrown* film gave students on campus a tangible sense of how their generation's pop music had influenced West Africa, and how hiplife music had become a whole new branch of hip-hop. I used my university resources to support one of my past student's work in my research field and exposed his artistry to the UC Davis campus. Regarding the theme of the "Spreading the Word" project, I wrote this in my journal: *I wanted to demonstrate the source of "the Word" in Africa—the continent's rhythmically potent word power now has the world performing the mind/body/spirit connection through hip-hop youth culture. It is truly a new "arc of mutual inspiration" growing from the internationalization of hip-hop.* Our closing Q&A with the student audience helped reveal the sociopolitical links—the connective marginalities—that are implicit within the globalization of hip-hop.

The second part of my "Spreading the Word" week happened that Saturday on the culminating Black Family Day, occurring annually on the grassy UCD Quad. I produced the Ghanaian emcee and band leader Blitz the Ambassador (Samuel Bazwule),[1] who had flown in from New York for the music gig and hooked up with his West Coast musicians to present his own brand of hiplife and Afrobeat music. Blitz is a consummate musician, who composes his own music, blending highlife, salsa, R&B, Afrobeat, and hip-hop. His rap style is rapid-fire in delivery laced with heavy social commentary, while his music production has a horn-based sound counterpointing his rap flow. His sound reminds me of the US hip-hop group The Roots and Nigeria's late Fela Kuti in one contemporary remix. The students loved his music, dancing on the grassy Quad area in front of a makeshift constructed stage. American and African students alike appreciated Blitz's unique blend of hip-hop featuring musical connections from throughout the African diaspora. At the end of Blitz's concert, I felt I had brought great art and my research together in a dynamic mix of events. In the process the music cultures produced by Africa and its diaspora were brought a little closer together, which is what I had been doing in different ways throughout my career. Now, I had a strong academic reputation and university resources behind that endeavor.

I used my UC Davis resources again when I produced "An Evening with Ntozake Shange" on February 22, 2011. Taking place in Freeborn Hall, the African Continuum and Campus Unions collaborated to honor one of my closest friends on campus. Ntozake, the famous poet-playwright, had given me my African name, had danced with me during the Black Arts Movement in the early seventies, and then went on to Broadway with her unforgettable *For Colored Girls Who Have Considered Suicide When the Rainbow Is Enuf* (chapter 4, *DinB*). Tyler Perry's movie *For Colored Girls* had recently premiered the year before with its all-star cast, including Loretta Devine, Janet Jackson, Kimberly Elise, Whoopie Goldberg, Thandie Newton, and Tessa Thompson. The national buzz around Ntozake and her most famous play was prominently in the air when she came to UC Davis, making it the perfect time to produce an evening with her on campus.

We made the event a part of the Leslie Campbell Legacy Speaker Series, and I worked closely with Lori J. Fuller, a member of the African Continuum and Student Affairs. Together we orchestrated a well-rounded event for my famous friend. After welcoming remarks, we opened with a "For Colored Girls Dance Tribute," poetry by students with whom I had been working, followed by my introduction of Ntozake that was both formal and personal, making sure everyone knew the special relationship we shared.

The centerpiece was, of course, Ntozake reading her selected poems, followed by a conversation between Ntozake and me. I asked her questions about her continuing prolific writing career as well as her past connection to the SF-Oakland Bay Area. She had moved back to Oakland in 2006 for a few years, which is when I became aware of her ill health in this part of her life. She had survived a stroke and, after a lengthy recuperation, was doing better. Even with her slightly slurred speech from the stroke, she was in good form, demonstrating her profundity and wit about all kinds of subjects from African diasporic culture to sexism, and from the joy of dance to the magic of poetry. Ntozake finished the event with a book signing, where audience members could chat with her. "An Evening with Ntozake Shange" turned out to be another of our treasured grand reunions during our lifetime friendship.

My dance and hip-hop work converged on April 26, 2011, when I brought the international-famous hip-hop dancer-choreographer Rennie Harris to campus for a dance workshop. The Artistic Director of Philadelphia's Rennie Harris Puremovement dance company delivered his street dance knowledge to my students in AAS/DRA 155 African American Dance and Culture of the US, Brazil, and the Caribbean course. I taught this cross-listed African American Studies and Theatre and Dance course every two years to students from both departments. Always blending theory and practice, I devised the lecture-based course with three required dance labs, abandoning the lecture hall and holding class in a dance studio to practice the dance from each of the three culture areas in the course content.

Rennie was perfect for the US dance lab, as his whole approach to hip-hop dance is its foundation in all the previous Black social dance forms. He combines Black social dance history with the hip-hop staples of locking, popping, elementary breaking, and house dance. His is not the popular hybrid video rap dance taught in many studios, but rather the authentic building blocks straight from the streets. Not only did he impress the students with his historical knowledge and rhythmic dexterity, but also the UCD director of dance who had come to observe his class. The late dancer-choreographer Della Davison was so impressed, she offered him a Granada Fellowship for the following year to set a work on the department's dance majors.

I had published a book chapter, "The Dance Archaeology of Rennie Harris: Hip-Hop or Postmodern?" about Rennie and his seminal contribution to dance: elevating hip-hop dance to a concert form:

> Rennie Harris is a hip-hop concert choreographer. If this sounds like an oxymoron, then you have not seen his critically acclaimed dance works. Harris shatters the high art (read ballet and modern dance) and low art (read popular street dance) paradigm in a definitive style that challenges our notions of modernism in dance.[2]

My dance and hip-hop scholarship converged with my practitioner's understanding of the art of dance in the Rennie Harris campus dance workshop.

The Ceremony of Black Graduation

I finished the 2011 school year by participating in the June "Black Graduation Ceremony," one of the specialized ethnic graduations that have become a tradition on many college campuses. Students participate in the regular baccalaureate, as well as a culturally focused one among their own culture group. Parents and the general community attend a Black-oriented ceremony that is not only culturally specific, but also acknowledges many of the particular challenges and triumphs in an inherently racist white educational institution. Most of the faculty in our African American and African Studies (AAS) Program attended, as we are often called on to become unofficial advisors to many of our African, Caribbean, and African American students, helping them matriculate to the point of graduation. Many of these students, particularly those in the sciences, complained of incessant microaggressions from faculty and fellow students, as well as outright racism. They would come to the AAS conference room to study in Hart Hall just to be in a supportive Black environment among other students who looked like them. Black graduation became a triumphant celebration over racial battles fought during their time at the university.

Held in Jackson Hall of the Mondavi Center for the Performing Arts, cultural specificity began immediately at the Black Graduation with the faculty, staff, and student processional into the venue and onto the stage. Although the faculty usually walked in a straightforward dignified manner, students danced to the accompanying celebratory rhythmic R&B music. They often sprinkled in Black fraternity and sorority stepping moves to announce their specific affiliations. During the diploma conferring ceremony, our students didn't just walk across the stage to receive their reward, they swaggered across stage while performing the latest Black social dance or culturally specific dances, such as the Eskista shoulder dance, a signature move of the Ethiopians.

Black dance becomes a cultural marker for the entire Black Graduation event. Performance Studies scholar Anita Gonzalez puts the typical Black graduation spectacle in perspective: "The arts provide representation and visibility for disenfranchised populations, promote wellness, and reinforce community bonds when people actively participate in them. Communities fighting for racial justice use the arts to humanize their experiences and tell stories of their struggle and resilience, which is important because it activates, creating empathy for those with differing life experiences."[3] Dance during our Black Graduation indeed became a celebratory healing tool, not just for the students, but for the entire community. It vividly offered a celebratory symbol of the triumph of the Black family, overcoming significant external and internal odds meant to dissuade this victorious event from ever happening.

I felt particularly proud sitting on stage with our graduating Black students. As I looked out at the sea of Black families, I realized they were all using this communal ceremony to acknowledge a meaningful step toward realizing the illusive "American Dream."

Returning to Galveston, Family Reunions, and Remembering Juneteenth

I need to backtrack in time to remember my family reconnections and to position my birthplace roots in my career story. Right after finishing the spring 2010 quarter, in early June I returned to Galveston, Texas, enabling Gene to experience the city of my birth that he had only heard about from my childhood stories. One main historical distinction about Galveston is that it is the first site of the celebration of Black freedom—the home of Juneteenth.

Juneteenth is an African American holiday commemorating the end of US slavery. Celebrated yearly on June 19, it was that day in 1865 that Major-General Gordon Granger of the Union army read General Order No. 3, commemorating the end of the Civil War to the enslaved Black people of Galveston, and they immediately began celebrating. Being an island just off the mainland coast near Houston, they were not made aware of the Emancipation Proclamation that was issued two years earlier during the Civil War. The deliberate withholding of freedom from Galveston slaves, in order get another season of free labor, became the impetus for the only celebration memorializing the end of the institution of chattel slavery in the United States.

The union army's victory and the freeing of mainland enslaved people could no longer be ignored. General Order No. 3 read:

> The people of Texas are informed that, in accordance with a proclamation from the executive of the United States, all slaves are free. This involves an absolute equality of personal rights and rights of property between former masters and slaves.[4]

With this notice, the Reconstruction era of Texas began, and Galveston Island became the home of what was eventually named Juneteenth because of the date Granger read the proclamation. However, it didn't become an official Texas holiday until 1979, nearly 115 years later. I was always aware of my birthplace's significance in African American history, particularly when I became more aware of Black history in my late teens and would periodically return to Galveston, seeing the plaques and historical markers everywhere commemorating Juneteenth.

Our 2010 trip was for a major family reunion. Brenda and her then fiancé Frank arrived from Los Angeles, and my father Leroy, who had moved back to his hometown of Bay City, Texas, all converged with Gene and me onto the family gathering. The family reunion was actually my stepmother's, Esther Franklin Anderson, my father's second wife from my childhood before we moved to San Francisco in the late fifties. Her family was having a huge Franklin family reunion in nearby Texas City, and we were there to support her. Esther and I were always very close; whenever I told her, "I love you," she always responded, "I love you more." A loving chocolate brown woman with a round face and prominent cheekbones, Esther was my second mother; Brenda and I truly loved her and wanted to show her that at the Franklin family reunion.

We arrived the day before the reunion, and Gene and I, along with Brenda and Frank, were able to take her out to dinner for some exclusive time before the family gathering. Our father Leroy joined us at the family reunion the next day. I remembered my Papa Leroy living in Houston after he and my mother Tenola had divorced when I was about five years old. She would put her daughters on a Greyhound bus in Galveston, and he and Esther would pick us up at the Houston bus station to spend the weekend with them. This entire Texas trip became a journey back into my deepest roots, to the young life of Janis Miller, before the career mission of Halifu Osumare was even conceived.

While in Texas, Brenda and I also visited our uncle Melvin, brother to Leroy. Melvin was a veteran of the Korean War who had lost his hearing during that conflict, and was now living in a nursing home in their hometown of Bay City. At eighty-three years old, my father had moved back there to be closer to his brother. But I could see that my father was not happy. He was the only child of his mother Ethel Wallace who had escaped the pettiness of the small southern town of Bay City, and was discovering it is not always possible to go back home harmoniously.

In hindsight, that return home to Texas, and Galveston in particular, was to further grasp my origins in the home of Juneteenth. Right after I got back home to Sacramento, there seemed to be a renewed interest in the commemoration as the only national remembrance of the end of the dark history of United States slavery. Sacramento's main newspaper, *The Sacramento Bee,* contacted me for an interview about the meaning of Juneteenth. The reporter,

Anna Tong, told me most people had heard the name but knew very little about its meaning. I told her I understood that the United States conveniently had what I call "historical amnesia" that facilitates the illusion of the American Dream. We expediently forget the horrors of the nation's past in favor of focusing on the lofty founding principles that we're still struggling to realize. This can be witnessed today in the anti-woke movement, where conservatives ban books to deliberately keep the populous from learning historical facts.

Tong used quotes from me as professor of African American and African Studies to highlight the US's problem with its sordid history: "[Juneteenth] isn't a part of our current-day popular memory," she said. "It's indicative of how we as Americans see slavery in this country as ancient history, yet it really isn't—it's only been 150 years."[5]

Luckily, the actual holiday of June 19 landed on a Saturday that year, and an Oya priest, Wanda Ravernell, called our spiritual community to a Juneteenth celebration at Oakland's Lake Merritt near the Boathouse Picnic Area. Wanda and her husband, bata drummer Tobaji Steward, founded the Omnira Institute, a cultural organization that sponsors an annual Juneteenth communal gathering. I attended as a Yoruba priest to this event and participated in the open-air ceremonial celebration. Wanda's vision for Juneteenth was multicultural, beginning with a First Nation chant by a Native American Elder. The ceremony continued with a libation to the ancestors, including calling the names of historic leaders and even names of recorded slave ships. Named "Juneteenth Jubilee!," the event was a serious ceremonial historical remembrance.

The centerpiece of the entire Juneteenth commemoration was an ancestral ring shout, the historical dance and song ritual blending Christian songs with a counterclockwise dance circle of celebrants, which began on the slave plantation. Wanda's ring shout participants were her organized priests and community people called Awon Ohun Omnira, who invoked the circular ceremony with the famous ring shout song "Kneebone Bent." The song refers to the difference between life and death, with its refrain "gimme de kneebone bent." When one dies, one is horizontal and the knees are straight and stiff; when one is alive and upright, the knees are bent, allowing the hips and the entire body to move freely to celebrate life. As historian Peter Woods has said:

> White masters probably heard this line ["gimme de kneebone bent"] as a compliant acceptance of the need for a Christian posture of prayer. But slaves themselves no doubt understood the phrase more fully as clear reinforcement of their own ancestors' values. Many West Africans believed that straightened knees, hips, and elbows epitomized death

and rigidity, while flexed joints embodied energy and life. The bent kneebone symbolized the ability to "get down."[6]

Wanda encircled the African ceremonial with prayers from many other traditions. After Yoruba and vodun prayers, which included Luisah Teish and Nedra Williams, there were invocations from other spiritual traditions. Hence, Juneteenth Jubilee! was culturally inclusive, commemorating the end of slavery of our African ancestors while including various spiritual observances of America as it has developed and come to be known.

With the inclusion of Abrahamic traditions, including Judaism, Christianity, and Islam, along with Asian traditions—Taoism and Siddha Yoga—I realized Wanda Ravernell's approach to Juneteenth was in the tradition of the way I had organized my Oakland dance center: celebrate Blackness in the context of its place in the multicultural reality of social change and justice. The latter component of social justice was in keeping with her Oya priesthood. One month later I celebrated my seventh Okuodon (ocha birthday) as Oyadamilola, "Oya Gives Me Wealth," and reflected on the changes in my life: a divorce, a new partner, a dream academic job, and my own beautiful home. I was indeed "rich."

The year 2011 started with another major change. My father Leroy had finally gotten enough of his relatives in Bay City and wanted to return to California to live with Gene and me. Leroy Miller had not been a father who nurtured me as a growing child (my stepfather had taken on that role). But I felt I needed to take care of him in his elder years. He arrived in January and moved into our ground-floor guest room with an adjacent bath. Because he and Gene had already established their relationship before he moved from Texas, we all settled into a live-and-let-live three-way relationship that was comfortable. In the beginning, he could take care of almost all his needs; I only had to manage his medical care and finances. He had a mild case of prostate cancer that he had never revealed, and I took him to Oakland for his regular urology appointments. I found him a Sacramento Black Baptist church that became his Sacramento community, members of which picked him up every Sunday for service. He had become more religious since his Mama Ethel died, and although he never said, I knew he had promised her that he would begin attending church again regularly.

Gene and I continued building our relationship while occasionally seeing after Bubber (Leroy's nickname). Gene was beginning to spend more time with his own painting and won first prize in The Art of Living Black annual exhibit that year. His "Looking In, Looking Out" 18" × 22" acrylic painting was a captivating headshot of a reflective Black man, which I interpreted as himself. Even though I became more aware of the aging process due to my growing osteoarthritis in my knees, my personal life was good, filled with family, and I was happy!

A Public Intellectual: Bringing My Scholarship to Community

As an academic, I always focused on the fact that ethnic studies dictate that one's scholarship must impact the community for social change; hence, I felt obligated to make my research relevant to my local community, offering several lecture-talks in Sacramento. In February 2011, a few days after the Ntozake poetry event at UCD, I gave a public presentation on what had become my central research concept: the importance of the Africanist aesthetic. It was at the Crocker Art Museum, which is Sacramento's largest art institution founded in 1872 and has become a California historical landmark. My talk, "The Africanist Aesthetic in Performing & Visual Arts," was a part of the museum's Open Art series and was presented in collaboration with the Kuumba Collective Art Gallery, in which Gene and I had become members, along with the Sacramento Chapter of the Links, Inc. My talk became one of the first lectures in the Crocker's 125,000-square-foot Teel Family Pavilion, a new modern addition to the Victorian-era museum.

My lecture illuminated the unifying artistic principles at the basis of African dance, music, sculpture, and textile design. The museum had recently featured "Mud Cloth Madness," an exhibit showcasing the famous Malian fabric with its intricate geometric designs made from dye with fermented mud. The Crocker's education director, African American Stacey Shelnut-Hendrick, brought me to give cultural context and philosophy behind African cultures producing the design concept. Although my expertise is in the performing arts, Gene and I both are collectors of African art. More importantly, I was steeped in African art historian Robert Farris Thompson's aesthetic concept of "African art in motion," connecting performing and visual art throughout the African continent.

A post-lecture article appeared in Sacramento's Black newspaper, *The Sacramento Observer*, which emphasized my connection to both academia and the community, as well as my ability to link African principles to contemporary popular culture: "Osumare demonstrated to attendees how art, dance and music are steeped in African traditional principles . . . The greater message of her lecture explored the connections between these arts forms and how they correlate to modern social and popular culture."[7]

I continued to make my research relevant to contemporary issues. A few months later, I wrote an editorial for The *Sacramento Bee* using my hip-hop scholarship. At the time, conservative pundits were using cultural double standards to criticize President Barack Obama's presumed cultural shift reflected in the artistic events he held at the White House. In Black communities the colloquial joke was that the Obamas had turned the White House into the "Black House." And it was common knowledge that Obama was a hip-hop fan, with a playlist including many commercial and so-called conscious emcees.

On May 11 of that year, the Obamas held an "Evening of Poetry" at the White House that included the well-known Chicago rapper Common (a.k.a. Lonnie Rashid Lynn). Fox News pundits Sarah Palin, Karl Rove, and Sean Hannity lambasted Common's inclusion as poor "judgement on inviting someone who would glorify cop killing during Police Memorial Week, of all times." They continued lambasting Obama's choice of Common as "lacking in class and decency," and calling the rapper "a ghetto radical," "a thug," and "dangerous."

My editorial article, "Attacks Against Rapper Are Smoke Screen for Larger Issues," was a rejoinder to this obvious racialized assessment of Common. My argument relied on the issue of the artistic license artists should be allowed, as well as comparing some of Common's objectionable lyrics to similar hyperbolic rhetoric used by right-wing politicos themselves. Specifically, the two raps objected to by the Fox News commentators were Common's "A Letter to the Law" (2007) and "A Song for Assata" (2008), the latter of which is about the convicted Black Panther exiled in Cuba. A line in "Letter" states, "Tell the law, my Uzi weighs a ton," and the artist also references George W. Bush: "Burn a Bush cos' for peace he no push no button." My critical analysis in "Attacks Against Rapper" reads:

> These lines [by Common] are being interpreted as a cop killing threat and suggested harm to the president of the U.S. But aren't metaphor and symbolism engaged in service to one's political worldview used on the Right as well? Did not Palin come under fire by using her popular phrase, "Don't retreat, reload," at a time when the Tucson, Arizona shooting of U.S. Rep. Gabrielle Giffords had people against talking about gun control? Yet Palin does not allow the same artistic license when assessing an artist whose field is known for hyperbolic imagery to make a point.[8]

I continued my rejoinder by using white political critic Tim Wise's comparative take on the disparity when conservatives give a pass to other music genres considered "white" music. I wrote, "Cultural critic Tim Wise noted on CNN that America has a 'racial disparity in how we view music,' calling our attention to how we do not hold country musicians, such as the late Johnny Cash, who had many lyrics about killing and use of guns, to the same standard. Instead, Cash was given a Kennedy Center Honor for Lifetime Achievement in the Arts."[9]

I used this editorial article in Sacramento's main newspaper to point out the racial disparities in how conservative commentators treated the two-term Obama administration. It became another example in the counterargument that we were far from a post-racial society, a concept that many, during that era, were toying with. This was nearly ten years before the 2020 brutal George Floyd murder and the era of US racial reckoning and protests. In this way, I occasionally used my hip-hop scholarship to publicly address contemporary cultural and racial inequities.

One of my most treasured memories of my public sharings in Sacramento was my involvement with the November 12, 2011 event "An Evening with Amiri Baraka and Ben F. Jones." The great poet and leader of the Black Arts Movement, Amiri Baraka was brought to Sacramento by Evolve The Gallery, a visual arts business owned by Brady and Michelle Blakeley. This couple had come to the city only a year earlier and took Black visual arts to a whole new level of professional visibility. Gene and I had been to several of their exclusive exhibits with high-end art, and he had bought several of their works. In the process we had all become personal friends. But the event with the late great Amiri Baraka (1934–2014) and the internationally renowned fine artist Ben F. Jones was of another caliber.

Michelle and Brady had rented a live-work space in Oak Park near Kevin Johnson's Underground Bookstore and the Guild Theater, turning their small studio space into a ground-level art gallery with the second floor as their well-appointed studio apartment. For the big event they rented the two-hundred-seat Guild Theater and it became a sold-out public event, followed by a VIP showing of Jones's art at their gallery. "An Evening with Amiri Baraka and Ben F. Jones" was truly a prestigious affair, including a panel discussion moderated by me with the two artists and a poetry reading by Baraka that included local award-winning jazz bassist Harley White, Jr.

Being a part of the Sacramento artistic and intellectual literati, Brady and Michelle invited Gene and me to a pre-event dinner at their studio home the night before, allowing us to talk and break bread with Baraka and Jones in a relaxed, casual setting. As a poet himself, Gene had previously founded his own Oakland poetry organization, and Amiri Baraka was one of his heroes. The Evolve gallery's VIP home dinner with the artists and board members allowed Gene to query Baraka about poetry, the Black Arts Movement, and contemporary politics. We all discussed the Obama administration as well as art and poetry and later received a preview of Jones's work on exhibit that focused on the fusion of spirituality and politics.

Listed on the program as "Scholar and Artist," I was honored to convene the public discussion with the two great artists on the stage of the Guild Theater the next afternoon. I had prepared my questions in advance because I wanted to make sure I covered key issues embedded in the work of these two great American artists. I focused my questions on the theme of "revolution and the revolutionary," exemplified in the Black political era of the sixties that used art as a recruitment tool into the political process. I also asked Baraka, in particular, about the place of the "Black Houses," cultural centers across the country during the late sixties and early seventies Black Arts Movement. I had first been introduced to that movement by him at the San Francisco Black House in 1966 (chapter 1, *DinB*). Also, Jones had spent much time in Cuba, and had developed a strong point of view about that country's revolution in relation to their artists.

I also wanted to make sure I got the two elder artists to discuss contemporary hip-hop, particularly whether Baraka thought it was the "new Black Arts Movement." As elder statesman, he articulated that his sixties Black Arts Movement was against the establish social order, whereas hip-hop had become a part of the established order. But I countered by listing those artists whose work was offering counternarratives, like Common, Mos Def, Lupe Fiasco, Lauryn Hill, and Jean Grae. Ben Jones talked about the work of Jean-Michel Basquiat, a New York artist coming of age in the early hip-hop era, as also critiquing the social order in painting after starting as a street graf artist. We arrived at the conclusion that hip-hop was far more complicated regarding resistance and complicity with the status quo. This complexity is central to the digital late capitalist era, making the concept of the Afrofuture equally multifacetedly intricate.

I also brokered the subject of the place of improvisation in Black culture, a major topic of Baraka, as he often read his poetry to live jazz music. He was known for improvising around the interplay of the two genres, often uttering his words like another musician. This is exactly what the audience experienced when Amiri Baraka ended the afternoon program with a reading of his latest poems to the improvisational stylings of bassist Harley White, Jr. The next day I wrote the following in my journal: *There were a few young artists in attendance, but the audience was primarily baby boomers who are trying to make sense of our previous revolutionary era and today's convoluted, complex globally interconnected capitalist world. This event was a great culmination of my public presentations. They have given me the chance to share my perspectives with the general public on our culture. I don't want my knowledge to remain only in the hallowed halls of academia, only being heard by a small cadre of scholars. I want to share my knowledge and perspectives publicly.*

Director of African American and African Studies

In September 2011 I assumed the role of director of my academic unit at UC Davis. African American and African Studies (AAS) was a program at the time, rather than a department. We were the last of the ethnic studies units in Hart Hall to apply to the Academic Senate for departmental status. Hence, my title was director instead of chair. As all Ethnic Studies departments in the US, our unit was the result of the late sixties fight for Black, Native American, Chicano/a, and Asian American Studies on college campuses, the activism for which started at my alma mater, SF State University (chapter 1, *DinB*). Assuming my directorship, I vowed to transition AAS to departmental status.

But almost immediately a campus "storm" emerged. A national protest took over the nation, with college campuses at the epicenter: "Occupy Wall Street." The following is what I wrote in my journal about it: *The American people have finally woken up enough to take class action, and it is no surprise that the "Occupy Wall Street" movement has found its epicenter in Oakland and the Bay Area, the home of the Black Panthers, the Free Speech Movement, and the ethnic studies movement. It is a class protest that has been long overdue. The richest 1 percent of the population has over 40 percent of the wealth; many corporations are firing Americans and outsourcing jobs abroad yet making record profits; the country has soaring unemployment, and corporate CEOs take home millions-of-dollar bonuses. It is time for the masses to say enough is enough, and students are a big part of the constituency of the nation-wide protests.*

On the UC Davis campus students had begun occupying Mrak Hall, the central administrative building, protesting increasing tuition hikes to balance decreasing state university funding of the UC system. As I watched the "Occupy" movement erupt on campus, with tents being set up on the grassy Quad right outside my office window, I was happy to witness another major student-led movement like in the sixties. Students began cutting class, and sympathetic faculty held alternative classes on the Quad, some in which I participated. Bruce D. Haynes, a Black sociology professor asked me to give a talk at one of his Quad classes on the history of student activism, and I joined his makeshift class, sitting in an egalitarian manner on the ground in the round. I shared my experience at SF State back in the ancient days of 1968, focusing on the place of the Black Studies movement in our historic protest. Students were truly engaged, asking many questions to clarify their contemporary protest approach. It was an exciting way to reinvent education, and I was all in!

What started as a national protest movement of unequal distribution of wealth, the place of Wall Street, and general class inequality also grew into a new attack on higher education itself. The UC and California state university campuses were all "occupied" with tent cities, teach-ins, and takeovers of central university administration buildings. The growing national movement all came to a head right at UCD on November 18, 2011, on the Quad: the infamous UC Davis "Pepper Spray Incident." After asking sit-in student protesters to leave a paved area of the campus Quad, a university policeman pepper sprayed a group of student demonstrators. A video of officer Lt. John Pike in the act of spraying went viral, with memes invented of him holding the can spraying everything from the Peanut cartoon's Snoopy to Sleeping Beauty and the Statue of Liberty itself. The level of media attention the UCD pepper spray incident garnered demonstrated the growing power of video and social media to make an ordinary person famous or, in this case, infamous. This incident became a defining moment in the entire occupy movement.

Although nowhere near the atrocity of the 1970 Kent State student massacre, after the UC Davis pepper spray incident, large protests spread across the nation against the use of that kind of attack against peaceful student protesters. Students felt UCD campus police had acted against the university administration's orders against any arrests or use of force. The pepper spray incident prompted public debate about the militarization of the police against peaceful protesters; of course, freedom of speech and First Amendment rights were also raised. The UCD chancellor at the time, Linda Katehi, apologized to the students, saying the police had acted against her orders, but the whole incident prompted her eventual undoing, as probes into her entire running of UCD came into question. In the end, after much legal wrangling in a federal lawsuit, the three dozen student demonstrators were collectively awarded a $1 million settlement by UC Davis, with individual students receiving $30,000, covering only one year of tuition.

For African American and African Studies and the other ethnic studies departments in Hart Hall, the UC Davis pepper spray incident became a rallying cry for equity and justice in higher education, as well as the freedom of students and faculty to participate in the free debate of ideas and reform of the nation. We formed the Hart Hall Social Justice Initiative Committee that brought the ethnic studies, women's studies, cultural studies, and American Studies departments and programs together in an unprecedented political unification. We held classes, seminars, and panels about issues of free speech and more racial justice in higher education. As director of African American and African Studies, I became a major player at our once-a-week meetings of the newly formed committee.

The Hart Hall committee worked for several months to convene a "Teach-In" on February 23, 2012, at the Arc Pavilion, the biggest venue on campus where graduation ceremonies occur, to an audience of over one thousand. The event was titled "Social Justice in the Public University of California: Reflections and Strategies," and we brought Professor Angela Davis to campus as our keynote speaker to illuminate contemporary issues growing out of the Occupy Movement around academic freedom, the so-called security state, the corporatization of the public university, and the history of people of color protest movements. The Social Justice Initiative Committee members in attendance at our momentous event were Amina Mama (Women and Gender Studies, now Gender, Sexuality, and Women's Studies), Inés Hernández-Ávila (Native American Studies), and me from African American and African Studies. Chicano/a Studies was also involved, but their chair could not attend the event. We got the dean of our academic units to contribute funds for the Teach-In, supplemented by small contributions from each department, to hire Angela Davis, who, for us, represented the quintessential academic example of an intellectual of color who had "paid her dues" in the trenches of protest, being on the FBI's 1970 Ten Most Wanted list, and forty years later had emerged as a UC Santa Cruz professor.

I was elected to be Mistress of Ceremonies and introduce my friend Angela, who had once been my dance student at Everybody's Creative Arts Center, and whom I had not seen since she gave her 1998 talk at the University of Hawai'i (chapter 2). In my introductory remarks I used a call-to-action phrase common at the time. I wanted to impress upon the large gathering of students, faculty, and staff the concept for which Angela had always been an exemplar: "Democracy is not a spectator sport."

Angela Davis galvanized the large crowd with her pithy analysis of the state of higher education and the need for academia to be on the side of social justice and freedom of speech. She also used personal anecdotes to drive home the point that social justice and change are, in fact, inevitable. Having grown up in Birmingham, Alabama, during apartheid-like segregation, her mother had always told her, "This is not the way things are supposed to be, and they will not always be this way." She had spent her whole life trying to make her mother's pronouncement come true. The Hart Hall Social Justice Teach-In in February 2012 became the culmination of the three-month long Occupy Movement on the UC Davis campus.

"Life is what happens in between the plans you make!"

I have always had an internal mantra that tells me, "Life is what happens in between the plans you make," and that certainly became true when Gene's mother, Frankie Mae Howell, passed away on December 14, 2011. In the midst 1) of my running the AAS program and planning the Teach-In, 2) Gene's mother had finally transitioned from Alzheimer's disease, and I immediately went into assistance mode for Gene. She had been diagnosed in 2005 and progressively deteriorated mentally and physically over the ensuing six years. I had met her soon after meeting Gene (chapter 4) and observed her slow decline. A month after, we held the memorial service at Colonial Chapel in Oakland.

Gene asked me to speak at her January 2012 funeral to talk about her spirit, and I was honored to be one of the few formal presenters at Frankie Mae Howell's funeral, calling my contribution "Affirmations of Body and Soul." Of course, her long-term partner James Rich was present as well as Gene's brother Rick and two sons Anyi-Malik and Armand-Toussaint and Frankie's two sisters. Gene's ex-wife also came to pay her respects, which was one of the few times I have met her.

I was impressed with the creative bent he orchestrated for his mother's homegoing celebration. Besides the usual sermon and benediction by Reverend Lorraine McNeal, he had several artistic presentations: my longtime friend and colleague, pianist and composer extraordinaire Jacqueline Hairston played her "Spiritual Roots, Classical Fruits"; several of his poet friends read their works; and he even presented praise dance by Power in the Blood Dance Troupe. I never saw him break down and weep, but I knew with the passing of his mother he had also lost one of his best friends and the single most influential person in his life. I was happy to become his new best friend and support; I tried to show him that I truly had his back.

I was starting the second year of my directorship of AAS with increased visibility as a campus leader, a strong supportive homelife with Gene, and fortified spiritual guidance. I had begun to truly synthesize my intellectual, emotional, and spiritual lives in an integrated manner in each situation I found myself. Now, at sixty-six years old, I was becoming keenly aware that I was entering the last years of working a formal job before some form of quasi-retirement.

8

The Sankofa Process

Afrofuturism at Home and Abroad

I embrace the way of Change—the flow of nature, for I know the dancing spirit never dies.

Halifu Osumare

If I had previously thought juggling teaching, research, and service was difficult, as director of the African American and African Studies Program at UC Davis, I now learned what it meant to have *administration* added to my job mix. Since I had founded several arts organizations, juggling a myriad of administrative tasks was not new, but being a responsible administrator while simultaneously being a full-time professor oftentimes became overwhelming. But over my three-year appointment as director, I learned how to manage the insanity of my multiple roles while simultaneously becoming a public intellectual on issues of Black popular culture.

On several occasions I was asked by the media to comment on the passing of key Black popular culture figures or on major political events in which Black popular culture was implicated. I remember when Don Cornelius, founder and producer of the influentially famous *Soul Train* television show, died in February 2012, the *Christian Science Monitor* called me to solicit my comments about his significance to America society. Their commemorative news article partly read:

The show was what Cornelius called 'the electronic drum'—a reference to the way African tribes communicated from one village to another. "There was no other way for this culture to be transmitted on a rapid basis, but Cornelius understood that TV was the medium of the day," says Halifu Osumare, director of African American Studies at the University of California, Davis and a specialist in hip-hop culture. "It brought these regional sounds and moves together to a national audience. You have an entire generation of teens, not just black, but all ethnicities, being socialized on Saturday mornings as they watched black culture from all over the country parading down that Soul Train line," Osumare says.[1]

I used my growing reputation as a public intellectual to illuminate Black people's "soul power" through music and dance. As a choreographer, I had emphasized one major point: what is culturally *American* about the United States *is* Black culture. Now as a spokesperson for the culture, I continued the same mission of illuminating my ancestral cultural legacy through my newfound *scholarly* voice.

In my shift from dance practitioner to academic pundit, my embrace of all-pervasive hip-hop culture prompted even more attention to my perspectives on Black culture. The same month as our UC Davis Social Justice Initiative event (chapter 6), a fatal incident galvanized national attention: the killing of seventeen-year-old Trayvon Martin on February 26, 2012, by self-appointed neighborhood watchman George Zimmerman. Again, I was asked to give my perceptions about the incident to the media, this time for *CNN Living*. They particularly wanted me to comment on the larger hip-hop context of the hoodie sweatshirt as a perceived "thug" image. As young Trayvon was wearing a hoodie at the time of his killing, his choice of attire and how it was socially perceived became a part of the story. In the online news article, they quoted me saying,

> The hoodie has become one of those cultural markers of the gangster outlaw. It is a part of the construction that happens within capitalism, in terms of how things are bought and sold in the marketplace. So now when people see a black man with a hoodie in the street, it becomes an image of a potential thug or gangster. You have those stereotypical images in mind, not of what [the man] is actually like, but what capitalism has promoted as part of this style trend . . . I don't think there is anything intrinsically sinister about hoodies, but for certain purposes, for certain types of people, the hoodie has a wide range of applications. . . . [It has become a] part of the demonization of the black male and the creation of the stereotypical image of him walking down the street in the hoodie . . . People don't see [the Trayvon Martin killing] as an isolated incident, they see it as a historic trend.[2]

My voice as a public intellectual was growing on perspectives related to Black people and the growing convolutions of hip-hop culture.

Life and Death Happens

Another death hit home even more personally. In March 2012 my sister Pat followed her beloved Tenola (chapter 6) and passed at the age of fifty-eight. Born Ledora Jeanne Hall, she had been the book nerd of Mama's five daughters, with an extremely high IQ. Whenever we were together at Mama's and played the game Trivial Pursuit, none of us could ever beat her; she was a vast repository of knowledge on many disparate subjects. A registered nurse all her adult life, Pat lived as a recluse in a studio apartment in the Upper Fillmore district of San Francisco near Pacific Medical Center, where she became clinical nurse manager of one of the primary wards of the hospital. Just the opposite of me in temperament, she rarely ventured out into the world, choosing instead a once-a-week taxi ride to Mama's house on weekends to have breakfast and spend the day with her.

But that weekly family visit eventually stopped after Tenola died. Pat became *seriously* reclusive, cutting herself off from the family. Nothing any of us did—calling, going to see her, or sending letters and gifts—made a difference. Pat was the definition of a loner, living in her own world most of her life and dying in a similar fashion. Becoming increasingly depressed after Tenola's death, she simply did not want to live any longer and stopped taking her diabetes medications or taking care of herself in general. We all agreed, as the saying goes, "She's in a better place where she is no longer unhappy."

Taking My Hip-Hop Scholarship to Brazil

As *The Africanist Aesthetic in Global Hip-Hop: Power Moves* circulated internationally, my reputation as a hip-hop scholar grew exponentially. University of São Paulo (UPS) education professor Dr. Monica do Amaral invited me to Brazil in April 2012 to present my work on global hip-hop at the "Culturas Jovens, Afro-Brasil, America: Econtros E Desencontros" (Youth Cultures, Afro-Brazil, America: Encounters and Disconnections) conference. Monica and members of the Faculty of Education of UPS had heard about my global comparative research on hip-hop and wanted me to give two lectures during the four-day conference, along with two other scholars from the US and one from France. So, I arranged for my teaching assistants to take over my classes during that spring quarter for a two-week period in April and went to São Paulo.

Gene wanted to use this opportunity to also experience Brazil, making it a joint adventure for us, and I made arrangements with Professor Amaral for his attendance at the conference. But we both felt that if we were going to Brazil, besides São Paulo, we also had to visit Salvador, Bahia, the Afro-Brazilian part of the country in the North. It was to be a two-city Brazilian working adventure.

We arrived in São Paulo on April 10 and stayed at a moderately priced Howard Johnson hotel in the heart of bustling downtown São Paulo, the most populous city in Brazil, and indeed all of South America. The other scholars were Martha Diaz, founder of NYU's Hip-Hop Education Center; William Smith, assistant professor of Music at North Carolina Central University (now Bowie State University); and Professor Christian Béthune from the Centre of Interdisciplinary Studies at University of Paris. The four of us, along with UPS education scholars doing work on Brazilian youth and hip-hop, constituted the scholarly component of the conference.

But the conference also included recognized youth practitioners and founders of Brazilian hip-hop from various communities in and around São Paulo. Monica do Amaral, as an education scholar, was using this highly visible academic conference to legitimize hip-hop in Brazil, bringing the "ivory tower" and the practicing community together to reveal the youth culture as a tool for revamping public education in Brazil.

"Cultura Jovens" was comprehensive and interdisciplinary, allowing me true insights into another example of hip-hop's internationalization. Monica and another colleague on the Faculty of Education at USP opened the conference with a warm welcome, followed by Professor Béthune's philosophical treatise, "Hip-Hop as a Youth Culture: What Rap Is in Relation to Culture." Having written philosophical texts on the aesthetic underpinning of jazz music in Western culture (*Adorno and Jazz* and *Jazz and the West*), he was now venturing into rap music with his current book, *An Aesthetic of Rap* (2004). Monica's research in education is based in a strong philosophical tradition that included Theodor Adorno's work as a post-WWII philosopher belonging to the Frankfort School of Cultural Studies. Therefore, her strategy was to have Béthune immediately establish the academic philosophical perspective underpinning the conference. His talk was in French and simultaneously translated into Portuguese and English with the audience wearing translation earphones, becoming the methodology of the entire multi-lingual international conference. It felt like the United Nations, with many languages being spoken with simultaneous translations.

The conference opening segued into community presentations and talks about the reality of Brazilian urban hip-hop. There was a freestyle battle by performers from Radio Bumba, a local pop culture station, followed by a panel of the originators of hip-hop in Brazil: King Niño Brown, an early hip-hop dancer who modeled his style on James Brown and is now the director of Casa do Hip-Hop, a community center in a suburb of São Paulo; and DJ Hum, the original deejay with rapper Thiade, one of Brazil's first recorded emcees in the 1980s. They both gave insights into the historical trajectory of hip-hop in Brazil. "Culturas Jovens" also included female emcee Tiely Queen, who helped found a Brazilian female collective of rappers that was celebrating its twentieth anniversary. Later in the conference, Tiely Queen battled with Chen Lo (Chentis Pettigrew), a New York emcee who Monica had brought to perform at the international convocation. These artists gave me a perspective on how long hip-hop culture had been deeply entrenched among the youth of Brazil. Monica do Amaral had convened a substantive international hip-hop conference with academic, local praxis, and cross-cultural collaborative hip-hop components.

That first evening of the conference, Gene and I went to a hip-hop concert in the city, and many of the same female emcees appearing with Tiely Queen were "throwing down" on stage. The concert had a packed audience of Black, brown, and white Brazilian youths all connected through hip-hop. The large warehouse-like club had a VIP section and a bar, but seemingly only one exit in and out. Gene kept his eye open for any possibility of problems so we could exit quickly if necessary. But it turned out to be a very educational event, with many emcees rapping about political and social change in Brazil. It was important to see the hip-hop community outside of the conference. The concert allowed us a sense of the *reality* of Brazilian hip-hop culture, and we found the event to be serious and substantive about the youths' social and culture issues.

All of the international scholars Monica brought to Brazil provided scholarly import from different academic niche perspectives. As mentioned earlier Béthune provided a strong philosophical basis for "Why hip-hop?" at this time in Black cultural development, while both Smith's and Diaz's foci were on hip-hop educational curriculum and aesthetic diasporic connections. I was the scholar offering the cross-cultural, *comparative,* international perspective. My first talk, utilizing a PowerPoint presentation with images and text slides, was "Global Hip-Hop and the African Diaspora." This talk was excerpted from my book chapter of the same title in *Black Cultural Traffic: Crossroads in Global Performance and Popular Culture* (2005).[3] In it, I compare Cuban and Brazilian hip-hop from cultural and political perspectives using my theory of connective marginalities of culture, class, historical oppression, and youth in the African diaspora (chapter 3). I used Niyi Afolabi's exploration of Brazil's notorious crime, abandoned children, and street people,[4] emphasizing that these social conditions separated it from socialist Cuba, where hip-hop youth may be poor but have basic needs such as shelter, education, and health care guaranteed by the government.

Brazil, as the African diasporic nation with the highest percentage of African descendants, is a complex morass of influential Afro-Brazilian culture markers, including samba, bossa nova, the *bloco Afros* of carnival, and *capoeira* martial art. But it also has a long history of deep poverty and a "throwaway" street youth population that are severely harassed and killed by the police. My "Global Hip-Hop and the African Diaspora" presentation did not retreat from exposing my perspective on the socio-cultural *duality* in Brazil that Brazilian hip-hop emcees make clear.

Now, actually *being* in Brazil, I was going beyond library research and news accounts, seeing firsthand the realities and the myths of Brazil's so-called *democracia racial* (racial democracy). A graduate student assistant of Monica's, Vinny Puttini, became friends with Gene and me, taking us to see the "real" São Paulo beyond the conference. Vinny showed us several *favelas,* poverty-stricken communities lining the periphery of São Paulo, and it was indeed eye-opening to see these hill neighborhoods adjacent to wealthy gated communities. The immorality of Brazil's income disparity became visually apparent. But São Paulo authorities also give legitimacy to hip-hop graffiti artists who graphically display some of their deleterious realties as well as Afrofuturistic fantasies. Vinny also took us to see "Graffiti Alley," two street-length walls with rotating colorful world-class artwork designated by the city as an outdoor art gallery for hip-hop youths, and we were extremely impressed at the quality as well as the permission to publicly exhibit the work.

Vinny Puttini, who teaches community English classes in São Paulo, took Gene and me deep into the neighborhoods of the city beyond the tourist sites. We learned how to drink Brazilian *cachaça* rum in a little neighborhood bar called Cu do Padre (Asshole of the Priest) that was situated behind a Catholic church, with its name and location demonstrating the ironic humor of urban Brazilians. Vinny is actually Italian and grew up in the famous Bexiga (or Bela Vista) district of São Paulo, known for its mixture of Italian, Portuguese, and African Brazilians. He took us to his favorite bar, the Place of Friendship, in his home district. The bar was a little hole-in-the-wall packed with working-class people of all colors who obviously knew each other. What was so memorable about the Place of Friendship is that it revealed the origins of the myth of *democracia racial* to us: the neighborhood people, no matter the color, were getting drunk and singing song after song together as a part of their common culture. I recorded the following in my journal about our Place of Friendship experience:

> As we sat and drank beer and listened to the samba songs of the older black
> and white Brazilians, we were able to observe how the racial democracy

of Brazil works at the micro-level. These people who have worked and struggled together see themselves as one *in their cultural identity; through their music they have the same class experiences, the same identity, the same humanity. But once one leaves these working-class neighborhoods, the resources are not equal; the power of decision-making is not equal. We see no Black Brazilians in real positions of power politically or in the media. At the macro-level, Brazil is in denial.*

Back at the conference, this inequality was also reflected. I was one of the few visibly Black scholars at *Culturas Jovens.* William, Martha, and I became *the* Black scholars of the conference; we were role models for the attending Afro-Brazilian students. At my lecture, I wore an African dress and headwrap that also impressed the Afro-Brazilian students. I discovered that less than one percent of Brazilians identifying as Black teach at the university level. Monica, as a white Portuguese Brazilian, told me that she was committed to having more Black intellectuals at her next conference, and that was one of the reasons she brought William Smith, Martha Diaz, and me to share our research at the conference.

My second talk, *The Hiplife in Ghana,* based on my second hip-hop book that was in press at the time, was a big hit at the conference because it discussed *Africa* as the aesthetic origins of the youth culture that we were all interrogating. As many Brazilians are still connected to their *specific* West and Central African family roots, several Afro-Brazilian university students approached me, struggling through their English to thank me for being there, and particularly for addressing the deconstruction of Brazil's sociopolitical and racial problems.

Visiting Salvador, Bahia

After the Culturas Jovens conference and our many São Paulo revelations, Gene and I were ready for the land of Afro-Brazilians: Salvador, Bahia. The first capital of Brazil, originally known as *São Salvador da Bahia de todos os Santos* ("Holy Savior of the Bay of All Saints"), Salvador was the original port of entry for the estimated four million enslaved Africans, representing 40 percent of the total population of Africans brought to the Americas during the transatlantic slave trade. As soon as one enters the city of over 2.9 million people, it becomes obvious this is the home of Black Brazilians, where the Portuguese first established themselves in the New World.

The Pelourinho district in the upper city is populated with colonial monuments, churches, and large cathedrals dating back to the eighteenth century.

Everywhere in the city the artifacts of the Yoruba orisas (or *orixás* in Brazil) are celebrated through artifacts bought and sold in the tourist marketplace. The commodification of the orixá belief system takes place particularly in the Pelourinho, still lined with its original cobblestone streets and containing many tourist shops and galleries selling Afro-Brazilian culture. Never before had I observed the public celebration, yet commercial trivialization, of my belief system, which is more hidden in the US. The Dique de Tororó, a lake at the base of a former dam near the new soccer stadium built for the 2014 World Cup and the 2016 Olympics, is a perfect example of the visually pervasive orixá belief system in Salvador. In the middle of the pond stands majestic large sculptures of the eight African powers—Esu, Ogun, Shango, Yemonja, Oshun, Oya, Nana, and Obatala—created by the artist Tatti Moreno. The orixás seemingly float spiritually on the water, testifying to the ubiquity of Afro-Brazilian religion and culture in Salvador.

But the public display of the African belief system is only the surface of the *actual* orixá religion pervasive in Brazil, particularly in Salvador. Isaura Olivera, my Afro-Brazilian friend and Yoruba practitioner then in Oakland, had given Gene and me several contacts in her Salvador home. Those personal contacts allowed us to get outside the tourist gloss to penetrate to a deeper level of Bahian culture. One of Isaura's friends, Isa Trigo, theater artist and professor at Universidade do Estado da Bahia (Bahia State University), took us to one of the oldest Brazilian candomblé religious compounds or *terreiro,* Ile Opo Afonja, located in the Cabula district. Upon arrival I was acknowledged as a fellow priest, and Gene and I were given a full tour by one of the main priestesses of Opo Afonja, showing us entire structures dedicated to each of the African powers built within the gated 1.5-square-mile compound. They also had an on-site elementary school for neighborhood children and a beautifully respectful bronze memorial to their founding priestess, Eugenia Anna Santos (1869–1938), better known as Mãe Aninha, who started their terreiro in 1910. At Opo Afonja, Gene and I both felt the public validation of the orisa belief system as a world-class religion that continues with vitality and relevance in Salvador.

I also managed to give my "Hip-Hop and the African Diaspora" academic talk at the Universidade Federal da Bahia (UFBA, Federal University of Bahia). My lecture was open to the public and was facilitated and translated by another contact made before arriving, Lisa Castillo, a white American scholar who had lived in Brazil for sixteen years. The Institute for African Diaspora and Oriental Studies at UFBA sponsored my talk, drawing a modest attendance of about fifty mostly young Afro-Brazilian college students and community people very adept in Brazilian hip-hop. My talk featured analyses of several popular Brazilian emcees, such as Rio De Janeiro's MV Bill and São Paulo's Racionais MCs, a rap group known for their critique of class and race in Brazil. Lisa was very helpful in simultaneous translation of my presentation, and I was able to effectively interact with the young Bahians in attendance about their youth culture.

Gene and I finished our one-week stay in Salvador with a visit to the notorious Candeal favela in the city. My long-term friend Rafael Gonzalez put me in contact with Collin, a Bay Area American living in Candeal. We spent a half-day with Collin, meeting people in that community, eating delicious Brazilian food that reminded me of Ghanaian stew-soups, and visiting the favela's community center built by the famous Brazilian pop singer Carlinhos Brown, who grew up in Candeal. We saw firsthand the poverty, but humanity, of the people in this poor Salvador community. We learned from Collin that the residents only want a *sincere* hand-up by the government to help in their life aspirations. But the severe poverty and resulting lawlessness is the reality for so many of the poor favelas like Candeal. Our visit gave us an up-close-and-personal view of Brazil's social inequality, where few make it into the relatively small middle class. That day in Candeal revealed Brazil's disparity between the haves and have nots and the convoluted repercussions plaguing the country. This stark reality of descendants of our African ancestors touched me and Gene deeply.

Right before leaving, I sat on the balcony of the Vila Galé Salvador hotel where we were staying, near the famous Barra coastline, watching the crashing waves of the Atlantic Ocean. The complex reality of Brazil prompted me to write this poem in my journal before leaving.

> Ancestral Waters
>
> The Ancestral Black Atlantic
> washes upon the shores of Bahia
> The Waters carrying my Ancestors
> crashes on jagged rocks
> with Force of Memory
> Blue waters carrying slave ships
> Human cargo destined as builders of the "New World"
> yet the "Old World" always beckoned
> pulling us back across the Ancestral Black Atlantic
>
> Freedmen and Freedwomen searching for home
> for Africa within
> These same waters became our graves

> Ancestral bones lining the ocean floor
> screaming out to be avenged
> sending messages from the past
> for the future
> in the present

> The Ancestral Black Atlantic
> washes upon the shores of Salvador
> with *Itaparica* standing strong in the Bay
> Ancestral memories loom large in Bahia
> always calling, always beckoning
> Waiting to be recalled, re-invoked, re-interpreted
> Relived in the Now
> As Time seeks its Completion

Brazil, as another part of the Black Atlantic, allowed me to make an even deeper connection with the African diasporic experience; and the side trip to Bahia invoked a sense of the Afrofuture in me. What is to be our future as long-suffering Black people on this planet? How does our enslaved past and our precarious present play into an unknown future? How can we shape that unknown for future generations? I kept returning to the Sankofa bird, and the sankofa process always leads me to the Afrofuture.

The Hiplife in Ghana: The Book Tour

My second book, *The Hiplife in Ghana: West African Indigenization of Hip-Hop* was published in September 2012, four years after the Fulbright residency in Ghana generating that research. With all the responsibilities of teaching, continuing to publish book chapters and journal articles, and all the incessant university and departmental meetings required of a tenured professor, not to mention now being director of my academic unit, I had written, edited, passed the peer review process, and finally got Palgrave Macmillan to publish the much-awaited second book. Back in June, when I finished the final galley proofs, I wrote in my journal: *I give thanks for all the support from so many, because despite appearances, this is not a solo endeavor: From Professor Nketia in Ghana and my Kenyan colleague Mwenda Ntarangwi, both of whom wrote book blurb endorsements, to Reggie Rockstone, who will appear on the cover, as well as the orisas, particularly Oya and Ochosi, who got me through several spiritual battles, I have done it.*

As Palgrave is an international publisher, *The Hiplife in Ghana* was simultaneously released in the US and Great Britain. But they gave me little promotion; I felt like an ant in the mill of thousands of other authors in their international publishing industry. Academic publishing is very different than the huge trade publishing industry, like Random House, Harper Collins, Knopf, Inc., etc. Plus, rarefied academic treatises, even if about a pop culture phenomenon like hip-hop, by a little-known writer like myself, makes self-promotion crucial for success. Hence, through my own administrative efforts, I was able to set up an international book tour. My friend and colleague Brenda Dixon Gottschild suggested I hire a publicist to help me promote the book, and recommended two Philadelphia women, with whom she had worked before, to do the job: Laura Henrich and Sacha Adorno.

The two women worked as a team, so I got a twofer for a reasonable fee. They came up with a professional press release that read in part: "*The Hiplife in Ghana* explores how hip-hop music and culture in Ghana West Africa has morphed over two decades into a whole new form of world music called hiplife. This groundbreaking scholarship investigates hiplife music as more than just an adaptation of hip-hop, but as a revision of Ghana's own century-old popular music known globally as highlife." Armed with a reputable international publisher and top-notch personal publicists, I was on my way to promoting my second hip-hop book, which I felt would insure my next promotion to full professor.

Mwenda Ntarangwi, Kenyan cultural anthropologist and author of *East African Hip Hop: Youth Culture and Globalization* (2009), wrote a succinct book blurb endorsement of *The Hiplife in Ghana* that I have always liked:

> Halifu Osumare has written a rich account of hiplife music in Ghana through a prism of what she has termed the "arc of mutual inspiration," and beautifully provides the reader with a picture of the intricate connections between highlife, US hip-hop, late capitalism, youth agency, and local cultural practices. In this regard hiplife is not only a window into a local music style mobilized by youth in Ghana but a medium through which dominant ideologies and global structural forces are simultaneously complied with and resisted by those mostly affected by the challenges and opportunities of economic and political processes of the twenty-first century.

I had read his *East African Hip Hop* and had been impressed with his understanding of how African youth agency and youth empowerment was central to understanding the African continent's adoption of American hip-hop. His work had influenced my thinking about Ghanaian youth and their negotiations for social and economic power through rap music and hip-hop dance in Accra. I was grateful for his interest in my work as an *American* scholar writing about African youth culture.

His assessment of the centrality of my concept of the "arc of mutual inspiration" was spot on, as I coined the construct as the principal connection between African American and West African youths in Ghana's hiplife phenomenon. Hip-hop's adoption in Ghana, I argued, is a part of a continual *circulation* of African cultural priorities, starting with the initial transatlantic slave trade into the Americas and persisting with West and Central Africa's "repatriation" of the resulting revised New World rhythms, dances, and styles. I positioned the entire phenomenon as the African diaspora reinventing its African traditions through New World sensibilities, which in turn, are consumed and reinvented in Africa.

The arc of mutual inspiration is indeed the foundational seed of the Sankofa process of reinventing the past to move forward into a hopeful future—the basis of Afrofuturism as I define it. In many ways this Sankofa process is what I had been choreographing and writing about my entire career. Hence, it was no surprise that I was now naming it from a scholarly perspective and weaving it into my analysis of hiplife music in Ghana.

I was now ready for an international book tour with *The Hiplife in Ghana*. With my own personal contacts and the marketing efforts of publicist Laura, we constructed a promotional tour on three continents. And what better place to start than in my own city of Sacramento. On September 29, 2012, I gave my first book talk at Underground Books, which had become my starting point for my book readings. Gene was my biggest fan, and he accompanied me throughout my promotional tour. He had become my trusty partner who always had my back, and for the Underground Books presentation he even made his famous sweet potato pie, which, according to the audience's reaction, threatened to *upstage* my reading. He had stayed up late making six of his pies to pass out slices at that first reading, which made an even more homey local feeling to my tour start.

My US PowerPoint presentation included a basic history of Ghana followed by reading specific book passages. Starting with my long experience in Ghana and the "Obruni" experiences allowed me to immediately position myself within the subject of Ghanaian hiplife. This approach opened the larger discussion about diasporans' relationship to the Motherland. Afrocentrists in the audience love this approach, and it usually invokes a lively interaction.

After the local reading, we were ready to embark upon a global tour that would take us to Ghana; Edinburgh, Scotland; London, England; and New York. I introduced Gene as my research assistant and bodyguard, to which he always smiled.

We started the international part of the book tour in Ghana, as the actual launching of *The Hiplife in Ghana*. It made sense to unveil the new book in the site of its subject matter. Before Gene and I arrived, I had already made arrangements with the Music Union of Ghana (MUSIGA) to schedule media interviews, as the union president was now Obour (chapter 5), the first hiplife artist to head the influential organization. It was in his self-interest to promote my book that would elevate this relatively new music genre in the country; plus, he was one of the artists featured in it. From VIP tickets to the Radio and Television Personality Awards on our first night to the dedicated chauffeured MUSIGA van to drive us to the media blitz of print, radio, and television interviews, Gene and I were treated like royalty. I also gave a regular book reading at the Silverbird Bookstore in the Accra Mall, and my Ghanaian "son," emcee Okyeame Kwame (chapter 6), appeared with me for that particular engagement. It was definitely a new level of international recognition, representing a new pinnacle in my career and ongoing relationship to Ghana.

Upon arrival in Accra on October 11, we were picked up from the airport by Obour's assistants, Bosco and Saykiwaa, who gave us a written media schedule. But it was Obour himself who pulled me aside to handle a delicate matter: I needed to give him a lump sum of cash that would be distributed to the various media people during my stay as the customary "dashing" in exchange for the interviews I would receive. I already knew about the not-so-underground bribing system to get things done on the streets, but I naively thought this would not be necessary at the upper echelon of Ghanaian society; I quickly realized this is exactly how everyday corruption and survival works in a poor society. I never saw the money exchange, but I knew that his staff was discretely dashing each interviewer after each television, radio, or newspaper session.

The Hiplife in Ghana book was embraced wholeheartedly, and I was treated like a celebrity. As I penetrated the big-time Accra media outlets, I began to realize Accra is actually a big village, and everyone in the media and entertainment industry knows each other. My pre-trip communications with Obour as president and Bosco as manager had paid off. Sakyiwaa Mensah, the publicist, set up a grueling, but fun, media schedule for me. I was on almost every television station in Ghana and several radio stations, along with numerous newspaper interviews. Being driven by a chauffeur in the MUSIGA van to my various interviews and presentations, I decided that Ghana truly embraced me and the book at a level that I had not really expected.

But the tour was not without its controversy that revealed an underlying self-esteem issue in Ghanaian society. Many of my interviewers would ask me, "Why has it taken a 'foreigner' to come to Ghana to legitimize our latest pop music?" This question was obviously seeded in the fact that as a non-Ghanaian researching and writing about their hiplife music, I explicitly made

Figure 8.1. Author in Ghana TV studio for *The Hiplife in Ghana* book interview. Photo courtesy of author.

Ghanaians realize how much they themselves had not taken their own contributions to world pop music that seriously. I simply answered, "Well, that is a question that only you as Ghanaians can answer. I am simply sharing with you my research and love of hiplife music, and as a result explaining how I see its importance." I well knew that Ghanaians, as do many Africans, often need Westerners to validate their Indigenous cultural production before they themselves will truly embrace its worth. This is one of the unfortunate legacies of colonialism. I hoped that my book would not only make it clear how much they were connected to us African diasporans but that their popular culture is worthy of acknowledgment and is globally influential.

The actual *official* launching of the book was October 18 at the Institute for African Studies on the UG Legon campus. DJ Black, one of Ghana's best hiplife deejays, brought an adept mix of hiplife music to start the event, and several hiplife artists were in attendance, including Obrafour and Tic Tac, whom I had written about. Obour, as the president of MUSIGA, co-hosted the event with me, and I acknowledged my research assistant, dancer-choreographer Terry Ofosu, for his invaluable support in my research. I was also honored to have the launching blessed by the attendance of the late Professor Kwabena Nketia (chapter 6), with the entire event taking place in the hall named for the then ninety-one-year-old. He was still very vital, and after I had given a chapter overview of the book, sprinkled with a few readings of passages, I introduced

Prof. Nketia as my academic father, as our professional relationship went all the way back to my initial Ghana visit in 1976, thirty-six years earlier.

Professor Nketia read from his own book of poetry he had written as a young scholar and told the audience if rap had been a cultural phenomenon during his youth, he might have been a rapper himself, as he loved poetry. Although I could not follow his reading in the Twi language, it was obviously witty because he generated a lot of laughter and head nodding during his recitation. The online media blog ModernGhana.com recorded his part of the book launch in this way: "Professor Nketia related how language and communication have always been a part of the ways by which people express themselves. He has a whole lot of books to his credit. He read one of the books he authored in his early twenties and got the audience intrigued with the creativity of his dialogue back then and its relevance to today's world. He mentioned that if hiplife had been around during this youth, he most probably would have been a hiplife artist, and that he is happy his grandson, musician Manifest, who was present at the event, is doing so well in the arts."[5] Little did I know that his grandson Manifest, a well-known international emcee, and I would actually work together the following year in the US, promoting the hiplife music phenomenon. The University of Ghana book launching was the centerpiece of my entire international book tour.

The next leg of the tour was to the colonizer of Ghana, the United Kingdom, first in Edinburgh, Scotland, followed by London, England. I was invited to give a book talk at the Africa in Motion (AIM) Scotland African Film Festival and Symposium in Edinburgh on October 27. I chose to focus on the book chapter on the generational aspect of hiplife music, calling my lecture "Youth Agency in Ghanaian Hiplife." The festival was attended by Scottish, British, and African artists and scholars doing work on Africa, including critics and African filmmakers whose work was presented in the festival. The film screenings of contemporary African films took place at the Filmhouse in town and included short documentaries on the then hot button topic of the Arab Spring rebellion that had begun the previous year in North Africa.

The symposium, however, happened at the University of Edinburgh, and my talk on youth agency in pop music in Accra fit very well into the festival theme of "Modern Africa." Gene and I loved walking through the streets of Edinburgh lined with buildings made of both old medieval stone masonry and contemporary modern architecture, testifying to the ancient and modern living side by side in modern-day Europe. The entire film festival represented the educated youth of the United Kingdom attempting to create a counterpoint to Europe's historical exploitation and stereotyping of the African continent.

Traveling southward to London, I gave a less formal book reading on October 28 at The Africa Centre, then located in the famous Covent Garden district of the city. The Africa Centre is one of the oldest nonprofit organizations on Africa and its diaspora in Europe, founded in 1964 during the heart of Africa's liberation movements. Publicist Laura Henrich had sent them *The Hiplife in Ghana* press release, and the staff jumped at the chance to present a book reading and signing for their London audience, which grew to about fifty people. It was very well-organized, as the staff had elicited a young Nigerian media journalist as the moderator, Alexis Akwagyiram, then with BBC Africa and now the Nigeria bureau chief for Reuters.

Alexis was well prepared, having read the book and ready with stimulating questions after my overview PowerPoint presentation. As a journalist he was known for interrogating the effects of hip-hop on Britain. Alexis's past research and writing on hip-hop led into a lively dialogue about the global implications of hiplife in Ghana, which, in turn, bled into a stimulating Q&A with the mostly young African audience regarding the place of youth in the growth of contemporary Africa. Afterward, Gene and I went to dinner with Alexis and several African and Caribbean sisters attending the book reading. They wanted to continue dialoguing about my work and our contemporary twenty-first-century times we are all navigating as African peoples. These are the kind of engaging interactions that are an author's dream after all the hard work to get the book in print. The book tour was really paying off in more ways than one.

Gene and I took advantage of being in famous London town by taking in some tourist sites. We took a walk along the River Thames in south London, along its paved boardwalk. As we looked across the wide river, we promised ourselves the next time we came to London we would visit Brixton, the well-known Black district with many Caribbean and African immigrants representing the British Commonwealth. Of course, we took an obligatory walk to the borough of Westminster to view the outside of Buckingham Palace with its pompous stoic guards.

As an artist, Gene wanted to visit the famous British Museum, as we realized it was not far from the boutique bed-and-breakfast where we were staying in the Bloomsbury district. The British Museum lived up to its reputation of grandeur with huge wings containing archaeological classic Greek, Roman, and Egyptian sculptures. We knew they also still had priceless West African artifacts hidden in their basement, particularly the Benin Bronzes from Nigeria, pillaged from the 1897 raid of the kingdom.[6] We contemplated that aspect of the museum's history as we ate lunch at the Court Café under the magnificent glass ceiling of its Great Court.

On our last day in London, I had an important radio interview for *The Hiplife in Ghana.* I appeared on the *Rita's World* show hosted by deejay Rita Ray, a Ghanaian female deejay and African pop music expert. The radio studio is housed in at the School of Oriental and African Studies (SOAS) of the University of London, one of the world's leading institutions for the study of Asia, Africa, and the Middle East. In preparing for my book tour, I had found an article about Rita and her radio show in the *New Africa* magazine. We conversed online and arranged for the interview date before we arrived in London. I later found out she had played a vital role in revitalizing the African music scene in London by deejaying at the Mambo Inn in Brixton.

Rita Ray did not disappoint; she had prepared a wide-ranging array of Ghanaian music to intersperse throughout my interview. As we discussed the book, she played everything from an early musical composition of Ghanaian choral music by Professor Nketia to an excerpt from the hiplife track "The Game," to which I had devoted an entire chapter in my book. The interview became a warm and free-flowing conversation between two Black sisters. We took a hiplife journey through Rita's selected music, from its beginnings with Reggie Rockstone to the intense use of highlife and traditional Ghanaian rhythms. I was able to share with her listening audience some of the book's in-depth concepts, allowing my *Rita's World* interview to substantively conclude my Great Britain part of the tour.

The concept of life happening in between the plans we make then hit us full force. The very next day a storm brewing in the Caribbean hit the US Eastern Seaboard on October 30. Hurricane Sandy was so bad that they called it a "Superstorm." It became one of the most devastating hurricanes in US history, with the highest waves ever recorded in the western Atlantic, causing storm surges that flooded New York and New Jersey. The superstorm caused $70.2 billion in damage, left 8.5 million people without power, and killed seventy-two Americans and a total of 233 people across eight countries, from the Caribbean to Canada.

We had been scheduled to leave London on October 31 for New York, as I had scheduled book events at New York University, the Schomburg Library in Harlem, and The Museum of Contemporary African Diaspora Art (MoCADA) in Brooklyn. But that day our American Airlines flight was canceled, and New York City, "the city that never sleeps," was completely shut down. We had to schedule an alternative British Airways flight to Denver to get back to Sacramento. I was so glad Gene insisted on flight insurance; what an end to the book tour.

Even with this devastating premature end to the tour, it was still a success. I realized that I had become the "Queen Mother" of hiplife in Ghana;

the Obruni outsider had finally transcended the "white professor" image in the colonial hierarchy to become one of "the people." My comradery with the musicians, deejays, rapper-producers, and fans of Ghana's contemporary pop music bestowed an honorary Ghanaian status on me, even if just for the time I was there. And the capstone was President Barack Obama being elected for a second term on November 4, right after we returned to the US.

Personal Reflections on the Aging Process

After *The Hiplife in Ghana* book tour, I experienced a milestone birthday: number sixty-five, the magic year when one is supposed to retire. Although I was still riding the successful wave of my academic career, including going up for full professor, I did begin to contemplate what retirement would look like. Even though I loved classroom teaching, leading young minds to critically think, I was becoming painfully aware that my undergraduate students were becoming lazier and more tied to their electronic gadgets. In earlier academic times, one could assume students understood the classroom as respected sacred space; now, I was forced to include "rules of conduct" in my syllabus: only using computers for taking notes rather than Googling everything I said, and silencing cell phones before class started. My standard joke, as I read through my rules of conduct on the first day of class, was "I don't want to hear Lil Wayne or Nicki Minaj as ringtones while I'm lecturing, even if I *am* the hip-hop professor." Also, as I was entering my third year as program director, I was tired of faculty recalcitrance on several administrative issues, as well as those incessant university meetings at every level. Although I was planning to take my first sabbatical after I stepped down as head of the program, I also began thinking about my retirement.

Personally, I was having to admit that I was no longer "middle-aged," but, in fact, I was now an Elder; I was old! I even started receiving social security, which I deposited into my retirement account. But on the other hand, we dancers always believe we are ten years younger than our non-dancer peers. The discipline of physical exercise and "dancerly" exertion does something for the endorphins that, in turn, can slow down the aging process. Plus, I still believed in the Aaliyah song, "Age Ain't Nothing But a Number," and although she was proclaiming that adage as a young teenager trying to act grown, I was claiming it as an Elder still feeling young. I had kept myself in healthy mind, body, and spirit, becoming vegetarian for a while, then only adding seafood and chicken back into my diet; red meat was something I had foregone for decades. I also continued regular meditation, did my Dunham breathing, and tried to maintain a healthy balance in my life.

That Christmas 2012 I went to Mom's for dinner as my family traditionally did. I arrived early to help with all the cooking and preparations, along with my sisters Brenda and Tracey. But with Pat now passed, we were all thinking of both she and Tenola having gone too soon, and were really missing them. Two out of my mother's five daughters were now gone. Mama Tenola always kept a stoic stance in the face of loss, but we knew she continued to grieve in private. As we said blessing at the table before eating, niece Theresa added her mother Tenola's name to the prayer, as she felt her mother's loss most. I stayed close to Theresa that day, as we opened presents and laughed and talked, because I knew she needed extra support. As I was not always around my family because of all my traveling, it was particularly rewarding to feel my family connections that Christmas day. It is poignant how death can bring a family closer, making us all cling to the miracle of life and appreciate each other even more.

Early the next year I had another reminder of my advancing age as well as my accomplishments that the decades had produced: a group of dancers at the Malonga Casquelourd Center in Oakland organized "Commune + Unity Dance Day: Reunion 2013," and I was invited as the founder of Everybody's Creative Arts Center/CitiCentre Dance Theatre to speak. It was a grand reunion of the Oakland Black dance community on January 13, with an entire day of dance classes and a sprawling photo exhibit of the building's artistic history, all concluding with remarks by me as a founding Elder. It was quite rewarding to witness the current-day generation of dance leaders continuing the inclusive dance community I had initiated back in 1977 after returning from my first trip to Ghana (chapter 6, *DinB*). The contemporary mantle was being assumed by several dancers who had formed the Kongo SQ West Kinship Society, the producer of the event. It consisted of Regina Calloway, who carries on the legacy of the late Carlos Aceituno of Foga Na Roupa; Muisi-Kongo Malonga, the daughter of Malonga continuing the legacy of Fua Dia Congo; and Janeen Johnson.

I spoke to the young dancers at the end of the day, and I was joined by some of my elder friends, forming a kind of Elder Council around me. Two of my oldest friends were with me: Sandra McGee, my oldest childhood friend, and Rafael Gonzalez, my friend from the 1970s with whom I have a deep spiritual connection. Gene stood on the side taking photos as he witnessed firsthand my Oakland dance legacy, which I had been describing to him since we met. I spoke from my heart that day about what I had observed. I let the remaining dancers know that the spirit of the "dance circle" I had started thirty-five years earlier was alive and well in them, and that our dance ancestors, like Malonga, were smiling down on us all. I reiterated that I would help Kongo SQ West

Kinship Society survive and thrive because they are carrying on the dancing spirit of the African diaspora in Oakland. They continue to make Oakland, California, one of the primary centers of African culture.

Continuing My Academic Teaching and Hip-Hop Scholarship

In the winter quarter of 2013, I taught one of my few *graduate* seminars while at UC Davis. Our AAS program (now a department) has a Designated Emphasis that allows students to specialize in African American, African, or African Diasporic Studies. Their AAS designated specialization appears on their diploma along with their major field, such as History, Anthropology, English, etc. I taught AAS 201, Critical Foundations in African American Studies to eight young bright graduate students from various fields around the campus, including music, performance studies, theater and dance, and history. We sat around a conference table and discussed a different classic text each week that gave them a broad perspective on the field, such as Henry Louis Gates's *The Signifying Monkey: A Theory of African-American Literary Criticism* (1988) and *The Black Atlantic: Modernity and Double Consciousness* (1993) by Paul Gilroy. Each week one student presented his/her in-depth analysis of one the course texts. It was intellectually stimulating to engage with a small group of advanced students with analytical skills, as opposed to large undergraduate courses populated with students of various academic skills and commitments to education.

I even had a Nigerian visiting artist with the Department of Theatre and Dance, Qudus Onikeku, audit the course. He was like a sponge, expanding his understanding of the African American experience as it dovetails with African contemporary issues. He presented a very provocative performance art piece, "Flash: A New Choreography" at the main theater on campus toward the end of that quarter, and we became friends; I even had he and his wife over to our home for dinner, where we engaged in discussions about the African diasporan past, present, and future, initiating a long-term friendship. Now, back in Nigeria directing a global performance think tank called AFROPOLIS, Qudus explores African culture and performance in relation to technology. His AFROPOLIS project has become one of the most forward-thinking Afrofuturist ventures on the African continent, which I explore in chapter 9.

Another important connection in my graduate course was with the dancer La Tessa Joy Walker (now Ayo Walker). She had been accepted into the Performance Studies Graduate Group, which I had a seminal hand in creating along with a group of faculty in Theatre and Dance and other fields from across the campus. She had applied to UCD Performance Studies because she wanted to work with me and focus her research on Black dance. When she was considering applying, Ayo came to campus and met with me in my office to ask if I would become her major advisor in Performance Studies with an AAS Designated Emphasis. As a Black student, she had not taken many African American Studies courses at that point, so after being accepted into the PhD graduate group in 2012, my grad course became a rigorous introduction to an intriguing new field for her. Her performance and academic career to that point had engaged teaching, choreographing, and performing dance while earning a master's degree in dance education from New York University. Although my grad course intensified her understanding of advanced African American Studies, little did I know then that our relationship would become multidimensional, which I'll explore later.

Publishing *The Hiplife in Ghana* expanded my conference presentations beyond popular culture, dance, and American Studies to the annual African Studies Association (ASA). I presented my exploration of African youth empowerment through hip-hop with my paper "Youth Agency in Ghanaian Hiplife Music." However, also in February 2013, I presented at "The Poetics and Politics of Hip Hop Cultures" conference at the University of Arizona in Tucson. That university had become the first in the nation to establish a Hip-Hop Studies minor degree, and they wanted to inaugurate the new hip-hop degree with a scholarly think tank. I was invited to present my Ghana hip-hop scholarship, along with several other scholars and artists, including Marcyliena Morgan, well-known linguistic scholar and director of Harvard's Hiphop Archive. Our hip-hop revolution in academia was seminal, and "The Poetics and Politics of Hip Hop Cultures" conference was another move in that direction.

What distinguished this conference was its exploration of the entire culture of hip-hop with an emphasis on its internationalization in France, with scholars presenting on graffiti art and rap in the context of slam poetry in France. The entire conference had a French hip-hop focus because it was conceived by French Professor Allain-Phillippe Durand, the then director of Africana Studies at the University of Arizona. As soon as the hip-hop minor was established at the university, it had come under attack for "diluting academic rigor"; hence his conference became evidence that Hip-Hop Studies was as academic as any other discipline in the academy.

Later that year, Marcyliena Morgan invited me to be a part of the Harvard University Hiphop Archive & Research Institute's "The Author Meets the Critics" series. The format is a recently published hip-hop book author presents the book with other scholar-critics in *that* field of hip-hop to explore the book's contributions. On November 6, 2013, "Author Halifu Osumare Meets

the Critics—The Hiplife in Ghana: West African Indigenization of Hip-Hop"
was convened at Harvard, with esteemed colleagues Eric Charry, Department
of Music at Wesleyan University and editor of *Hip Hop Africa* (2012); Dawn-
Elisa Fischer, hip-hop scholar in SF State's Department of Africana Studies;
Kenyan hip-hop author Mwenda Ntarangwi, mentioned earlier; Patricia
Tang, Department of Music at MIT and author on Senegalese sabar music; my
friend Alain-Philippe Durand from University of Arizona; and Anthropologist Jesse Weaver Shipley from Haverford College, the only other academic
authority on Ghanaian hiplife music. I had read Shipley's in-depth journal
articles on hiplife in preparation for my Fulbright research; but my book had
been published one year before his *Living the Hiplife: Celebrity and Entrepreneurship in Ghanaian Popular Music* (Duke University Press, 2013).

One never knows how such a public forum convened to critique one's
book by peers will actually play out. Will it be a critical roast of the work or
a balanced analysis of your contributions to the field? Held in the relatively
small reception room of the Hutchins Center, which also houses Harvard's
W.E.B. DuBois Institute, the seating capacity is only about fifty people. But
one always knows that it will be a quality audience of hip-hop aficionados at
Harvard; hence, one had better come prepared. All of the invited scholars had
read *The Hiplife in Ghana* and came primed with written statements exploring
my concepts and research findings. As it turned out, each scholar praised *The
Hiplife in Ghana* from different perspectives. I was particularly thankful that
Shipley respected the work, as he was the one scholar who had worked among
the same artists and culture in Accra as I. The scholars let me know that they
considered me a serious scholar whose work helps explain the complex intersections of race, class, culture, and history, and most importantly my analyses
of Ghana's latest popular music contribution were well crafted on an astutely
established premise.

The Harvard event kicked off a small East Coast book tour, as Gene and I
went on to New York for two more important events: a reading in Brooklyn
at the Museum of Contemporary African Diasporan Art (MoCADA) and a
presentation in Harlem. The next two days I gave presentations at the Hip-
Hop Education Think Tank 3 conference taking place at Harlem's Schomburg
Center for Research on Black Culture. On this leg of the tour, I was happy to
meet up with my UC Davis mentee, Ayo Walker, who was also attending the
conference. We were growing closer into a personal mother-daughter relationship, as I continued to help her through her Performance Studies PhD
program. Organized largely by hip-hop education scholar Martha Diaz of
NYU's Hip-Hop Education Center, the conference explored the diversity of
hip-hop school programs and the importance of hip-hop pedagogy for engag-

ing and retaining Black and brown youth in public schools as well as in higher education.

The conference attendees were an international cadre of educators, not only from the US, but also from Holland, Brazil, China, Australia, Mexico, and Senegal, several of whom were already using my *Power Moves* book in their curriculum. I learned that each global site was at a different stage of their utilization of hip-hop: youth in Senegal used rap and graffiti to become politically active in critiquing the government and electing officials; in China they were fighting severe repression and lack of access to important hip-hop sites on the internet; in Amsterdam, they were emerging from an arts-only movement to one engaging sociopolitical implications of art through hip-hop; in Brazil, a hip-hop representative in the Ministry of Culture had been appointed; and the Mexican contingent of educators wanted the US participants to become more engaged in what was happening in hip-hop south of its border. Besides presenting my work on Ghana at the Hip-Hop Education Think Thank 3, I became even more enlightened about contemporary issues in various international hip-hop sites.

Becoming Full Professor and Dancing the Afrofuture

In May 2013 I had gotten word from our dean that I had been promoted to full professor. At a research-1 (R1) institution like UC Davis, reaching full professorship usually means one must have a second book or a whole slew of highly regarded journal articles. I had accomplished that hurdle with *The Hiplife in Ghana,* but stepping up and assuming directorship of our program, significantly increasing my service profile, also aided the new promotion.

I saw this new academic status in the context of my entire scholarly journey and wrote about that process in my journal: *My ancestors led me to the field of hip-hop, and more specifically international hip-hop. They knew that this field would catapult me into the fast track of promotion as Hip Hop Studies gained greater currency in academia through becoming central to American capitalism. From 1997 at the University of Hawai'i, where I had to choose a dissertation topic, to getting my first assistant professorship at BGSU, to earning tenure in 2007 at UCD, to the obstacles around gathering a full professor promotion committee, finally, arriving at the success of the moment. It has been my journey. Our Journey!* In June I had what I called "Halifu's Promotion Barbecue Party" in our backyard to celebrate with family and friends.

That same month Albirda Rose and I produced the 2013 Dunham Certification Workshop at Laney College dance department, returning to the same site of our 2006 Dunham memorial events (chapter 5). This would become the first certification workshop separate from the annual Dunham Seminar. After a lack of acknowledgment of our autonomy and separate mandate from Miss Dunham, Albirda and I had chosen to extricate our organization and begin the process of incorporating the Institute for Dunham Technique Certification (IDTC) as its own 501(c)(3) nonprofit organization.

At Laney we started with a symposium, covering the history of IDTC and the Dunham legacy, and gave emerging young scholars—Elizabeth Chin, Saroya Corbett, and Sukie Keita—an opportunity to present their developing Dunham scholarship. Albirda taught an important masterclass, and candidates for certification taught classes for their Dunham pedagogy methods to be critiqued by a committee of certified instructors. We also gave important Dunham legacy awards to community members—Yvonne Daniel, Lynn Coles, and my friend Linda Goodrich—all of whom had spent a lifetime promoting the Dunham legacy. We were proving that IDTC, the last organization Miss Durham had authorized, could stand alone and generate the next generation of holistic Dunham Certified Instructors.

Ending 2013, I reflected on the chapters of my life. I had become full professor, successfully making the transition from dancer-choreographer to academic-scholar. I had also accrued more financial security for retirement than dance could have offered me. I found my partner for the elder years of my life in Gene Howell. At sixty-seven years old, and drawing social security, I had, in a sense, already lived several lifetimes. From the young naïve Black hippie bravely leaving the pioneering Bay Area and becoming an American expatriate in Europe while building my first credits as dance artist, to dancing professionally in New York with the Rod Rodgers Dance Company. From discovering my dance roots living in West Africa and in the process ridding myself of any remnants of the "slave mentality" to returning to my Bay Area home to create the legendary Oakland Black dance center, Everybody's Creative Arts Center/CitiCentre Dance Theatre, now the Malonga Casquelourd Center for the Arts. And from teaching dance for twelve years at Stanford University to moving to Hawai'i, achieving my doctorate, and re-creating myself into an academic, all while studying and performing Hawaiian hula.

I was now the hip-hop professor at the University of California, Davis. It indeed felt like several lifetimes, and it was all worth it. I felt self-actualized and fulfilled, both as an artist and academic. I revealed to the world that African-descendant people were great contributors to world culture and indeed *central* to world popular culture. During my entire life I had been truly "Dancing in Blackness," and now I was "Dancing the Afrofuture."

9

We Got Next!

From the Afro-Present to the Afrofuture

Dance is at the center of regaining Buntu—humanity. Remembering how to rhythmically move together with heart, breath, and sincere connection is at the core of our collective human future.

Halifu Osumare

As I finish this account of my life in the summer and fall of 2021, it is impossible to ignore the dual crisis in the US, and indeed the world, which we endured for nearly two years: the COVID-19 pandemic health crisis and the racial reckoning resulting from what has been called the "George Floyd Moment," but actually from the last four hundred years of antiblackness. These crises have been global, even planetary, often reminding me of what we in the sixties used to call the "dawning of the Age of Aquarius." But back then we saw the so-called coming of the New Age as gloriously visionary, sitting in San Francisco smokey marijuana-filled rooms on floor pillows around "trippy" psychedelic lava lamps while uttering clichés like, "Far fucking out, man" and "The future is a trip!" The Fifth Dimension's 1969 song "The Age of Aquarius (Let the Sunshine In)" captured the times with lyrics like:

This is the dawning of the Age of Aquarius
The Age of Aquarius
Aquarius! Aquarius!

Harmony and understanding
Sympathy and trust abounding
No more falsehoods or derisions
Golden living dreams of visions
Mystic crystal revelation
And the minds true liberation[1]

We naively assumed we would be done with racism after the *second* racial reckoning since post-slavery Reconstruction: the Civil Rights and Black Power movements. And the fact that The Fifth Dimension were Black singers made the New Age even more poignant for me. We innocently calculated that we were going to end the continuous US foreign wars of imperialism, represented then by the Vietnam War, while at the same time challenging social, gender, and sexual norms that were all-pervasive. Today, I remember what Toni Morrison once said, "You want to fly, you got to give up the shit that weighs you down." She poignantly posed that existential equation with the ambiguity of her final scene in *Song of Solomon,* when her protagonist Milkman takes a flying leap off a tall mountain to escape being shot by his best friend. Did he die, or did he truly take flight?

We Got Next

I can ask the same question about today's twenty-first century dilemma: Will these earth-shifting health and racial justice crises wake us up and moves us forward, or will we dig deeper into entrenched ignorance and racism that weighs us down, moving us deeper into vicious cycles of division and death? Either way, I am a true believer that Black people—African-descendant peoples—is "who got next." The basketball court slang phrase referring to the person or group who has the court after the group currently playing the game, can be a metaphor for Black people who are clearly at the center of this moment in global transformation. Whether examining the so-called George Floyd Movement or the disproportionate effect of the coronavirus virus on Black and brown communities, we got next. African-descendant peoples and *"perceptions"* about us are at the crux of the potential for change on the planet.

And, as I have been saying throughout this memoir, Black cultures have the vitality and the perseverance to carry the burden of being "next." I am not a Christian, but in Matthew 19:30, Jesus said, "Many who are first will be last, and many who are last will be first." This biblical pronouncement was in the context of his encounter with a young rich ruler who was unable to give up his great wealth. Race and class are at the center of our current dilemma in this transformative period on the planet, and Black folks—those enslaved for 250 years—are at the center of our contemporary contested transition.

The (un)United States is an unkept promise, teetering at a crossroads, a real dilemma, in the first half of the twenty-first century. Our present predicament is made more urgent because African Americans, as former slaves who continue to be "contingent citizens" in the US, are also a part of the colonial history of the world. We are survivors of the sustained resistance to the racializing colonial project, and as humanitarian Uppinder Mehan calls us, "essentially a colonized nation within a larger nation."[2] That is why when George Floyd was so callously murdered for nine minutes and twenty-nine seconds on May 25, 2020, in Minneapolis by Derek Chauvin, the whole world responded. Connective marginality became obviously apparent. People of all races in cities across the nation, as well as regions of the entire world, responded. People in Africa, Asia, Europe, South America, the Caribbean, Australia, and New Zealand organized street protests to demonstrate their outrage and solidarity with US Blacks for social justice, all shouting "Black Lives Matter." For a brief moment, there was *human* connection across the planet joining forces for the plight of Black people as well as for their own marginalized groups and local injustices, drawing attention to the continued privileging of the global colonizers.

Even before the pandemic, there were dire twenty-first century end-of-the-decade assessments about sociopolitical ambiguity moving into 2020. *The Guardian*'s Washington correspondent, David Smith, wrote an article, for which he interviewed me, called "The Decade That Shook America." His byline for the title was "2010–2020 was a contradictory decade that will confound future historians with a simple question: how did America go from Obama to Trump?" In the article, Smith draws a picturesque dichotomy between the influence of Lin-Manuel Miranda's musical megahit *Hamilton* and the rise of Donald Trump to the US presidency. On one side, one has a "hip-hop, jazz, blues, rap, R&B . . . Broadway recast [of] America's founding fathers as people of color in a hymn to the immigrant nation," and on the other, one has "Trump [who] smashed and grabbed his way into the political class, and the White House, with a nationalist, nativist message that promised to build a border wall to keep Mexicans out and make America great (white) again."[3]

The Trumpian side of the American persona appears as an anti-Obama backlash that reeks of racism to its core. Smith quoted me as saying, "I think that Barack Obama was a rupture in the master narrative of the white, wealthy male being the only possible leader for this country. . . . It really shows the extreme schizophrenia of this country and how race is still very much a part of the two-faced 'original sin' portraying itself to the world as the beacon of democracy always looking at the inalienable rights of the individual, while at the same time reinforcing racial difference and hierarchy."[4]

Another pronouncement Smith made could not have been more prescient as to how the racial reckoning was going to grow into what I dub the "third Reconstruction in America," with the Civil Rights Movement as the second. "As 2019 drew to a close, America's existential crisis was the yawning, ever-growing chasm between these two tribes."[5] The January 6 insurrection on the congressional Capitol building, repressive state voting laws, the incessant killings of unarmed Black people, and the banning of Critical Race Theory and the 1619 Pulitzer Prize–winning journalism project from public school curricula all point to a sociopolitical chasm that has grown and a crisis that expanded exponentially.

The 1619 Project deserves some exploration because it centralizes the four hundred years of recorded enslavement and marginalization of African peoples in the United States. The project will forever be associated with the "cultural revolution" associated with the 2020 George Floyd global protests. On August 18, 2019, *New York Times* journalist Nikole Hannah-Jones edited a supplement to the iconic newspaper along with a *New York Times Magazine* edition devoted to "the 1619 Project." The front of the newspaper supplement read, "We've Got to Tell the Unvarnished Truth," which is plastered over an archival bill of sales for enslaved Africans. On the inside cover in large letters is written: "We are committing educational malpractice," as an indictment of the US educational system not teaching the reality that "slavery is the foundation on which this country is built." This seminal journalism project kicked off the commemoration of an important juncture in American, and indeed, world history, while simultaneously reframing the United States' strength based on the historic enslavement of millions of Africans.

The project's premise was not anything new to me or any other African American Studies scholar, for we had been emphasizing this point of view in Black history courses since the late sixties' development of the Black Studies field. I had taught the significance of the twenty-odd slaves arriving in the British colony of Jamestown, Virginia, in 1619 for many years. In my AAS 51, History of Black Dance course, for example, I used Lynne Fauley Emery's text *Black Dance from 1619 to Today* (1988, 1972) that chronicles that 1619 arrival of Africans as the beginning. I taught the customary portrayal of those first twenty Africans as more like indentured servants because the institution of lifetime chattel slavery would not emerge until about the 1640s. But, for the general US public, the entire 1619 Project became a revelation and a major source of debatable public discourse.

The *academic* objections were predictably about historically specific inaccuracies, such as emphasizing that those 1619 Africans were arguably not really considered "slaves." However, the major scholarly objection was the portrayal of slavery itself as the "true founding" principle of America, rather than our sacrosanct 1776 "war of independence from Britain" narrative. As Stanley Kurtz states in his review of historian David Wood's rejoinder book *1620: A Critical Response to the 1619 Project,* "That [founding principle] would make

American exceptionalism shameful rather than 'great.'"[6] In truth the US was founded on the shameful *ambiguity* of both "individual freedom" and "racial difference," and the debate between which principle was more foundational will probably rage on into the future.

In my UC Davis history courses, I allowed my students to debate this very issue as an assignment. The US motto *e pluribus unum* provides a succinct debating argument: Is the country truly focused on the unum (unity of one) or pluribus (the unequal many)? And I taught students to substantively argue both sides vigorously. In my own dance career, I focused on racial *misrepresentation* underlying historic Black cultural contributions. The point of my many iterations of "The Evolution of Black Dance" is that the descendants of enslaved Africans established the tone of the *cultural* identity of America.

The Brazil Exchange

That year I was pleased to host Dr. Monica do Amaral from Brazil at UC Davis while she was on a US research trip. I felt like I was returning the favor, in a small way, for her bringing me to Brazil as a part of her 2012 hip-hop conference in São Paulo (chapter 7). I presented her lecture "Contemporary Aesthetics of Resistance by Urban Youth in Brazil," in our AAS Brown Bag Series, offered during the lunch hour. Monica's lecture offered a poignant look at the linkages and disconnections of poor Black urban youth in São Paulo in comparison to hip-hop youth in the US, all through the lens of philosophy. I felt fulfilled in introducing the campus to how the American youth culture was affecting other countries regarding race and class. As she was not confident in her English at the academic level, I enlisted the help of Dr. Leopoldo Bernucci of the Department of Spanish and Portuguese as translator. While Monica was at UCD, I also shared African American culture by taking her to a Black quilt exhibit by the UCD Design Department, and also African culture by taking her to the Spirit of Uganda concert at the Mondavi Center. In this way, I was able to repay her for the generosity she had shown Gene and me in Brazil.

My scholarly exchange with Monica do Amaral did not stop when she left UCD because she brought me back to Brazil two years later to the 2014 COPENE conference—Congresso do Brasilero Pesquisadores Negros (Congress of Brazilian Black Researchers). Gene and I stayed at the Hilton Belem in Para state in northeastern Brazil near the beginning of the Amazon River, allowing us an entirely new view of the country. The COPENE conference, held at the Universidade Federal do Para, was a chance for me to meet *Afro-*

Brazilian scholars working in various academic areas, and Monica felt like my comparative international hip-hop research would be particularly relevant. I became a featured scholar in the grand auditorium that July 30 with my talk, "Keeping It Real: Race, Class, and Youth Connections through Hip-Hop in the U.S. and Brazil." It was extremely well received, with young Brazilian students gathered around me afterward in front of the stage, wanting to query me about my research.

This occasion became another validation of the relevancy of my chosen field of hip-hop youth culture. Monica told me that only a few scholars were given the largest conference venue for their presentations, and I had been chosen as one of them; I was profoundly honored. Even the translator sitting in the booth deciphering my talk into Portuguese approached me afterward, wanting to stay in contact via Twitter. I was building a reputation in Brazil as a scholar among the growing cadre of Black Brazilian researchers in COPENE.

UCD Achievements and Graduate Students in Dance and Performance Studies

One of my prized achievements as director of the AAS program is the establishment of the Goss Academic Achievement Award that supports students in their junior year to ensure matriculation. Darryl and Lois Goss, UCD Black alumni and husband and wife team, are models of *giving back* by the Black upper class. Daryl Goss was then vice president and general manager of BioReliance Corporation, managing the company's UK multinational operations, and was an African American Studies major during the eighties while attending UCD. The Gosses and I became friends, meeting several times to hash out the particulars of the award, and I got our then Student Affairs Officer, Kayton Carter, to construct the criteria and establish an award announcement process. This award became an incentive for our AAS majors to excel, and we were proud that the annual award gift came from one of our own former Black majors.

Fast-forward to February 2021, and Daryl and Lois Goss created a presidential chair in the now *department* of African American and African Studies at UC Davis to provide funding for teaching, research, and outreach about the history and culture of communities of African descent around the world. Their donated endowment was $1.5 million, which was supplemented with $500,000 from the UC Presidential Match for Endowed Chairs. The Gosses' donation was the first endowed chair in our department and represented recognition of our departmental efforts since its beginning in the sixties' movement for Black Studies.

Working with graduate students in dance and performance studies at UCD allowed me to bring my two worlds—dance and academia—into a mutual interdependence. Although I was not officially associated with the Department of Theatre and Dance, I did offer several Dunham workshops for the department and mentored several of their graduate students. Additionally, I was one of the founding UCD faculty members of the Performance Studies Graduate Group, discussed in chapter 7. The PhD degree-granting graduate group grew out of a previous departmental PhD program that focused solely in theater and dance, founded in 1996 by Susan Leigh Foster, Sue-Ellen Case, and Barbara Sellers-Young as faculty in the Department of Theatre and Dance. The new Graduate Group, with which I was affiliated, began in 2009 with faculty from not only dance and theater, but also media, literature, women and gender studies, technoculture, music, design, classics, history, and me from African American and African Studies. We had taken two years to create a program curriculum that could compete with the well-established Performance Studies departments at NYU and Northwestern University. However, what attracted international students to our particular performance studies approach was its interdisciplinary diversity.

UCD's Performance Studies Graduate Group was the program into which Ayo Walker was accepted, allowing me to mentor and advise her for the four years she was at UCD. She would eventually become my "adopted" daughter and remains so until today. Just as my previous relationship with Erica, now Yoruba priestess Osundara (chapter 3), our personal mother-daughter relationship grew from our academic relationship. But I also mentored two other Black dancers in the Department of Theatre and Dance: mayfield brooks (then known as Mary Ann Brooks) and Raissa Simpson. These three dancers—Ayo, mayfield, and Raissa—were my last protégés I mentored at UCD, and all three focused on concepts of performance as research in relation to the Black experience. I was training them to become the next generation of Black dance artists-scholars who would continue the deconstruction of dance and race, but also move us into the Afrofuture with their art and scholarship.

I mentored each student-artist from the perspective of their individual inquiries into the Black experience, their foci at that point in their careers providing direction for my guidance of their culminating degree projects. Because my own experience and interests are so varied, I was able to give each what they needed to push the boundaries of their artistic and academic inquiries. With Raissa Simpson, for example, her performance piece and written thesis, *Dancing in Sepia,* explored both a choreographic piece, originating from her undergraduate work at SUNY Purchase, as well as her written intellectual theory of (Black) dance. The subtitle of her thesis, "Choreographing

Race, Empathy, and Intersectionality," addressed the body as a site of racial discourse, investigating how Black people have embodied movement for their survival. She used anthropology, philosophy, and dance to work through a "redefinition of identity and to acknowledge the body as a site for social change."

The choreographic performance of *Dancing in Sepia,* in which Ayo also performed, was a visually stunning abstraction of that concept from the auction block of slavery to the mythological freedom of literally flying. Both her intellectual acumen and choreographic skills demonstrated a Black artist pushing the envelope of Afrofuturism. After her graduation in 2016, she continued to develop that theme in her choreographic explorations and hired me as her dramaturg to work with her San Francisco–based PUSH Dance Company.

mayfield brooks, whose pronouns are they/them, did an Interdisciplinary MFA in Theatre and Dance, graduating in 2014. I was on their graduation committee and advised them in their performance art piece "Improvising While Black: Chronicling a Black Aesthetic." Previously they had taken my graduate course, Critical Foundations in African American Studies, which deepened the intellectual grounds for their performance focus. They explained "Improvising While Black" as an inquiry into racial representation, spontaneous movement creation, and survival. They articulated their resulting performance art piece as the exploration of many questions, including "What is blackness in a world where most things Black and/or African are reviled, demonized and erased while at the same time desired, coveted and appropriated?"

The culminating work was site specific, moving through various campus locations with the audience traveling along with their multiracial cast of dancers, and ending in the Arena Theater of Wright Hall. They used multimedia projection, props, and costumes brilliantly to contextualize their many genres of movement, including postmodern, tap, and areal work. They also brought together performance as research to explore America's complex ambivalence around Black people and blackness, as well as that historical ambivalence's effect on Black people and their performance. mayfield brooks went on to become a much sought after movement-based artist teaching workshops and creating performance-based improvisatory modes of dance as resistance within the frame of Improvising While Black.[7] I perceived this kind of work necessary to chip away at the deep-seated collective racial psychology to help ensure the Afrofuture could actually become a shift in the world paradigm.

Ayo Walker's culminating graduate work was strictly academic to achieve a PhD in Performance Studies (PFS). However, she was very much a dance practitioner who had choreographed several works while at UCD. For example, her "Do Hashtags Make Black Lives Matter" used an original soundscape created from radio interviews and statements of family members of victims from the multiple police killings of unarmed Black people.

Throughout her two years of coursework in PFS at Davis, she had grown increasingly conscious of the inequalities implicit in dance in higher education, based on the absolute Eurocentric focus of most dance departments at the university level. The majority of the degree-granting dance departments privilege European classical ballet and (white) modern dance, with Black dance forms as peripheral electives. As she approached the dissertation-writing phase of her graduate work, she chose the subject of academically proving the cultural bias inherent in higher education dance; hence, the title of her dissertation became *Towards Entercultural Engaged Pedagogy: Revisioning Curricula in University Dance Studies from a Black Dance Aesthetics Approach.* Ayo not only wanted to prove the accepted bias and outright racism in dance education, but was adamant about conceiving a theoretical pedagogical model as an antidote to the pervasive problem in dance education. She created a student-oriented multicultural approach to dance education that she calls "entercultural engaged pedagogy."

Her dissertation abstract explains her theory in relation to the overall problem. "This dissertation argues for a greater understanding for developing and implementing a revisionist history of the discipline via the Black dancing body within the context of 'enterculturalism' for a complete curricular overhauling to ensure students receive a more comprehensive cultural literacy in higher education dance."[8] Hence Ayo's dissertation was both *reactive* to the explicit cultural bias in dance in higher education, beginning in the early twentieth century with Margaret H'Doubler and the Bennington College years,[9] but was also *proactive,* offering a new teaching method recognizing a student's own culture and their previously acquired movement knowledge as a part of the dance education process.

I became the chair of her dissertation committee, working with Ayo very hard on her four chapters. She included a quantitative fieldwork study of eight dance departments in several regions of the United States, and in June 2016 she was awarded her doctorate in Performance Studies. I retired right afterward, feeling like I had fully completed my academic mission with Ayo's graduation. In a sense, I felt like I had replicated myself. She wrote about our relationship in her dissertation dedication: "Especially for Dr. Halifu Osumare, my Iya Mi Keji La T'owo Iya Mi—my second mother from my mother's hand;

you taught me to resist oppression through my purpose, walk in my destiny, and to be unapologetically Ayo."

As I drew to the end of my directorship of African American and African Studies (AAS), I reflected on many of my accomplishments during that three-year period (2011–2014). I had achieved some practical tasks, like obtaining campus funding to renovate our conference room, but I was most proud of starting the process to achieve departmental status for our program. The difference between a program and department at UC Davis was ostensibly not that much; however, the *perception* of a full-fledged department as opposed to a precarious program that can be easily eliminated during hard times of university defunding, loomed large. Plus, all the other ethnic studies units in Hart Hall—Chicana/Chicano, Asian American, and Native American Studies—had all transitioned into departments since their late 1960s founding.

I was determined to start the paperwork to become a department, beginning a year-long review for approval by the Academic Senate. I called a day-long retreat of the faculty to discuss and assign tasks of writing about our various historical achievements and contemporary challenges and opportunities. I followed up with each of our faculty members—Wale Adebanwi, Moradewun Adejunmobi, Milmon F. Harrison, Bettina Ng'weno, and Elisa Joy White—to accomplish the extensive form to apply for departmental status, submitting the paperwork before I stepped down on June 30, 2014.

I completed my leadership role looking forward to a well-deserved sabbatical. My graduate students Ayo and Mary Ann (mayfield) took me out to dinner to celebrate the end of my administrative appointment. But my celebration was tempered by another national political event: the August 2014 killing of Michael Brown, another unarmed young Black male murdered by a policeman, this time in Ferguson, Missouri. He had just recently graduated from high school, and large ongoing protests ensued. Thus, the Black Lives Matter Movement was launched.

Two Crises: The Pandemic and Race

Returning to the present, the chasm between the races in the US was made extremely apparent with the COVID-19 pandemic's effect on Black people. A May 2020 *New York Times* article revealed, "The data, which shows death rates in each of [New York's] ZIP codes, underscores the deep disparities already earthed by the outbreak . . . Neighborhoods with high concentrations of black and Latino people, as well as low-income residents, suffered the highest death rates, while some wealthier areas—primarily Manhattan—saw almost no deaths . . ."[10] These findings by the New York City Health Department could be replicated throughout the nation, as racism and the lack of health care resources, exacerbated by dense living quarters for poor people of color, have always been factors in health and wellness. The bottom line becomes, as the article exposed, "race and income have proven to be the largest factors in determining who lives and who dies."

In the twenty-first century Black culture itself is on an often precarious footing. If Black people in the US are actually a colonized nation within a nation, then *Culture,* I argue, becomes our land—our country—the only thing we really own. But some say we really don't own our cultural production either, as appropriation of Black culture has abounded from minstrelsy to Broadway, and from television and Hollywood to now YouTube and TikTok on the World Wide Web. But Black folks have fiercely clung to our "land" through our bodies, movements, slang, style, and Africanness.

The *hyphenated space* between African and American becomes crucial, for it is where the diasporic past, the present political dilemma, and the future possibilities—the Afrofuture—based on our continued resistance to oppression, as well as our connection to our communities, become our tools of survival. I'm not referring to some kind of "racial authenticity," but about human souls connected to spiritual forces that have allowed us to survive, and sometimes thrive, against all odds, against unthinkable oppressions. In this historical scenario, *Performance* becomes a requirement for survival, and dance—rhythmic motion coming through our sentient beings—is at the heart of our survival.

And to be an initiated priest in the Yoruba tradition gives me access to what Afrofuturist Daniel B. Coleman calls a pluriverse. "To be a spiritual practitioner of these Afro-diasporic traditions that became Afro-diasporic upon crossing the Atlantic, is to practice Astro-Blackness in a Afrofuturist pluriverse."[11] I realize I have been dancing the Afrofuture most of my life as a self-defined Black woman who has access to spiritual forces far beyond what many understand, particularly my so-called oppressors. This is what *Dancing the Afrofuture* reveals.

The pandemic forced Black dancers and choreographers to slow down and use technology to continue disseminating their choreography, like all other dancers, and also reflect upon our lives and careers in the context of all this history. One example of that slowing-down reflective process was Black Dance Stories (BDS) lived-streamed on YouTube by dance historian and performer Charmaine Warren and her BDS team. With nearly fifty episodes, featuring more than ninety dancers and dance producers crossing generations and dance genres, our laptops, iPads, and smartphones allowed Black dance artists to dialogue with each other while reflecting on our personal and professional lineages. In the process unexpected connections between individual's personal stories emerged. During my episode, number twenty-nine, I communed with dancer-choreographer Earl Mosley, founder of Long Island's Diversity of Dance; and Coco Killingsworth, then co-interim president of Brooklyn Academy of Music. The three of us found loving supportive connections in telling our stories individually and dialoguing about our many correlations and links, several "amens" spontaneously uttered during our one-hour session. Our BDS episode became a group therapy session that we didn't know we needed, and I personally felt rejuvenated and inspired after our online Black dance stories.

A *New York Times* article on the series revealed the larger significance of "Mama Charmaine's" vision for the online series. "[She] began envisioning Black Dance Stories in the early days of the pandemic, when so many in the dance world were stuck at home with no work, their usual routines and social circles fractured. The murder of George Floyd, she said, heightened her desire to bring Black dance artists together to share their stories."[12] Again, the dual crises precipitated Charmaine's pondering a remedy or respite, a "kind of a salve, a salve of community." In Hawai'i they call it "Talk Story"; telling one's story in connection to one's community can be healing by bringing the collective together to renew links to a shared history, a shared story.

Eva Yaa Asantewaa, a senior curatorial director at the Gibney, a New York dance organization, captured the needed end result of Black Dance Stories: ". . . it also does the vital work of allowing Black artists to speak for themselves, as opposed to being talked about and defined by other people."[13] Asantewaa's poignant observations continued: "Our need to document what we do as Black creatives in this society is always an issue because so much information is lost or distorted, or other people take credit for things. So, to be able to connect with artists who are telling their own stories in their own way and dialoguing with one another about their lives is invaluable—and not only now, but also down the line, for future artists and future fans of dance."[14] Indeed, in our attempt to cope with the dual crises—the pain and loss of 2020–2021—initiatives like Black Dance Stories emerged that will undoubtedly serve a larger purpose for a salutary Afrofuture.

In the middle of the pandemic, I wrote a poem about the irony of the long-standing racial *mask* that Black folks have had to wear for survival—captured in Paul Laurence Dunbar's famous nineteenth-century poem—in relation to the ubiquitous *forced masking* during the pandemic. My poem captures the

Afro-Present, our continuing need for duplicity to survive systemic racism while longing for a *maskless* Afrofuture:

A Contemplative Moment, or We Wear the Mask
May 14, 2020

Dunbar's Mask returns
New form of masking, masquerading
This time for healing, for caring?
We have always worn the mask of disguise
Grinning rather than Grimacing
Laughing rather than Crying
Survival always meant accruing
"This Debt we pay to human guile
while hurting all the while"
Could "the world be otherwise
in counting all our tears and sighs?"

The Old Normal disguising pain
deep wounds of terror
Could the New Normal
take us beyond the Past,
beyond the brutality and no gain?

Are we capable of truly caring?
walking in another's historical footsteps?
Can we wear a mask of compassion and protection?
instead of fear and oppression?
Can we stop the charade
to find a joyous parade?

A spectacle of Love
with a new Mask
Symbol of a new normal?
Or a veneer covering old disguise
Why do we wear any Mask?
Why do we disguise the True Self?
wanting to live free
A Virus dictates a Mask of Protection,

But what happens to the old Mask?
Does it continue to hide "A Dream Deferred?"

Inspired from: Paul Laurence Dunbar's "We Wear the Mask" (1896)
and Langston Hughes's "A Dream Deferred" (1951)

The Afro-Present Becoming the Afrofuture

I am convinced in the infinite potential for options in what I have been calling
the Afrofuture. The preponderance of Afrofuturist websites, a renewed interest in Octavia E. Butler's prescient science-fiction novels, and several digital
futuristic projects emanating out of Africa all lead me to this conclusion. The
Biden administration has even created a national office of Science and Technology Policy (OSTP) and positioned a top Afrofuturist, Dr. Alondra Nelson,
as deputy director for science and society. Nelson is known for her work in
bioethics and racism in science and medicine, and her choice for this national
position has received praise from Black Afrofuturist scholars and the scientific community alike.

Alondra Nelson is well known for her writings and talks about Black people's culture and the future. "Part of the resilience of Black culture and Black
life is about imagining the impossible, and a better place, a different place." She
also notes, "Black people have lived the alienation that science fiction writers
imagined; Blacks as the alienated [citizen] are the original aliens."[15] Nelson
positions the African American experience at the junction of science and
technology, just as Butler did in her award-winning science fiction novels—
Parable of the Sower and *Parable of the Talents*—what Kerry James Marshall
did in his "Keeping the Culture" painting depicting a Black family traveling
on a spaceship carrying an ancient Dogon sculpture, and how singer Janelle
Monáe portrays herself as a messianic android on her *Metropolis* EP (2007)
and her debut *Archandroid* album (2010). But as my past Stanford University
student, the famous astronaut Dr. Mae Jemison, once told me, "You got to stay
rooted even when you're in space."

Ironically the term "Afrofuturism" was coined by white pop culture critic
Mark Dery in 1994. In his chapter, "Black to the Future" in his edited volume
Flame Wars: The Discourse of Cyberculture, he laid out its parameters. Dery
defined Afrofuturism as "speculative fiction that treats African-American
themes and addresses African-American concerns in the context of 20th
century technoculture—and, more generally, African-American signification
that appropriates images of technology and prosthetically enhanced future.
[This] might, for want of a better term, be called 'Afrofuturism.'"[16] That a white

cyberculture theorist was propelled to include an analysis of the artistic and cultural practices of a people reared on a terroristic past and an inequitable present speaks to the *centrality* of those people who *had* to conjure imaginary worlds beyond the brutal reality of past and current dynamics of their lived experience in order to survive. Black cultural critics, like Greg Tate and others, also expounded upon the term to denote what Black artists like Sun Ra, George Clinton and Parliament Funkadelics, and early futuristic disco-funk divas LaBelle were already exploring musically decades earlier.

British-Ghanaian scholar and filmmaker Kodwo Eshun has written poignantly about Afrofuturism, positioning it within the historical erasure of Africa from the entire Enlightenment project. "To establish the historical character of Black culture, to bring Africa and its subjects into history denied by Hegel et al., it has been necessary to assemble countermemories that contest the colonial archive, thereby situating the collective trauma of slavery as the founding moment of modernity."[17] Of course, this is not a new revelation, as Paul Gilroy (1993) and novelist Toni Morrison are well-known promoters of the counternarrative of African descendants being at the center of modernity.

Eshun argues that a futurity positioning Africa in its rightful place was initiated at the beginning of African independence from European political colonialism. For example, he claims Nkrumah's Pan-African attempt to create a United States of Africa was one such "counterfutures." I would add Léopold Senghor's Negritude philosophy of African Socialism, situated differently than European Marxism, as another example. Senghor once wrote, "Negro African society is collectivist, or more exactly, communal because it is rather a communion of souls rather than an aggregate of individuals. Africa had already realized socialism before the coming of the Europeans. But we must renew it by helping to regain its spiritual dimension."[18] However, with neocolonialism in all its forms, such as Western promoted coups and European financial aid to Africa attached to sworn allegiance and continued mineral resource exploitation, African futurist efforts waned.

Eshun argues for a twenty-first-century revival of Afrofuturism that builds on those past Africanist philosophical countermemories. While acknowledging continuing forms of neocolonialism, he also insists "that power now operates predictively as much as retrospectively. . . . [It] also functions through the envisioning, management, and delivery of reliable futures."[19] What he means is that "the future" is now for sale in science fiction, in its various forms within literature, comics, film, music, and dance, all creating a twenty-first-century "New Economy." He says, "Science fiction capital is the synergy, the positive feedback between future-oriented media and capital. The alliance between cybernetic futurism and 'New Economy' theories argues that information is a direct generator of economic value. Information about the future therefore circulates as an increasingly important commodity."[20]

To understand Afrofuturism in the context of this "New Economy" and its unique contributions to the larger field of science fiction, one need not look any further than the blockbuster 2018 *Black Panther* film as discussed in the introduction. The movie created a futuristic vision of Wakanda, a fictious African country, based on the original Marvel comic book superhero of the Black Panther, allowing Black people, as well as the rest of the world, to step into a futurist view of Africa. The film gives us science fiction possibilities of a future led by a technological intelligence emanating out of Africa, and a vision of how the future will be necessarily related to the pain of the past. The film's main characters of T'Challa, played by the late great Chadwick Boseman, and Killmonger, portrayed by Michael B. Jordan, are cousins whose fathers, as brothers, were estranged due to an attempted coup in Wakanda. Killmonger's father was banned from Wakanda and had to raise his son in Oakland, California, of all places. Directed by Oakland native Ryan Coogler, the first Black director of a Marvel Studios film, he situated Killmonger as a product of the rough streets of the Black ghetto who wants to get revenge for he and his father being deprived of their rightful place in the advanced African society of Wakanda. Hence, Coogler used *Black Panther* to situate a futuristic African society containing advanced computer technology with the coveted "vibranium" mineral against the deprivations of the present-day African American urban experience in a city I know all too well.

In Afrofuturism, the past/present cannot be ignored, even in a futuristic society where Africa represents the pinnacle of advanced society. Futurist countermemories are rendered more potent against the sociopolitical dilemma of the present and the exploitative past. The cybernetic future is more fully understood in relation to the colonial past and the contentious present—the *Sankofa* process, looking backward to the past as one consumes the futuristic egg. As theater and film director Peter Brook has said, "People in the past have done what we're trying to do infinitely better. That's why, for one's own sanity, to keep one's own sense of proportion, one must regularly go back to them."[21]

In addition, *Black Panther* also offers a revealing lens into Eshun's concepts of "science fiction capital" and the "feedback between future-oriented media and capital." The marketing and merchandising of the film expose how much science fiction's media hype pushes today's late capitalism. For example, the first poster produced for the *Black Panther* film shows T'Challa as African royalty on a massive throne dressed in his Black Panther suit. The merchandizing items that followed were hoodies, jackets, helmets, and T-shirts, not to mention the upsurge of the comic books sales as well as the social media dialogue and hype. As Chadwick Boseman said in a pre-release interview, "It's taken on a life of its own, looking at what people have created on their own from the inspiration of the movie, with the re-creation of our posters and the GoFundMe campaigns. It's amazing to watch it; the 'moviement' of it all! I've never seen anything like it in my life." During the same interview Michael B. Jordan added, "It's massive on a whole other level; obviously when you deal with Marvel globally and how much it means to so many people. Eighteen movies in, this being the nineteenth one, it raises the bar of the scale [of marketing and hype]."[22] What the two actors pondered about the marketing experience of their then latest film is what Eshun calls "the futures industry," defined as "the intersecting industries of technoscience, fictional media, technological projection, and market prediction." And these intersections have fueled "the desire for a technology boom,"[23] with Afrofuturism as central.

Many other Black television series followed *Black Panther* in the popular Afrofuturism genre including HBO's 2019 *Watchmen* and its 2020 horror series *Lovecraft Country*. The Emmy award–winning *Watchmen* was a nine-episode series that was an antiracist pulp thriller remix loosely based on a subversive 1986 DC comic book series and a previously made 2009 (white) science fiction movie. Created by film and comic book writer Damon Lindelof, the series takes place in an alternate futuristic universe, but premised on white supremacy and contemporary racial violence, centralizing the infamous 1921 Tulsa race massacre. It, therefore, introduces a new generation to that important often-erased part of America's violent past, becoming another example of life imitating art, when a year and half later in May 2021 the entire nation was fixated on the one hundredth anniversary of the Tulsa "Black Wall Street" massacre, serving as another crucial history lesson for America.

The *Watchmen* television series emphasized an Afrofuture attempting to exorcise the racist past that necessarily must be re-examined first. One tellingly prophetic scene was portrayed in the final ninth episode: Lou Cosset's character, Will, the elderly lone survivor of the original Tulsa massacre, is now an old wheelchair bound Black man. He tells the female protagonist Angela Abar, played brilliantly by Regina King,[24] who won an Emmy for Best Actress for a Limited Series, "You can't heal under a mask; wounds need air." The masks that Black people have *had* to wear for survival is questioned, proclaiming that the racial and personal wounds we bear from the past must be revealed to allow the future to truly free us.

Afrofuturism and Dance

Afrofuturism isn't limited to film and television and literature; dance has taken its seat at the futuristic table as well. Black choreographers are taking direct and indirect approaches to examining the possibilities of African-descendant peoples in the future. Afrofuturist dance artists are not only concerned with past and present injustices but are, in fact, seizing control of future narratives. As sociologist Robin D.G. Kelley has said, "The most radical art is not protest art but works that take us to another place, envision a different way of seeing, perhaps a different way of feeling."[25] Futuristic visions are a part of the Black Radical Tradition that has sustained us and drives us beyond the overt terror of the past and the tenuous terror of the present.

Several dance artists embrace Afrofuturism directly, embedding it within their aesthetic by creating entire projects exploring the concept's possibilities. Choreographer and dance educator D. Sabela Grimes, a 2014 Rockefeller Artists Fellow, directly appropriates Octavia Butler's concept of earthseed—"God is Change"—as the organizing principle for his "Earthseed Movement." His pedagogical approach to alignment and groundedness reveals a commitment to the physical and metaphysical efficacies of Afro-diasporic cultural practices. He lodges his movement practices in Butler's philosophy of change as the only constant leading toward the ultimate truth of destiny. His Los Angeles–based Afrofuturistic dance theater projects, like *World War WhatEver, 40 Acres & A Microchip, BulletProof Deli,* and *ELECTROGYNOUS,* physically ruminate on metaphysical histories while balancing the deconstruction of masculinity and conceiving a "womynist" consciousness.

On the East Coast, the Brooklyn-based Renegade Performance Group, founded by André Zachery, blends choreography and technology while utilizing a hip-hop aesthetic. Zachery's "Drexciya Redux: An Afrofuturist Cabaret" captures the company's aesthetic in an opening solo of an androgynous male-like hooded figure invoking a New Age disco with hip-hop tutting movements segueing into a rapping deejay, all in front of a rolling projection backdrop of current news headlines and evocative phrases. A poet enters and asks, "At what frequency do we change; at what frequency do we activate? Only the water can understand the call of La Siren or Olokun." His usage of Haitian and Yoruba spirituality in relation to a futuristic call for transformation consciously invokes mythologies associated with the past, but which never actually passed, and instead invokes future visions in us. These two dance Afrofuturists—Grimes and Zachery—situated on opposite US coasts represent the continuum of past and present that is irrevocably tied to an envisioning future.

Two Black female Afrofuturist choreographers explore that continuum through the prism of Octavia Butler's influential science fiction writings. New York–based Trinidadian choreographer Makeda Thomas has taken Butler's Hugo award–winning short story about a future world, "Speech Sounds," as her impetus for a trio choreographic piece of the same name. She explores Afrofuturist metaphors of art and technology that, like Zachery, simultaneously invoke the orisas as forces of nature circulating throughout the African diaspora. Her choreographic approach depends on improvisations of three dancers moving through multiple variations of the work, an approach that mirrors Butler's story that "is about the spaces between selves; of how individuals connect and disconnect; of isolation and companionship . . ."[26] Thomas's interdisciplinary choreographic work reflects a child of the diaspora, with research for her "Speech Sounds" dance piece moving through West Africa, Europe, the US, Venezuela, Grenada, and Trinidad. Her use of orisa movements is based on how "unique syncretisms of those distinct cultural histories [become] manifestation[s] of the divine through human movement."[27]

Staycee Pearl is another female Afrofuturist dance artists. Pearl is an Ailey-trained dancer who created STAYCEE PEARL dance project & Soy Sos (SPdp&SS), along with her husband and sound designer Herman "Soy Sos" Pearl in 2009. They became the resident dance company of the Kelly-Strayhorn Theater in Pittsburg. In 2011 Pearl began focusing her choreography on Butler's literary canon creating *Octavia: Bringing a Literary Inspiration to Life*. For the aural soundscape Herman used a Jimi Hendrix–inspired 1983 piece from his *Electric Ladyland* album, claiming Hendrix as an early Afrofuturist, who aurally aligns with Butler's work. Staycee tackled the choreographic translation of Butler's work this way:

> The . . . question that stood out in my mind was how could we have each socially pregnant conversation through movement? We found that it was easiest to tackle the bigger ideas and most fun to play around with the lesser elements such as shape shifting and alien sex. The harder stuff was supremacy, racism, and apartheid, all of which she so expertly mirrors for us in literature.[28]

Pearl's *Octavia: Bringing a Literary Inspiration to Life* demonstrates the rapprochement of dance and literature through an Afrofuturist vision that exposes devastating human shortcomings while illuminating Butler's extraterrestrial foresight of future possibilities.

New York Times dance critic Gia Kourlas captured New York choreographer Kyle Marshall's Afrofuturism aesthetic in the title of her exposé on him: "A Choreographer Finds His Way, Getting Lost in the Stars." Turning thirty years old during the pandemic in 2020, Marshall used his "downtime" to continue his research after graduating in dance from Rutgers University, dancing with the Trisha Brown Dance company, and forming his own company in 2014. He used the quarantine to examine the potential of improvisation in his work, spurred on by his exploration of jazz music. "I also thought improvisation would be a helpful way for performers to get back into material after not being onstage for so long."[29]

Out of his "woodshedding" came two new works, one of which is *Stellar,* screened at the Baryshnikov Arts Center. Marshall reveals the work was "inspired by Afrofuturism, jazz and science fiction."[30] Watching the piece online, I felt a sense of discovery and wonderment at what many young Black choreographers are exploring in the twenty-first century. They are looking upward beyond the muck and mire of the Afro-Present to the stars, perhaps to the North Star of freedom. Perhaps looking to the stars again will guide us to a new kind of Promised Land. Kourlas writes about *Stellar* this way: Marshal conjures a universe, meditative and otherworldly, in which three dancers, Bree Breeden, Ariana Speight and Marshal himself, move to a dreamy score by Kwami Winfield . . . There's weightlessness to them; at times, they seem like particles.[31]

Marshall is inspired by jazz musician Sun Ra's approach to music, and his "Space is the Place" motif was a great inspiration for *Stellar.* As young artists like Marshall discover past Afrofuturist artists like Sun Ra, we witness the current generation continuing the journey into the black hole of space as an expedition into the Self. Marshall's music composer, Kwami Winfield, draws the direct connection: "Sun Ra represents an alternative vision of the future—the potential to be more than what we're born into as humans and specifically Black people in America . . . something that Kyle and I talked about specially was the way Sun Ra treats his keyboard like the controls of a spaceship."[32] As an older Black artist who experienced the Sun Ra Arkestra live, I am heartened to see young Black choreographers exploring his music and grabbing the Afrofuturist baton to continue the marathon of Black exploration of inner and outer space. Kyle Marshall is one of these current Black choreographers who is regenerating past tenets of Afrofuturism into new visions of possibilities.

Raissa Simpson's Bay Area Dance Afrofuturism

During the pandemic lockdown in 2020 I assumed several online consultancies, as digital lectures, classes, rehearsals, organizational meetings, and webinars as Zoom and other platforms became standard. My former UCD graduate student, Raissa Simpson, approached me in the fall of that year about me becoming choreographic dramaturg for her San Francisco PUSH Dance Company. As I had already been her advisor on her *Dancing in Sepia* UC Davis graduate thesis and concert, I was familiar with her Afrofuturist choreographic approach and accepted the one-year consultancy. As I was then beginning to research Afrofuturism, I thought working with a dance artist on a practical level would ground my understanding of how the concept manifested in a particular choreographic approach. Beginning the dramaturg consultancy, I met online with Raissa and the company members once a week. The dancers were working out their assigned movement problems individually, either in their homes or at outdoor sites, and submitting them to Raissa online through the Dropbox platform, to which I was given access. It became an interesting process to research her themes, evaluate the movement manifestations of the dancers, and discuss the evolution of the work at our weekly Zoom meetings.

Raissa founded her PUSH Dance Company in San Francisco in 2005, after dancing with two of the city's well-established companies: Robert Moses's Kin Dance Company and Joanna Haigood's Zaccho Dance Theatre. Her dance company consists of eight dancers of Black and Asian descent (Raissa herself is Black and Filipino), with long-term company member Ashley Gayle as the rehearsal director (now associate artistic director). Raissa's dancers span the training gamut from university and conservatory to street improvisers, allowing her to explore contemporary modern to hip-hop dance approaches in her Afrofuturist quest. Her own training in the SUNY Purchase dance department, with Kevin Wynn as one of her mentors, was strictly modern and ballet; but when she returned to the West Coast and began auditioning for various dance opportunities, she realized that broadening her dance repertoire into Afro-diasporic forms, including hip-hop, was absolutely necessary in the twenty-first century. This understanding became the seed for her current Afrofuturist approach to her movement studies, as she told me, "I shift current dance practices from homogenous depictions of Black bodies on stage to imagery of otherworldly beings." In so doing she explores the contemporary concept of Afrofuturism from an embodied dance praxis.

During her MFA concert at UC Davis, she had her dance company perform along with university student dancers to achieve *Dancing in Sepia,* and it eventually became part two of a trilogy of dance pieces called *Mothership.* The entire larger work began her artistic journey into Afrofuturism. As she says on her website, "*Mothership* is a trilogy work that challenges cultural traditions and identities through the lens of Afrofuturism—an artistic movement that emerged in the mid-1990s and drew heavily on composer musicians like

Sun Ra and Parliament Funkadelics. Afrofuturism re-imagines and reclaims the past, present, and future for Black lives."[33]

Raissa's *Mothership* trilogy allows the intersections of past, present, and future to dialogue in aesthetic ways that engage the sociopolitical history underpinning time. About *Mothership 1,* premiering in 2016, she says, "It was born out of questions surrounding national identity, race and xenophobia. Through the lens of Afrofuturism, the ten-minute performance challenges traditional notions of race and gender. Most of the queries are rooted in the African diaspora with constant play in shifting viewpoints on historical context of slave ownership and the revisionist theory of the Founding Fathers."[34] The dancers wear eighteenth-century white European wigs of the early US colonies along with contemporary dancerly shorts and tops, performing modern dance shapes and configurations. In *Mothership 1* Raissa blends the past and present in iconography and movement phrases to interrogate the logic of colonial ideology that allowed people to own other human beings.

Mothership II (M2), as an elaboration of *Dancing in Sepia,* became a complete commitment to Afrofuturism as a lens through which to envision a world beyond the present terror for BIPOC (Black, Indigenous, and People of Color) people. She writes about *M2* on her website: "M2 centers on speculative fiction and anti-colonialism to transport the viewer into a world filled with ritual, spirituality and Indigenous practices. Simpson's multimedia design draws upon Afrofuturism as a social movement, to utilize Sun Ra's 'Space is the Place' quote, to imagine a future free from racial and gendered harm."[35] Her celestial planetary multimedia moving backdrop is juxtaposed with archival footage of slavery and, along with her self-composed synthesized music, does indeed draw the audience into a vision of futuristic possibilities beyond the trauma of the past. A small moving platform, for example, serves as an auction block on which dancers ambiguously posed for view, as well as a spaceship to transport them to other worlds, all while moving it around the stage throughout the dance. The imaginary of "flying Africans" during slavery is invoked in twenty-first-century choreography.

Premiering in September 2017 in Raissa's self-produced annual PUSHfest weekend of concerts, along with other dance companies, *M2* was an important step forward in Raissa Simpson's exploration of Afrofuturism. Her annual PUSHfest concert took place before the pandemic at ODC Theater, one of San Francisco's most active venues for contemporary dance. I took advantage of her annual concert weekend to showcase my own re-emergence onto the choreographic scene after retirement. I presented my 2017 choreographic piece *In the Eye of the Storm,* which I had set on Sacramento Black Art of

Dance (S/BAD) at California State University, Sacramento (CSUS) for Linda Goodrich's retirement concert and the twenty-fifth anniversary of S/BAD. Raissa's PUSHfest allowed me to bring my new choreographic work, further explained later, to the larger dance world of San Francisco, providing me a choreographic re-entry to my home city at seventy years old.

Raissa's *Mothership III* (*M3*) premiered in 2019 at ODC, and curiously enough, the third part of the trilogy represents the *present,* as *M2* was about the future. In this third part of her trilogy, she focuses on Octavia Butler's vision of "stories for Black People in present day life." Raissa is curious about what many perceived as Butler's conundrum: "[Butler] was confronted with the question of why is it necessary to have Black characters in her narratives even if extraterrestrials are omnipresent in science-fiction, and made it a point to insert them into her futuristic stories."[36] Hence, after having her audience confront the colonial past in *M1* and then catapulting them into a futuristic vision of possibilities based on that treacherous past in *M2,* Raissa finally deposits us in *M3* in the present, forcing us to interrogate current-day social movements while engaging what she calls "defamiliarizing what is socially familiar." In *M3* the dance's star-filled backdrop and self-composed electronic score is like an ever-present drone reminding us that even in the ambiguous contentious present, we remain on a life-giving planet revolving around our sun, with human connections to the other stars in the universe.

Raissa's view of the present is based on her deep involvement with San Francisco's growing inequality of gentrification. In 2014 Raissa premiered the *Point Shipyard Project,* a work growing out of her teaching dance and exploring the stories of the predominantly Black youth in the Bay View Hunter's Point district of SF. Raissa's *Point Shipward Project* integrated her company members with the youth participants, allowing a collaborative artistic process to emerge and forming the basis for the choreography. Raissa Simpson, as an Afrofuturist choreographer, is still connected to the reality of inequality in her present-day city that supports her company.

In a published book chapter on her aesthetic and futuristic choreography, Raissa sums up her choreographic motivation in relation to Bay Area social dynamics, as manifested in both *Point Shipward Project* and *Codelining,* another of her works that combined technology with the issue of real estate redlining:

> Dance isn't just an art; it's a form of survival. While San Francisco presents itself as a progressive and tranquil city, Black bodies are forced to remain in constant vibration. As Black communities face gentrification in San Francisco dance has become an integral part of preserving

complex relations and representation of Black embodiment. Through visceral and physical gestures, I situate my dances as an archival gathering of a dwindling community . . . Always considering the underlying motif of Afrofuturism, these present-day depictions [in my dances] are lifted off into the cosmos by reframing ritual dances with technology.[37]

Raissa Simpson uses Black and BIPOC dancing bodies through her PUSH Dance Company to explore the ancient-future paradigm of Afrofuturism. She is concerned with the Afro-Present as well as the Afrofuture, bringing into conversation the ancient that is not so past with the ignorance and inequalities of the present, all to explore the possibilities of the future as now, which my generation first called the Age of Aquarius. From my perspective, Raissa Simpson has become like a contemporary Afrofuturistic Katherine Dunham. She merges her dance and scholarship with a deep concern for the future of Black people and humanity in general.

Technology, Dance, Digital Blackness, and the Promise of the Afrofuture

Contemplating the technological shifts over my lifetime is mindboggling, for I am old enough to have lived the analogue to digital cultural, social, and political transition. Although the government might have been experimenting with huge computers occupying entire rooms back in the sixties, the general public could have never conceived of individuals owning a small personal computer, let alone carrying around a small handheld mobile cellphone that doubles as a computer. We could not have conceived of having copious information at the click of a mouse (A mouse in your house? Those were meant to be killed!), or something called a "search engine" leading to instantaneous vast arrays of knowledge that once took weeks to discover in a physical library. I never imagined my cherished library card catalogues becoming extinct; how would I do my research? Back in the day we had to pay dearly for an international long-distance call to communicate with someone in another country, and even then the connection was not all that clear. A real-time conversation "online" through social media could not even be imagined. In fact, we have redefined the term "social media"; it used to mean the gossip column in the local newspaper. As digital journalist for *60 Minutes for Quibi,* Laurie Segal says, "The world is becoming a chat room, and we are becoming our own avatars."[38] Today, there is little difference between "online" and "offline."

In the first three decades of my life—the fifties, sixties, and seventies—and even most of the eighties, we lived in an analogue world. It wasn't until the late eighties that I got my first clunky Apple MacIntosh computer with a floppy drive and limited memory bought through my faculty discount at the Stanford University Bookstore. Little did I know that in my elder years, today in my seventies, I would live in a whole new digital world where the "future" would be parceled out to the general public by global digital capitalist corporations and new Silicon Valley start-ups like the packaged rations given to astronauts floating in spaceships. I particularly examine these life-changing technological shifts from the perspective of how they have affected dancers, African-descended people, and Blackness itself.

More than 4.2 billion people currently use the internet globally, which makes it the single most important piece of technology of the twentieth and twenty-first centuries. As we adapt to digital technology, it has *literally* changed the way we live our lives. Indeed, the COVID-19 pandemic alone has driven the technological shift home to us: we replaced physical meetings and in-person employment with digital Zoom meetings from the waist up, as office workers and managers telecommuted to work. In the dance world, we went from physical dance rehearsals in studios and performing on stage to posting individual videoed choreography created in one's living room, moving our furniture to create needed dance space.

We now live in a world where Technology with a big "T" has generated the power to shape media and culture itself. As Segal pronounced, "[There are various] niche media platforms where people can live out their own truths."[39] And when truth becomes that *relative,* manipulated by anyone online with a strong voice, no matter how insane the context, then as my Aunty Gladys in Hawai'i (chapter 2) would say, "We're in some deep kimchee." Large tech companies have become so powerful that "governments are moving simultaneously to limit the power of tech companies with an urgency and breadth that no single industry had experienced before."[40] Of course the motivations for trying to control Big Tech—Apple, Google, Facebook, Twitter or X, etc.—varies, depending on the country: The US and Europe are concerned with these companies stifling capitalist competition and spreading misinformation and purposeful "disinformation," as well as invading individual privacy; Russia's provocation is to silence protest movements and enforce more political control; while "in China it is some of both."[41]

The underlying concern, as usual, is power. The ten largest tech firms, which have become gatekeepers in commerce, finance, entertainment, and communications, now have a combined market capitalization of more than $10 trillion. In gross domestic product terms, that would rank them [together] as the world's third-largest economy. The growth of tech companies has produced troubling ramifications, not the least of which is our individual privacy, as they allow advertisers of all kinds to "harvest" (a new tech-business word) our personal data. The *original* intent of the internet was a borderless digital space where free-flowing ideas of all kinds could be consumed unencumbered. To keep any semblance of that original motivation alive today, a lot more is at stake, not the least of which is big money.

As the cliché goes, "at the end of the day," only we are in control of our interaction with this life-shifting technology. But we have gotten caught up in *virality,* the condition of rapidly spreading popular communications with each other through the internet. Now we are burying ourselves in misinformation and purposeful disinformation, with governments looking for ways to curb intentional lies that are literally killing us, such as false information about the vaccine for the novel coronavirus. During the pandemic social media has become an accelerator for extremism, with groups of people cornered within their own cultural silos feeding each other conspiracy theories of all kinds.

But beyond the large political, economic, and social effects of social media, I am also interested in how the digital age has affected dance. One major boom or bust for dance and pop culture, depending on how one looks at it, is the TikTok social media platform. TikTok is a video-sharing networking service founded in 2012 and owned by the Chinese company ByteDance. Global consumers use it to make various short-form videos on different subjects, but dance routines are the most popular medium. #DanceVideo on TikTok has become a real "thing" through users uploading fifteen-second to one-minute videos of dancers and dance enthusiasts around the world. The "dance challenge," where young dancers upload their choreography to the same latest pop song, has become a major feature of dance on TikTok, providing young people a chance to "go viral" and become "instant celebrities."

With thousands, and often millions, of views, a TikTok dancer can build their platform to become a "TikTok Star" in what is now called "the TikTok dance community." For example, Charli D'Amelio, a young white female dancer, adept at Africanist hip-hop dance moves, started the "Get Busy" dance challenge in 2020 by reviving the 2003 Sean Paul dancehall hit song of the same name. The TikTok dance phenomenon generated millions of users grooving to the Jamaican hit, with even Hollywood actors getting into the act, which in turn, boosted the virality of the entire dance-song spectacle. But I ask, do global TikTok users really understand the Black dance aesthetic or the historical struggles of the Black people creating it? Globalization of the hip-hop aesthetic is at the center of much of TikTok's popularity, but few know the evolution of those Africanist movements in the Western world or the history of their appropriation. As I said in *The Africanist Aesthetic in Global Hip-Hop,*

"... the Africanist aesthetic plays a crucial role in hip-hop's commercialization in the postmodern era [and is a major] insinuation in economic, technological, and social dynamics in the era of globalization."[42]

The concert dance scene is also utilizing new technology, often as a central impetus, not simply for content delivery. For example, white dancer and choreographer Catie Cuan, a doctoral student in mechanical engineering at Stanford University, experiments with Artificial Intelligence (AI) in the form of dancing with robots. One of her pieces translates "basic jazz and ballet vocabulary into robot joint angles, ... creating what she calls a ballet for swarms of robots, mapped onto robot morphology that leverages their innate nature."[43] Explaining what she means by their "innate nature," she says robots can be made to have "distinctive movement qualities" using "the precise torques of their joints," as "they have no muscles to contract or relax [and that] totally changes the perception of weight placement and bodily distribution." Cuan views her entire creative process with AI as "a choreographic tool that can disrupt the habitual dancing-making process."[44]

Collaboration between AI technology and dance is growing exponentially. One major sign of its growth is the creation of a division of Google called Google Arts and Culture that has been collaborating with well-known companies like Bill T. Jones/Arnie Zane Company and the Martha Graham Dance Company to explore these new kinds of dance aesthetics. As this new dance field called "choreographics" emerges, it depends heavily on the computation that creates "digital avatars that dance along with live performers."[45]

But Africa and its diaspora is not left out of exploring the digital age, thanks to a few Afrofuturists on the continent. One of the main dance artists in this field is Nigerian Qudus Onikeku, whom I introduced in chapter 7 as a visiting artist at UC Davis who audited one of my graduate courses. Born in Lagos, he was trained in France at the National Higher School of Circus Arts in Chalons-en-Champagne. Besides his native Nigeria, his performance art has been presented in the US, Europe, and the Caribbean, combining Yoruba-based choreography with movement philosophies of hip-hop, capoeira, and the Nigerian masquerading traditions into what he calls "An African Futurist Dance Experience." His choreography often explores themes of memory, identity, and exile. After training in Europe and touring the world with pick-up companies, he returned to Nigeria to form Q Dance Company and his umbrella organization AFROPOLIS, a name derivative of the ancient Greek acropolis, where the Parthenon was built on its high ground.

Conceived in 2014, Qudus views AFROPOLIS as a multimodal creative incubator art project "working exclusively with creative young people to have our place in the future, by disrupting borders separating the African diaspora through visas and the systematic blockages that disallow exchange and collaboration."[46] He creates a creative synergy through a technological "distributed network of global Africans in a specific global city as well as in a virtual space."[47] In early August 2021 the city of Barcelona, Spain, was a site of his choreography, and by mid-August Qudus's "danceGATHERING 2021" project was in Lagos, with dance artists around the world logging in. In this way Qudus is able to achieve his creative dance interaction through technology on a global scale, becoming one of the few African dance artists consistently creating international collaborations. This is Afrofuturism at its most productive, creatively stimulating the African diaspora through technology to envision and actually create our collective future through dance in the now.

Qudus's vision of AFROPOLIS.org is very Dunhamesque because it bridges the arts and humanities, bringing together dancers, with visual artists, scholars, and journalists during online virtual Zoom panels. He proclaims these online panels "radically shift the boundaries of knowledge in various fields and locations" by exploring the concept of virtuality within an African worldview. For example, in the summer of 2021, Qudus formed a panel discussion called "Oruko Mi Ni: Reinterpreting Ibeji" to explore the meaning behind birth twins that the Yoruba consider sacred. The panelist consisted of Qudus, representing AFROPOLIS; Oluwasayo Taiwo Olowo-Ake, curator of an exhibit of the same name at the University of British Columbia; Dr. Kole Ade Odutola of the University of Florida; and playwright and theater director Professor Ahmed Yerima. The panel focused on a *deconstruction* of the Western interpretation of the Yoruba cosmological concept of Ibeji; most curatorial exhibits and anthropological literature present the Yoruba conception of Ibeji through a colonial primitivist lens. This discussion was significant to Qudus, as he uses Yoruba cosmology, such as the sacredness of Ibeji, as the foundation for his choreography and themes. Hence, it is important for him to host humanities-based projects to re-educate the world about the Yoruba philosophy that underpins many of his choreographic themes. This is the goal of many Afrofuturists, rehistorizing the past to promote a salutary future.

There are also Afrofuturist groups established to make sure that the inequities of the Afro-Present are not carried into the Afrofuture within the new technological arenas. One such organization is Black in AI that focuses on increasing the presence and inclusion of Black people in the field of AI by creating space for sharing ideas and fostering collaborations with mentorships and general advocacy for African-descendant people in new technology. Black in AI's website reads: "While artificial intelligence (AI) has the potential to solve an incredible spectrum of problems and challenges in our lives, our work and our world, there is a widening disconnect between the people who are introducing and deploying AI-based solutions and those who set policies for when and how these solutions are used."[48] As "[t]he big thinkers of tech say AI is the future. It will underpin everything from search engines and email to the software that drives our cars, directs the policing of our streets and helps create our vaccines."[49] Interjecting sociological concerns into the quickly growing technological field of AI is crucial because the past has not passed, but is actually gaining new ground in Big Tech.

Another tech organization established to monitor and advocate for Black people in this futuristic industry is Data for Black Lives, focusing on data as protest and accountability. Central to its programs is the conceptualization of "Big Data" emerging from Big Tech and calling it out for its deleterious effects on Black people. The organization views Big Data as a part of "a long and pervasive historical legacy of scientific oppression, aggressive public policy, and the most influential political and economic institution that has and continues to shape U.S. economy."[50] Their website reads:

> Big Data is more than a collection of technologies, more than a revolution in measurement and prediction . . . It has given legitimacy to a new form of social and political control . . . Algorithms and other data technologies are the engines that have facilitated the ongoing evolution of chattel slavery into the Prison Industrial Complex.[51]

These are strong accusations against Big Tech generating Big Data, but they are borne out by documentary films and literature that are increasingly focused on inequalities found in the new technology. For example, Cathy O'Neil's *New York Times* bestseller *Weapons of Math Destruction: How Big Data Increases Inequality and Threatens Democracy* (2016), emphasizes usage of algorithms that result in discriminatory actions against some people by weaponizing Big Data. One of the biggest culprits of this particular bias is Face Recognition Surveillance technology, which has been responsible for numerous Black men being wrongly identified and jailed by police authorities for crimes they did not commit. A 2019 national study was conducted on over one hundred facial recognition algorithms and found that they did not work as well on Black and Asian men.

This finding of facial recognition technology is backed up by Black female coder Shalini Kantayya's 2020 Netflix documentary *Coded Bias*. Premiering at the Sundance Film Festival to an enthusiastic audience, the film systematically demonstrates how data reflects our history. In the film, Kantayya analyzes that, "The past dwells within our algorithms, and the data is showing us the inequalities that have been here. This kind of technology is highly susceptible to bias."[52] Algorithms are not impartial and can affect civil liberties, particularly those of BIPOC people. What Kantayya's film tells us is that coding is not detached from real-world discriminations.

This is why Afrofuturism is important for African-descendant people; we need to envision our own future on our own terms, becoming another way of realizing FUBU, For Us By Us. No matter how one views new technology in the third decade of the twenty-first century, whether through the lens of Black performance artists utilizing it to advance Afrofuturism or the lens of tech organizations founded to ensure people of African descent aren't harmed or excluded from the futuristic tech field as it grows exponentially.

For example, what has been dubbed "Black Twitter," the collective identity of Black users on that platform even after the Elon Musk takeover, has also initiated or facilitated new Black tech start-ups and social movements like Black Lives Matter. Black Twitter has also provided a boon to the careers of hip-hop artists like Drake and Megan Thee Stallion, driving their popularity to new heights. Black uses of technology and social media is changing the game of the digital communication age while insinuating us into every aspect of the futuristic industry.

A Black cyberculture has developed, which Black digital media scholar André Brock Jr. argues has engendered "the virtuality of race." He maintains that virtual culture adds a "technical-technological-digital dimension to Black identity."[53] Brock conceptualizes this technological Black perspective not from "America's [familiar] antiblackness [that] overdetermines Blackness," but from the point of view of what he calls "pathos," into which he incorporates analyses of "Black digital practice engendered by joy, sexuality, playfulness, anger, and politics." He understands "Blackness as a discourse in conversation with, but not wholly subject to, whiteness as epistemology."[54]

Thus, new tech and social media enhance the proverbial *agency* crucial to negotiating Blackness, and which is crucial to being seen and heard. Black Twitter and other social media platforms, if used properly, can also aid in resisting being used for the purposes of others, a deleterious aspect of the public sphere Black artists, in particular, know all too well. We got next because the Black Afro-present predicament necessitates continually redefining ourselves through available media, becoming a built-in coping mechanism to project ourselves *past* present hypocrisies to embrace future clarity and lucidity—the Afrofuture.

Bringing an African-Centered Approach to the Quagmire of Technology

In the face of exclusionary inequities already creeping into the implementation of new technology aimed at futurist human growth, I ask, "How can Black folks bring an African-centered approach to the quagmire of technology and the future of AI?" How can African philosophical perspectives, particularly through dance, potentially solve the seeming separation between humanism and technology? Besides the work that Qudus Onikweku's AFROPOLIS is exploring, another project posing answers to these questions is AI 4 Afrika, conceived by S. Ama Wray and her colleagues with a philosophy called Cosmo-Ubuntu. AI 4 Afrika is a team of innovative artists, technologists, philosophers, and community organizers with a clear belief in the need for an African perspective in the development of new technologies: "We believe Afrikan voices, perspectives and experiences matter in the artificial intelligence discourse. For too long we've been ignored. AI 4 Afrika is working to fix this. Afrika is at the table. Our goal is to make AI more inclusive and aware of Afrikan perspectives."[55]

At the core of the AI 4 Afrika philosophy is Cosmo-Ubuntu, based in a humanist view of the cosmic world. Spearheaded by team member José Cossa, a Mozambican education scholar at Pennsylvania State University, Cosmo-Ubuntu is "a humane, theoretical, and solutionary approach to technological innovation and policies that address issues of global justice."[56] The word Buntu is associated with the Niger-Congo language-speaking people of Central and Southern Africa, and the etymological derivation of the word simply means "human." The AI 4 Afrika team uses this philosophy to connote "a sustainable, inclusive, and global alternative framework for understanding personhood or human in AI praxis [while expanding] the normative reliance on a Europeanist understanding of 'human,' which remains insufficient for technological solution beyond Euro-modern worlds."[57] Ultimately, Cosmo-Ubuntu is a twenty-first-century African-centered philosophical intervention intent on inserting humanism into new technology discourse, particularly artificial intelligence, by "remembering" ancestral knowledge that centralizes *embodied* knowledge, emphasizing past knowledge is the seed for future progress—the Sankofa Process.

At various AI 4 Afrika presentations and panel discussions dance scholar S. Ama Wray's *Embodiology* concept (chapter 7) is engaged to physicalize the concepts of Cosmo-Ubuntu, bringing an embodied humanism that must remain at the foundation of any beneficial futurism. "Embodiology is a movement-led improvisation and performance praxis that works alongside music [to] . . . to expand thinking . . . to optimize human performance whether or not the subject is or is not an artist."[58] The movement system originates in Wray's study of Indigenous West African performance practices, from which she has culled six principles of communication; she has, in turn, applied and tested these principles in Western performances and educational settings. Wray says Embodiology is an "innovative decolonizing proposition" that opens consciousness to human breath, heartbeat, and polyrhythmic capacity to engage with other humans.

What sets Embodiology apart from other movement systems is its potential interdisciplinarity: "[It] is a complex and emerging field of inquiry [that] welcomes the engagement of neuroscientists, psychologists, neurochemists, physiologist, cognitive scientists, dance therapists, and engineers."[59] She often has scientists co-facilitate her Embodiology workshops, adding scientific dimensions by explicating the embodied experience of the participants.

For my purposes, Embodiology has a significant contribution to both Black Studies and Dance Studies. Wray states, "This is also important to the field of dance because Embodiology emerges out of Black excellence and the advocacy for Black scientists, who potentially bring a cultural instantiation to this work . . . Dance Studies has a strong presence in the field of dance therapy but there are little to no practices that recognize the presence of Africanist dance forms; this is a space that this work will inevitably contribute to."[60] Simultaneously, Wray advocates for Embodiology's universality: "This work should not be understood as only being of benefit to African descended people; quite the contrary, in view of the broad range of people that have gravitated towards this work to date."[61] With twenty-first-century organizations like AI 4 Afrika, futurist work continues to explore the need to investigate human inner space as we aim toward Octavia Butler's concept of "destiny among the stars" of outer space.

The work of Afrofuturism in the twenty-first century is the continual deconstruction of the hierarchical *mindset* of race, culture, high and low art, and capitalist hoarding of resources while simultaneously dismantling the colonialization of the *geographical* world. The mentality developed over the last five hundred years driving colonial domination by Europe and the Western world is not only destroying us, but also Mother Earth herself. I argue that the wisdom of the Ancestors can aid our twenty-first-century deconstruction efforts. An Afrofuturism accessing the *wisdom* of Africa has an important place in dismantling the edifice of the colonial mindset, *and dance is at the center of regaining Buntu—humanity.* Remembering how to rhythmically move together with heart, breath, and sincere connection is at the core of our collective human future.

Epilogue: Retirement and *Dancing in Blackness*

Viewing my own life and career through a technological lens, I can see the trajectory of the analogue late twentieth century morphing into the digital twenty-first century, from the old selectric typewriting to rudimentary personal computing, and from microchips to social media and Artificial Intelligence. At the beginning of my fifty-year career, starting in the late sixties before computers, I was pecking out my press releases on electric typewriters and hiring typesetters to create promotional flyers; I recorded my dances on reel-to-reel tape that eventually changed into Super 8 video; I thought I was "big-time" when I promoted my community dance concerts through local access cable TV. Today's choreographers publicize their work directly to thousands of followers around the world through Instagram Live.

Living this long has allowed me to not only experience these technological shifts that changed all our personal and professional lives, but to also compare and analyze the effects and meaning of these changes on humanity and the planet. These socio-cultural changes in our lifestyle have provided more personal and collective agency, but have also created more human alienation, "groupthink," and destructive environmental problems. Moreover, these large technological shifts have not ameliorated racism, sexism, and homophobia; instead, they have accentuated them.

In 2015 much happened to me personally as I approached retirement. After fourteen years of being together, that September Gene and I got married by driving up to the Sierra Mountains to Reno, the Nevada quick-wedding capitol. My dear Congolese friend and dancer Mabiba Baegne, who lived in Reno at the time, agreed to be our witness. Our marriage came on the heels of my sister Brenda, after twenty-five years, marrying her longtime mate, Frank Dawson; I guess we Miller sisters are just not wired to jump into marriage. I also had my fiftieth high school reunion in San Francisco, becoming a real indication I was getting "old."

Another indication of my aging was the celebratory dedication of the Alice Street Mural that visually showcased the history of the African and Chinese communities making up the Alice and 14th Street community in downtown Oakland. The colorful and history-filled mural by muralists Pancho Peskador and Desi Mundo and their Community Rejuvenation Project captured the history of the efforts growing out of Everybody's Creative Arts Center/Citi-Centre Dance Theatre. The mural commemorated so many of my past artistic colleagues—Malonga Casquelourd, Carlos Aceituno, Deborah Vaughan, Moshe Milon Sr., Dr. Zak Diouf and Naomi Washington Diouf, Jose Loren-

Figure 9.1. Oakland's Alice Street Mural at 14th and Alice Streets, with Ruth Beckford as centerpiece, representing the city's Black Dance Legacy. Photo courtesy of author.

zo—and most importantly, the mother of Bay Area Black dance, Ruth Beckford, as centerpiece. Miss Beckford, then ninety years old, appeared with the aid of her walker, giving an important dedication speech about the legacy of Black dance in the Bay Area. It was fulfilling seeing my own dancing image on the wall, taken from a photo during my 2008 Fulbright trip to Ghana when I danced Bamaya with the Afrique Dance Theatre (chapter 6).

The Alice Street Mural has now been sadly covered over as a result of gentrification and Oakland's so-called downtown development efforts. However, a new mural called "AscenDance," by the same artists headed by Desi Mundo and his Community Rejuvenation Project, has been painted in the same district on the west side of the Greenlining Institute's 360 Center on 14th Street. Also, a documentary film, *Alice Street,* created by filmmaker Spencer Wilkinson forever commemorates the Alice Street Mural and its captured history.[62]

The Alice Street Mural in its full visual form, along with the documentary film, memorialize my years of dance and cultural activism in Oakland and the community I helped create. I wrote in my journal: *As I approach 70 years old, my legacy is being solidified. I knew Malonga was smiling down from the ancestral realm.* And that spirit realm became even more real for me in 2015 with several deaths hitting me hard: my former mother-in-law whom I loved dearly, Betty Woodward, passed, as well as my Ghanaian dance colleague, Nii Yartey, who was the same age as me. He died suddenly while his dance company was on tour in India. At this point I frequently contemplate the fragility of life.

Of course, my biggest concluding event that year was my own retirement from UC Davis on July 1, 2016. The department produced an event appropriately called "Sankofa Celebration" that also commemorated the AAS program becoming a *department*. My colleague, sociologist Milmon Harrison, who was chair at the time, arranged the celebratory testimonial at the Center for African Diaspora Student Success, featuring drumming and key tributes to my accomplishments. I had taught at UC Davis for eleven years, and now I was finishing that part of my academic career. I had created popular new hip-hop courses, revived the Black Dance History course, and wrote the proposal for AAS to become a department; I felt fulfilled.

And then on September 16, 2016, I had my last duty on campus: I accompanied Ayo to the Graduate Division office to file her finished dissertation, "Towards an Entercultural Engaged Pedagogy." I had helped her achieve her doctorate in Performance Studies and, in the process, had become her second mother. Now I was truly finished. Gene and I were free, and we vacationed in Barbados, having a wonderful time in the tropical sun of the Caribbean.

I followed up in November by planning a major retirement and seventieth birthday bash at the Hilton Garden Inn in Sacramento, not far from our home. Renting a banquet hall on the hotel grounds, I had Deejay and Chef Kuran both cater and provide party music for my celebratory bash, with my family and a large cadre of my friends attending. Linda Goodrich and Ayo were the co-hostesses who greeted everyone at the front door with name tags that Gene had designed; Linda and Ayo became the Mistresses of Ceremony for the three-hour birthday-retirement event, and Ayo performed a beautiful tribute dance.

The highlight of the party was heartfelt testimonials from my family members and friends about our personal relationships. It was touching seeing my sisters Brenda and Tracey and niece Anjelica give their family tribute to me as the first-born daughter of Tenola Hall. Although my mother was not able to make the trip from San Francisco, I did arrange for my ninety-year-old father Leroy to be brought from his assisted living facility to the party. He even danced down the culminating Soul Train line with his signature dapper cool, framed by all my friends. It was a memorable party with so many of the important people in my life: Sananda, Selimah, Susheel, Bobbie Bolden, Brenda Waters, Gloria Weinstock, Rafael Gonzalez, Jacqui Hairston, Yvonne Daniel, and Albirda Rose all came to celebrate with me. Each of them represented a special part of my life story, and I was grateful. Of course, Gene was right by my side, like the solid rock that he had become in my life.

The year continued with my returning to choreography, when Linda G. asked me to choreograph for her twenty-fifth anniversary of Sacramento Black Art of Dance at Sacramento State University. I remember saying, "I haven't choreographed in eleven years, do you think I can still do it?" and she answered, "Once you know how to swim, when you jump back into the water, you'll remember." She was right! I knew I had to create a major piece chronicling how I felt about the times as a tribute to Oya, portraying her as a spiritual force of change necessary in contemporary times that has us immersed in the eye of a national and international storm, a storm of change and shifting energies, politically, culturally, and spiritually. I chose nine Sac State dancers to help me realize *In the Eye of the Storm* that premiered that February. I wrote this in my journal about my choreographic motivation: "*In the Eye of the Storm" speaks to the need for social justice in the face of tyranny. It is dedicated to Oya-Yansa, my orisa who creates the winds of change to allow the potential for social and spiritual growth. And she guides me in the creation of the dance.*

My greatest joy in creating the piece was having my daughter Ayo dance the Oya figure and guiding her spiritually as well as artistically. For the performances, I got "permission" from Oya to allow Ayo to use my actual consecrated rattle, sword, and horsetail as props, with the stipulation that only

Figure 9.2. *In the Eye of the Storm* with Ayo Walker as the deity Oya, Sacramento State University, February 2017. Photo: Tony Nguyen.

she could touch them. All stagehands knew that only Ayo could handle *those* props backstage. Ayo came regularly to my shrine room to pray to Oya before the premiere, and the piece was well received by both the public and the Yoruba spiritual community.

The year ended somberly on November 29 with my father Leroy "Bubber" Miller making his transition at ninety-one years old to the ancestral realm. I was grateful that he waited until two days after my birthday so those dates would not be linked. We held his memorial service at Sacramento's Macedonia Baptist Church, which I had discovered for him in 2011 just a few months after he arrived to live with us, and in which he had become a beloved deacon. I created a slideshow of his life for the memorial service that was appreciated by all, as our family and friends gathered to honor my father. To process my grief, I wrote in my journal: *Leroy Miller was a unique man. He was his own man, a leader among men, and he gave that quality to me. Our spirits will always be linked. I took care of him during the last six years of his life, and because he did not raise me, we grew closer. He was a man of few words with a big heart. People were always attracted to him because of his warmth and acceptance of everyone. He will be missed by many. I will miss him.*

My father was a World War II Black man from Bay City, Texas, who never went past the eighth grade. He became a gambler, hustler, waiter, maître d', and even restaurant owner for a short time. He did what he had to do to survive in racist America while never becoming bitter, leaving two successful daughters. He always empowered me as a Black woman, giving me a lifetime mantra: "Remember, you can do anything you're big enough to do."

As 2018 danced into existence, I was anxiously awaiting the publication of *Dancing in Blackness: A Memoir*. I eagerly anticipated seeing my early dance life story in print. The University Press of Florida (UPF) had accepted it, and I had gotten several good peer reviews for revisions. Publishing is a long process, and my third book was going to be personally intimate, not my objective erudite analysis of hip-hop like the last two. This one would reveal many of the details of my *personal* life underlying my *artistic* life as "a professional dancer's journey over four decades, across three continents and twenty-three countries, and through defining moments in the story of black dance in America," as the UPF marketing team summarized. That marketing statement continued with, "In this memoir, Halifu Osumare reflects on what blackness and dance have meant to her life and international career." I had become a scholar who was known for her unique take on Black popular culture—hip-hop—that had become central to global youth identity. Now, a personal autobiography would make me vulnerable in a way that my previous publications had not.

When *Dancing in Blackness* was finally in print, I was amazed at how strong and dynamic its cover was. The photographic dance image from my 1984 *Rites of Passage* twenty-minute solo appears iconically "Black." The cover photo shows me in a side developé movement, with my left arm painfully wrapped around my stomach, as the right arm stretches out behind me in a metaphoric *scream*. I seem to anguishly gaze up to the gods, framed by a backdrop of African-like masks hanging behind me. The photo, taken by the late great Oakland dance photographer Harry Wade, was now to become my signature dance pose, a movement statement of sorts of my dance story. I realized how appropriate the image that UPF had chosen for the cover really was.

The book's back cover contains several of my colleagues' testament blurbs about *Dancing in Blackness*. Susan Manning at Northwestern University wrote, "Osumare reveals an astonishing ability to evoke and to historicize her professional journey," while Thomas DeFrantz at Duke University wrote, "An unapologetic, rapturous travelogue detailing life, love, and an abiding mission to further the place of black dance in global histories."

Fairly soon after its February 2018 publication, UPF got important academic reviews for my memoir. Noted dance scholar Nadine George-Graves wrote a stellar review for the *British Journal of Aesthetics* that reads, "[*Dancing in Blackness*] . . . serves as a primer on black dance history of the late twentieth century as Osumare met and worked with just about everybody. She is an intellectual and creative hub connecting generations of concert dance makers and knowledge workers. Ultimately this text is about aesthetics, society and social justice history as much as it is about living an international artistic and scholarly life."[63] These kinds of assessments and reviews of *Dancing in Blackness* set the stage for my 2018 international book tour.

My book tour became a reunion of sorts with many components of my past life and current career converging. I called upon past friends and institutions with which I had worked throughout the country to sponsor public readings. Gene told me he was all in as my traveling companion and tour assistant and would accompany me on all my scheduled dates. He became essential, as several venues were not able to order and sell books on-site. Gene took charge of bringing and selling books from our own stash after several of my readings.

The national tour covered Sacramento and the Bay Area in Northern California, as well as Southern California, including Los Angeles, Santa Monica, and San Diego, continuing to Chicago, NYC, Harlem, and Brooklyn. Gene and I ended the tour internationally in Barbados at the University of the West Indies, Cave Hill, where I was the keynote speaker for the third biennial International Dance Conference, chaired by Cuban dancer and scholar Neri Torres.

Signs that the tour was to become a reunion with my past started immediately in Sacramento at Underground Books: one of my early dancers from Aquarius Rising Dance Theater (chapter 6, *DinB*), Zebia Pecot, showed up enthusiastically in the audience. I actually created a reunion reading event with my fellow CitiCentre Dance Theatre company members Linda G., Roger Dillahunty, and Daniel Giray (Debra Floyd, who lives in Washington, DC, could not attend). That reading became a pre-show event to the annual Collage des Cultures Africaines dance concert of Diamano Coura West African Dance Company at Laney College Theater in early March. That reading was an *orchestrated* reunion, as we four dancers had not been together since 1988 when we disbanded the company (chapter 6, *DinB*). I ended that PowerPoint reading with CitiCentre Dance Theatre's early publicity photo, and afterward we formed a panel on stage to reminisce about the company and its 1980s meaning to Oakland.

The Chicago and New York leg of the book tour expanded the readings out of my home state. Susan Manning brought us to Northwestern University in Evanston, a suburb of Chicago, for a special roundtable reading with graduate students in Performance Studies that included the well-known scholar E. Patrick Johnson. It was always stimulating to interact with an *academic* audience, allowing me to delve deeper into the theoretical and sociopolitical aspects of

Figure 9.3. Reunion photo of CitiCentre Dance Theatre Company members, Laney College Theater, March 2018, Oakland, CA. (*Left to right*: Roger Dillahunty, Linda Goodrich, the author, Daniel Giray; not pictured: Debra Floyd). Photo courtesy of author.

the memoir. For the New York readings, I was blessed to have dance scholar Carol Ann Webster as my New York agent, coordinating readings and publicity. She is a Jamaican-born dancer who works at the interactions of "race," ethnicity, gender, and religion, and at that time she was a postdoc at Institute of Religion Culture and Public Life at Columbia University. Given the glut of New York's artistic activity, it is difficult for an "outsider" to produce events, and Carol Ann provided the needed help finding book reading venues in the saturated New York market.

I ended up with three New York readings in May 2018: Gavin Brown Art Gallery in Harlem, where I appeared with dancer Ruthlyn Solomons; Greenlight Books in Brooklyn, where I read with the MacArthur award–winning dancer-choreographer Jawole Willa Jo Zollar of the Urban Bush Women; and most importantly Hunter College, where I appeared with my late friend poet-playwright-novelist Ntozake Shange. I treasure that particular reading now because it was the last time I saw Ntozake before she passed five months later.

Our joint reading at the Roosevelt House on Hunter College's midtown campus was a true culmination of the US part of the tour, as well as my friendship with Ntozake. It was as if fate had brought Ntozake and I together one more time to publicly shine together. The reading was appropriately sponsored by Hunter College's Dance, Women and Gender Studies, and English Departments. I read from my book using prompts and colorful photos in my PowerPoint presentation, followed by Ntozake taking the stage and wowing the audience with a reading from her last book of poetry, *Wild Beauty, New and Selected Poems by Ntozake Shange* (2018). We finished by sitting together on stage fielding questions from the high-powered academic and artistic audience, including New York dance luminaries like Noel Hall, my former dance colleague in the Rod Rodgers Dance Company; and Mary Barnett, an early Alvin Ailey rehearsal director. All of New York seemed to file by our signing table to buy our books, and Gene snapped a treasured photo of us holding our respective books, which I framed and hung on my office wall. Today, I view it daily and invoke Ntozake as my ancestor.

Gene and I left New York and went straight to Barbados to finish the *Dancing in Blackness* book tour. Having been to the island two years earlier, we were a bit familiar with the island. This time instead of the Hilton Barbados near the capitol Bridgetown in St. Martin parish, we stayed at the Discovery Bay Resort in Holetown in St. James parish; but the biggest difference was, *this* time, everything was completely paid for by the University of West Indies (UWI). We made Barbados into a working *vacation* because my sister Brenda and her husband Frank decided to join us, as he wanted to visit his relatives in Barbados, making it a family affair.

Figure 9.4. The author and poet-playwright Ntozake Shange at joint book reading, Hunter College, New York City, May 2018. Photo: Gene Howell.

But we were in Barbados to attend the dance conference "Decolonizing Bodies: Engaging Performance," produced by Neri Torres and replete with UWI scholars from all disciplines, along with international dance scholars and artists. In attendance were dance professor Henry Daniel from British Columbia, Canada, and filmmaker Miguel Angel Rosales from Spain. It was an honor to present my keynote address, "Dancing in Blackness as Decoloniz-ing the Mind," tying my book into the entire conference theme. I centralized VèVè Clark's concept of "diaspora literacy" to explore how Black resistance across the African diaspora has been facilitated through dance and the body. It became a rare opportunity to have my sister Brenda, along with Frank and his sisters, experience my dance scholarship.

The entire 2018 *Dancing in Blackness* book tour elevated my combined dance and academic careers to a whole new level. The tour allowed people who only knew me as a scholar since the late nineties to mingle with my earli-er dance colleagues pre-graduate school. Although I did not imagine this hap-pening in advance, in hindsight it was inevitable. It was like a meeting of my *two selves* that my life story joined together, tied in a neat little "Black" bow.

The book received several awards. The Selma Jeanne Cohen Prize in Dance Aesthetics, the American Book Award, the 2019 Dance Scholars Award from the International Association of Blacks in Dance, and the 2020 Dance Stud-ies Distinction in Dance Award for Artistry, Scholarship, and Service to the

Field, all brought increased attention to my life and career. These awards allowed me to reflect on the *totality* of my contributions to dance: my dance and choreography in the 1970s and 1980s became the basis for an *embodied knowledge* approach to both my Dance and Hip-Hop Studies scholarship. In turn, I began to understand the symbiosis between praxis and theory undergirding Black dance activism throughout my life.

I see myself in a long lineage of Black/African women who have fought for what's *right!* From Ya Asantewaa in the Gold Coast becoming Ghana and Queen Nzinga in what became Angola to Harriet Tubman and Sojourner Truth in the (dis)United States, there has existed a "Black Girl (Woman) Magic" that goes way beyond a millennial meme.[64] I see myself as a part of that *Black* magic; my fight is not on the literal battlefield, but in the arts—in dance and Black popular culture. And within this performance battlefield, I also acknowledge the validity of other cultures and their right to also co-exist. In Hawai'i, I swiveled my hips in the *ami kuku,* just as I had done in the Congo *zebola,* and felt the connection between earth-based dance cultures that reflect Mother Nature in all her glory. I have fought for the acknowledgment of all dance cultures to take their rightful place as human expressions of the divine, beyond Eurocentric hierarchies.

As I reflect on this in my current home in Sacramento, California, that was once the sacred lands of the Patwin Southern Wintu native peoples, I acknowledge the breadth of my career over time—five decades—and space—"three continents and twenty-three countries." As a Cherokee prayer says, "May I live long enough to know why I was born." *Dancing in Blackness: A Memoir,* published in 2018, was my first conversation with myself to answer that question, and now *Dancing the Afrofuture: Hula, Hip-Hop, and the Dunham Legacy* continues that answer.

The time one has is precious, and as Toni Morrison once said, "Definitions belong to the definers, not the defined."[65] In my memoir writing, I define myself, discovering how I am forever growing and shifting, relinquishing any sense that I am in control. The seed for the theme of this book, Afrofuturism, was buried in my acceptance speech for the 2020 Dance Studies Association Distinction in Dance Award: "I can imagine ourselves (African-descendant people) in a future not tied to a narrative of oppression, but a future where we are free to completely express ourselves as we are becoming." Personal and collective agency must be seized by us to radically change the current definitions so new meanings can be born.

In my life, *Dance* is a subject, an agent, and a method. I've used dance as a strategy for my own liberation as well as my lens into the world. Dance became the way I perceive life itself. My approach was first revealed in the revolutionary seventies, when, rather than marching, I insisted on dancing the Black story—*The Evolution of Black Dance*—as my contribution to the (r)evolution. After a year living in Ghana, when I founded Everybody's Creative Arts Center in Oakland in 1977, I made the organizational motto: "Dance is Life and Life is a Dance!" "Rhythmic movement by sentient beings" is how Katherine Dunham defined dance; carrying on her legacy, that definition has mapped the cartography of my life. From the SF-Oakland Bay Area to Europe; from Boston and New York to Africa; and from Hawai'i to the Caribbean, I have danced across the globe, and in the process mapped out a life that charted a creative path to myself.

My life has spanned the analogue to the digital. I have lived through the polaroid instant picture to the mobile phone selfie, and in each era I looked myself straight in the eyes and saw my reflection. I have made the world my stage, as Shakespeare wrote in *As You Like It,* and it is so true. Today, Performance Studies has made a discipline of the performance of life in all its dimensions from the political to the personal, and in our digital age the personal has become synonymous with the political. The proscenium stage cannot contain all that needs to be said and danced; taking the dance to the people where it first started, as Alvin Ailey told us, is important particularly in *these* times of the digital global connection, yet utter personal alienation. I urge all of us to take to the streets and dance the carnival of life with Afrofuture intentions, where class, "race," ethnicity, gender, and sexuality disintegrates into the bacchanal of our collective human identities. And as Amanda Gorman, the youngest national poet laureate has said, "And so we lift our gazes not to what stands between us, but what stands before us. We close the divide because we know to put our future first, we must first put our differences aside."[66]

Notes

Introduction

1 Quoted in Amy Abugo Ongiri, *Spectacular Blackness: The Cultural Politics of the Black Power Movement and the Search for a Black Aesthetic* (Charlottesville: University of Virginia Press), 15.

2 Thomas F. DeFrantz and Anita Gonzales, "Introduction: From 'Negro Expression' to 'Black Performance,'" in *Black Performance Theory,* ed. Thomas F. DeFrantz and Anita Gonzales (Durham, NC: Duke University Press, 2014), 5.

3 Karen Nicole Barbour, *Dancing Across the Page: Narrative and Embodied Ways of Knowing* (Bristol, UK: Intellect, 2011), 49.

4 For a comprehensive list of Dunham choreography across all these genres, see Ruth Beckford, *Katherine Dunham, A Biography* (New York: Marcel Dekker, Inc. 1979).

5 "About the Black Lives Matter Network," Black Lives Matter Website, http://blacklives matter.com/about/.

6 As noted by Jane Alberdeston Coralín, "African Diasporic Arts and Social Change." Live webinar by University Press of Florida, April 13, 2022.

7 According to Marilyn Armour of the Institute for Restorative Justice and Restorative Dialogue at the University of Texas at Austin, School of Social Work, "restorative justice is a fast-growing state, national, and international social movement and set of practices that aim to redirect society's retributive response to crime . . . It attends to the broken relationships between three players: the offender, the victim, and the community." https://charterforcompassion.org/restorative-justice/restorative-justice-some-facts-and-history.

8 Misty Copeland with Charisse Jones, *Life in Motion: An Unlikely Ballerina,* (New York: Simon & Shuster, 2014), 3.

9 Brenda Dixon Gottschild, *The Black Dancing Body: A Geography From Coon to Cool* (New York: Palgrave Macmillan, 2003), 222–223.

10 Ntozake Shange, *Dance We Do: A Poet Explores Black Dance* (Boston: Beacon Press, 2020), 49–50. Copyright © 2020 by Ntozake Shange. Reprinted with permission from Beacon Press, Boston, Massachusetts.

11 Halifu Osumare Official Website: https://www.hosumare.com/

12 VèVè A. Clark, "Performing the Memory of Difference in Afro-Caribbean Dance: Katherine Dunham's Choreography, 1938–87," in *History & Memory in African-American Culture,* eds. Geneviève Fabre and Robert O'Meally (New York: Oxford University Press, 1994), 195.

13 Katherine Dunham *Stormy Weather* break on YouTube: https://www.youtube.com/watch?v=7djiH_kKrkE.
14 In Womack, Ytasha L., *Afrofuturism: The World of Black Sci-Fi and Fantasy Culture* (Chicago: Lawrence Hill Books, 2013), 144.
15 Amanda Gorman, *The Hill We Climb* (New York: Viking—Penguin Random House, 2021), 14.
16 Ibid., 108–109.
17 See for example Amos Tutuola, *My Life in the Bush of Ghosts* (New York: Grove Press, 1954).
18 Renegade Performance Group. http://www.renegadepg.com/ephemera.html.

Chapter 1. Dancing Out of the Bay Area

1 Melissa V. Harris-Perry, *Sister Citizen: Shame, Stereotypes, and Black Women in America* (New Haven, CT: Yale University Press, 2011), 33–43.
2 Halifu Osumare, "'The Fierce Freedom of Their Souls': Activism of African Dance in the Oakland Bay Area," in *Hot Feet and Social Change: African Dance and Diaspora Communities,* ed. Kariamu Welsh, Esailama G. A. Diouf, and Yvonne Daniel (Urbana & Chicago: University of Illinois Press, 2019), 143–165.
3 Robert Farris Thompson, *African Art in Motion* (Los Angeles: University of California Press, 1974), 41, quoted in Halifu Osumare, "'Aesthetic of the Cool' Revisited: The Ancestral Dance Link in the African Diaspora," *UCLA Journal of Dance Ethnology* 17, 1993: 2, 4.
4 Ibid., 41.

Chapter 2. Dancing in Hawai'i: Scholarship and Black Dance

1 The fear of volcanic eruptions from Kilauea is real. In May 2018 the lower Puna eruption became a worldwide volcanic event. Lava fountains rose to three hundred feet and flowed with toxic gases into Leilani Estates, along with substantial earthquakes. Having moved from Hawai'i in 2000 and sold the house in 2009, I watched these events unfold from afar. I sympathized with the local homeowners who endured this volcanic event, with many losing their property. There is indeed a price for paradise.
2 One of Kathryn Waddell Takara's major contributions to the history of African Americans in Hawai'i is her *Oral Histories of African Americans.* Honolulu: Center for Oral History-Social Science Research Institute, University of Hawai'i at Manoa, 1990. The text is a 406-page opus of interviews with African Americans, past and present, living in the islands.
3 Elisa Joy White, "Representations of Blackness and the Popolo Problematic in Hawai'i," in *They Followed the Trade Winds: African Americans in Hawai'i* (2nd Edition), ed. Miles M. Jackson (Honolulu: University of Hawai'i Press, 2013), 269.
4 Barack Obama, *Dreams from My Father: A Story of Race and Inheritance* (New York: Broadway Paperbacks, 1995, 2004), 23–24.
5 Ibid., 27.
6 For further exploration of *Southland*'s controversy, see Halifu Osumare, "Socialization Through the Arts: Katherine Dunham as Social Activist," in *Sentient Performativities of*

Embodiment: Thinking Alongside the Human, ed. Lynette Hunter, Elisabeth Krimmer, and Peter Lichtenfels (London & New York: Lexington Books, 2016), 297–315.

7 "Las Danzas De Haiti," *Acta Anthropologicia* 11:4 (November 1947) and *Les Dances D' Haiti* (Paris: Fasquelle Editeurs, 1957).

8 Cleo Parker Robinson, Personal Correspondence, September 1994.

9 For an important critique of DuBois's concept of the talented tenth, see Henry Louis Gates, Jr. and Cornel West, *The Future of the Race* (New York: A.A. Knopf, 1996).

10 Halifu Osumare, "Conflicting Epistemologies: Historic Ambivalence of Black Intellectuals about African (American) Performance." Unpublished manuscript, University of Hawai'i, Manoa, March 13, 1997.

11 Kevin D. Kim, "Dance Instructor Crosses Cultural Bounds." *Ka Leo o* Hawai'i, 23 September 1994, 12.

Chapter 3. Dancing in Hawai'i: Performing Hula and a Hip-Hop Doctorate

1 (http://www.Hawaiianhuladance.com/#!)

2 Adrienne Kaeppler, *Hula Pahu: Hawaiian Drum Dances,* Vol. 1 (Honolulu: Bishop Museum Bulletins in Anthropology, 1993), 3.

3 Robert Farris Thompson, *African Art in Motion: Icon and Act* (Los Angeles: University of California Press, 1974), 13.

4 For a detailed perspective of laws banning the hula, see Dorothy B. Barrére, Mary Kawena Pukui, and Marion Kelly, *Hula: Historical Perspectives* (Honolulu: Bishop Museum, 1980).

5 Osumare, "The Politics of the Body," unpublished manuscript, 1996.

6 Ibid.

7 See Haunani-Kay Trask, "The Birth of the Modern Hawaiian Movement: Kalama Valley, O'ahu," *The Hawaiian Journal of History* XXI (1987). http://hdl.handle.net/10524/144.

8 Hilo is also home to the prestigious Halau O Kekuhi, headed by famed kumu hula Pualani Kanaka'ole Kanahele and her younger sister Nalani Kanaka'ole, both daughters of the famed kumu hula Edith Kekuhi Kanaka'ole (1913–1979). This revered hula family set the standard for the 1970s Hawaiian Renaissance, with hula at its foundation. Pualani also helped establish Hawaiian Language Studies at UH-Hilo, which in turn spurred the Hawaiian language emersion programs in the public schools to ensure the continuation of the islands' Indigenous language.

9 Katherine Dunham, "Notes on the Dance," in *Kaiso! Writings By and About Katherine Dunham,* ed. VèVè A. Clark and Sara E. Johnson (Madison: University of Wisconsin Press, 2005), 519.

10 Ngugi wa Thiong'o became the focus of an international rescue campaign in 1997 when he was arrested by Kenyan authorities and held without being charged. Designated a prisoner of conscience by Amnesty International, his release was secured a year later. As he was in constant danger of re-arrest and barred from teaching in Kenya, he had been living in exile since 1982 and moved to the United States in 1989. In 1992 he became a professor of comparative literature and performance studies at New York University, and in 2015 he became Distinguished Professor of Comparative Literature and English at the University of California, Irvine.

11 Robert M. Rees, "Going to Extremes at the University of Hawai'i," *Honolulu Weekly*, February 25–March 3, 1998, 5.

12 Halifu Osumare, *The Africanist Aesthetic in Global Hip-Hop: Power Moves* (New York: Palgrave Macmillan, 2008), 1.

13 Ibid., 131.

14 VèVè A. Clark was the Dunham scholar who edited, along with Sara E. Johnson, the last text on Katherine Dunham before the dance doyen's death in 2006, *Writings by and About Katherine Dunham* (Madison: University of Wisconsin Press, 2005). Since Clark's own death in 2007, her memory was honored by having UC Berkeley's Caesar Chavez Center name one of its rooms the VèVè Writing Lounge in 2020.

15 Tanya Schevitz, "This is College? Classes on Popular Culture like Hip Hop, 'Simpson' Bursting into Academia." *San Francisco Chronicle*, 16 May 2000, A18.

Chapter 4. Dancing in Ohio and Nigeria

1 David Dupont, "Hip-Hop on Over to a New Course at BGSU," *Sentinel-Tribune*, 26 May 2001.

2 For a fuller explanation of the postmodern dance movement, refer to the classic text: Sally Banes, *Terpsichore in Sneakers: Post-Modern Dance* (Hanover, NH: Wesleyan University Press, 1987, 1977).

3 Halifu Osumare, "The Dance Archaeology of Rennie Harris: Hip-Hop or Postmodern," in *Ballroom, Boogie, Shimmy Sham, Shake: A Social and Popular Dance Reader*, ed. Julie Malnig (Urbana & Chicago: University of Illinois Press, 2009), 271.

4 Brenda Dixon Gottschild, *Digging the Africanist Aesthetic in American Performance: Dance and Other Contexts* (Westport, CN: Greenwood Press, 1996), 51.

5 One can find information on the documentary *Free to Dance* online. https://www.thirteen.org/freetodance/resources.html.

6 Barbara Browning, "Global Dance and Globalization: Emerging Perspectives," *Dance Research Journal: Congress on Research in Dance* 34/2 Winter 2002: 13.

7 Halifu Osumare, "Global Breakdancing and the Intercultural Body," *Dance Research Journal: Congress on Research in Dance* 34/2 Winter 2002: 32.

8 André Brock, Jr. *Distributed Blackness: African American Cybercultures* (New York: New York University Press, 2020), 13.

9 Nyama McCarthy-Brown, *Dance Pedagogy for a Diverse World: Culturally Relevant Teaching in Theory, Research and Practice* (Jefferson, NC: McFarland & Co., Inc., 2017), 28–29.

10 Takiyah Nur Amin, "Foreword," in *Dance Pedagogy for a Diverse World*, 2.

11 The dynasties of the Ooni go back centuries to 1200 and 1300 AD. The current Ooni is Adeyeye Enitan Ogunwusi Ojaja II and is the fifty-first Ooni of Ife. He became the ruler after the Ooni Obakun Ade Sijuwade, whom we met, died in 2015.

12 Judith Gleason, *Oya: In Praise of an African Goddess* (San Francisco: HarperSanFrancisco, 1992), 47.

13 Ibid., 48.

Chapter 5. "Dancing" in Sacramento and Davis

1 E. Bolayi Idowu, *Olódumarè: God in Yoruba Belief* (Brooklyn, New York: A&B Books Publishers, 1994), 5.
2 Nadine George-Graves, *Urban Bush Women: Twenty-Years of African American Dance Theater, Community Engagement, and Working It Out* (Madison: University of Wisconsin Press, 2010), 6.
3 As my book *Black Choreographers Moving: A National Dialogue* (1991) was self-published and personally distributed with a grant from the California Arts Council, *The Africanist Aesthetic in Global Hip-Hop* was my first book published by a press.
4 *African-Haitian Dance Class: Dunham Technique.* DVD. (New York: Insight Media, 1971). YouTube: https://www.youtube.com/watch?v=IR4VGFVCyQE.
5 Jack Anderson, "Katherine Dunham, Dance Icon, Dies at 96," *New York Times.* 23 May 2006.
6 Hedy Weiss, "Pioneering Dancer, Author, Activist," *Chicago Sun-Times,* 23 May 2006.
7 Sarah Kaufman, "Moving the World: Katherine Dunham Choreographed a Life That Stretched Beyond the Stage," *Washington Post.* 23 May 2006, C01.
8 Brenda Payton, "Fitting Tribute to a Dance Pioneer," *Oakland Tribune,* 2 June 2006.
9 Halifu Osumare, "Socialization Through the Arts: Katherine Dunham as a Social Activist," in *Sentient Performativities of Embodiment: Thinking Alongside the Human,* eds. Lynette Hunter, Elisabeth Krimmer, and Peter Lichentenfels (New York: Lexington Books, 2016), 303.
10 Halifu Osumare, *The Africanist Aesthetic in Global Hip-Hop,* 122.
11 Ibid., 142.
12 Leslie Fulbright, "VèVè Clark—Expert on African Diaspora," *San Francisco Chronicle,* 14 December 2007.
13 Linda Goodrich, Email Communication, April 12, 2020.
14 Joanna Dee Das, *Katherine Dunham: Dance and the African Diaspora* (New York: Oxford University Press, 2017), 36.
15 Thomas F. DeFrantz, *Dancing Revelations: Alvin Ailey's Embodiment of African American Culture* (New York: Oxford University Press, 2004), xiii.

Chapter 6. Hip-Hoping Back to Ghana

1 André Brock Jr., *Distributed Blackness: African American Cybercultures* (New York: New York University Press, 2020), 241.
2 DuBois was not a supporter of Marcus Garvey, but Nkrumah was impressed with Garvey's Black world entrepreneurial spirit. The grand parade square in the middle of Accra is called Black Star Square, named after Garvey's Black Star Line shipping company, which linked the US, Caribbean, and West Africa between 1919–1922. In his "Kwame Nkrumah, George Padmore and W.E.B. DuBois," Research Review NS, Vol. 7, Nos. 1&2, 1991, 1, Kwadwo Afar-Gyan says Nkrumah was "perhaps most deeply inspired by the pan-Africanist ideas of Marcus Garvey, a Jamaican who had gone to America in 1916 and had subsequently found and led the largest Black movement of his time. Interestingly, Garvey's ideas and modus operandi were highly objectionable to both Padmore and Du Bois."

3 Paul Harris, "Obama Deeply Moved by 'Evil' Slave Fortress," *The Guardian,* 11 July 2009. https://www.theguardian.com/world/2009/jul/12/barack-obama.

4 Staff Writer, "Obama Grandpa in Cape Coast," *Daily Guide—NDP News,* 14 July 2009. https://www.modernghana.com/news/227104/obama-grandpa-in-cape-coast.html.

5 Halifu Osumare, *The Hiplife in Ghana: West African Indigenization of Hip-Hop* (New York: Palgrave Macmillan, 2012), 39. For an in-depth exploration of the development of highlife music, also see John Collins, *West African Pop Roots* (Philadelphia, PA: Temple University Press), 1992.

6 Ibid., 21.

7 Jesse Weaver Shipley, *Living the Hiplife: Celebrity and Entrepreneurship in Ghanaian Popular Music* (Durham, NC: Duke University Press, 2013) 48–49.

8 Karin Barber, foreword in *Popular Culture in Africa: The Episteme of the Everyday,* eds. Stephanie Newell and Onokome Okome (New York: Routledge, 2014), xix.

9 Osumare, *The Hiplife in Ghana,* 169; Also see pp. 34–35 for a complete delineation of Obour's five distinct hiplife stages.

10 Ibid., 107.

11 Ibid., 108.

12 Association for the Study of the Worldwide African Diaspora mission statement, http://aswadiaspora.org/mission-and-constitution/.

13 Joanna Dee Das, *Katherine Dunham: Dance and the African Diaspora* (New York: Oxford University Press, 2017), 169.

14 Halifu Osumare, *Dancing Blackness, A Memoir* (Gainesville: University Press of Florida, 2018), 193–194.

15 Francis Nii Yartey, "Development and Promotion of Contemporary Choreographic Expression in Ghana," in *FonTomFrom: Contemporary Ghanaian Literature Theatre and Film,* ed. Kofi Anyidoho and James Gibbs (Amsterdam and Atlanta: Rodopi, 2000), 126.

16 Osumare, *The Hiplife in Ghana,* 98.

17 Panji Anoff, Personal Interview, Ouagadougou, Burkina Faso, October 18, 2008.

18 For an explanation of *nommo* in relation to rap, see Osumare, *The Africanist Aesthetic in Global Hip-Hop: Power Moves* (New York: Palgrave Macmillan, 2007), 31–36.

19 Ali Diallo, Personal Interview, Ouagadougou, October 18, 2008.

20 Osumare, *The Hiplife in Ghana,* 102.

Chapter 7. Becoming a Public Intellectual and Celebrating Blackness

1 Blitz the Ambassador is also a noted filmmaker, and was a co-director of Beyoncé's 2020 *Black Is King* visual album, along with Emmanuel Adjei and Ibra Ake. Multi-talented, Blitz also published a popular novel, *The Scent of Burnt Flowers* (2022), and is the director of the musical production of *The Color Purple* film (2023).

2 Halifu Osumare, "The Dance Archaeology of Rennie Harris: Hip-Hop or Postmodern?" in *Ballroom, Boogie, Shimmy Sham, Shake: A Social and Popular Dance Reader,* ed. by Julie Malnig (Urbana and Chicago: University of Illinois Press, 2009), 261.

3 "Arts Scholar and Leader to Join Georgetown as Co-Lead of New Racial Justice Institute," *Georgetown University News Story,* February 22, 2021. https://college

.georgetown.edu/news-story/arts-scholar-and-leader-to-join-georgetown-as-co-lead -of-new-racial-justice-institute/.

4 "Juneteenth Historical Marker," Galveston.com, https://www.galveston.com/whattodo/ tours/self-guided-tours/historical-markers/juneteenth/.

5 Anna Tong, "Juneteenth Marks Black Freedom," *Sacramento Bee,* 18 June 2010, 6.

6 Peter H. Wood, "'Gimme de Kneebone Bent': African Body Language and the Evolution of American Dance Forms," in *The Black Tradition in American Modern Dance,* ed. Gerald E. Meyers (Durham, NC: American Dance Festival, 1989), 8.

7 Delgreta B. Brown, "Crocker Hosts Lecture on 'African Aesthetic,'" *Sacramento Observer,* March 2011, E-4.

8 Halifu Osumare, "Attacks Against Rapper Are Smoke Screen for Larger Issues," *Sacramento Bee,* 22 May 2011, E5.

9 Ibid.

Chapter 8. The Sankofa Process

1 Gloria Goodale, "'Soul Train' Icon Don Cornelius Changed the Beat of the Nation," *Christian Science Monitor,* February 2, 2012, 1–2. http://www.csmonitor.com/USA/ Society/2012/0202/Soul-Train-icon-Don-Cornelius-changed-the-beat-of-the-nation.

2 Emanuella Grinberg, "Hoodie's Evolution from Fashion Mainstay to Symbol of Injustice," *CNN Living,* March 27, 2012, 3. http://www.cnn.com/2012/03/27/living/history -hoodie-trayvon-martin/index.html.

3 Halifu Osumare, "Global Hip-Hop and the African Diaspora," *in Black Cultural Traffic: Crossroads in Global Performance and Popular Culture,* eds. Harry Elam and Kennell Jackson (Ann Arbor: University of Michigan Press, 2005), 266–288.

4 Ibid., 281. I quote Niyi Afolabi, "Brazilian New Wave: Hip-Hop and the Politics of Intervention." Conference Paper, Modern Language Association, Washington, DC, December 2000, 3–4.

5 Bismark Omari Somuah, "Book on Hiplife Launched," *Myjoyonline.com,* reposted by ModernGhana.com, November 18, 2012. https://www.myjoyonline.com/book-on -hiplife-launched/.

6 For a contemporary exploration of this unresolved issue between Britain and its former African colonies, see Nosmot Gbadamosi, "Is It Time to Repatriate Africa's Looted Art?" *Foreign Policy News,* July 28, 2020. https://foreignpolicy.com/2020/07/28/time -repatriate-africa-looted-art-artifacts-cultural-heritage-benin-bronzes-nigeria-ghana -europe-british-museum/.

Chapter 9. We Got Next!

1 AQUARIUS/LET THE SUNSHINE IN
Words by JAMES RADO and GEROME RAGNI Music by GALT MACDERMOT
© 1966, 1967, 1968, 1970 (Copyrights Renewed) JAMES RADO, GEROME RAGNI, GALT MACDERMOT, NAT
SHAPIRO and EMI U CATALOG, INC.
All Rights Controlled by EMI U CATALOG, INC. (Publishing) and ALFRED MUSIC (Print)
All Rights Reserved
Used by Permission of ALFRED MUSIC

2 Uppender Mehan, "Final Thoughts," in *So Long Been Dreaming: Postcolonial Science Fiction & Fantasy,* eds. Nalo Hopkins and Uppender Mehan (Vancouver, Canada: Arsenal Pulp Press, 2004).

3 David Smith, "The Decade That Shook America," *The Guardian,* 21 December 2019, 1–2. https://www.theguardian.com/us-news/2019/dec/21/decade-that-shook-america -donald-trump-barack-obama-us-politics-race-division.

4 Ibid., 3.

5 Ibid., 2.

6 Stanley Kurtz, "A Book For Our Times: Peter Wood's 1620 Skewers 1619 Project," *The National Review,* November 16, 2020. https://www.nationalreview.com/corner/a-book -for-our-times-peter-woods-1620-skewers-1619-project/.

7 For an excellent article on mayfield brooks's work see, Zena Bibler, "Disorientation as Critical Practice: Confronting Anti-Black Perceptual Regimes and Activating the Otherwise in mayfield brooks's Improvising While Black Pedagogy," *Dance Research Journal* 54/1, April 2022, 30–49.

8 Ayo Walker, *Towards Entercultural Engaged Pedagogy: Revisioning Curricula in University Dance Studies from a Black Dance Aesthetics Approach,* PhD dissertation, University of California, Davis, 2016, 2.

9 For a succinct article on Margaret H'Doubler, see Rachel Rizzuto, "Margaret H'Doubler—1889–1982," *Dance Teacher,* September 1, 2015. https://dance-teacher.com/ margaret-hdoubler-1889–1982/. For a summary of the Bennington dance years, see Susan Green, "How Modern Dane Took Root in Vermont," *Bennington College Institutional News,* March 5, 2012. https://www.bennington.edu/news-and-features/how -modern-dance-took-root-vermont. Also see Kate Mattingly, *Shaping Dance Canons: Criticism, Aesthetics and Equity* (Gainesville: University Press of Florida, 2023).

10 Michael Schwirtz and Lindsey Rogers Cook, "These N.Y.C. Neighborhoods Have the Highest Rates of Virus Deaths," *New York Times,* 5 May 2020. 1.

11 Daniel B. Coleman, "Countering Afropessimist Ontological Nihilism: Afrofuturist and Afro-Diasporic Cosmological Rejoinder," *The Black Scholar* 53:2 2023, 55, DOI: 10.1080/00064246.2023.2177950.

12 Siobhan Burke, "Black Dance Stories: By the Artists, for the People," *New York Times,* 29 June 2021, 3.

13 Ibid., 5.

14 Ibid.

15 Alondra Nelson, "Afrofuturism," https://www.youtube.com/watch?v=IFhEjaal5js&t= 8s.

16 Mark Dery, "Black to the Future: Interviews with Samuel R. Delaney, Greg Tate, and Tricia Rose," in *Flame Wars: The Discourse of Cyberculture,* ed. by Mark Dery (Durham, NC: Duke University Press, 1994), 179.

17 Kodwo Eshun, "Further Considerations of Afrofuturism," *CR: The New Centennial Review,* Vol. 3, No. 2, Summer 2003, 288.

18 Léopold Sédar Senghor, *On African Socialism* (New York: Praeger Publishing, 1964), 36.

19 Eshun, "Further Considerations of Afrofuturism," 290.

20 Ibid., 291–292.

21 Alan Riding, "Theater; Peter Brook Prefers His 'Hamlet' Lean," New York Times, December 10, 2000, Section 2, 5.

22 "Black Panther's Michael B. Jordan & Chadwick Boseman on Cultural Impact and Identity," MTV News, February 14, 2018. https://www.youtube.com/watch?v=PHa7D3t-gGg.

23 Eshun, "Further Considerations of Afrofuturism," 290.

24 For a good analysis of Regina King's character Angela Abar in the Watchmen television series, see Caitlin Gallagher, "Angela Abar Is the Perfect Update to the 'Watchmen' Universe," Bustle Entertainment, 20 October 2019. https://www.bustle.com/p/regina-kings-character-angela-abar-isnt-in-the-watchmen-comics-19223716.

25 McKayla Sluga, "Dreams of Freedom and a Life That Matters: How the Black Lives Matter Movement Is Reimagining America" in Skin Deep: Contemporary Engagements with American Memory, Race, Immigration, and Contested Spaces. http://skindeep.leadr.msu.edu/race-and-social-movements-today/dreams-of-freedom-and-a-life-that-matters/. Sluga uses Robin D. G. Kelley, Freedom Dreams: The Black Radical Imagination (Boston: Beacon Press, 2002).

26 As quoted in Yanique Dawkins, "Afrofuturism-inspired Dance Theatre Performance Explores Art, Technology," Atlanta Blackstar Blerds, January 27, 2015. https://blerds.atlantablackstar.com/2015/01/27/afrofuturism-inspired-dance-theatre-performance-explores-art-technology/.

27 Ibid.

28 "Across the Floor: Anniversary Edition #2," PearlArts Studios, May 10, 2020. https://www.pearlartsstudios.com/blog/2020/5/16/across-the-floor-anniversary-edition-2.

29 Gia Kourlas, "A Choreographer Finds His Way, Getting Lost in the Stars," New York Times, 3 June 2021, 2.

30 Ibid.

31 Ibid., 3.

32 Ibid., 4.

33 Raissa Simpson, "Mothership Trilogy," PUSH Dance Company. https://www.pushdance.org/motherlode/.

34 Ibid.

35 Ibid.

36 Ibid.

37 Raissa Simpson, "Writings on Dance: Artistic Reframing for Celestial Black Bodies," in Critical Black Futures: Speculative Theories & Explorations, ed., Philip Butler (New York: Palgrave Macmillan, 2021), 103.

38 Laurie Segal, "60 in 6 Correspondent, 60 Minutes for Quibi," CBS This Morning, January 18, 2021.

39 Ibid.

40 Paul Mozur, Cecilia Kang, Adam Satarino, and David McCabe, "A Global Tipping Point for Reining in Tech Has Arrived," New York Times, 20 April 2021. https://www.nytimes.com/2021/04/20/technology/global-tipping-point-tech.html?searchResultPosition=1.

41 Ibid.

42 Halifu Osumare, The Africanist Aesthetic in Global Hip-Hop, 149.

43 Genevieve Curtis, "Dances With Robots, and other Tales From the Outer Limits," *New York Times,* 5 November 2020.

44 Ibid.

45 Ibid.

46 "About Us," AFROPOLIS, https://www.afropolis.org/about.

47 AFROPOLIS Email Newsletter: "One Epic Journey-Europe Tour."

48 Black in AI. https://blackinai.github.io/#/about.

49 Cade Metz, "Who Is Making Sure A.I. Machines Aren't Racist?" *New York Times,* 15 March 2021. https://www.nytimes.com/2021/03/15/technology/artificial-intelligence -google-bias.html?searchResultPosition=2.

50 Data for Black Lives. https://d4bl.org/programs.html.

51 Ibid.

52 Shalini Kantayya, *Coded Bias,* Documentary film, 2020. https://www.codedbias.com/.

53 André Brock Jr., *Distributed Blackness*, 23.

54 Ibid., 36–37.

55 Home page, AI 4 Afrika, https://www.ai4afrika.com.

56 "Cosmo-Ubuntu, Machine Translation And Cognitive Code Switching," AI 4 Afrika Panel, AI for Good Conference, July 2020, Geneva Switzerland. https://aiforgood.itu .int/event/cosmo-ubuntu-machine-translation-and-cognitive-code-switching/.

57 Ibid.

58 S. Ama Wray, "An Interdisciplinary Symposium Exploring Embodiology: From Ancient Movement Practices to Phenomenal Being," Paper Presentation at Center for Neurobiology Learning and Memory; Institute for 21st Century Creativity, University of California, Irvine, December 2, 2021.

59 Ibid.

60 Ibid.

61 Ibid.

62 See *Alice Street* film website that captures the vitality and activism of the mural, what it meant for Oakland, and how gentrification threads our community-based cultures: https://alicestreetfilm.com/.

63 Nadine George-Graves, "Book Review, Dancing in Blackness: A Memoir," *The British Journal of Aesthetics,* 2021, 1.

64 Brenda Dixon Gottschild conceived this phrase in her unpublished essay "Why Black-Space."

65 Toni Morrison, *Beloved* (New York: Random House, 1987), 225.

66 Amanda Gorman, *The Hill We Climb: An Inaugural Poem for the Country* (New York: Viking Press, 2021), 16.

Bibliography

Afar-Gyan, Kwadwo. "Kwame Nkrumah, George Padmore and W.E.B. DuBois." *Research Review NS,* Vol. 7, Nos. 1&2 (1991): 1–10.

Anderson, Jack. "Katherine Dunham, Dance Icon, Dies at 96." *The New York Times.* 23 May 2006.

Atlanta Blackstar Blerds, January 27, 2015. https://blerds.atlantablackstar.com/2015/01/27/afrofuturism-inspired-dance-theatre-performance-explores-art-technology/.

Banes, Sally. *Terpsichore in Sneakers: Post-Modern Dance.* Hanover, NH: Wesleyan University Press, 1987, 1977.

Barber, Karin. "Foreword," in *Popular Culture in Africa: The Episteme of the Everyday,* edited by Stephanie Newell and Onokome Okome, xv–xx. New York: Routledge, 2014.

Barbour, Karen Nicole. *Dancing Across the Page: Narrative and Embodied Ways of Knowing.* Bristol, UK: Intellect, 2011.

Barrére, Dorothy B., Mary Kawena Pukui, and Marion Kelly. *Hula: Historical Perspectives.* Honolulu: Bishop Museum, 1980.

Beckford, Ruth. *Katherine Dunham, A Biography.* New York: Marcel Dekker, Inc. 1979.

Bibler, Zena. "Disorientation as Critical Practice: Confronting Anti-Black Perceptual Regimes and Activating the Otherwise in mayfield brooks's Improvising While Black Pedagogy." *Dance Research Journal* 54/1, April 2022, 30–49.

Brock, André, Jr. *Distributed Blackness: African American Cybercultures.* New York: New York University Press, 2020.

Brown, Delgreta B. "Crocker Hosts Lecture on 'African Aesthetic,'" *Sacramento Observer,* 3–9 March 2011.

Browning, Barbara. "Introduction: Global Dance and Globalization: Emerging Perspectives," *Dance Research Journal: Congress on Research in Dance* 34/2 Winter (2002): 12–13.

Burke, Siobhan. "Black Dance Stories: By the Artists, for the People," *The New York Times,* 29 June 2021.

Butler, Octavia E. *Parable of the Talents.* New York: Grand Central Publishing, 1998.

Clark, VèVè A. "Performing the Memory of Difference in Afro-Caribbean Dance: Katherine Dunham's Choreography, 1938–87." In *History & Memory in African-American Culture,* edited by Geneviève Fabre and Robert O'Meally, 188–203. New York: Oxford University Press, 1994.

Clark, VèVè A. and Sara E. Johnson, editors. *Kaiso! Writings by and about Katherine Dunham.* Madison: University of Wisconsin Press, 2005.

Coleman, Daniel B. "Countering Afropessimist Ontological Nihilism: Afrofuturist and Afro-Diasporic Cosmological Rejoinder," *The Black Scholar* 53:2, 2023, 48–57.

Collins, John. *West African Pop Roots.* Philadelphia, PA: Temple University Press, 1992.

Copeland, Misty. *Black Ballerinas: My Journey to Our Legacy.* New York: Aladdin, 2021.

Copeland, Misty, with Charisse Jones. *Life in Motion: An Unlikely Ballerina.* New York: Simon & Shuster, 2014.

Curtis, Genevieve. "Dances With Robots, and other Tales From the Outer Limits," *The New York Times,* 5 November 2020.

Dawkins, Yanique. "Afrofuturism-inspired Dance Theatre Performance Explores Art, Technology."

Dee Das, Joanna. *Katherine Dunham: Dance and the African Diaspora.* New York: Oxford University Press, 2017.

DeFrantz, Thomas F. *Dancing Revelations: Alvin Ailey's Embodiment of African American Culture.* New York: Oxford University Press, 2004.

DeFrantz, Thomas F. and Anita Gonzales. "Introduction: From 'Negro Expression' to 'Black Performance.'" In *Black Performance Theory,* edited by Thomas F. DeFrantz and Anita Gonzales, 1–18. Durham, NC: Duke University Press, 2014.

Dery, Mark. "Black to the Future: Interviews with Samuel R. Delaney, Greg Tate and Tricia Rose." In *Flame Wars: The Discourse of Cyberculture,* edited by Mark Dery, 179–222. Durham, NC: Duke University Press, 1994.

Dixon Gottschild, Brenda. *Digging the Africanist Aesthetic in American Performance: Dance and Other Contexts.* Westport, CN: Greenwood Press, 1996.

Dunham, Katherine. *A Touch of Innocence.* Chicago: University of Chicago Press, 1959, 1994.

———. *Dances of Haiti.* Los Angeles: UCLA Center for Afro American Studies, 1983.

———. *Island Possessed.* Chicago: University of Chicago Press, 1969, 1994.

———. *Journey to Accompong.* New York: Henry Holt Company, 1946.

———. "Las Danzas De Haiti," *Acta Anthropologicia* 11, no. 4 (November 1947).

———. *Les Dances D' Haiti.* Paris: Fasquelle Editeurs, 1957.

———. "Notes on the Dance." In *Kaiso! Writings By and About Katherine Dunham,* edited by VèVè A. Clark and Sara E. Johnson, 514–519. Madison, WI: The University of Wisconsin Press, 2005.

Dupont, David. "Hip-Hop on Over to a New Course at BGSU," *Sentinel-Tribune,* 26 May 2001.

Eligon, John, and Audra D. S. Burch. "Questions of Bias in Covid-19 Treatment Add to the Mourning for Black Families." *New York Times,* 11 May 2020.

Eshun, Kodwo. "Further Considerations of Afrofuturism," *CR: The New Centennial Review,* Vol. 3, no. 2 (Summer 2003): 287–302.

Fulbright, Leslie. "VèVè Clark—Expert on African Diaspora." *San Francisco Chronicle,* 14 December 2007.

Gates, Henry Louis, Jr., and Cornel West. *The Future of the Race.* New York: A.A. Knopf, 1996.

George-Graves, Nadine. "Book Review, Dancing in Blackness: A Memoir," *The British Journal of Aesthetics* (2021): 1–10.

———. *Urban Bush Women: Twenty-Years of African American Dance Theater, Community Engagement, and Working It Out.* Madison: University of Wisconsin Press, 2010.

Gleason, Judith. *Oya: In Praise of an African Goddess.* San Francisco: HarperSanFrancisco, 1992.

Gorman, Amanda. *The Hill We Climb.* New York: Viking—Penguin Random House, 2021.

Gottschild, Brenda Dixon. *The Black Dancing Body: A Geography From Coon to Cool.* New York: Palgrave Macmillan, 2003.

———. *Digging the Africanist Presence in American Performance: Dance and other Contexts.* Westport, CN: Greenwood Press, 1996.

Green, Susan. "How Modern Dance Took Root in Vermont," *Bennington College Institutional News.* March 5, 2012. https://www.bennington.edu/news-and-features/how-modern-dance-took-root-vermont.

Hanna, Judith Lynne. *To Dance Is Human: A Theory of Nonverbal Communication.* Chicago: University of Chicago Press, 1987.

Harris, Paul. "Obama Deeply Moved by 'Evil' Slave Fortress." *The Guardian,* 11 July 2009. https://www.theguardian.com/world/2009/jul/12/barack-obama.

Harris-Perry, Melissa V., *Sister Citizen: Shame, Stereotypes, and Black Women in America.* New Haven, CN: Yale University Press, 2011.

Hazzard-Gordon, Katrina. *Jookin': The Rise of Social Dance Formations in African-American Culture.* Philadelphia: Temple University Press, 1990.

Idowu, E. Bolayi. *Olódumarè: God in Yoruba Belief.* Brooklyn. New York: A&B Book Publishers, 1994.

Kaeppler, Adrienne. *Hula Pahu: Hawaiian Drum Dances,* Vol. 1. Honolulu: Bishop Museum Bulletins in Anthropology, 1993.

Kaufman, Sarah. "Moving the World: Katherine Dunham Choreographed a Life That Stretched Beyond the Stage." *Washington Post.* 23 May 2006.

Kelley, Robin D. G. *Freedom Dreams: The Black Radical Imagination.* Boston: Beacon Press, 2002.

Kim, Kevin D. "Dance Instructor Crosses Cultural Bounds." *Ka Leo o* Hawai'i, 23 September 1994.

Kourlas, Gia. "A Choreographer Finds His Way, Getting Lost in the Stars." *New York Times,* 3 June 2021, 2.

Kurtz, Stanley. "A Book For Our Times: Peter Wood's 1620 Skewers 1619 Project." *The National Review,* November 16, 2020. https://www.nationalreview.com/corner/a-book-for-our-times-peter-woods-1620-skewers-1619-project/.

Linly, Zack. "Trump Wants to Include Funding for His White History Curriculum in Tik-Tok Purchase Deal." *The Root,* September 20, 2020. https://www.theroot.com/trump-wants-to-include-funding-for-his-white-history-cu-1845122148.

Malnig, Julie. "Editor's Note," *Dance Research Journal: Congress on Research in Dance* 34/2 (Winter 2002): 5–7.

Manjoo, Farhad. "Only You Can Prevent Dystopia." *New York Times,* 1 January 2020. https://www.nytimes.com/2020/01/01/opinion/social-media-2020.html?searchResultPosition=1.

Mattingly, Kate. *Shaping Dance Canons: Criticism, Aesthetics, and Equity.* Gainesville: University Press of Florida, 2023.

McCarthy-Brown, Nyama. *Dance Pedagogy for a Diverse World: Culturally Relevant Teaching in Theory, Research and Practice.* Jefferson, NC: McFarland & Co., Inc., 2017.

Mehan, Uppender, and Nalo Hopkins, editors. *So Long Been Dreaming: Postcolonial Science Fiction & Fantasy.* Vancouver, Canada: Arsenal Pulp Press, 2004.

Metz, Cade. "Who Is Making Sure A.I. Machines Aren't Racist?" *New York Times,* 15 March 2021. https://www.nytimes.com/2021/03/15/technology/artificial-intelligence-google-bias.html?searchResultPosition=2.

Morrison, Toni. *Beloved.* New York: Random House, 1987.

Mozur, Paul, Cecilia Kang, Adam Satarino, and David McCabe, "A Global Tipping Point for Reining In Tech Has Arrived." *New York Times,* 20 April 2021.

Obama, Barack. *Dreams from My Father: A Story of Race and Inheritance.* New York: Broadway Paperbacks, 2004.

Ongiri, Amy Abugo. *Spectacular Blackness: The Cultural Politics of the Black Power Movement and the Search for a Black Aesthetic.* Charlottesville: University of Virginia Press.

Osumare, Halifu. "'Aesthetic of the Cool' Revisited: The Ancestral Dance ink in the African Diaspora." *UCLA Journal of Dance Ethnology* 17 (1993): 1–16.

———. "Attacks Against Rapper are Smoke Screen for Larger Issues." *Sacramento Bee,* 22 May 2011.

———. *Black Choreographers Moving: A National Dialogue.* Self-published and distributed, 1991.

———. *Dancing Blackness, A Memoir.* Gainesville: University Press of Florida, 2018.

———. "Global Breakdancing and the Intercultural Body." *Dance Research Journal: Congress on Research in Dance* 34/2 (Winter 2002): 30–45.

———. "Socialization Through the Arts: Katherine Dunham as a Social Activist." In *Sentient Performativities of Embodiment: Thinking Alongside the Human,* edited by Lynette Hunter, Elisabeth Krimmer, and Peter Lichentenfels. New York: Lexington Books, 2016, 207–315.

———. *The Africanist Aesthetic in Global Hip-Hop: Power Moves.* New York: Palgrave Macmillan, 2007.

———. "The Dance Archaeology of Rennie Harris: Hip-Hop or Postmodern." In *Ballroom, Boogie, Shimmy Sham, Shake: A Social and Popular Dance Reader,* edited by Julie Malnig. Urbana & Chicago: University of Illinois Press, 2009, 261–281.

———. "'The Fierce Freedom of Their Souls': Activism of African Dance in the Oakland Bay Area." In *Hot Feet and Social Change: African Dance and Diaspora Communities,* edited by Kariamu Welsh, Esailama G. A. Diouf, and Yvonne Daniel. Urbana and Chicago: University of Illinois Press, 2019, 143–166.

———. *The Hiplife in Ghana: West African Indigenization of Hip-Hop.* New York: Palgrave Macmillan, 2012.

Payton, Brenda. "Fitting Tribute to a Dance Pioneer." *Oakland Tribune,* 2 June 2006.

Rees, Robert M. "Going to Extremes at the University of Hawai'i." *Honolulu Weekly,* February 25–March 3, 1998.

Rizzuto, Rachel. "Margaret H'Doubler—1889–1982." *Dance Teacher,* 1 September 2015. https://dance-teacher.com/margaret-hdoubler-1889-1982/.

Schevitz, Tanya. "This is College? Classes on Popular Culture like Hip Hop, 'Simpson' Bursting into Academia." *San Francisco Chronicle,* 16 May 2000.

Schwirtz, Michael, and Lindsey Rogers Cook. "These N.Y.C. Neighborhoods Have the Highest Rates of Virus Deaths." *New York Times,* 5 May 2020.

Segal, Laurie. "60 in 6 Correspondent, 60 Minutes for Quibi." *CBS This Morning,* January 18, 2021.

Senghor, Léopold Sédar. *On African Socialism.* New York: Praeger Publishing, 1964.

Shange, Ntozake. *Dance We Do: A Poet Explores Black Dance.* Boston: Beacon Press, 2020.

Shipley, Jesse Weaver. "Aesthetic of the Entrepreneur: Afro-Cosmopolitan Rap and Moral Circulation in Accra, Ghana." *Anthropological Quarterly* 82, no. 3 (Summer 2009), 633–678.

———. *Living the Hiplife: Celebrity and Entrepreneurship in Ghanaian Popular Music.* Durham, NC: Duke University Press, 2013.

Simpson, Raissa. "Writings on Dance: Artistic Reframing for Celestial Black Bodies." In *Critical Black Futures: Speculative Theories & Explorations,* edited, Philip Butler. New York: Palgrave Macmillan, 2021, 93–113.

Sluga, McKayla. "Dreams of Freedom and a Life That Matters: How the Black Lives Matter Movement Is Reimagining America." On website Skin Deep: Contemporary Engagements with American Memory, Race, Immigration, and Contested Spaces. http://skindeep.leadr.msu.edu/race-and-social-movements-today/dreams-of-freedom-and-a-life-that-matters/.

Smith, David. "The Decade That Shook America," *The Guardian.* 21 December 2019, 1–2. https://www.theguardian.com/us-news/2019/dec/21/decade-that-shook-america-donald-trump-barack-obama-us-politics-race-division.

Staff Writer, "Obama Grandpa in Cape Coast," *Daily Guide—NDP News,* 14 July 2009. https://www.modernghana.com/news/227104/obama-grandpa-in-cape-coast.html.

Takara, Kathryn Waddell. *Oral Histories of African Americans.* Honolulu: Center for Oral History-Social Science Research Institute, University of Hawai'i at Manoa, 1990.

Thompson, Robert Farris. *African Art in Motion: Icon and Act.* Los Angeles: University of California Press, 1974.

Tong, Anna. "Juneteenth Marks Black Freedom," *Sacramento Bee,* 18 June 2010, 6.

Trask, Haunani-Kay. "The Birth of the Modern Hawaiian Movement: Kalama Valley, O'ahu," *The Hawaiian Journal of History* XXI (1987):126–153.

Tutuola, Amos. *My Life in the Bush of Ghosts.* New York: Grove Press, 1954.

Walker, Ayo. *Towards Entercultural Engaged Pedagogy: Revisioning Curricula in University Dance Studies from a Black Dance Aesthetics Approach.* PhD dissertation, University of California, Davis, 2016.

Weiss, Hedy. "Pioneering Dancer, Author, Activist." *Chicago Sun-Times,* 23 May 2006.

White, Elisa Joy. "Representations of Blackness and the Popolo Problematic in Hawai'i." In *They Followed the Trade Winds: African Americans in Hawai'i* (2nd Edition), ed. Miles M. Jackson. Honolulu: University of Hawai'i Press, 2013, 269–275.

———. "Representations of Blackness and the Popolo Problematic in Hawai'i," in *They Followed the Trade Winds: African Americans in Hawai'i* (2nd Edition), edited by Miles M. Jackson. Honolulu: University of Hawai'i Press, 2013, 269–275.

Womack, Ytasha L. *Afrofuturism: The World of Black Sci-Fi and Fantasy Culture.* Chicago: Lawrence Hill Books, 2013.

Wood, Peter H. "'Gimme de Kneebone Bent': African Body Language and the Evolution of

American Dance Forms." In *The Black Tradition in American Modern Dance,* edited by Gerald E. Meyers. Durham, NC: American Dance Festival, 1989, 7–8.

Yartey, Francis Nii. "Development and Promotion of Contemporary Choreographic Expression in Ghana." In *FonTomFrom: Contemporary Ghanaian Literature Theatre and Film,* edited by Kofi Anyidoho and James Gibbs. Amsterdam and Atlanta: Rodopi, 2000.

Index

Halifu Osumare is professor emerita of African American and African Studies at University of California, Davis. She has been a dancer, choreographer, educator, cultural activist, and scholar for over fifty years. She is author of *Dancing in Blackness: A Memoir; The Africanist Aesthetic in Global Hip-Hop: Power Moves;* and *The Hiplife in Ghana: West African Indigenization of Hip-Hop.*